The Gender of Globalization

School for Advanced Research
Advanced Seminar Series

James F. Brooks
General Editor

The Gender of Globalization

Contributors

Mary Anglin
Department of Anthropology, University of Kentucky

A. Lynn Bolles
Department of Women's Studies, University of Maryland

Karen Brodkin
Department of Anthropology, University of California, Los Angeles

William L. Conwill
Counselor Education Department and African American Studies Program, University of Florida

Ulrika Dahl
Gender Studies, Södertörn University College

Akosua K. Darkwah
Department of Sociology, University of Ghana, Legon

Nandini Gunewardena
Human Services Program, Western Washington University

Faye V. Harrison
Department of Anthropology and African American Studies Program, University of Florida

Ann Kingsolver
Department of Anthropology, University of South Carolina

Louise Lamphere
Department of Anthropology, University of New Mexico

Mary H. Moran
Department of Anthropology and Africana and Latin American Studies, Colgate University

Annapurna Pandey
Anthropology Department, University of California, Santa Cruz

Rhacel Salazar Parreñas
Asian American Studies and the Graduate Group of Sociology, University of California, Davis

Sandy Smith-Nonini
Department of Anthropology, University of North Carolina, Chapel Hill

Barbara Sutton
Women's Studies, State University of New York at Albany

The Gender of Globalization

Women Navigating Cultural and Economic Marginalities

Edited by Nandini Gunewardena and Ann Kingsolver

School for Advanced Research Press

Santa Fe

School for Advanced Research Press

Post Office Box 2188
Santa Fe, New Mexico 87504-2188
www.sarpress.sarweb.org

Co-Director and Editor: Catherine Cocks
Manuscript Editors: Ann D. Brucklacher, Kate Whelan
Design and Production: Cynthia Dyer
Proofreader: Sarah Soliz
Indexer: Catherine Fox
Printer: Publishers Graphics

Library of Congress Cataloging-in-Publication Data:

The gender of globalization : women navigating cultural and economic marginalities / edited by
Nandini Gunewardena and Ann Kingsolver. – 1st ed.
    p. cm. – (School for Advanced Research advanced seminar series)
 Includes bibliographical references and index.
 ISBN 978-1-930618-91-6 (pa : alk. paper)
 1. Poor women–Cross-cultural studies. 2. Globalization–Social aspects–Cross-cultural studies.
3. Globalization–Economic aspects–Cross-cultural studies. 4. Culture and globalization–Cross-
cultural studies. 5. Marginality, Social–Cross-cultural studies. I. Gunewardena, Nandini.
II. Kingsolver, Ann E., 1960-

HQ1161.G464 2007
305.48'9694209–dc22

                            2007031821

Contents

Figures

Foreword

Reflections on the Production of Differentiation

Karen Brodkin

Gender, ethnicity, race, class, religion, sexuality—in our everyday lives we think of these as "categories," facets of social personality, funds of experience that shape our lives and perspectives. All too often they become explanations for why particular groups are the ways they are and for the ways in which they are subordinated. At worst, they become ingredients in a global game of blaming the subordinated for their own subordination.

But these categories are less about describing intrinsic attributes and more about describing globally structured relationships of domination and subordination—the wealthy over the workers, whites over people of color, men over women, foreigners over locals, and so on. This is the point that William Conwill makes so forcefully in challenging category-like views that male violence is integral to African American culture. He shows how socially structured domination of and discrimination against black Americans are also gendered and underpin black women's lack of alternatives to the bad domestic relationships hardly unique to African American communities.

Thanks to the latest phase of capitalism's globalization, differentiations based on gender, race, class, religion, sexuality, ethnicity, and more ways of locally structuring domination and subordination are familiar worldwide, especially in their category-like guises. Not all these differentiations are recent products. As Mary Moran's chapter reminds us, current globalization builds on patterns created by centuries of colonialism and imperialism interacting with local systems of domination.

But these forms of global and local domination are not simple. We cannot always predict who will be on top, what cultural attributes will adhere to the dominant and the dominated to explain their relationship. The patterns and language of global inequality are like good jazz. They take a simple and familiar tune and produce a seemingly infinite number of variations on its theme, often with jarring riffs. But underneath, we can still recognize the theme—domination and its explanations as produced by the flaws of the dominated.

The authors in this book have put gender, and especially women, in the foreground. Of course, gender is a very differentiated category in terms of what attributes are imputed to women and men of specific classes, regions, races, and religions. In the same way, and not unrelated, gender is also incredibly differentiated as relationships of domination and subordination. That is what the ensemble of case studies in this book shows so well. On the one hand, we read an essay and say, "That's such a familiar way of stereotyping and debasing women," but then, on the other hand, we read the next essay and say the same thing about a very different, almost opposite stereotype of women.

For example, compare what Nandini Gunewardena terms "discourses of reproach" with the similar set of stereotypes described by Annapurna Pandey. In Gunewardena's example, urban Sri Lankans view Sinhala women factory workers as sexually promiscuous and wild, whereas in Pandey's example, upper-caste Hindus stereotype upwardly mobile tribal Kond women who have, thanks to national affirmative action programs, entered the educational system. Both the Sri Lankan factory workers and their more middle-class counterparts in Orissa have to struggle against negative stereotypes designed to justify sexual and economic violence against them, largely because they have left their ethnoracially subordinate "place." Barbara Sutton describes a similar set of negative gender stereotypes that are applied to women who are not ethnically or racially subordinated but who are "othered" along class lines. Women who work in the informal economy have to work at night, use public transportation, and inhabit dangerous terrain. Here, too, negative, gendered, class stereotypes serve to demean them and to justify their oppression by those in less precarious economic straits.

In sharp contrast, Ulrika Dahl tells of the ways that rural white Swedish women have stereotyped Swedish Thai women as racially subordinate. In the discourse of white women, Swedish Thai women, often married to white Swedish men, appear as "traditional" and submissive, in contrast to white Swedish women, stereotyped as liberated and progressive. White Swedish women in this discourse would not put up with the male domination that Swedish Thai women allegedly embrace.

All these discourses share the attachment of negative attributes to women. However opposite they appear on the surface, they are all racialized, spun to the detriment of women who are subordinated by race and ethnicity. They also are deployed to sanction sexual violence and economic discrimination. Sinhala factory workers face victimization on the street and at work and fear shame from their families. Kond women struggle against sexual violence that is designed, at least in part, to keep them from competing for middle-class economic gains. Swedish Thai women are excluded from the entrepreneurial activities of their white counterparts and from any support to struggle against domestic violence and subordination.

When we step back and look at gender as a socially structured relationship of unequal power in a particular locale, we can begin to see the rich and repulsive repertoire for rationalizing domination that global capitalism has unleashed upon the world, shaping new experiences of womanhood (and manhood) in local contexts. The theme and its variations explain that dominance of a few is natural, inevitable, and therefore morally justified. These attributes work as more than explanation. They also divide the differently subordinated against one another and urge identification with those who dominate them in other aspects of life, as Pandey, Dahl, Moran, and Conwill show.

However, not all differentiation is about the production of discourses that justify gender subordination. Globalization is the latest phase in five-hundred-year-old capitalism, which, as Mary Moran reminds us, has fashioned its systems of domination in conjunction with local structures of inequality. As in the past, globalization today impacts different groups of people very differently. Moran argues persuasively that the impact of globalization on "women" as a generic category must consider the local class-status system, as well as the age and kinship identities of individuals. Sutton shows clearly how the crash of Argentina's economy under neoliberal reforms hit women especially hard as they denied themselves in efforts to provide for their families. But women's sacrifices were varied and far from equal across the class spectrum.

Some of that differentiation process has also opened new possibilities to women around the world. Bolles, Moran, Darkwah, Parreñas, and Dahl examine the lives of women in West Africa, Western Europe, and the United States who are not heavily constrained and subordinated by such discourses and images. In Lynn Bolles's analysis of a family-owned business, we find unexpected sources of power for women even as they struggle against corporate control in local regions. Akosua Darkwah shows how globalization and neoliberal policies in Ghana enabled Ghanaian women entrepreneurs to expand their businesses by importing clothing. The white Swedish women Dahl describes were able to use NGO and economic development funds to build successful businesses. Rhacel Parreñas describes the global migration of middle-class Filipino women who become domestic child and elder caregivers. All of these are new opportunities.

But some of these groups also face formidable structural constraints. Parreñas shows how spiritual homelessness is a shared experience among Filipina home caregivers in Rome and Los Angeles. They are drawn to migrate by higher wages and the economic improvements they bring to their families in the Philippines. But they are also excluded from Italian society by racism, set apart from the more affluent Filipino American community in Los Angeles by class, and isolated from one another in their work. The lack of social space and place keeps them tied to their homeland, but also their need to work and send remittances keeps them away from home. Meanwhile, Darkwah reveals how the global prices of imports and the tight budgets of customers weaken the bargaining ability of Ghanaian female traders, harming the social relations by which they build their client base and squeezing their ability to make a living.

Not all is bleak. Lynn Bolles shows how Jamaican women entrepreneurs have capitalized on local specificity and the Internet and are continuing to build a successful economic base in the face of corporate tourism. Both Ann Kingsolver and Sandy Smith-Nonini deal with the possibilities for organized resistance that globalization brings. Kingsolver analyzes the very different impacts of neoliberal policies, especially those in the United States and Mexico as a result of NAFTA. Like Moran, she finds that such policies have improved some women's lives but have had a decidedly negative impact on other women. However, Kingsolver argues that the openings and constraints do more than pit women against one another. Rather, these create conditions in which groups of women may find themselves in alliances for their mutual benefit. Smith-Nonini gives us one such example in the support by middle-class San Franciscans and several national professional associations (including the American Anthropological Association) for the strike by HERE (Hotel and Restaurant Employees Union), representing mainly Latina/o hotel workers. These chapters introduce two important points. First, neoliberalism creates interstices that allow some groups of women to use the master's tools to good effect. Second, globalization's concentration of wealth and spread of (different kinds of) misery can create alliances among those who seem to be most unlike one another in specific interests.[1]

About the Author

Karen Brodkin teaches anthropology and women's studies at UCLA. She works on social movements in the United States, and her new book is titled *Making Democracy Matter: Identity and Activism in Los Angeles.*

Note

1. I thank Pat Zavella for her reading and comments on this piece.

The Gender of Globalization

1

Introduction

Nandini Gunewardena and Ann Kingsolver

The gender of globalization has been obscured by "neutral" analytical lenses that overlook the powerful incongruity between women's key roles in the global labor force and their social and economic marginalization, as well as their persistent efforts to navigate the processes that produce this incongruity. Our main concern in this volume is to understand, via the lenses of gender and cultural analysis, the ways in which women participate in, become drawn and incorporated into, are affected by, and negotiate their encounters with contemporary forms of global economic restructuring commonly referred to as globalization. We bring together ethnographic case studies from diverse locations in the global South and the global North, analyzing economic globalization as a *gendered* process. Our purpose is to move beyond the naturalization of gender in our analysis of globalization;[1] we illustrate how local and global constructions of gender are employed in the operations of transnational capital to exacerbate women's economic and social vulnerabilities.[2] Collectively, the ethnographic case studies in this volume analyze globalization not merely as an innocuous and inevitable (see Gibson-Graham 1996) historical phenomenon, but also as a set of processes with distinct, gender-specific implications. These ethnographic essays "pivot the center" (Collins 1991) by focusing on the "subjective," agentive perspectives of those who are most marginalized by capitalist globalization, rather than on the "objectifying" language of econometric analyses. By using ethnographic methods, the authors (from several disciplines) illuminate the often invisible dimensions of social and economic disempowerment that women encounter in globalization, contrary to the arguments put forward by globalization's proponents. We seek to document the complex realities of women's lives, often referred to as the hidden face of globalization, masked by the impressive macroeconomic performance measures that have rallied the fervent devotees of globalization.

The ethnographic essays collected here tell of disruptions fueled by globalization in the situated lives and lived experiences of women, from their own perspectives.[3] We illustrate the confluences of gender, race, ethnicity, class, caste, color, religion, and regional ascriptions within the construction of marginality in specific social contexts and examine the interactions and intersections of these axes of differentiation between local and global constituencies. Simultaneously, we argue that the increasing and deepening economic marginality experienced disproportionately by women in globalized contexts does not necessarily rob them of their capacity for agency, individually or collectively.

The analytical vantage point of this volume, then, questions normative notions of agency and augments the body of feminist literature that explores its paradoxical aspects, by illustrating the complex and contradictory ways in which women's agency and subordination are manifested. The insights on women's agentive acts documented in this volume strengthen feminist understandings of the divergent ways in which women confront material oppression and of the multifaceted dimensions of agency. In this manner, this volume deconstructs several monolithic, unitary concepts—the naturalization of gender in globalization, the uniform effects of globalization, the essentialist notions of gender, identity, and location (for example, what constitutes the local, as compared with the global, and the global North versus the global South), the homogeneity of power and oppression, and the singularity of agency (as always leading to empowerment). Our concern is to show how the operations of capitalist globalization have led to uneven shifts and reconfigurations of these categories beyond binaries and universals.

Collectively, these chapters provide insights into women's own assessments of social and economic marginality and the wide range of strategies they deploy in challenging and subverting their subordination. We strive to provide insights into the diversity of women's experiences of marginality as we highlight the parallels and differences in the ways in which they travel across the spaces and processes often conceptually elided as the global North or South, gendered experience, and globalization. That is why we discuss plural globalizations and plural marginalities in this volume.[4] As such, the ethnographic cases document the different trajectories women traverse in straddling the various social and political borders they encounter and the often parallel, sometimes different, strategies they resort to in defending their integrity and defining their identities as autonomous beings. We use the notion of "navigation" to refer to the myriad encounters women grapple with in globalized contexts and their efforts to exercise agency *within constraints*. The ethnographic material in this collection provides a far more nuanced understanding of agency, beyond the reduction of agency to empowerment.

The ethnographic analyses trace how emergent forms of marginality are related to and build on existing forms and bases of power, subordination, and disempowerment. Many authors in this volume incorporate a Foucaultian (see Foucault 1979) understanding of power relations—in this case, capitalist power relations—as constantly asserted and contested in daily interactions. To this end, the authors explore reconceptualizations of marginality that problematize fixed "margins," given the emerging evidence of the diverse strategies women deploy to make these margins more malleable. The use of the ethnographic approach allows incisive documentation of such assertions and contestations, and that is the central contribution of this project to the broader conversation on globalization. In addition to the multiple vantage points of the authors (many from marginalized social locations themselves), the voices of and interpretations by women marginalized by globalization come to the fore in this book as women narrate their own experiences.

ORIENTATIONS AND DIRECTIONS

We are indebted to feminist anthropologists who have articulated foundational ideas that guide our analyses. Key works include those on the cultural construction of gender (for example, as collected by Gero and Conkey [1991]; Reiter [1976]; and Rosaldo and Lamphere [1974]; and discussed by Visweswaran [1997]), women's work and relationship to capital and capitalism (for example, Nash 1979; Sacks/Brodkin 1974, 1979), and the political economy of gender and globalization as historically contingent and reflected in the material realities, social institutions, and cultural ideologies that shape women's incorporation into globalization in relational and unequal manners along markers of race, ethnicity, caste, and class.[5] Our use of the lens of gender includes documentation of both men and women's experiences in analyses of gender and globalization (see Derné 2002; Gutmann 1997). Many feminist anthropologists, as well as scholars in related fields,[6] have documented how the current wave of economic globalization (with its neoliberal governance) has had disproportionately negative impacts on women in terms of aggravating women's social and economic marginality.[7]

The landmark volume on globalization by Fröbel, Heinrichs, and Kreye (1980) discusses a significant instance of capitalist globalization in the twentieth century—the emergence of export-oriented industrialization in the 1970s chartered by transnational corporations (TNCs) and spurred by neoliberal economic policies. The three decades since have proven that women, placed as low-end, poorly paid, assembly-line workers, have been critical for the burgeoning growth of export processing and production for a global market. Rapid technological developments in the communication and transportation sectors in the 1980s hastened the processes of globalization even as the widespread importation of neoliberal economic philosophies facilitated the liberalization of markets in production, trade, and finances. Attesting to the multiplication of TNCs during this period, Sassen (2006) documents how foreign direct investment (FDI), the magic bullet formula of neoliberal economics instrumental in propagating export production (via TNCs), grew three times faster in the 1980s than export trade.[8] Yet, contrary to predictions, particularly those related to the now highly contested "trickle-down" economic theory, economic globalization has deepened rather than narrowed the social and economic divides between the global North and South, as documented even by leading economists such as the former chief economist for the World Bank, Joseph Stiglitz (2002). Less well documented are the particularly damning gendered consequences of globalization—a lacuna this volume attempts to fill.[9]

Given that women represent more than 80 percent of the unskilled labor force in transnational production and services, Sassen's discussion of not only the exponential growth of TNCs but also their strategic role in the globalized world economy signals the daunting implications for our understanding of women's increasing roles in economic globalization. As she notes, "by far the largest numbers of affiliates [of TNCs] are in developing countries, because they are a mechanism for TNCs to enter the global South. Their number went from 71,300 in 1990 to 580,638 in 2003" (Sassen 2006:27).

During the 1980s and 1990s, scholars from a range of social science disciplines—notably, anthropologists and sociologists intrigued by the implications of the large-scale recruitment of young single women by transnational firms—documented various aspects of women's productive work within globalized contexts. In the new millennium, however, we understand globalization from a broader perspective—within and across locations—as determined by, as well as influencing, transnational labor migrations (legal and illegal, such as trafficking), agentive consumption (in addition to production) practices, entrepreneurial activities, and collective organizational efforts. Women's overrepresentation in these global circuits, including the impoverishing role of macroeconomic policies such as structural adjustment, trade liberalization, and FDI that compel women to participate in the global economy, has also been previously discussed by Sassen (2006), Harrison (1997a), and Chant and Craske (2002), among others.

This literature amply documents how these policies have reduced local purchasing power parity and subsistence security and led women to adopt compensation strategies at the expense of their self-exploitation to ensure household and family survival. A World Bank (2006) document on revenue generated by transnational immigrants (predominantly a female workforce) reveals a staggering figure of $230 billion in global remittances. The chapters in this volume add to this body of literature, analyzing how these processes are distinctly gendered. The richly textured descriptions of the lived realities of women experiencing these forces illustrate how women of diverse ethnic, racial, caste, class, and other identities (as well as intersectional social locations) encounter and respond to the forces of globalization in unique and differentiated ways.

Scholars interested in the economics of globalization, particularly from a macroeconomic perspective, including issues related to those discussed above, will find Sassen's volume and other texts of great interest. In contrast, the purpose of this volume is to address the range of concerns that the macroeconomic perspective does not illuminate. As Benería notes (2003:40), the very recent incorporation of feminist theory in the field of economics, for example, with the establishment of the International Association for Feminist Economics in 1992,[10] has brought new attention to women's unpaid and undercounted labor. This is a significant shift because macroeconomic data often obscure the detrimental aspects of globalization, experienced particularly by society's most marginalized members.

MAPPING THE SPECIFICS OF GLOBALIZATION

Our use of the term *globalization* builds on the definition outlined by Appadurai (1996), Inda and Rosaldo (2002), Naples and Desai (2002), Lewellen (2002), and others as a set of social and economic processes that entail intensified global interconnectedness (and subsequent changes in local livelihoods), via the mobility and flows of culture, capital, information, resistance, technologies, production, people, commodities, images, and ideologies. Contemporary processes of globalization in their cultural and economic manifestations can well be considered the most formidable forces of the twenty-first century. The intensification of late-modern capital's fluidity and mobility, the deregulation of trade, the widespread influence of neoliberal logic, and the ensuing cultural and economic transformations that constitute globalization merit further inquiry, especially in terms of their implications for women's well-being and survival. Emerging evidence suggests that, contrary to the economic gains and social benefits women are expected to reap from their engagement in a global economy, women's incorporation into global production systems and forms of cultural representation has worked counter to their well-being, survival, security, autonomy, and empowerment.

A sizeable body of analytical work produced on globalization over the past several decades generates insights into the myriad processes that are labeled, in much too totalizing a way (Gibson-Graham 1996), as "globalization." Anthropologists, including Wolf (1982) and Drake (1987, 1990), have demonstrated that the globalization of capitalist relations is not new and that assertions of marginality written into the history of global capitalism must be met with counterhistories that feature the specific mechanisms of capitalist subjugation and narratives that do not naturalize Europe and the United States as the world's "center." In this project, we join those theorists who have focused on problems associated with development and the "global factory" (including the human rights violation of offering less than a living wage) and stemming from capitalist logic and practice (see Robbins 2005; Rothstein and Blim 1991; Ward 1990). Critical Marxian analyses of capitalism, far from being outdated, have never been more relevant than in the current moment (see Nash 1997; Roseberry 1997; Wood 1997).

As many scholars have argued (see Alexander and Mohanty 1996; Brodkin 2000; Buck 2002; Collins 1998a; Harrison 1995, 1997a, 1997b, 2002; hooks 1984; Kingsolver 2001; Mohanty 2003a; Sarker and De 2002; Steady 2002; Torres, Mirón, and Inda 1999; Yelvington 1995; Zavella 1997), research on globalization must consider the central role of racial/ethnic exploitation in capitalist globalization and the intersection of gender with other markers of difference and subjugation, such as race, ethnicity, class, and caste. Given the widening social and economic disparities evidenced in the processes of globalization and the new and redemarcated lines of social stratification implicated in such processes, we are compelled to consider the multiple and overlapping systems of subordination and exploitation that have emerged or been reified in globalized contexts, especially in the global South.[11] The case studies included in this volume explore the dynamics by which ascriptions of gender, race, ethnicity, class, caste, color, religion, and regional locations in the global South and North are configured in specific social contexts to construct marginality. They inform us of the particular contours of local disparities created by the interaction and intersection of the aforementioned axes of differentiation, and of the socioeconomic power differentials between local and global constituencies.

DELINEATING DIFFERENCE AND MARGINALITY IN GLOBALIZATION

The theoretical conversation engaged by this volume puts forward an explanatory framework for understanding local and global patterns of hierarchization of needs and social valuations formed by globalization along axes of gender, race, ethnicity, class, caste, color, and regional location. Our collection addresses several questions on the dynamics of gendered marginality and disempowerment evidenced in the current manifestations of economic globalization (for example, under neoliberal policy regimes). Individual chapters document the shifting ways in which women currently participate in or are incorporated into local and local-global workforces, as well as women's perceptions of their positioning in economies reconfigured through globalization. Several chapters document the new and sometimes worsened forms of vulnerabilities to which women are subjected, ensuing from threats to their survival and well-being in contemporary forms of economic globalization; others denote processes that lead to the creation and deepening of social distance and exclusionary practices, locally and globally; and some document the ways that women are critiquing (and finding alternatives to) capitalist rationales for organizing social and economic relations and employing alternative logics successfully in resistance movements.

The reconstructions, redefinitions, alternative representations, and reconfigurations of women's roles ushered in by the dramatic restructuring of economic and social orders illustrate the lack of uniformity in the unfolding of globalization processes. While emerging reports continue to document the widening social and economic disparities set in motion by globalization, the ethnographic material in this volume provides vivid accounts of the multiple ways in which such disparities affect women's lives and, in turn, women's divergent responses to the disempowering consequences of globalization. Women's confrontations with these processes lead us to further examine the hegemonic nature of transnational economic

9

structures, policies, and practices that embody neoliberal economic philosophies. The chapters in this volume grapple with the fact that even as these new economic and social orders undermine traditional patriarchies, they often introduce novel hierarchies. To identify the gendered impact of contemporary capitalist globalization, the case studies explore how globalization processes intersect with various, often preexisting, forms of social inequality. They cite evidence of how such inequalities are inevitably exacerbated by globalization and reproduce existing patterns of subordination along gendered axes. These case analyses also document how the unfolding of these processes impacts the realms of culture and morality, politics and discipline, labor and economy.

The ethnographic insights collected here suggest that women are intimately affected by the intensification of economic deprivation and widening income disparities ushered in by economic globalization in its current form(s), contrary to globalization's promise of poverty reduction and prosperity. Trade liberalization, for example, the cornerstone of the current regime of globalization, is promoted with the stated goal of reducing poverty and bringing about prosperity and freedom in the global South. Yet, volumes of evidence indicate that the power differentials inherent in the organization of global trade and production are being deepened, reified, and even justified in the practical unfolding of neoliberal economic policies. Those who are most affected by these policies are often individuals with the least to say about their implementation and about how and where these will unfold in both the global North and South. Hence women, particularly those already occupying marginal social locations, are inevitably entangled in the related processes of disempowerment.

As Naples points out, "feminist scholars offer insights into the contradictions associated with globalization by exploring how gender, sexuality, racialization, and region are mobilized to reinscribe differences through market relations" (Naples 2002:9). This volume builds on the concern expressed by Naples and many others, that racially and ethnically marked women are disproportionately subjected to economic and social dislocations. Accordingly, the primary focus of this volume is to document the encounters with transnational capitalist relations by low-income women situated at the margins of racialized, ethnic, class, caste, and regional hierarchies, women who often lack strong political representation of their interests. In addition to discussing the shifting demarcations of class, race, color, ethnicity, caste, age, and regional location, and the heightened marginality these confer, we explore women's agentive acts in their efforts to overcome such marginality.

NAVIGATION AND AGENCY

The chapters in this volume are grounded in the formative work of feminist anthropologists on the significance of women's agency (Ahearn 2001; Collier 1974) in engaging in resistance practices that challenge and subvert their marginalization and subordination (for example, Naples and Desai 2002; Rowbotham and Linkogle 2001; and many others). We reference the concept of "navigation" to capture the nuanced ways in which women of diverse social locations and identities (ethnic, racial, indigenous, caste, class, religious, and political affiliations and as formed at the intersection of these identity designations) exercise their personal and collective agency in resisting and challenging the disempowering aspects of globalization they encounter and experience.[12] Although the concept of agency is a pivotal one in gender and women's studies theorizing, given its significance for overcoming various forms of subordination, many transnational feminists (for example, Abu Lughod 1998; Fernandes 1997; Sunder-Rajan 1993) have helped us better understand how agency is far more complicated than a mere assertion of self-empowering will. Benería (2003:55–56) points out that assumptions of boundless agency may be traced to rational choice theory. Feminists, through a critical lens, have seen that not everyone is as free to choose among options as the "rational economic man," which ran so freely through so many classrooms and boardrooms in the last half of the twentieth century.

Our use of the concept of navigation also refers to the understanding that agency may not be conceived as a priori or as instantaneous, all-transforming, autonomous actions, but rather, as Butler (1999) has urged, that agency is revealed via inquiry into the conditions of its possibility. As such, the chapters in this volume explore and document the complex, contradictory, and controversial aspects of agency as the subjects of our inquiry often challenge the gendered power systems that subordinate them, sometimes registering a seeming accommodation to such power structures and sometimes displaying ambivalence toward them. Our concern in this volume is to add a nuanced understanding of agency in a way that allows room for a recognition of how, in many instances, women's agency may often be restricted by the cultural, social, and economic constraints and contradictions that undermine its potential for enactment, particularly in the ways in which current processes of globalization yield a gendered impact. The ethnographic chapters may be read for the ways in which marginalized women perceive and manage the constraints to, and possibilities of, their own agency.

An abundant body of scholarly work highlights the increased feminization of local and global labor forces and women's transnational activism in response to the numerous forms of economic and social disempowerment.13 This volume augments that corpus of research with ethnographic cases that illustrate the explanatory power of gender as a conceptual paradigm for understanding how local-global patriarchies collude with the operations of transnational capital in gendering globalization—although we see these relationships as being much more complex than a binary model of patriarchal capitalist oppression and resistance to it. In this manner, we are currently witnessing a moment in which women in the global South are able to exercise their social agency in an effort to challenge traditional forms of patriarchy and emerging forms of subordination imposed by "new" forms of patriarchy inherent in the workings of late-modern capital. Moreover, the expanded opportunities for transnational social action in a globalized world have created space for women's individual and collective resistance practices. In the ongoing violence after September 11, 2001 ("9/11"), women have also increasingly positioned themselves as community strategists, engaging issues that now have local and global relevance, including global peace movements, in ways that social scientists must better understand.

Within this volume, our collective aim is for readers to engage with both the analyses of the researchers authoring each chapter and with the analyses of the marginalized women to whom they listened. The epistemological project advanced by this volume is not simply to talk *about* how women navigate cultural and economic marginalities, but also to—as we have stated—provide a milieu in which those women narrate their own (however constrained) agentive acts and analyses. We take very seriously the critiques that charge that the words of already marginalized individuals are further exploited and commodified through ethnographic projects such as ours. We ask readers to consider the analyses of globalization offered in these pages by women who face various forms of marginalization to be just as salient as more privileged academic analyses. Thus, the examples of marginalized women's narratives of their experiences in this volume not only illustrate the complex dynamics of capitalist globalization but also represent a specific epistemological argument. In sum, marginalized women are not discussed in this volume as passive objects under the ethnographic lens, but as active collaborators in epistemological engagements of complex and multidimensional capitalist processes increasing inequities in global-local contexts.

NARRATIVES OF MULTIPLE ENCOUNTERS WITH GLOBALIZATION

With that epistemological project in view, we foreground the narratives of women navigating cultural and economic marginalities woven throughout the ethnographic essays in this book, reflecting junctures and disjunc-tures in their experiences. By following the threads of the narratives of these and other women in this collection, readers can trace cross-regional differences and similarities in the gendered experiences of globalization. The comments by Dammi and Manike, the garment workers in Sri Lanka's export processing zones, for example, resonate with those by Cherry, Jovita, Mila, and other domestic workers in Los Angeles and Rome on their subjective experiences of marginality in city spaces. Their positioning and incorporation in diverse transnational labor processes (seemingly a result of choice, but also determined by the impoverishing effects of structural adjustment policies and the gendering of low-wage and care work) reflect a not too dissimilar subjection to the structural violence evidenced in Mary and Louise's experiences of domestic violence in the United States as com-pounded by city, state, and federal policies. The diverse ways in which these women are racialized, and thereby encounter compounded forms of dis-empowerment (at the intersections of race, class, caste, ethnic, and geo-graphic locations), are echoed in the narratives of the Kond tribal woman, Sandhyarani Naik; Sybil, the tourism entrepreneur in Jamaica; Wanja, the Thai immigrant who operates a small business in Sweden; and Saraswati, the Tamil tea plucker in Sri Lanka. Their experiences inform us of the emerging discourses and frameworks sprouted in globalized contexts that help construct their marginality. For example, Sandhyarani Naik and other Kond women discuss how they navigate nationalist policies such as *swadeshi*, framed around Hinduizing (*Hindutva*) concepts of belonging that impose exclusionary practices on tribal people. Dammi, Manike, and other gar-ment workers reflect on their nonbelonging in the class hierarchy of cos-mopolitan Colombo, the reduction of their identities to unskilled workers, and their transgressive acts in response.

The reflections by women in these ethnographic case studies on their strategies of resistance show that agentive acts are empowering from a sub-jective perspective even when they are unlikely to transform the oppressive material realities that constrain women in their encounters with globaliza-tion processes. Sybil decides to reestablish the family business in a manner that could well compete with larger, better funded hotel chains (and suc-cessfully develops a strategy to do so). Ghanaian female traders like Sisi, who represent a long historical tradition of female trading in West Africa, take up transnational trading as a means of surviving the compressive effects of structural adjustment and, equally important, find ways to take advantage of trade liberalization policies. The women in this volume also ruminate on the varied impacts of neoliberal policies on their survival capacities and social positioning. Diana and Dot, in Mexico and the United States, for example, offer their analyses of NAFTA, which may be compared with Saraswati's narrative about SAFTA. Similarly, Eva, Mona, and other women in rural Sweden critique the contradictory effects of EU gender equity policies on their local context. Wanja discusses her characterization as a Thai immigrant in Sweden and how EU economic policies affect her small business operation. Cherry, Jovita, Mila, and other domestic workers reflect on the ways in which immigration policies in Los Angeles and Rome are implicated in and aggravate the xenophobia they encounter in these cities. Vilma Campos and Anthony Lee draw connections between US policy in El Salvador and the Asian financial crisis and their experiences of marginality as transnational workers in the hotel and restaurant industry in San Francisco. The manner in which their physical bodies bear the strains and stresses of globalization is evident in the latter narratives, as well as those of Luz, Candela, Fanny, Luna, and Alondra in Argentina, who contribute vital insights on the impact of longer working hours but decreased standards of living ushered in by Argentina's economic crisis.

Some of the insights provided by women marginalized in globalization are offered through material discourses (and discussions of them), as in what the cloth displayed by women at funerals in Liberia represents, shedding light on the history of colonization, offshore European textile production, migrant labor, and import-export policies that are part of the longer history of globalization. Collectively, they represent the tensions evident in the disempowering social and material consequences of globalization that women experience in diverse locations in the global North and South and their strategic acts of agency. Implicit in these strategic engagements is a call for a collective, transnational response to globalization, as voiced by Saraswati, the Tamil tea plucker in Sri Lanka.

ETHNOGRAPHIC INSIGHTS ON GENDERED MARGINALITY

The ethnographic essays in this volume augment the existing literature on globalization by providing vivid accounts of women's diverse experiences in globalized social contexts and by making space for the voices of women in globalized contexts to narrate their own particular experiences. We bring together multidisciplinary ethnographic documentation by scholars positioned socially and physically at many global locations, acknowledging both the situatedness and partiality of knowledge (see Collins 1991), as Lamphere, Ragone, and Zavella (1997) have emphasized in their collection. In terms of methodology, we provide a space for recognizing the diversity of voices and perspectives as a critical way to avoid the erasure of difference in the production of knowledge, as Mohanty (1991, 2003a), Collins (1991), Hurtado (1996), Hale (1991), Brah (2003), and Sandoval (2003) have cautioned against. Methodologically, we agree with Burawoy and others (2000) and Williams (1996) that we need to ground our analyses of globalization in documentation of the connections between our everyday milieux and transnational processes (as with the analysis of the labor conditions in the hotels where anthropology meetings are held). We bring together ethnographic evidence that traces the numerous processes and factors instrumental in the exacerbation of marginality and disempowerment in the operations of globalization along the contours of gender.

A number of scholars have called for anthropological analyses of globalization (see, for example, Kearney 1995; Tsing 2000) and of capitalism (Blim 2000) that draw on the close observational and listening skills of ethnography to document the variously situated interpretations and experiences of globalized capitalism(s), and for specific attention to gender in relation to globalization (see Freeman 2001; Yelin 2004). The proliferation of the ethnographic method into other disciplinary domains speaks to its powerful capacity to capture the complex dynamics of social relations. As the various disciplinary analyses represented in this volume attest, ethnographic methods are not necessarily the exclusive province of anthropologists. Sociologist Ali Rattansi (2005:287) has noted the particular usefulness of ethnographic approaches, or "thick descriptions," in understanding "the lived experience of racialized interactions." Moreover, sociologist Raka Ray's (2003:110) essay on what she learned from listening to a domestic worker, Lakshmi, about her life and work in Calcutta, points out the importance of listening to what women say about their circumstances and also to the silences of what women do *not* say. In this regard, the ethnographic vantage point of this volume not only puts marginalized women of color at center stage but also allows for the amplification of their voices. As Aguilar (2004:16) argues, "to speak of globalization without center-staging women of color would be a grave mistake." Finally, echoing the persistent concerns with gender essentialism and representation that women's studies and anthropology have long engaged, the ethnographic descriptions also capture the diversity in women's encounters with globalization and the unique and often parallel dimensions of inequities that configure their lives.

POINTS OF DEPARTURE AND CONVERGENCE

This volume represents the culmination of a two-year effort devoted to the theme of women and globalization by the Association for Feminist

Anthropology (AFA), launched during Lynn Bolles' (2002–2004) term as president and continued under Mary Anglin's term as president (2004–2006). As part of this effort, AFA members compiled bibliographies and syllabi, mentored students, and organized sessions at the annual meetings of the American Anthropological Association (AAA) (2003). Many of the chapters in this volume are drawn from a panel on women and globalization ("The Other Side of Peace: Women and Globalization"),[14] organized by Lynn Bolles and Nandini Gunewardena at the 2003 annual meetings of the AAA. Several chapters were recruited from the session "Global Apartheid, Environmental Degradation, and Women's Actions for Sustainable Well-Being," organized by Faye Harrison for the 2004 meetings of the International Congress of Anthropological and Ethnological Sciences (ICAES). This collection brings together essays on women's experiences in several globalized social contexts in the global South, including Ghana, India, Jamaica, Liberia, Mexico, the Philippines, and Sri Lanka, as well as comparative analyses of marginalized regions and sectors of the global North (for example, the US South, a rural Swedish district, and service work in California and Rome). The collection represents a transnational and interdisciplinary collaboration among scholars from five continents in the global North and South.

We are indebted to the School for Advanced Research (SAR) for extending the funding support that made it possible for a group of senior feminist scholars to convene on the SAR campus in April 2005 to engage in extensive discussions about the nature and scope of the book. Thanks to the foresight and flexibility of SAR Press co-director Catherine Cocks, we were able to depart from the usual week-long seminar format required by the SAR for book projects.[15] In our case, ten project advisers (including several past presidents of the AFA) corresponded virtually about the ethnographic chapters already assembled and then met on the SAR campus for condensed discussions establishing themes for additional essays. The participants included Mary Anglin (then president of the AFA), Lynn Bolles, Karen Brodkin, Catherine Cocks, Nandini Gunewardena, Faye Harrison, Ann Kingsolver, Louise Lamphere, Mary Moran, Sandi Morgen, and Patricia Zavella.

The seminar enabled us to discuss the contributions of feminist and ethnographic perspectives to political economic analyses of globalization. One of our concerns was to incorporate diverse perspectives on unique and parallel experiences of globalization processes by women in different social and spatial locations. We reached a consensus that it was imperative to allow the voices of culturally and economically marginalized women to resonate critically throughout the text via the ethnographic documentation of the individual authors, who, themselves, embody such diverse social and spatial locations.[16] We also agreed that this volume must avoid naturalizing women's participation in globalization and analyze critically how local and global gender constructions may collide in the ways women experience globalization processes. Our aim is to contribute to a more nuanced understanding of women's social locations at, and navigation of, the intersections of racial, ethnic, class, caste, indigenous, and other markers of marginality.[17]

From the start, this volume has been rooted in a political economic analysis of women's specifically gendered locations and actions in relation to the current dynamics of global geopolitics and reflecting a multitude of power relationships—in households, communities, organizations, nations, and transnational contexts. As a project of the Association for Feminist Anthropology, this volume brings to broader political economic discussions of globalization particular attention to the subjective voices of those marginalized from, and by, academic privilege and critiques naturalized categories, colonial, patriarchal, and white lenses, and entitlement. The construction and negotiation of culture is also a tenet of ethnographic analyses brought to the volume, but we wanted to emphasize—in focusing on how women navigate particular marginalities—the constraints on agency, as well as the possibilities for women experiencing convergent forms of oppression with capitalist globalizations.

STRUCTURE OF THE VOLUME

This book may be read and used in a number of ways, but we have organized the chapters by clustering them according to thematic concerns that encourage readers to take up the discussions begun by the authors. The first cluster, for example, focuses on production, distribution, and consumption—in this case, of cloth and clothing—as central to current and historical analyses of globalization. In the section "Producing Threads, Consuming Garb: Women Traversing Global Clothing Markets," Nandini Gunewardena's chapter focuses on women workers in a garment factory in Sri Lanka; Akosua Darkwah discusses women trading cloth in the transnational market between Europe and Ghana; and Mary Moran considers the shifting meanings of cloth and its consumption in Liberia from the colonial period. This cluster facilitates discussion of the gendering of globalizations through a focus on commodity chains and the lives connected through those chains (see Collins 2003).

The second cluster of chapters, "Racialized Policies, Scarred Bodies: Women Transposing Neoliberal Violence," documents the dichotomous categories that have fostered the hierarchical racialization, subordination, and paternalistic marginalization of groups of people through capitalist economic and cultural relations. This cluster also allows readers to look critically at the ways in which historical, development, and neoliberal discourses are used to promote and mask active marginalization, including physical violence. The chapters in this section are Ulrika Dahl's discussion of marginality related to nationality and gender in rural Sweden, William Conwill's analysis of domestic violence and economic marginality in the United States, and Barbara Sutton's documentation of the embodied effects of neoliberal policies on women facing harsher working conditions and less access to food and health care.

The third section, "Servicing Leisure, Serving Class: Women Transgressing Global Circuits of Care," focuses on service work as a lens to study women's marginalities, and their contestation of these, in global circuits. Lynn Bolles discusses women workers and entrepreneurs in the tourist sector in Jamaica; Rhacel Parreñas focuses on domestic workers from the Philippines who navigate urban spaces in the United States and Italy; and Sandy Smith-Nonini writes about the union activism of workers from many nations who service San Francisco's hotel and restaurant industry, which hosts groups such as the American Anthropological Association.

The last cluster of ethnographic essays, "Contesting Marginalities, Imagining Alternatives: Women Transforming Global Coalitions," focuses on something that all the chapters in the volume address—agency in relation to conditions associated with economic globalization. Ann Kingsolver's chapter includes a discussion of the conceptual contributions of women's plurinational organizing to broader alliances against neoliberal free trade policies in Latin America. Annapurna Pandey looks at the use of the concept *swadeshi* by women in India to resist negative aspects of globalization in their regions.

The foreword, chapter 2, and the concluding chapters introduce other ways of reading across and beyond the collected ethnographic essays, taking up the themes of structure and agency, the role of states, the paradoxes of globalization, processes of differentiation, patriarchal capitalist and other power relations, and ethnographic and coalitional approaches to understanding gendered globalizations and how women navigate economic and cultural marginalities.

The authors engage theories of cultural and economic marginalization that bridge political economic, feminist, critical race theory, and other approaches to discuss individual and collective experiences of power that distinguish among agency, autonomy, and hegemony. We examine expressions of agentive, oppositional discourse and strategies for alternative knowledge practices and political mobilization to contribute to theoretical analyses of marginalization, vulnerability, and social exclusion in relation to economic globalization.

About the Authors

Nandini Gunewardena is a practitioner anthropologist with a Ph.D. from the University of California, Los Angeles. She has more than 14 years of pragmatic experience addressing the concerns of women in several impoverished nations in Asia and more recently the Middle East and North Africa through her work with a number of bi- and multilateral agencies. Her expertise includes community-based research, project implementation, outcome assessments, and policy reform. She returned to academia in 1998, teaching in the departments of anthropology, women's studies, and international development studies at the University of California, Los Angeles. She is currently a faculty member in the human services program at Western Washington University. Her ongoing research focuses on the inequities generated by neoliberal globalization (including the feminization of poverty), women's work in transnational factories, and suicide as a response to economic stressors.

Ann Kingsolver, associate professor of anthropology at the University of South Carolina, has been interviewing men and women about their views on globalization since 1986 in the United States, Mexico, and, most recently, Sri Lanka. She wrote *NAFTA Stories: Fears and Hopes in Mexico and the United States* (2001) and edited *More Than Class: Studying Power in US Workplaces* (1998). She is general editor of the *Anthropology of Work Review.*

Notes

1. Kaufman (2003:153) notes that the "acceptance of oppression as natural and normal by oppressed and oppressor alike is especially striking in the gender-based forms of oppression." Attention to this problem by feminist theorists has enabled us to recognize other forms of naturalization, as in capitalist market rationality being seen as "natural" or "logical."

2. We acknowledge here that there is a separate literature on vulnerability, which those interested in marginalities might want to investigate critically. Kirby (2006:11), for example, argues that discussions of vulnerability by organizations such as the World Bank need to be expanded to include explicit attention to violence. Authors in and beyond this volume have also addressed the physical violence of neoliberal policies, for example.

3. See Lamphere, Ragoné, and Zavella 1997 (pp. 451–469) for more on this concept.

4. As Bergeron (2001:991) notes, "many feminist accounts of globalization remain partly inscribed within mainstream discourses of economic and political space even as they are reconfiguring them." In this volume, the state and capital are not viewed as monolithic, but as experienced and configured differently, thus our use of plural globalizations.

5. See, for example, Basu et al. 2001; Channa 2004; di Leonardo 1991; Harrison 2002, 2004b; Lamphere, Ragoné, and Zavella 1997; Lancaster and di Leonardo 1997; Ong 2000; Ortner and Whitehead 1981.

6. Feminist analysis itself has multiple strands. See Hawkesworth 2006 (pp. 25–28) for an excellent history of plural feminisms. Moraga (2002) has referred to an "expanded feminism" to acknowledge the shift beyond the narrow roots of feminist analysis in a predominantly white and "First World" context.

7. See, for example, Aguilar and Lacsamana 2004; Balakrishnan 2002; Benería 2003; Bolles 1996a; Fernandez-Kelly 1997; Harrison 1997a; Kingfisher 2002; Ong 1987; Piven et al. 2002; Safa 1995; Wolf 1992.

8. Sassen (2006:16–17) discusses how "in the 1980s and 1990s, the growth in FDI took place through the internationalization of production of goods and services, and of portfolio investment (buying firms)."

9. Hawkesworth (2006:3) discusses well the situated effects of globalization on women "within particular races, classes, ethnicities and nationalities"; other projects are also closely allied with ours in this volume. The ethnographic examples collected here are intended to contribute particularly to that shared project.

10. Barker and Feiner (2004:2) describe a feminist economic approach as reframing economic questions and priorities: "Neoclassical economics insists on seeing each as essentially the same: they are all rational economic agents seeking to maximize their utility within the dual constraints of time and income. The feminist alternative holds that gender, race, ethnicity, and nation are analytical categories, not mere descriptors attached to rational agents who are in all other regards identical" (Barker and Feiner 2004:5).

11. We use the term *global South* to refer to the shared vulnerabilities experienced by developing nations that have been drawn into neoliberal globalization processes in oppressive and disempowering ways, and in solidarity with "South–South" collaborative efforts to bring about social justice and equity. We are cognizant of the parallel vulnerabilities that exist within pockets of the global North, to the extent that they may be included in our framing of the global South. In similar fashion, we recognize that sources of oppression operant across the globe collude in constituting the marginalities and disempowerment in this wider notion of the global South.

12. As Chang (2004:231) points out, women of color have been most affected by capitalist globalization because of its extension of earlier forms of marginalization; sev-

eral of the ethnographic essays in this volume include historical analyses precisely because of the compound, gendered effect of earlier forms of oppression.

13. See, for example, Keating 2004; Kelly et al. 2001; Marchand and Runyan 2000; Naples and Desai 2002; Rowbotham and Linkogle 2001; Staudt, Rai, and Parpart 2002.

14. The AAA theme for 2003 was organized under the rubric of "Peace: Affinities, Divisions, and Transformations." In coining the title for that session, we drew upon the phrase in the much respected Palestinian human rights activist and scholar Hanan Ashrawi's book *This Side of Peace* to capture the troubling aspects of globalization for women.

15. We are grateful to Catherine Cocks for her vision and support of this volume and to Ann Perramond for her insightful copyediting.

16. We agree with Arturo Escobar (1995:223), who has argued that ethnography is not the only way to investigate alternatives to capitalist modernities but that it is vital to attend ethnographically to insights from those most affected by hegemonic configurations, outside academic contexts.

17. There is a vast literature on intersectional approaches. Cindi Katz, for example, has used the term *topography* as "grounded by translocal politics [that] offers at the very least the possibility of countering the ways that the maneuvers of globalized capitalism exacerbate and build upon gendered, racialized, nationalist, and class axes of oppression and inequality in different historical geographies" (Katz 2001:1231).

2

Feminist Methodology as a Tool for Ethnographic Inquiry on Globalization

Faye V. Harrison

It has been suggested that leading scholars of globalization (such as Anthony Giddens and David Harvey) have tended to write from the vantage of "a privileged airspace above the world they theorize" (Burawoy 2000b:340; see also Lewellen 2002:95 on anthropologists who analyze transnational and global concerns). This observation certainly does not discount the value and usefulness of this body of theoretical discourse generated by sociologists, geographers, and other social scientists. It does, however, emphasize the importance of documenting, elucidating, and explaining the complexities and intricacies of global "forces, connections, and imaginations" (Burawoy 2000a:28, 2000b:342) from a diversity of partial perspectives, grounded in lived, embodied, and differentially situated knowledges (Haraway 1988). Such culturally diverse knowledges and the socially negotiated experiences on which they are based are among the concerns of *ethnographic inquiry* and the theories and analytical perspectives that inform and constitute this approach. As much more than a genre for writing and textualizing culture (Behar and Gordon 1995; Clifford and Marcus 1986), ethnography has long inspired sociocultural anthropologists and, increasingly, researchers in other fields (for example, Brown and Dobrin 2004).

SEEKING A VIEW FROM THE BOTTOM UP THROUGH GENDERED LENSES

The ethnography of globalization typically builds its view of historically contingent phenomena from the bottom up rather than from the top down, a perspective made possible by dialogic relationships cultivated between ethnographers and ordinary, often economically and politically marginal, people who struggle to negotiate the everyday conditions of the changing world. The contributors to this volume analyze globalization's gendered character, particularly the ways in which women across diverse local, translocal, and transnational fields of culture, power, and political economy exercise agency, engendering and negotiating the dynamics of globalization from below. The contributors achieve this ambitious goal by employing tools promoted by feminist methodologies for producing knowledge that can be linked to advocacy and activism for women's rights and, more generally, human rights and social justice for all.

Proponents of feminist methodologies have long debated how best to deploy techniques from established methodological toolkits, including the empiricist tradition, in order to meet their research and advocacy objectives. Ethnographic inquiry shares a great deal in common with the research priorities of many feminist and women's studies scholars. Although feminist research is generally a heterogeneous enterprise that includes survey research, some have insisted that feminist research should ideally embrace an egalitarian ethic of care that promotes face-to-face, hands-on, reciprocal relations between researchers and those being researched. Feminist research, according to this view, should redress the exploitation of women as objects of research. Those who subscribe to this view assert that feminist research should represent an alternative approach that emphasizes the experiential, takes a contextual and interpersonal approach to knowledge, is attentive to the concrete realm of everyday life and human agency, and is conducted with empathy, connectedness, dialogue, and mutual consciousness raising (for example, Nielsen 1990; Reinharz 1992).

Ethnography seems to be a most suitable approach to these criteria. However, debates over the years have shown that in even its feminist applications, ethnography does not automatically resolve the power disparities involved in women studying women (Stacey 1988). Although feminist anthropologists still struggle over this issue, ethnographic methods are certainly amenable to deploying a "logic-in-use" (Pelto and Pelto 1970:3) consistent with a feminist methodology that underscores the value of women's voices, experiences, and agency and the sociocultural and political-economic contexts in which they are situated.

To identify, probe, and interpret the gendered dimensions of globalization, anthropologists and allied social researchers must use appropriate tools to illuminate lived and embodied experiences, as well as the workings of various kinds of global flows, markets, corporations, unions, NGOs, states, and the policies that the latter mandate. Feminist anthropologists (for example, Freeman 2000; Nash 2001) have already set some impressive precedents for thinking critically and creatively about matters of methodology and gender—as it is embedded in wider matrices of inequality and power.

THE IMPORTANCE OF NOT CONFLATING METHOD AND METHODOLOGY

Because this chapter focuses on feminist and pro-feminist researchers' deployments of method and methodology, it may be useful to clarify my understanding of the meanings of these two interrelated terms—which are sometimes used synonymously. In my view, it is important not to conflate them, although they are mutually constituted. Methods are the specific procedures, operations, or techniques for identifying and collecting the evidence necessary to answer research questions. In and of themselves, they are not feminist or non-feminist. Therefore, there are no "feminist methods" per se. However, there are "feminist methodologies," because methodologies articulate conceptual, theoretical, and ethical perspectives on the whats, whys, and hows of research and the production of knowledge—from "low-order propositions" to "middle-range and general theory" (Pelto and Pelto 1970:3).

Methodologies provide the philosophical or logical rationale for the links researchers make among theory, pragmatic research strategies, evidence, and the empirical world. In simpler terms, a methodology is "a theory and analysis of how research does or should proceed" (Harding 1987 quoted in Naples 2003:3). A feminist methodology clues us in on which combination of methods is likely to be most suitable for meeting the pragmatic and ethical objectives of a feminist research project. Feminist research, on a whole, is a heterogeneous enterprise supporting a wide range of projects; consequently, there is ample room for both survey research and qualitative investigations such as historical and ethnographic case studies.

IS ETHNOGRAPHY A METHOD OR A METHODOLOGY?

To understand globalization in its fullest human dimensions—including those that are gendered, as well as raced and classed—critical learning and research communities should, to the extent possible, seek both evidence that provides general or generalizable answers and documentation that illuminates the many ways in which culturally diverse and geographically dispersed human beings make meaningful sense of, experience, and shape the rapidly changing world. These particular interpretations and experiences are often conveyed through the discursive and, as Barbara Sutton's chapter makes clear, bodily practices of everyday life. These are identified as data to be gathered, interpreted, and explained by social researchers whose toolkits may include the techniques, procedures, and strategies we associate with ethnography.

It is important to note that although ethnography is typically characterized principally in terms of qualitative methods, its methodological repertoire may indeed include quantitative techniques, particularly those appropriately and meaningfully triangulated with the styles and procedures that are ethnography's traditional cornerstones—participant observation and various kinds of intensive interviewing (Bernard 2005). Ethnography, therefore, is a multimethods approach that may comprise both qualitative and quantitative techniques and strategies to "[learn] about the social and cultural life of communities, institutions, and other [social] settings" (LeCompte and Schensul 1999:1).

We might even claim that ethnographic methodologies cover the range of research theories that consider experience-near participant-observation or participatory-immersion approaches central to the process of asking researchable questions, finding the best answers by some combination of techniques, and producing new layers of knowledge from analyzing and theorizing the research results. Given the common threads that bind together the chapters of this book, I would argue that similar feminist methodologies inform the gendered ethnographic analyses here. In other words, ethnography has been conceptualized and deployed as a feminist methodology.

THE INTELLECTUAL AND SOCIOPOLITICAL VALUE OF WOMEN'S STORIES AND PRACTICES

The ultimate symbiosis and complementarity between qualitative and quantitative research methods is too often discounted in research and policy-making arenas in which numerical data and statistical calculations are presumed to be more accurate, reliable, and useful than the "anecdotes" and "stories" accumulated through intensive ethnographic fieldwork. However, sociocultural anthropologists understand that stories can be a rich and invaluable source of knowledge and theory. For example, in accessible non-elitist language, Ann Kingsolver has written that "theory" can be viewed as "the stories we tell ourselves to make sense of life and to determine where we are as we navigate social space" (Kingsolver 2001:4). All human beings, from social science and policy experts to ordinary folk, narrate socially situated yet "differentially empowered" (2001:24) stories. Anthropologists are "ethnographic listener[s] and storyteller[s]" who weave together larger patterns of stories to develop social analyses, often those that link complex macrostructural forces to the intricate micropolitics of everyday lived experiences (2001:26). All of the chapters in this book make these kinds of conceptual and analytical connections.

Postmodernism amplified long-standing tensions between so-called hard and soft social scientific approaches. However, contrary to the fear that postmodernism would lead anthropology to a full-fledged retreat from solid empirical evidence and rigorous fieldwork, as anthropologist Ted Lewellen has observed, "many anthropologists regularly apply postmodern concepts in the interpretation of *meticulously collected empirical data*" (Lewellen 2002:47, emphasis added). He goes on to write that "[w]hat is impossible in radical postmodern philosophy—namely the blending of materialist, social-scientific practices with postmodern assumptions—is actually quite routine in practice. Realism, defined as the belief that entities exist independently of our perceptions or theories about them, can be reconciled without a great deal of difficulty with the postmodern emphases on reflexivity, situated knowledge, and social constructionism" (Lewellen 2002:47).

The integration of interpretive and materialist approaches has been a productive strategy for a number of feminist anthropologists who have integrated culture and political economy or interpretive political economy approaches, producing significant outcomes (for example, di Leonardo 1991; Kingsolver 2001; Nash 2001). The chapters here also reflect this approach to synthesizing the discursive and the material, the performative and the structural. For instance, Nandini Gunewardena's insightful cultural analysis of the aesthetically resonating self-presentation styles and the performance of modern identities among Sri Lankan female factory workers is clearly situated in the political economy of Sri Lanka's export-driven development. The "arranged marriage" or "marriage of convenience" between Sri Lankan workers and global capitalism is the stage upon which the flamboyantly adorned young women perform. Mary Moran's analysis of the production and marketing of textiles in the West African context points to the significance of these commodities for both the world system and West Africans, for whom gendered meanings of cloth have had considerable currency within changing status hierarchies.

INSIGHTS FROM CONTRIBUTORS' ETHNOGRAPHIC PRAXES

Some of the chapters in this collection focus more centrally on methodological issues. They raise important questions relevant across and beyond the volume: for instance, the ethical challenges involved in negotiations for informed consent, addressed in Akosua Darkwah's chapter on Ghana's transnational traders. This is an issue that Darkwah obviously manages effectively; however, negotiations for informed consent, which must be ongoing during the course of fieldwork, are not unproblematic matters. This matter-of-fact issue can be laden with serious ethical dilemmas in parts of the world where anthropology and ethnography are often maligned, viewed as remnants from the colonial past, and not conducted in the best interests of local communities. Darkwah's fieldwork places her in her home country, where, to negotiate informed consent, she had to convince the traders of the relevance of contemporary anthropology as a tool for illuminating their worldly experiences in constructive ways.

Sandy Smith-Nonini's chapter addresses the ethics and politics of ethnographic research in a particularly compelling way. The case she presents implicates and challenges US-based anthropologists to do the kind of serious "homework" (Williams 1996) that should force more of us to recognize our responsibility in working to resolve the conflicts and social suffering that globalization exacerbates. In her analysis, ethnographic fieldwork is a tool for building politically engaged advocacy for economic justice and human rights.

The chapters reveal that field sites proliferate beyond the conventional features of ethnographic maps. Although several chapters make reference to communities being affected by structural adjustment programs, neoliberal public policies, tourism development, and globalization-induced shifts in status and stratifications systems, sites more clearly in the foreground include websites and online associations, NGOs, plurinational organizational networks, political coalitions, union picket lines, the American Anthropological Association (AAA) and its dispersed membership, the multisited mobility of transnational traders and domestic workers, commodity chains and flows, the landscapes of big and small tourist hotels, and even marriage and family therapy sessions.

Ethnographic research is conducted across transnational spaces, often following research participants or consultants as they move from place to place, both intranationally and transnationally, in pursuit of livelihoods, economic development, and alternative political and policy outcomes. The contributors deal with the location of their research in interesting and innovative ways. For instance, Ulrika Dahl contributes an ethnography of what might be considered an oxymoron, a northern European periphery in which men are culturally assigned to tradition and women to modernity. Gunewardena's study of female factory workers is sited not "at the point of production" but in after-work activities, the practices and performances of social reproduction and female bonding. Rhacel Parreñas' study of Filipina domestics in Rome and Los Angeles describes the "placelessness" they experience in the former setting when they congregate and interact during their off-work hours. Parreñas adopted snowballing and shadowing techniques to map Filipina domestics' movements across the urban landscape, as well as the unofficial and often shifting venues in which they spend their leisurely and regenerative time together.

Issues of positionality are particularly relevant to the discussions in this volume. In pointing out that Parreñas' mother's social network was helpful in a nonprobability (snowball) sampling, for example, Parreñas acknowledges her own relationship to Filipino "community" or "communities" in Los Angeles and transnationally. Interestingly, she is quite explicit about the data-gathering methods used to carry out her study. We know the type of interviews conducted, the number, and the average length of time spent with the interviewees. We also know that she herself has experienced xenophobia in ways not unlike those confronted by her research subjects. We might also infer that the ways she experienced and confronted those assaults were inflected somehow by class privileges that her informants do not enjoy. Parreñas presents a balanced picture of her quasi-insider positionality and the methodical strategy she executed to carry out her fieldwork. In other words, she helps readers revisit her research route in order to offset the suspicion (should anyone have it) that her knowledge claims are largely grounded in her insiderness, her status as a "native anthropologist."

Her chapter shows that her fieldwork adhered to sound methodological guidelines that can be evaluated as a component of her ethnographic analysis. She reveals that her view of herself as an ethnographer is clearly not shaped by any essentialized notion of being native or subaltern (Narayan 1993). The same applies to a number of other contributors. Annapurna Pandey, for example, did her fieldwork in her home province of Orissa, India, where her research involved, to some extent, negotiating differences along lines of caste, class, and the tribal–Hindu divide. Natives are always heterogeneous and fractured, so to establish rapport and build relations of reciprocity and solidarity, the ethnographer has to pay dues of some sort to gain access to the organizations on which her ethnographic research focuses. Negotiating difference is an integral feature of all the research projects represented in this book.

Finally, I wish to re-stress that ethnographic inquiry is not restricted to anthropological praxis. The anthropology of gendered globalization is part of a wider interdisciplinary conversation among intellectual allies sharing overlapping interests and goals. William Conwill's chapter on the impact of neoliberal policies on African American families, households, and marriages represents the gendered and pro-feminist perspective of a research clinical psychologist who recognizes the similarities between ethnographic observation, listening, and dialogue and the psychosocial case study method that therapists use to develop appropriate therapies to promote individual and community mental health and to heal the wounds afflicted by neoliberal globalization's psychosocial assaults. He juxtaposes his qualitative analysis of a few counseling cases with his analysis of aggregate data from a national, publicly available survey conducted by other researchers. His chapter attests to ethnography's usefulness in multimethodological research based on principles of triangulation. He also points to the usefulness of situating ethnographic results in wider interdisciplinary contexts that include critical analyses and assessments of quantitative data sets, recognizing their limits and partiality despite their representativeness in statistical terms.

Representativeness, however, does not adequately elucidate nuances of sociocultural meaning and experience that can be seen through ethnographic lenses. The bodily inscriptions and embodied responses to Argentina's structural adjustment that Sutton's ethnography highlights, the shifts in the language of market bargaining that Darkwah's participant observations expose, the playful performances of gendered identity that Gunewardena's research foregrounds, and the unspoken placelessness that Parreñas encountered in Rome would most probably be lost to the measurements of survey instruments.

REFLECTIONS ON A LARGER PROJECT

Feminist methodologists, cognizant of the limits of the partial perspectives that any particular method or methodology yields, have advocated a multimethodological approach. This approach can be strengthened by epistemological and methodological coalitions among feminists who recognize the value of cross-pollination and collaboration. Methodological diversity among differentially positioned feminists, especially when they share basic ontological assumptions about the world, can enhance our ability to achieve a more comprehensive and robust understanding of the world (Naples 2003:202). This kind of coalition building is consistent, I believe, with the web of connections that Donna Haraway envisions for connecting and stimulating dialogues among diverse, situated knowledges. Working constructively and productively with the epistemological and methodological implications of our varying positionalities will better enable us to address issues of power that complicate and sometimes sabotage our best intentions as ethnographic fieldworkers, theorists, and social justice advocates.

Because we understand that gendered globalization also implicates racializing and classed differentiations, it is important for us to acknowledge that feminist ethnography should be in meaningful dialogue and active solidarity with potentially allied projects, especially those of critical ethnography, the methodology of the oppressed, and the decolonizing methodologies of indigenous, subaltern, minoritized, and anti-racist researchers (Brown and Dobrin 2004; Sandoval 2000; Smith 2005; Twine and Warren 2000). Together with these critical projects, feminist ethnographers should be better able to retheorize their ethnographic practices in ways that allow self-critical reworking and refinement to remove whatever problems or contradictions might limit ethnography's capacity to evoke socially meaningful and responsible intellectual, emotional, and political responses.

About the Author

Faye V. Harrison is professor of anthropology and director of African American Studies at the University of Florida. Her research on the politics and political economy of intersecting dimensions of social inequality is focused on the African Diaspora. She has conducted research in the United States, Great Britain, and the Caribbean on the gendered division of labor in the informal economy, the everyday effects of neoliberal globalization, and the many faces of structural violence. She has also written on the raced and gendered history and politics of anthropology. She edited *Decolonizing Anthropology* and *Resisting Racism and Xenophobia: Global Perspectives on Race, Gender, and Human Rights* and is the author of *Outsider Within: Reworking Anthropology in the Global Age.* She chairs the Commission on the Anthropology of Women, a section of the International Union of Anthropological and Ethnological Sciences.

Part I

Producing Threads, Consuming Garb
Women Traversing Global Clothing Markets

3

Disrupting Subordination and Negotiating Belonging

Women Workers in the Transnational
Production Sites of Sri Lanka

Nandini Gunewardena

In the current phase of capitalist globalization, foreign direct invest-ment prescribed by neoliberal policies has spurred the growth of transna-tional production, leading to global increases in women's labor force participation rates. Although new employment opportunities in the "mod-ern" sector[1] promise to confer economic benefits, evidence provided by several scholars points to attendant processes of disempowerment experi-enced by women.[2] Young women workers in Sri Lanka, like those in transnational production sites in Southeast Asia and Central America, have eagerly sought work in this "modern" sector as a way to escape the drudgery of agricultural work,[3] as well as to secure economic and social autonomy.[4] Yet, as elsewhere,[5] factory work in the export processing zones (EPZs) of Sri Lanka has, ironically, served more as a source of social and economic subordination for women workers. The denial of collective bargaining and the absence of standards mandating a living wage have diminished women's economic gains. Furthermore, oppressive disciplinary measures within and beyond the factory walls have robbed them of their humanity and aggravated their social marginality. While in transnational factories tyrannical management strategies designed to exact optimal pro-ductivity reduce women workers to labor commodities, in public spaces stringent scrutinizing practices intended to regulate women's behavior ren-der them morally suspect subalterns.[6]

On the bustling streets of Sri Lanka's capital city, Colombo, women factory workers are hailed as *Juki badu* (Juki things) or *garment badu*, regardless of whether they are associated with garment or other production outfits.[7] These incriminating jeers implicate a double marginality by relegating women's factory work to the feminized domain of garment production and signifying multiple levels of objectification with the tag term *badu* (which literally means "thing"). Considering the significance of the garment industry in generating foreign revenue for the country (the foremost source),[8] such characterizations also betray an erasure of women workers' humanity and productive capacity.

This knotty entanglement of class and sexual objectification hints at the subversion of women factory workers' identities to the interests of capitalist production and patriarchal sexual desire. Seemingly innocuous, such street parlance carries a heavy, negative symbolic load, invoking distancing practices along gendered class boundaries, conferring a further layer of social marginality to women factory workers. These demeaning street discourses are part of the repertoire of reproach encountered by factory girls in Sri Lanka, embodying the disjunctions of gendered morality between the rural periphery and urban middle-class society. The young women who traverse these boundaries are indicted as morally suspect subalterns while simultaneously consigned as labor commodities. Acutely aware of their stigmatized status, women factory workers engage in diverse strategies to reclaim their dignity and disrupt their assignment to the margins of society.

In the following, I examine the ways in which women workers in Sri Lanka's transnational factories are subjected to numerous practices of moral and labor disciplining that reinforce their social subordination along the contours of gender and class, as well as women's responses in resistance to the constraints of such practices. I document how such women workers (predominantly migrants from remote, peripheral rural villages) are subjected to disciplinary regimes on the shop floor and, outside the factory, to the moral surveillance of society. I discuss how these processes occur via gendered representations that castigate women for lacking morality and self-restraint, and I argue that such negative characterizations are instrumental in justifying their placement as subordinates in the workplace and beyond.

My concern is to examine how these processes ultimately result in distancing practices that deepen women's social marginality along local and global demarcations of power, class, and gender. Assessing the constraints on their social agency and the possibilities of resistance, I document how they navigate and negotiate hegemonic Sinhala gender ideals and class ascriptions. Because Sinhala women constitute the majority of the work-force in Sri Lanka's transnational factories (Rosa 1989), this chapter focuses exclusively on ethnically Sinhala[9] women workers.

METHOD AND CONTEXT

This chapter draws upon informal discussions with women factory workers in Colombo, Sri Lanka, over the course of about a year in 1994. These interviews took place outside the work setting and may not be considered a representative sample, filtered as they are through the narratives of a handful of young women workers. The chapter privileges the stories of these young women workers, via the case studies of two women, as the lens through which the collective experiences of women factory workers across urban spaces in Sri Lanka may be narrated.[10] My introduction to the world of women factory workers came through a fortuitous reacquaintance with two young women, Dammi and Manike (pseudonyms), from a distant *chena* farming (shifting agriculture) village in Moneragala. Considered among the poorest districts of the country, Moneragala is located in the southeast and was the field site for my dissertation research nearly a decade earlier.

The chapter relies on information I gathered as a participant-observer in the informal gatherings of young women at the end of their workday. Visiting one another to listen to music while they ironed clothes, sewed a hem, or prepared a special treat to be shared with co-workers the following day, the women chatted about the daily events in the factories where they worked. It was evident that for the young women who engaged in them, these discussions served as a means of unburdening themselves of the day-to-day tensions and stresses experienced on the shop floor, allowing them to share with friends and co-workers the seemingly incomprehensible behavior of management and to make sense of the shop floor environment, as well as their not-so-positive experiences in the city spaces of Colombo.

Aware of my return to Sri Lanka, Dammi wrote me a letter about their recent move to Colombo. The translation from Sinhala reads as follows:

> Dear Sister,
> A few months ago, Manike and I moved to Colombo to work in a garment factory. It was a difficult decision because of all the gossip in the village about garment girls. But the cost of growing sugarcane is so high that elder brother Karu simply can't make ends meet, and younger brother Jaye just finished his A-levels and wants to go on to a technical college. If our father was alive,

we wouldn't be poor and helpless, but what can be done—such is our Karma! We miss home, and especially the meals of millet and maize that you, too, used to enjoy, if you recall, but we have made a few new friends and at least we don't have to get burned under the sun, planting and cutting cane. We are now modern girls. Please come and see us.

Blessings of the Buddha,

Dammi

Several ideas expressed in this letter require explication because they reveal the common dilemmas faced by young women who opt for factory work, the factors that prompt their decisions to migrate to the city, and the repertoire of cultural notions they utilize in framing those decisions. The comment pertaining to "the gossip about factory girls" in their home village, for instance, reflects the prevailing discourse, which constructs factory women as morally suspect, and the extent to which these two young women were conflicted about their decision to join the factory workforce. Previous studies by Rosa (1989) and Lynch (1999) document similar kinds of character judgments imposed on women factory workers. One woman interviewed by Rosa (1989:5), for example, commented, "The villagers look at us with suspicion. The rumor that reaches the village is that FTZ [Free Trade Zone] women are 'loose' women." A male factory manager interviewed by Lynch made the following comment, revealing how this moral suspicion is articulated as a betrayal of tradition and of the moral purity expected particularly of women: "When village girls migrate to Colombo for work they go bad and get caught up in fashion (vilasitawa), whereas villagers pay more attention to customs (gati), and ways (sirit)" (Lynch 1999:56). Fear of being characterized in a similar manner by the village community haunted Dammi and Manike throughout their stay in Colombo and was a topic of constant discussion in the evening gatherings. This fear also informs us of the dearth of "respectable"[11] jobs in close proximity to the homes of young rural women from impoverished backgrounds.

Their use of the word *girls* (*kello* in Sinhala) to refer to themselves echoes the common use terminology in the society for young women, although, technically, *kello* refers to premenstrual females. This term alludes to the juvenile status ascribed to these young women, despite the financial responsibilities they bear, and is indicative of the societal reluctance to acknowledge fully the significant economic contributions they make to their natal households. Their claim to modernity reflects a choice they have made to embrace an alternative (albeit stigmatized) identity in an effort to distance themselves from the orientalist relegation of rural populations to the "backward" (nonmodern) social groups in this deeply class-stratified society. Unlike in Thailand,[12] where urban and rural classes alike embrace a celebratory discourse of modernity, in Sri Lanka, modernity is imbued with distinct meanings by the elite and middle classes[13] in Colombo and by the rural populations. For the former, it is a highly sought-after attribute that confers a belonging in a global, technologically sophisticated world, signaled by the choice of cosmopolitan dress and adornment and freedom from the fetters of tradition and superstition.

For village society, on the other hand, modernity has more mixed connotations. Rural dwellers may aspire to modernity as a means of shedding the orientalist caricatures to which they are held, but they simultaneously lay claim to the pristine identity ascribed to them in romanticized depictions of the village as the locus of authentic, unspoiled Sinhala culture characterized in nationalist projects. In this sense, they have also succumbed to the gendered symbolism surrounding modernity that perceives women as the embodiment of tradition and cultural purity. As exposure to city life deepens village girls' awareness of this divide, they are confronted with the dilemma of either acceding to the moral purity ideal, including its attendant connotations of "backwardness," or yielding to their newfound sense of autonomy and redefining their identities. They are compelled to grapple simultaneously with two tasks: bridging the social distance between themselves and urban society and contesting the negative attributes of modernity that attach to them in urban spaces.

In a similar vein, given the classification of factory work as part of the "modern" industrial sector, the girls' incorporation of the English word *modern* (in a shortened version, *mod*)[14] into their vernacular to characterize factory work and their identity as factory workers also reflects their preference for factory work to the drudgery of work in the cane fields—the only other employment available to them.[15] Their tendency to invoke the notion of karma as an explanatory device for their situation not only captures the prevalent notion in Buddhist Sri Lanka that one's lot in life is due to the karma accrued in previous lives, but also draws on the cultural explanation for gender and social subordination (that is, a woman's lot in life) as determined by one's karmic fate. Their unquestioning acceptance of engaging in productive work as a role norm provides insights into the discrepancies between the gender role expectations specified in middle-class Buddhist ideals,[16] which prescribe women's role as restricted to the domestic sphere (presumed to be a domain where women do not "work"[17] and are dependent on a male provider), and the gender norms in Sinhala areas of rural

Sri Lanka, which recognize and value women's diverse productive contributions to the livelihood of the family and household.

Despite Sri Lankan women's historical participation in informal and formal labor forces—in family farming, the plantation economy of the nineteenth century,[18] and recently in the manufacturing sector—middle-class Buddhist ideals still hold women to the "traditional" valorized role of wife and homemaker. This demarcation represents a conundrum for lower income groups, who find it nearly impossible to attain, given their economic marginality and related reasons. Deepening poverty in the country since the adoption of economic liberalization policies in 1977 has compromised household subsistence security enough to prompt more than one income earner to join the labor force.

MEDIATING CLASS AND GENDER: BEYOND THE BINARY OF DISEMPOWERMENT AND AGENCY

Scholars who have researched the plight of women factory workers in Sri Lanka (that is, Hettiarachchy and Schensul 2001; Hewamanne 2003; Lynch 1999; and Rosa 1995) have well documented the ways in which these young women workers are constructed as morally questionable simply because of their lone mobility in the big city, beyond the confines of home villages, which are perceived to afford protective surveillance by family and community. These studies have captured women's vulnerability to sexual overtures based on their construction as women with "loose" morals. I suggest that the perceived lack of patriarchal protection is at the root of this kind of characterization. At global production sites elsewhere, Ong (1987), Fernandez-Kelly (1997), and Mills (1998) have documented similar attributions. As Ong notes, for example, Malay factory girls are constructed as "hot subjects," implying sexual excess or laxity. Mills (1998) documents the ways in which Thai women workers in Bangkok's manufacturing sector negotiate rural "standards of feminine deference, modesty and virginal purity" in the face of prevailing concerns about their sexual reputations in the city.

Two strands of thought are discernible in the previous research on women factory workers in Sri Lanka—the depictions of women as subordinated by this kind of moral branding (Lynch 1999) and as agents engaging in various forms of cultural (Hewamanne 2003) or political resistance (Rosa 1995). Lynch focuses on the ascription of the "good girl" identity to which factory women aspire, in conformity with notions of respectability, self-restraint, and moral purity attached to dominant constructions of gender in strands of Sinhala Buddhist identity formulations. Lynch's concern is to document the ways in which women factory workers are pressured to acquiesce to the ideologies of respectability, whereas Hewamanne (2003:72) explores their engagement in oppositional cultural practices that entail a refusal to "perform the ideals of respectability,"[19] and represent a form of resistance. Although Lynch takes pains to historicize gendered identity constructions, there is a need to interrogate further the ways in which social class emerges as a critical variable in the formulation of different gendered identities. In the case discussed here, we must consider the notions of gender subscribed to by the Sinhala Buddhist middle classes in their preoccupation with delineating a legitimizing social space for their class identities as distinct from the rural "other."

To reconcile these divergent perspectives, I suggest that we view women's responses in non-essentialist ways, evidenced by the wide range of strategies they deploy in coping with the intense moral scrutiny to which they are subjected. Characterization of women workers' responses as either conforming or resisting entails a binary framing: women are portrayed as wholly antagonistic or fully compliant to the gender norms of the day. Such a dichotomy, in my view, effectively masks the far more nuanced dynamics of social interactions that occur at the intersections of gender and class. Furthermore, rather than pose class and gender as separate forms of social inequality, I suggest that we analyze them in relational terms, as intersectional[20] variables that constitute power relations in a given social context. In this case, the power vested in gendered class identities has significantly shaped the responses of women factory workers, endowed with little power, to the structured inequalities in society. Thus, their responses represent, in my view, an attempt to grapple with their subordinate placement in the class and gender hierarchies of their society.

In my long-term ethnographic observations of the gender–class interactions across rural and urban Sri Lanka, ambivalence is a far more common response to encounters with power than is wholesale antagonism,[21] as alluded to in previous studies.[22] I also suggest that women's myriad strategies may, in fact, be responses to the destabilization of the meanings of belonging in social contexts increasingly incorporated into capitalist globalization, which, in turn, prompt attempts to craft new and alternative conceptualizations of belonging.

As a way to reconcile these distinctions, I draw upon Foucault's conceptualization of "disciplinary power"[23] to explore how the female body is targeted at this global production site as an object to be manipulated and trained in the production of docility. Given the problematic aspects of his notion of docility,[24] however, my aim is not only to explore the imposition of power on women factory workers but also to cite the transgressive gestures that form a set of resistance practices they engage in, which offer a counter-narrative to the notion of docility. I situate my argument on the idea that marginal space is a site for witnessing repression, accommodation, *and* resistance simultaneously, given the dialectical relationship among these forces. Hence, my purpose is to explore how women's relegation to marginal social locations entails strategies of repression, while also evoking parallel strategies of resistance.

LOCATING THE WORLDS OF FACTORY WOMEN

My first glimpse into the residential lives of women factory workers launched this research inquiry. One evening, well after the end of their dayshift, I followed the directions they had sent me, walking along narrow streets that circled a solid-waste disposal site at the edge of the city, to the boardinghouse occupied by 19-year-old Dammi and her 17-year-old sister, Manike. I found them in a tiny, windowless, mosquito-ridden room, sharing one outdoor toilet and bathing at a common well with six other girls.[25] I listened to them narrate with resignation an account of their daily routine of waking up at 3 a.m., preparing their breakfast and lunch over a kerosene oil stove, and catching a 5 a.m. bus (the only one with an empty seat, given the heavy usage by the working masses traveling into the city) to the factory site. Their monthly pay was a mere 3,000 rupees, placing them below the poverty line[26] ("actually, 4,500 with overtime," Dammi was quick to interject—the equivalent of about $40 at the time).[27]

Appalled at their living conditions, I invited Dammi and Manike to move into a spare room in the little apartment I had rented. (Dammi insisted that she would have to wait until replacements filled their slots, to avoid overburdening their roommates with the extra boarding fees.) After their move, our shared residence (partly because of the electrical conveniences it housed) soon became the evening gathering place for groups of factory girls who would stop by to share a cup of tea at the end of their workday, use the electric iron, store perishables in the fridge, or simply listen to some music. This chapter draws upon the daily reports and anecdotes about life within and beyond the factory recounted by Dammi, Manike, and their co-workers over the course of the following year.

WOMEN AND WORK AT GLOBAL PRODUCTION SITES IN SRI LANKA

The introduction of economic reforms in the late 1970s[28] is generally considered to mark the turn toward Sri Lanka's incorporation into contemporary (neoliberal) globalization processes (Hettige 1998), resulting in rapid and massive economic, social, and political transformations. The ensuing shift to a reliance on export production led to the creation of Free Trade Zones (FTZs),[29] which attracted and accommodated many well-known transnational corporations (TNCs),[30] such as the Gap, Nike, and Liz Claiborne, as well as scores of less well-known ones primarily of North American origin. Their massive recruitment efforts[31] spurred the migration of young women from the rural periphery in hitherto unseen numbers to urban areas surrounding the FTZs and other factory complexes.

Classified as "unskilled" labor, women factory workers in Sri Lanka earn a meager 13 cents per hour, endure the indignities of class ostracism in public spaces, and suffer the humiliations of intimidation, scolding, sexual harassment, and corporal punishment in the workplace. They put up with overcrowded, makeshift residences that often house as many as 20 women in a 50-sq-ft room, all to repay a family debt, help meet the educational costs of a younger sibling (as in the case of Dammi and Manike), fund seasonal cultivation expenditures, or provide the entire subsistence needs of their natal households.[32] Compelled to migrate for work from distant rural areas because of household poverty and family indebtedness,[33] these young, mostly single, women workers navigate the dimly lit, poorly paved roads bordering the FTZs and other global production sites around the country, tolerating the jeers that cast them as disrupters of the moral order and the TNCs' tendency to characterize them as producers with little capacity for expressive, creative consumption.

The workweek typically includes weekends and regular holidays such as full moon days (the *poya*).[34] Yet, at peaks in the production cycle, when a seasonal line needs to be completed and shipped out, these young women often work continuously for two weeks at a stretch to meet production targets, some days on 12-hour shifts.[35] Dammi and Manike would negotiate an occasional poya holiday with factory management when it coincided with the obligatory almsgiving for their father's death anniversary or a similar ritually significant occasion. The 5 p.m. bus out of Colombo would bring them, after a sleepless night of travel, to their village some 200 km away by 8 a.m. the following morning. They had to catch a return bus to Colombo within 24 hours for fear of being laid off.

On such occasions, Dammi would approach me hesitantly to borrow 1,000 rupees to purchase some dry goods for the almsgiving and a few gifts for her mother and cousins. Barely saving enough to remit home to meet the cultivation costs each season, Dammi was often short of change for her bus fare to work, even though I supplied all their meals, with no charge for

43

the room. Theirs was not a unique situation, as I learned, but the common experience of most factory girls. Glad to have the convenience of a gas stove, instead of the time-consuming and smoky firewood hearth she had to cook over in her home village, Dammi would awaken at dawn (something to which she was not entirely unaccustomed at home) to prepare breakfast and lunch and wrap up leftovers to share with less fortunate factory girls, who did not have any protein in their diets.

SURVEILLANCE AS A DISCIPLINARY TOOL: THE COLLUSION OF FACTORY DISCIPLINE AND THE MORAL GAZE

Women on the factory floor are subjected to routine physical surveillance by mostly male supervisors, who monitor their production quality and output. According to the accounts of the women workers I interviewed, this overbearing scrutiny forms the primary source of tension on the shop floor. Although other sources of tension surround the repressive strategies deployed by TNCs to discourage and prevent the formation of unions,[36] as well as to maintain the low pay rates, which are far below a living wage,[37] it is the resort to coercive tactics that women factory workers found unbearable. These tactics included verbal admonishments and abuse, threats, and intimidation designed to yield excessively high production quotas, a regime of corporal punishments for noncomplying workers, and excessive monitoring and disciplining of workers' uses of time, not only in terms of punctuality and attendance but also in terms of prohibitions against conversation and co-mingling with fellow workers.

These women workers found this confluence of shop floor conditions—including the expectations of an uninterrupted, machine-like pace, impossible-to-achieve quotas and targeted output, and limitations on worker interaction—to be the most oppressive and unjust. One glaring example of the implications of these strictures is a 1998 incident in which a woman's hair got entangled in a high-speed machine in a Sri Lankan factory in the Katunayake FTZ. A stipulation against going to the aid of a fellow worker delayed those working beside her from helping her extract herself, resulting in her scalp being torn off (World Socialist website 1998).

During her initial months at work, Dammi would return home feeling dejected and humiliated because she had been "pulled up" (reprimanded, often in an abusive way) throughout the day for her inadequate cutting skills. Eventually, she negotiated a "checker" position in which she was in charge of pulling remnant threads and ensuring the final finish of the completed garment. Although worker compliance to the dictates of line supervisors was naturalized as per the customary cultural expectations of conformity to male authority, individual women found different ways to circumvent the strict rules. For example, as the spoiled younger sibling, Manike relied on her elder sister, Dammi, to take up slack for her—adding to Dammi's fatigue and resentment. Alternatively, Manike resorted to "charming" the supervisor into excusing her deficiencies, as Dammi would confide to me with irritation, simultaneously cautioning Manike about the dangers of such a strategy. Other women workers often carried special treats (such as homemade traditional sweets) or resorted to mild flirtations with male supervisors as bargaining tactics designed to flex the stringent rules and expectations.

In addition to the pace of work and the demands in production output (both quality and quantity), stringent policies about breaks, lunch schedules, days off, and toilet breaks were considered the most imposing and constraining by the women workers I interviewed, echoing the accounts of women workers in factories around the world. The women I interviewed commented with resignation about the monitored breaks and, with their customary humor, about the curious policy of limited and measured bathroom visits. Enforced by a card (dubbed the *choo* card, or "pee" card) marked by a supervisor tallying the number and duration of toilet visits per day, this practice was the subject of much joking, particularly capturing the antics of those who had a difficult time "holding it."

The excessive humor on this topic suggests a masking of the difficulties this practice imposed, but many of the women offered evidence of the ways in which they maneuvered around the choo card. Manike, for example, claimed that she would simply run to the toilet without waiting for permission—readily believable, given her customary brazen ways. Others reported dashing past the supervisor before he could stop them, with a smile and a quick "No problem, no, sir"[38] as a common strategy, or finding a way to the toilet without being seen. One of the women I interviewed reported a more extreme strategy used by a co-worker in her former workplace, who would simply shout as loudly as possible, "Sir, if I don't go now, I will explode on these very garments," which promptly yielded an annoyed nod of agreement by the supervisor.[39]

These strategies suggest that women factory workers have far more room to negotiate the pace and expectations at the work site, but these need to be interpreted with caution. They may only reflect the policies and practices in a particular factory and long-term relationships cultivated between supervisors and women workers that may have softened the harshness of the typical disciplinary regimes at other production sites. As the anecdotes above and below reveal, the physical abuse endured by one worker and the enforcement of rules in more rigid manners at other sites may have less serendipitous outcomes.

CONSTRUCTING IMAGES OF DOCILITY AND MANAGING PRACTICES OF "DEVIANCE"

To potential investors, the national Board of Investment (BOI) portrays the Sri Lankan worker as "well trained, docile and ambidextrous."[40] Self-discipline and obedience are specific characteristics attributed to and boasted of Sri Lankan workers. Following Foucault, it appears then that the construction of global factory workers as "disobedient subjects" by transnational management provides a justification for the exaction of "obedience" by resorting to temporal and corporeal disciplining.[41] The shop floor demeanor of factory girls, however, departs significantly from the BOI projection of docility. They display less of an acquiescence to the compliance expected of them and more of a contested negotiation of their duties, rights, and disciplining, as the above narrative reveals.

In many cases, however, the response by supervisors and management is to construct such contestations as culturally deviant (for example, as transgressing gender norms) and consequently to resort to culturally salient disciplinary strategies such as scolding, humiliating remarks, verbal reprimands, and often corporal punishment (beatings).[42] In a country where corporal punishment is commonly accepted as a routine part of disciplinary strategies in the school system, it may be no stranger in the disciplinary regimes of the workplace, especially where women workers are conferred "juvenile" (hence subordinate) social status. In one incident documented by Weerasuriya (2000:1), "a supervisor assaulted a woman worker from behind forcing her to increase her production target blinding her as her head hit the machine and sending the machine wire into her eye." In another account, "a women worker had lost her power of speech, as she was constantly verbally abused using very bad language for the purpose of increasing production. She could not speak for several months" (Weerasuriya 2000:1).

REINSCRIBING SOCIAL AND MORAL HEGEMONY

The regimes of labor disciplining on the shop floor and the moral-symbolic disciplining in public spaces that Sri Lankan women factory workers face provide some glimpses into the gendered anxieties regarding the larger numbers of women entering the labor market in recent years. The FTZs in Sri Lanka, for example, recruit primarily young (72 percent are below 25 years of age) and single (88 percent) women. Because of the high proportion of women workers and their residence in the zone, the major FTZ, Katunayake, has been referred to as *Stripura* (the City of Women). Reflecting the moral castigation of these young, unmarried, women workers, the name for the zone became the "whore zone" (*Vesa Kalapaya*) via a neat linguistic twist of the Sinhala term for *Free Trade Zone* (*Nidhahas Velanda Kalapaya*). Drawing on a liberal (albeit depraved) connotation of freedom (*nidahas*), the term suggests moral lascivity and trade/sale (*velanda*), as in the flesh trade.

This damning representation echoes the prevailing patriarchal discourse, which characterizes women as being inclined to sexual excesses unless they are controlled, supervised, and guided by morally superior men. This kind of characterization reveals the preoccupation with ideals of feminine purity espoused by emergent, influential, chauvinistic segments of the local intelligentsia that consider themselves the moral guardians of Sinhala Buddhist culture. It also serves to establish and renew the moral hegemony of a newly resuscitated set of ideals, embraced and propagated as authentic and traditional Buddhist norms, that prescribe a gendered code of respectability.[43]

Simultaneously, this characterization betrays the class stereotypes and presumptions surrounding the work habits, self-disciplining capacities (or the purported lack thereof), and unregulated sexual compunctions of rural and low-income populations held in an increasingly class-polarized society. The classic colonial stereotype of the "undisciplined native" has been used to explain and attribute blame for the social and income disparities of the haves and have-nots. It is now invoked in a neocolonial context in characterizing factory girls hailing from rural areas as undisciplined beings capable only of physical labor and requiring appropriate control in the exaction of such labor and in terms of their sexuality, via disciplinary regimes on the shop floor and beyond. These perceptions also serve to justify the relegation of women workers to the social margins in order to service privileged sections of the population in meeting their consumption desires.

THE CRISIS OF MASCULINITY AND CONSTRUCTIONS OF MORAL DEVIANCE

Why is there the compulsion to construct factory women as morally deviant? Sri Lankan women factory workers, like their sisters who migrate out as domestic workers, seem to present challenges to the traditional dominance of men, who, in the patriarchal, postcolonial cultural context of contemporary Sri Lanka, are expected to fulfill the gender ideal of provider. Ironically, the provider role was not a gender-differentiated role in premodern Sri Lanka but emerged as a male role via a conflation of Victorian-colonial influences and has been recently revived as an intrinsically local Buddhist construction. Thus, the recent entry of wives, daughters, and sisters to the formal workforce, and their ability to significantly augment or in some situations provide the sole sustenance for a family, can be perceived and construed as a personal failure by men.

I see the misogynist discourses that surround factory girls and women migrant workers as stemming, in part, from this crisis of masculinity in Sri Lankan society. Males who feel that they are no longer privileged as the sole provider can claim a moral high ground and assert their dominance and authority by invoking a moral superiority simply by virtue of their gender and thereby assault the dignity of young women workers with sexual slurs. The aspersions about factory women's sexual excesses permit the reification of a neo-Buddhist[44] gender hierarchy in which virtuous and therefore morally superior males can exert control over, supervise, and discipline "deviant,"[45] and therefore morally inferior, women.

The construction of urban spaces as privileged along class and gender (being the proper domain of urban elites and middle classes, primarily male) leads to the perception of women's entry into such physical spaces as disruptive. I suggest that women's incursions into the symbolic spaces of work and provider, previously the preserve of class- and location-privileged males, is thus perceived as a threat. City spaces endowed with place- and gender-specific identities reveal the power relations in the society. Women's visibility in these spaces poses a challenge to the meanings with which these have been imbued and thereby the place-specific relations of power with which the city is endowed.

Accordingly, the occupational stratification on the shop floor reflects the gender hierarchies prevalent in the society: Women occupy the bottom rung as machine operators, assembly-line workers, and packers, taking on tedious and monotonous piecemeal tasks (such as button sewing and fabric cutting), skills that are naturalized as feminine. Men are assigned the more complex technical tasks, as well as managerial positions.[46] Data from 1995 from the Sri Lankan Department of Census and Statistics show that women represented 12.9 percent of plant and machine operators (skilled work) and males represented 87 percent of the workforce in this category (Gunatilaka 1999). As Bender (2004) has noted, sexual harassment at the work site is ultimately a tool for the policing and naturalization of sexual difference at work. Extending Bender's argument about the centrality of sexuality (either in the form of sexualized characterizations of women workers in public spaces, as in the present case, or in the form of sexual harassment at the work site) in the maintenance of gender hierarchies at work, I suggest that such depictions are also instrumental in urban Sri Lanka in demarcating social distance along class and gender and in maintaining gender hierarchies in urban spaces, as discussed below.

NEGOTIATING BELONGING AND DISRUPTING SOCIAL EXCLUSION

The acute sensitivity of factory girls to these anxieties, tensions, and representations, however, has helped shape a range of responses, both accommodating and resisting, that helps them negotiate the contours of belonging and exclusion and ultimately disrupts their stigmatized identities. Navigating the tensions between economic deprivation and servitude and social subservience, women workers at global production sites are acutely conscious of the caricatures of their existence. A key strategy in their responses to this marginality is to disrupt their relegation to the role of producer and to insist on their capacity for creative expression by laying claim to their consumption capacities. Why insist on one's consumption capacity? As noted above, in globalized contexts flooded with consumer items, consumption capacity is associated with social power because only those who are class-privileged can afford to engage in making market choices. Factory workers' attempts to mimic the consumption practices of the privileged may thus be read as a strategy to disrupt their marginal social placement, unlike those without disposable income, who are robbed of the power to consume.

Moreover, the claim to consumption is, in effect, an assertion and a display of their access to disposable income. Factory women are wont to flaunt such access, despite the reality that it is an elusive element in their struggle for economic survival. Corresponding to their striving to conform to the markers of modernity set by urban middle-class society,[47] factory girls refrain from a conspicuous display of gold jewelry that at other times and social settings serves as the pro forma status symbol. Paradoxically, their desire to convey such status vis-à-vis village society means that most factory girls first invest in a gold chain, earrings, and a pair of bangles. Their claim to consumption and their resort to particular consumption practices are more a means of unsettling their marginal social placement.

Miller (1995) has noted that consumption also represents an entry into self-conscious modernity. The choice of Coca-Cola over mango juice, ice cream over curd,[48] and sausages over dried fish (a typical village food), are examples of the consumption choices made by factory girls that represent their increasing tendencies to purposefully craft "modern" identities. Building on Miller, I suggest that such practices inform us of the way factory women who do not have access to the goods they produce—the garments they make are destined primarily for the US and European markets and are beyond their means—assert consumption choices that help mask their intended social and class designations.[49] Alternatively, some women workers manipulate the domain of personal aesthetics (as documented by Hewamanne 2003) as transgressive acts, choosing overly conspicuous dress and adornment as celebratory markers of difference that appear to reject any aspirations to class mobility.

Despite women workers' contrasting levels of accommodation, at the heart of these strategies is the need to register their consuming capacity and challenge their relegation to the constrictive role of workers and producers. This is vividly evident in the shopping districts of Colombo, the habitual preserve of the middle classes. Rejected factory goods make their way to retail shops in Colombo's elite shopping districts, where name-brand apparel with slight irregularities and undetectable mistakes is sold at affordable prices for local consumers. Garment factory workers also frequent these outlets, in effect, asserting their modernity and attempting to bridge the class gap that distances them from Colombo's middle classes. They do so in the face of the class hostility to which they are subjected in such spaces, evidenced in snide remarks by middle-class women about the "uncouth" mannerisms of factory girls.

In a deeply class-hierarchical society like Sri Lanka, where clothing serves as a marker of status distinctions, where the judgmental gaze of the social hierarchy falls upon the minutest details of one's attire for the purpose of reaffirming class identity, exercising social distance, and creating subservience, factory girls are carving inroads of belonging by attempting to appropriate its most visible cues. Although society condemns their conspicuous fashion tastes as *vaivarana* (flamboyant), in contrast to the sober colors and minimalist aesthetic norm of Sinhala Buddhist ideals, these choices are no doubt a way for factory workers to thumb their noses at middle-class ideals, by flaunting the very opposite in a gesture of oppositional affirmation of their marginalized class status.

The adornment of "garment fashion" (as it has come to be termed) seems to suggest a purposeful class insubordination, an insistence by factory girls that they, too, are consumers, not only in an oppositional embrace of their stigmatized identities and as a powerful gesture of resistance, but also to disrupt their placement exclusively as producers with no expressive and creative capacities. In this manner, factory girls' leanings toward "garment fashion" offer a critique not merely of the specific fashion tastes of the dominant and elite middle classes in Sri Lanka, but also of the very construction of class and its correlations with consumption. As such, the fashion statements made by their choice of colors and adornments are, in effect, an empowering gesture disrupting the neat boundaries between manual and mental labor that global capital attempts to delineate, as well as a claim to their emergent identities as complex, multiple, shifting, and contested subjectivities.

Similarly, the "boisterous" behavior ascribed to garment girls, such as loud talk and laughter and rough (*ralu*) language,[50] suggests a kind of gender insubordination, a refusal to register compliance with Sinhala Buddhist middle-class ideals of feminine demeanor, which call for a soft step, quiet voice, and so on.[51] For example, "appropriating masculine language," according to Hewamanne (2003:81), represents "a powerful subversion of middle-class notions of feminine discipline and respectability." I suggest, however, that these terms of address are not necessarily masculine as much as the general forms of address (*umba/bang*) commonly used in rural areas and typically employed by the underclasses. More significantly, given the class condemnation these evoke, factory women's insistence on such terminology registers the intraclass camaraderie they paradoxically want to convey.

The use of such terms of address, I argue, is in effect an attempt to subvert the class boundaries between rural and urban, instead of a mere reflection of resistance to middle-class gender ideals, and a disruption of the multiple dimensions (gender, class, rural periphery versus urban center) of postcolonial notions of belonging prevalent in the society. Factory women's purposive choice of "rough" terms, despite their familiarity with "respectable" forms of address, is a further indication of their refusal to acquiesce to the "proper" gendered demeanors expected of them. Although these may be considered intentional strategies of oppositional identity creation, premised on a critical assessment of genteel, gendered forms of middle-class respectability that are beyond the reach of factory women, their power lies in the gestures that overturn the cherished neocolonial adaptations of Victorian mores treasured and embraced by the postcolonial middle classes. Factory women, in other words, are engaging in a social critique of the structuring of class privilege and its contours in contemporary Sri Lanka, while disrupting its gender norms and expectations.

Laying claim to the domain of creativity is also a way to assert control over the (negative) representations that objectify, vilify, and demean factory women's subjective experiences. One vehicle that has emerged for women workers to engage in such creative expression is a newsletter titled *Dabindu* (literally meaning "drops of sweat"), launched in the FTZs in 1984. *Dabindu* publishes original poetry, critical essays, short stories, and commentaries by women workers. Currently distributed throughout the country,[52] this newsletter serves as an avenue for articulating workers' subjective experiences and is eagerly consumed by factory girls as a source of advice, guidance, and information exchanges on worker rights, nutrition, and intimate relations.[53] As Rosa (1989) notes, *Dabindu* also represents a political mechanism through which women workers can voice workplace grievances. Even though its primary purview is purportedly that of creative expression, *Dabindu* has also been instrumental in raising awareness of the injustices endured by women factory workers, and, on occasion, resolving certain grievances, by assuming an advocacy stance on these issues. As such, it serves the important function of an arbiter, otherwise absent, and a campaigner for women workers' invisible rights. Rosa notes, for instance, that

> the newspaper has campaigned on many issues related to the FTZ workers. These have included the employment of women on the night shift; long unpaid hours of work; inability to obtain entitled leave; unjust dismissal; false propaganda; implying workers in the Zone have no right to organize; the issue of sexual harassment on the factory floor and on the journey home; transport difficulties. The [Dabindu] collective has also joined other groups in the area in campaigns, and the newspaper has been important in popularizing these. The wide variety of persons and organizations that the paper reaches, both inside and outside the area, has been an important element in this process. Manike was a woman worker who was dismissed for writing a poem in the newspaper on the grounds that she had told lies about the factory. After months of campaigning—involving the different centers, as well as national and international campaign by the paper—Manike was reinstated with full back pay. [Rosa 1989:22]

CONCLUSION

The disciplining of women factory workers' morality and physical bodies at the work site and beyond in Sri Lanka returns us to Engels' fundamental question whether wage work has any emancipatory potential for women and the neoliberal argument that market forces will automatically confer economic empowerment on women. This chapter has explored this question in terms of the gender and class inequalities emerging from the incursion and structuring of transnational production in one globalized locale: Sri Lanka. As shown, it is difficult to trace the portended economic autonomy and agency that wage work was expected to confer on women, but only because of the inherent dispossession embodied in transnational production, not because diminished autonomy and agency are the inevitable consequences of wage work.

In this specific social context, as young factory women are compelled to shuttle back and forth between their home villages and urban work spaces, role tensions are aggravated as they are confronted with managing contrasting gender role expectations and social class positionings. This case study reveals the nuanced ways in which gender at the intersection of class and capital functions to structure and legitimize power relationships. Although factory women have not been completely excluded from the newly energized Sinhala moral order, the threat of outright social exclusion operates as a lever that attempts to regulate their behavior.

An all-pervasive moral ideology based on middle-class notions of respectability has not deterred women's influx into the urban wage labor force, or their increasing participation rates. These norms have been mediated in the (re-)construction of women's proper role in society to the extent that they influence exclusion-inclusion processes in the central institution that confers respectability in the society—marriage. As such, women's entry into manufacturing labor has not sufficiently disrupted gendered power relationships in the family, community, and nation.

I have attempted to document how the processes of subordination to which women factory workers are subjected occur along several axes: first, by disciplining women's sexuality; second, by delineating binary identities of producer and consumer ascribed along local and global class, race, and gender axes; third, by constructing the norm of "industriousness" and "optimal productivity" as the universal expectation of workers that helps justify the disciplinary apparatus of global capital; and, fourth, via the translation and appropriation in local settings along gendered norms governing the work ethic, productivity, and worker conduct in order to generate value. Further examination of the patterns of moral surveillance in social spaces and their collusion with disciplinary strategies on the shop floor reveals that they rely on local constructions of gender and draw upon idealized attributes of femininity such as patience, endurance, self-discipline, and submission.

I have suggested that these disciplining practices, within and beyond the factory walls, may be instrumental in justifying the placement of women who enter the global labor force merely as workers with little creative or consuming capacity, and hence designated to serve and service the local and global consuming elite. I have attempted to map how global capital, driven by the need to extract the optimal capacity of workers' bodies, their skills and productivity, colludes with local capital in devising mechanisms of social control on the factory floor and how these converge with the moral regimes of the society at large via ideologies that operate at the intersections of class and gender positionings. I began by problematizing low-income women's incorporation into global production at the lowest rung of the occupational hierarchy—primarily as unskilled assembly-line workers. I then explored how this placement and the corresponding influx of women workers into city spaces raise questions of "belonging" based on notions of proper conduct and appropriate domain. I also illustrated how attendant disciplinary strategies are deployed to establish class and social distance via micropractices of inclusion and exclusion, which in turn compel factory women to engage in a reworking of the boundaries of belonging along the contours of gender and class.

When Dammi and Manike return home, they are careful to shed their "modern" clothes and joke about the scrutinizing eyes of their village community, ever watchful for evidence of their succumbing to the moral corruption reputed of factory girls. They plan ahead and report back to me how they emphasize the fact that they are living under my roof to extended kin, whose fears are immediately assuaged. They leave out the details about public taunts and the workplace regime, the tedium and fatigue, the cycle of pawned jewelry,[54] and the constant cycle of borrowed money that never gets repaid.

Dammi is careful to avoid any mention of her encounter with a young soldier, the flurry of letters exchanged between them, the pledges of love, and, finally, the pain of being rejected by his family as an inappropriate partner because of her status as a factory girl.[55] Her anguish was even more deepened by the revelation that her boyfriend's parents were not the least bit impressed by her caste affiliation (*govigama*, the highest caste) and her inheritance of 2 acres of land. These attributes do not seem to ward off the taint of her identity as a woman from a rural and underdeveloped (*pitisara*) part of the country. Like many factory women, Dammi and Manike traverse one reality that reduces them to bodies instrumental in the production of commodities, yet accused of commodifying desire, and another world in which they are expected to live up to the moral meanings of their names, "precious jewel" and "little jewel."

Notes

1. Manufacturing work in factories in export processing zones (EPZs) is considered "modern," in contrast to work in the agriculture sector, which is associated with "backwardness." See, for example, Mills 1998 for similar connotations of modernity and backwardness associated, respectively, with these two sectors in Thailand.

2. See, for example, Lee 1997; Lynch 1999; Mills 1998; Ong 1997; Pena 1997.

3. The primary alternative available to those without tertiary education.

4. For example, as a way to escape the patriarchal controls of traditional home communities, as documented also by Ong (1997) and Lim (1983).

5. See, for example, Chant and McIlwaine 1995; Fernandez-Kelley 1997; Lee 1997; Safa 1981; Wolf 1992.

6. See also pioneering work by Ong (1987) on Malay factory workers and more recent studies by Mills (1998) and Silvey (2000), respectively, on Thai and Indonesian EPZs.

7. *Juki* refers to the brand of industrial sewing machines that is widely used in the garment industry, and *badu*, plural for *baduwa*, is a slang word in Sinhala, literally translated as "thing." Like the sexual slur "piece" in North America, it is standard male street parlance in reference to a female targeted for male sexual appropriation.

8. The other two main sources of foreign revenue, which, coincidently, also rely on a predominantly female labor force, are remittances from migrant (domestic) workers in the Persian Gulf countries and elsewhere and the tea industry, Sri Lanka's foremost export product.

9. The ethnically Sinhala population constitutes approximately 76 percent of the population of Sri Lanka; the Tamil ethnic group constitutes about 18 percent. Given these demographic proportions, the clustering of the Free Trade Zones (FTZs) in predominantly Sinhala residential areas, and the general undesirability of such work, as well as the political patronage that often plays a role in securing factory jobs, the workforce in most transnational factories is disproportionately Sinhala.

10. A review of the existing literature (that is, Hewamanne 2003; Lynch 1999; Rosa 1989) confirms the parallels in the experiences of women workers reflected in the data I collected.

11. For example, teaching or civil service work that conforms to middle-class notions of "respectability" ascribed to women (documented by de Alwis [1997] and elaborated by Lynch [1999] and Hewamanne [2003]).

12. See Marybeth Mills' 1998 work on Thai women labor migrants, which discusses the meanings and representations of modernity embodied in the notion of *thansamay* and accessible indiscriminately to urban and rural populations, with few negative connotations.

13. Although it is customary to conceptualize the middle class as one homogenous category, I am using the term in the plural in recognition of the multiple

socioeconomic groups that fall into this class and exemplify diverse social and economic aspirations, hold differing social values, and subscribe in varying degrees to the hegemonic Buddhist gender ideals.

14. This embrace of modernity is a curious reversal from perceptions in past years. In the course of my previous field research in rural Sri Lanka, I encountered young women using the word *mod* in a mocking manner to refer to others who attempted to follow the "modern" fashions depicted in women's magazines emanating from Colombo.

15. A study by Gunatilaka (1999) notes that nearly one-fifth of the female working-age population in Sri Lanka have at least a ninth grade education, are unemployed, and aspire to work as teachers, nurses, or clerical workers in public employment but that none seek work in the agricultural or fisheries sectors.

16. See de Alwis 1997 for further reading about middle-class constructions of gender.

17. The value of women's social reproductive work is discounted, and "work" is typically perceived as that which brings in a cash income.

18. See Kumari Jayawardena 1986 for a discussion of the important role women played in the (British) colonial plantation economy of the nineteenth century.

19. Because previous works by Lynch (1999) and Hewamanne (2003) extensively discuss these ideologies, I reserve my commentary on this topic to a brief summary. Middle-class notions of respectability defined via a gender lens have been instrumental in constructing an idealized image of the Sinhala Buddhist woman that emerged as part of the nationalist project of the late nineteenth to early twentieth centuries and paradoxically reflected more conformity with Victorian notions of femininity and associated attributes of domesticity, purity, and passivity. The popularization of these elite notions among the middle classes has led to their wide acceptance as the norm for all Sinhala women, contravening the starkly contrasting gender norms and ascriptions that have prevailed in the rural periphery.

20. Scholars forwarding intersectional analysis (for example, Coomaraswamy 2000; Crenshaw 1989; Glenn 2002; Ontario Human Rights Commission 2001) have pointed to the intersections of race, ethnicity, class, and gender as the axes of subordination, but I am using only two of these dimensions (gender and class) as applicable to this case. The two women whose stories form the central frame of the personal narratives originate in a remote region of Sri Lanka where people claim indigenous heritage, referring to themselves as *Vanni* (a strand of indigenous identity that is considered to be the "true," untainted Sinhala people). I refrain from including this self-classification as part of the axes of subordination because not all factory workers hail from this region.

21. It is possible that this kind of class antagonism is a reflection of the degree of politicization of women workers in the FTZs. Given their concentration in residences surrounding the FTZs and their common stance vis-à-vis the zones themselves, they

have forged a collective identity. An interview I conducted with an FTZ woman worker during her visit home to her village, however, did not reveal any such acute class antagonism. This leads me to believe that class ambivalence is more common than class antagonism. Women who work in global factories elsewhere in the city or in other parts of the island may not have an opportunity to forge such a collective identity because they are not clustered in the manner that FTZ workers are.

22. See, for example, Hewamanne 2003.

23. Foucault's conception of power is that, essentially, power is a relationship between people in which one person affects another's actions. Power differs from force or violence, which affect the body physically. It involves making a free subject do something that he or she would not otherwise do: power therefore involves restricting or altering someone's will.

24. There is already an abundant literature that contradicts Foucault's notions of docility, as well as a rich body of ethnography on the resistant practices forged by workers at global production sites.

25. Similar living conditions are noted by Rosa in her 1986 and 1989 studies.

26. The 1995 poverty line established for Sri Lanka by the World Bank was Rs. 4,000/month.

27. In 2002, the monthly wage for a skilled garment worker was still about 3,000 rupees (US$31) and with 60 hours of overtime would reach only 5,000 rupees (US$52), still hovering about the poverty line if inflation is taken into account (Gunadasa 2002).

28. Including the liberalization of imports, foreign direct investment, and other privatization measures.

29. Also often referred to as export processing zones (EPZs).

30. A strategy pursued as a means to generate employment and thereby reduce national poverty.

31. It should be noted that the recruitment of a predominantly female labor force in Sri Lanka, as elsewhere, rests on gender-specific notions about women's suitability for factory work, including inherently feminized attributes such as ambidexterity and presumed dispositions such as docility.

32. See Rosa 1989 for comparative reasons provided by women workers for seeking factory work; see also the work of Hettiarachchy and Schensul (2001), which documents similar findings.

33. Hettiarachchy and Schensul's (2001:127) study confirms that this pattern, evident in the population of women workers drawn to work in the FTZs of Sri Lanka, who emanate "exclusively from the poorest sectors of rural villages."

34. Poya days are considered sacred in Sri Lanka and hence a day of worship because it was on a full moon day that the Buddha gained enlightenment.

35. As reported by Saman Gunadasa (2002), "A young female worker from Fashion Wear Garments told a correspondent from the World Socialist Web Site, 'We do overtime to earn more money as our wages are not enough to live on. With these

new laws, we will not even be able to get sick leave. Even without these laws, we can hardly get sick leave. We are not free to go home if the day's target is not finished. Even pregnant sisters face the same situation. If we work until nine at night and do not complete the target, we do not get overtime payments. If we got at least 6,000 rupees a month, we would manage without overtime. But we don't get such a wage or have such freedom.'" The Sri Lankan government imposes longer hours on female workers. See the World Socialist website, http://www.wsws.org/articles/2002/sep2002/sril-s04.shtml.

36. See Rosa 1989 for a discussion of the legal regulations and the military environment in the country that have constrained trade union activity. These include the heavy presence of police and security personnel charged with the mandate of quelling any form of "unrest" under the emergency regulations that have prevailed in the context of the ethnic conflict and the youth insurgency of 1989, as well as the specific mandate against trade union activity in the FTZs and other global production sites and factories in the country.

37. This includes a consideration of the costs of living beyond the typical consideration of basic consumption expenses.

38. The term *sir* is commonly used by workers to address their superiors at the transnational production sites in Sri Lanka.

39. I have not been able to confirm the veracity of this story because on many occasions stories were conjured up for the bemusement of the anthropologist and the amusement of the interviewees.

40. Sri Lanka was one of the first South Asian countries to shift to an export-oriented economy in 1977, primarily as part of a neoliberal prescription to reduce rural poverty. The country's first FTZ was set up in Katunayake in 1978, about 40 km north of Colombo and within easy proximity to the Colombo International Airport. Since then, three other FTZs have been established in Sri Lanka, at adjoining Biyagama and farther along the southern coast at Koggala. By 1998, 890 export factories were operating in the FTZs. Women constituted 86 percent of the labor force in the FTZs in 1983; of this number, 70.8 percent worked in the garment industries. By 1998, the number of workers in the FTZs had increased to 280,000, of which 88 percent were single women, mostly below 25 years of age. In addition, five export-processing parks were completed around the country so that "by 1999, 1070 enterprises with an investment commitment of Rs. 145,795 million were in commercial operation" (Alailima 2001:15). Moreover, "the expansion of the garment industry has been the cornerstone of export-oriented industrialization with about 90 percent of the jobs in the garment sector and about 80 percent of the EPZs being for women" (that is, women's employment; Alailima 2001:16).

41. Foucault's discussion of power is central to *Discipline and Punish*. He thinks that power is a strategy, or a game not consciously played by individuals but one that operates within the machinery of society.

42. See the following web article by the Dabindu Collective (n.d.) for a discussion of the coercive tactics: http://www.amrc.org.hk/Arch/3804.html.

43. The large influx of rural women to the urban labor force has raised questions about women's "proper" domain, as defined by the ideals of feminine respectability prevalent in the society. The result, instead of an accommodation of women's evolving role in a modernizing society, has been the resurgence of nationalist ideologies that assume a retrogressive stance demarcating more stringently the domestic arena as the feminine sphere. See de Alwis 1997 for an elaborate discussion of this kind of revival of middle-class Buddhist notions of respectability.

44. By this term I am referring to the attempt by cultural revivalists in postcolonial Sri Lanka to borrow from supposedly Buddhist notions to demarcate a novel form of nationalist identity that is constitutive of a strictly demarcated gender hierarchy.

45. *Deviant* meaning stepping beyond the boundaries of the domestic sphere and associated gender roles to which women have been relegated in the society.

46. Jayaweera (1991) attributes this tendency to the gender streaming in government-sponsored vocational training programs, which has limited women's access to technical know-how and hence to employment in technical types of work. It is clear from global production sites elsewhere, however, that gender is used as a device in structuring the occupational hierarchy of the shop floor.

47. The lack of visible gold adornment on the city streets reflects a shift in middle-class sensibilities: gold jewelry is now reserved primarily for weddings and other such auspicious occasions. I suggest that factory women mimic this pattern.

48. A local form of yogurt, made from buffalo milk.

49. In Miller's (1995:156) article on consumption and commodities, he noted that anthropologists have the task of discovering "how people using goods that they did not produce and that they experience only as consumers nevertheless struggle to create social and cultural identities."

50. See also Hewamanne 2003, which documents this phenomenon.

51. See also de Alwis 1997 on the attributes accorded to the notion of respectability.

52. The Dabindu Collective publishes this monthly newsletter highlighting the injustices in the FTZs. Publication of the newsletter continues to be the collective's core activity and provides opportunities for workers to express their views. Dabindu has facilities in two towns housing the main FTZs and supports women workers through workshops, awareness raising, and other programs.

53. Dabindu Collective (n.d.). A report including personal testimony from Dabindu workers, presented at the Maquila Solidarity Network conference. Posted online at http://www.maquilasolidarity.org/resources/maquilas/pdf/ExchangeEng-part6.pdf.

54. Gold jewelry is one of the first significant purchases made by factory women because of its cultural significance as a marker of status, femininity, and respectability. Although they spend their first savings on this item, as time progresses and expenses

(including remittances home) overtake income, pawning their gold jewelry becomes the customary habit.

55. Lynch (1999:66) notes the wide concern about the reputation of women factory workers and the aversion to marry them, reflected in the newspaper marriage advertisements (common throughout South Asia), which often specifically state "no garment girls."

4

Making Hay while the Sun Shines

Ghanaian Female Traders and Their
Insertion into the Global Economy

Akosua K. Darkwah

Sisi is a 45-year-old Ghanaian woman who engages in what has become known, since the Ghanaian trade liberalization reforms of 1983, as the "Accra-London-Accra" business. This trade was originally initiated by a group of women who traveled from Accra to neighboring countries of West Africa to purchase consumer items, which were sold to their Ghanaian customers upon their return. This group of enterprising women has now extended its purchasing destinations beyond the West African subregion to London, New York, and, in recent years, Asian cities such as Bangkok and Hong Kong. They buy a variety of consumer goods, ranging from shoes, bags, dresses, hair accessories, children's clothing, and bedsheets, to kitchen items such as food processors, toasters, fryers, and dinner sets, and the like, which they then resell in Ghana for profit.

Sisi was originally trained as a hairdresser and worked in hair salons in Ghana and later in Germany, where she and her husband had immigrated. In Germany, she amassed enough savings to set up her own salon in Ghana. She ran the salon until her husband got a job with an accounting firm in New York City and he moved to the United States. It was at this point that Sisi began to consider seriously the possibility of engaging in transnational trade as a means of earning a living.

The year was 1995, twelve years after the implementation of structural adjustment programs in Ghana. Structural adjustment programs can best be described as Janus-faced. Many aspects of the programs, such as work-force retrenchment and the removal of health care subsidies, have taken a toll on the Ghanaian populace. Other aspects, such as the trade liberaliza-tion component, which included the removal of price and import controls, a simplification of tariff schedules, and the abolition of the 10 percent sales tax, as well as a legalization of foreign exchange transactions, have made it much easier for Ghanaians to start lucrative import businesses (Aryeetey 1994:1218). Sisi was among the women who took advantage of such employ-ment opportunities provided by the trade liberalization component of structural adjustment.

Having her husband in New York City provided Sisi with a home in the Western world to which she could return when on a purchasing trip. Not having to spend money on hotel bills meant that Sisi had more capital at her disposal on each purchasing trip. On average, Sisi purchased between US$5,000 and US$10,000 worth of consumer items from wholesale shops in New York City, which she then sold for a profit upon her return to Ghana. Sisi usually traveled twice a year for two-week periods to purchase her items. While she was away in New York City purchasing more items, her father, a retired civil servant, supervised her shop. For the rest of the year, Sisi stayed in her shop, overseeing its day-to-day operations.

Success in this type of enterprise depends on a loyal base of customers who consistently purchase goods from a particular trader. Some of these customers might buy the goods for retail sale in faraway towns and villages; others might buy the goods for their own consumption. The ability of these customers to purchase goods is directly linked to their purchasing power. In a developing country such as Ghana, purchasing power is often on the decline because the value of the local currency vis-à-vis major world curren-cies, such as the American dollar, declines without an attendant increase in earnings. Sisi is well aware of the fact that her business thrived far better in the past than currently, but she knows that this is neither her fault nor that of her customers. The structural adjustment program that made it possible for her to trade with ease is the same program undermining her customers' purchasing power and therefore her business efforts.

The currency devaluation aspect of structural adjustment makes Ghana's currency highly unstable. Indeed, the Ghanaian cedi more often than not depreciates against the American dollar. Sisi makes the most of a deteriorating situation by capitalizing on the two periods in the year when all Ghanaian consumers, regardless of how meager their earnings, make an effort to make some purchases: the Christmas and Easter seasons. Sisi ensures that her shop is stocked to full capacity during these two seasons when sales are highest. This way, although her profit margins are consistently on the decline, she can earn enough to fund her trips to and from New York, as well as live comfortably in Ghana.

Hers is a story that can be retold by various women, not just in Ghana but also in places such as Cape Verde (Marques, Santos, and Araújo 2001) and Jamaica (Harrison 1997a; Ulysse 1999a, 1999b), in slightly different forms. This new type of Ghanaian market women, who are able to engage in a new form of economic enterprise as a result of the opportunities provided by globalization, presents an opportunity to assess the debate on the benefits or drawbacks of globalization from a fresh perspective—an elite perspective that has often been ignored in the literature that analyzes the merits and demerits of globalization.

Globalization, defined here as the worldwide adoption of capitalist economies, is often touted as the panacea for the woes of the Third World. It offers economic returns to big businesses, both local and foreign, as well as to importers of various items (Babb 1996:36). These profits are eventually supposed to trickle down the socioeconomic ladder (Harrison 1997a:456) so that everyone will enjoy the positive impact of globalization. Structural adjustment policies were introduced by the International Monetary Fund (IMF) and implemented by national governments in much of the Third World during the 1980s with the objective of allowing the Third World to partake of the benefits of globalization.

Numerous writers (for example, Afshar and Dennis 1992; Benería and Feldman 1992; Elson 1991; Gladwin 1991; Sparr 1994) have assessed the impact of structural adjustment and come to the general conclusion that these policies have not benefited the Third World. These writers, focusing primarily on citizens and particularly women located at the lower levels of the socioeconomic ladder, have noted how these individuals' economic circumstances have worsened with the introduction of such policies. However, this scholarship on the impact of globalization on the poor tells only half the story because it focuses on the indirect beneficiaries of globalization. Neoliberal theory expects the rich to gain from globalization in the short run. Through a trickle-down process, the poor are then assumed eventually to gain from globalization.

Much less analysis has examined the impact of globalization on Third World elites. This task is equally important because elites, specifically business owners, are supposed to be the direct beneficiaries of globalization. According to the legalist perspective (De Soto 1989), globalization is a good thing because it forces states to remove regulatory and legal barriers that hinder the smooth operation of business enterprises in the Third World and frustrate the efforts of the elite. When these barriers are removed, business owners prosper and transfer these benefits to the poor through more employment opportunities and philanthropy.

This chapter departs from the dominant literature on the impact of structural adjustment on the poor and focuses instead on the elite. Specifically, I turn my attention to women located fairly high up the socio-economic ladder—a group of Ghanaian female traders who travel across the globe buying consumer items that they then return to Ghana to sell. I ask to what extent globalization has benefited these women who, as owners of businesses, are supposed to benefit from the structural adjustment policies that have removed trade barriers in the developing world.

I argue here that the neoliberal ideology that has underpinned Ghana's development policies for more than 20 years has had contradictory effects. Components of this ideology, such as trade liberalization, are liberating for the traders under study here. Indeed, they owe the explosion in their numbers to the liberalization programs of the late 1980s (Aryeetey 1994). However, other components of this ideology, such as currency devaluations that raise the cost of imported goods, limit the extent to which these traders in global consumer goods can attain financial success. In an environment where earnings rarely rise to match inflation, increasing the cost of items simply means a decrease in the purchasing power of consumers, as Harrison (1997a) highlights in discussing the diminished ability of Jamaican women workers in the informal sector to make ends meet, given the higher cost of living with the devaluation of the Jamaican dollar and the removal of subsidies on food items. A citizenry with decreased purchasing power buys less, which invariably decreases the turnover of global consumer items and, in the long run, the traders' profits. Traders of global consumer items therefore find themselves in a very tenuous position financially because they are subject to the vagaries of the global capitalist system.

To survive this tenuous position, Ghanaian women apply agency by changing the very nature of the manner in which trading takes place. Thanks to the trade liberalization programs of the late 1980s, all manner of consumer items are available on the Ghanaian market. Yet, as I will illustrate in my discussion on bargaining styles, traders in their bid to coax consumers to spend their meager earnings on their products have had to redefine the nature and purpose of bargaining for consumer items. Bargaining no longer serves a negotiative function; it is ritualistic. In general, one cannot bargain to get a price reduction in the consumer goods market; one bargains because that is what is expected in the traditional market setting. Nevertheless, this ritualistic coping strategy is not very effective, for it simply maintains the profit margins of traders and does not ensure that consumers can buy the goods.

This work draws from my dissertation research project, which sought to uncover the advantages and disadvantages of neoliberal economic policies for transnational traders in global consumer items (Darkwah 2002). My interest in the lives of transnational female Ghanaians was borne out of both academic and personal experience. I consider myself a transnational female Ghanaian scholar, one who was raised on Ghanaian soil and acquired higher education in the United States. My life since graduation has also been highly transnational; I spend the school year in Ghana and breaks in various countries, presenting papers or working with other scholars. My social location, both as a Ghanaian and as a female, has also given me a unique opportunity to explore the questions of interest to me here.

This project, which began in June 2000 and ended in December 2001, utilized standard ethnographic techniques of inquiry. It entailed the systematic use of unstructured interviews and participant-observation of Ghanaian female traders at work in the Makola Market in Accra, the capital city of Ghana. Makola Market is the largest wholesale and retail market for global consumer items in the country. My entry into the market was greatly facilitated by my serendipitous encounter with a trader of global consumer items who was four years older than I and had an undergraduate degree. Beyond her appreciation of my academic interests, we discovered that we had acquaintances in common. This woman took me under her wing as a sister and greatly shaped my ethnographic experience. She introduced me to her circle of friends and convinced them that my work was for purely academic reasons. Each of her friends, in turn, took me in as her sister or daughter and opened up to me in ways that allowed me to gain in-depth insight into their lives as traders. I spent countless hours in the shops of four of these women and have maintained my relationships with them to varying degrees since the project ended. The bargaining dialogues discussed here were taped in these shops with permission from both the traders and the consumers.

TRADING LOCALLY, TRADING GLOBALLY

Ghanaian women's trading activity has long been noted. In 1853, for example, Cruickshank, a Scottish merchant writing a travelogue about his experiences in the then Gold Coast, noted:

> The whole population are traders to a certain extent. It is the
> delight of the African women to sit in the market-places under

the trees, exposing their wares for sale, or to hawk them through the streets from door to door, and from village to village. [Cruickshank 1853:II, 280–281]

Daniell, writing three years later, also remarked on the centrality of both markets and women in Ghanaian trading activity:

Markets are held on every day of the week...either at the entrance or termination of one of the principal streets adjoining some cleared space of ground, or in localities habitually frequented by a concourse of people....The whole [all] are vended under the patient instrumentality of women and children who, squatted in regular lines along the sides of the streets, or beneath the shade of the adjacent houses, dispose their effects to the greatest advantage. [Daniell 1856:29]

Colonialism served to define trade further as a women's niche in the country's economic life (Robertson 1995). From the outset of colonial rule in Ghana in the late nineteenth century, jobs in clerical services were provided solely for men. As a result, all aspects of trade in Ghana were left, for the most part, to women (Robertson 1995). Some of the women who traded in the early part of the twentieth century, either as sellers of farm produce or retailers for large, foreign trading firms such as the United Africa Company (UAC), were able to generate quite substantial sums of money for themselves. Even in colonial times, some women had lines of credit with overseas firms to the tune of thousands of pounds sterling (Galleti, Baldwin, and Dina 1956). The fortunes of these traders were to change dramatically with the advent of independence.

As has been noted by writers on the informal sector in Africa (Eames 1988; Kerner 1988; Robertson 1983), Asia (Lessinger 1988; A. Smart 1988; J. Smart 1988), and the Americas (Babb 1988; Spalter-Roth 1988), there has long been a hostile relationship between some workers in the informal sector, such as traders, and the state. Beginning with Ghana's first president, Kwame Nkrumah, who had socialist leanings, a series of rules and regulations were put in place that greatly limited the extent to which women could trade in imported goods with ease. These policies included strict import licensing regimes, surcharges on imports, and state-enforced price controls (Rimmer 1992). All of this was to change in 1983. That year, Ghana became the first African country to initiate a structural adjustment program. Among other things, the program called for trade liberalization.

Trade liberalization is based on the neoclassical economic principle that countries prosper most when free trade thrives. Although the extent to which trade liberalization allowed for the easy trade of Ghanaian goods on international markets is doubtful, trade liberalization undoubtedly had an immediate impact on Ghanaian consumers in terms of increasing their access to a variety of consumer goods. Trade liberalization made the importation of goods less cumbersome and encouraged traders with the financial means, many of whom were women, to try their hand at transnational trade. As a result, since 1985 there has been a steady growth in the distributive trade sector of the economy (Aryeetey 1994:1218). The growth of this sector is clearly apparent in the markets of Ghana, particularly Makola Market, which has now become the largest consumer goods market in the country. At this market, one can find all kinds of goods—hair care and beauty products, clothing, shoes, bags, belts, fabrics, kitchen equipment, electronics—brought in from countries in Europe, the Americas, Asia, and the Middle East, including Italy, France, Germany, Mexico, Brazil, China, Thailand, and Dubai. Language and distance seem not to have deterred the traders in their quest to make global consumer goods available to the ordinary Ghanaian.

These traders are located at the apex of the indigenous trading hierarchy.[1] They are usually Ghanaian women of a high social standing with the resources to own and operate a shop. Two-thirds of the women I interviewed had mothers who themselves had traded in items such as fabrics and processed foods produced in local factories. Their mothers' shops served as training grounds where they learned the mechanics of successful trading. In addition, the majority of these women got their start-up capital, which averaged about US$4,000, as gifts from their mothers. The women discussed here are therefore among the most advantaged of traders in the Ghanaian distribution system. They wholesale and retail goods that they themselves have gone outside the country to locate, as well as those provided by suppliers or friends who have traveled abroad for various reasons and brought back some items to sell on a trial basis or have items originally acquired as gifts that they would rather sell.

Known in Ghanaian circles as businesswomen, these women represent a veritable extension of the West African female trade that is such a part of the lives of many West African women (Clark 1994). Their shops are registered with the attorney general's office, and they pay income taxes. On average, these women command working capital of anywhere between US$5,000 and US$20,000. They have bank accounts, usually both foreign and local ones, and have a long history of savings with a formal credit institution, a requirement for acquiring visas to various countries for purchasing trips. Their association with the formal banking system also provides them with the opportunity to take out bank loans if they so desire. These women provide a valuable service to Ghanaian consumers by giving them access to goods that are often not produced in Ghana. Unlike their counterpart informal commercial importers in the Jamaican context, who are looked down upon either for their efforts to move up the economic ladder or because of the perception that they are drug traffickers (Harrison 2004a; Ulysse 1999a, 1999b), traders in the Ghanaian, indeed the West African, context are quite highly respected for their ingenious ability to make huge sums of money as traders.[2]

The consumer goods section of Makola Market, in which these traders operate, is a recent phenomenon in Ghana, compared with the much more established foodstuffs section. There is a clear class distinction between the traders in consumer goods and the traders in foodstuffs. The former are more likely to come from wealthier families than are the latter. It is this family wealth that determines their choice of goods in which to trade. Yet, the consumer goods section of the market retains much of the flavor of the older, traditional foodstuffs section. Both of these markets are fairly gendered spaces. Although men are not necessarily banned from participation in market activities either as traders or buyers, the Ghanaian market, be it for foodstuffs or consumer items, is a predominantly female space. Traders and buyers are much more likely to be female than male. The absence of males is, however, much more conspicuous in the foodstuffs section because food-related activities are generally seen in the Ghanaian context as a female activity.

These two markets are also similar in the arrangement of goods, the employment of family members as workers, the development of personalized ties between traders and regular customers, and the persistence of bargaining before a sale. However, I will argue here that the tenuous position in which traders in the consumer goods market find themselves as a result of their insertion into the global economy has led them to develop a unique form of bargaining in order to survive. This new form of bargaining has become their tool of agency in the globalizing world. Thus, the nature of bargaining as a prelude to a sale in the consumer goods market is distinctly different from that which occurs in the traditional foodstuffs market. The difference lies primarily in the arguments that traders marshal in defense of the prices at which they intend to sell their goods. Inherent in the arguments that the traders raise in their defense is their awareness of the limits of the so-called benefits of globalization.

TRADITIONAL BARGAINING IN GHANA

Uchendu (1967:37) defines bargaining as "a process of price forma-tion which aims at establishing particular prices for specific transactions, acceptable to both buyer and seller, within the 'price range' that prevails in the market." In and of itself, bargaining is not a new phenomenon. Although it is often conceived of as a practice that persists primarily in Third World markets around the world, particularly in West African and Caribbean markets, Garfinkel (1967) experimented and found that bar-gaining with positive results was possible even in the markets of a devel-oped country like the United States.[3] In Third World countries without consumer protection agencies and shops with nationwide retail outlets, however, buyers in a market are suspicious and uncertain of the value of commodities available at the market. Khuri (1968) argues that bargaining is crucial because it serves as a price-regulating mechanism. This explains its pervasiveness in Third World markets.

In fact, in Ghanaian markets, traders perceive buyers who fail to engage in bargaining before purchasing a product as having truncated the purchasing process. Invariably, such buyers would also end up paying far more for the product than the trader intended, for Ghanaian traders set their prices much higher than the going price, knowing full well that potential buyers will ask for a price reduction. This way, they can afford to give the buyers a price reduction without incurring a loss. Buyers who fail to demand the price reduction therefore give the traders a much higher profit margin than the traders intended.

In Ghana, bargaining takes place both at the consumer goods market and at the foodstuffs market. As I will show later, there are distinct differ-ences between the kind of bargaining that takes place in the global con-sumer goods market and that which occurs in the traditional foodstuffs market. In the local foodstuffs market, two types of traditional bargaining take place: quantity bargaining and price bargaining (Clark 1994). In quantity bargaining, a potential buyer requests that a few more items be added to whatever amount the trader has packaged for the price that the trader quoted. This form of bargaining is common with goods that are small, divisible, and sold in piles, such as tomatoes and plantains. For exam-ple, if a trader quotes that four tomatoes are going for the price of 4,000 cedis (US$0.44), a potential buyer may request five at the same price. With larger foodstuffs, such as yams, which are sold roughly by size, a buyer engaged in quantity bargaining would initially demand the price of a yam of a certain size and, when told the price, request that a slightly bigger yam be sold at that price.

Alternatively, especially with food items that are divisible into very small units, such as beans, a buyer could purchase the item at whatever price the trader quoted, after which the buyer would request that a few more of the same item be added on for free. This add-on system, known locally as the *to-so* system, of bargaining is very common. Whether the buyer requests the add-on before or after paying for the items, the logic under-pinning the quantity bargaining process is the buyer's desire for a volume discount.

Quantity bargaining is used much more extensively in the small-scale retail of foodstuffs. Clark (1994) argues that quantity bargaining has a more personalized flavor than price bargaining, by which she means that buyers are more likely to engage in quantity bargaining with traders with whom they have a personalized relationship.

With price bargaining, on the other hand, a potential buyer requests that the cost of an item be reduced. In the traditional foodstuffs market, price bargaining is more likely to be used in the wholesale of foodstuffs, where the fixed wholesale units defining the price make it impossible for buyers to request a variation on quantity. Price bargaining, Clark (1994) argues, involves the use of economic arguments to substantiate buyers' or traders' respective claims to reduce or maintain a price. Such economic arguments include claims that other traders are selling for less or that the buyer cannot afford to buy an item at such a price. Traders' counterclaims include statements that if other traders are selling for less, then it is because those goods are of an inferior quality.

THE NEW FORM OF BARGAINING

In the global consumer goods market, one would expect quantity bar-gaining, based on the fact that much of what gets sold in this market is on a retail basis. In reality, even when goods are sold directly to consumers, only price bargaining exists, because global consumer items are generally not divisible into smaller units, as is the case with foodstuffs. However, the nature of price bargaining in this market is quite different from that which prevails in the local foodstuffs market. This is primarily because in Ghana the traders of global consumer items are in a unique position compared with the traders of local foodstuffs. That is, unlike their counterparts in the foodstuffs trade, traders of global consumer items are inserted into the global economy. By purchasing in foreign lands the goods they sell locally, they trade at the interface of local and global markets. To be able to trade at a profit, the traders have to consider economic conditions operating in both the country from which they purchase their items and the one in which they sell their products. As a result, these traders' decision-making processes regarding price setting and bargaining strategies are quite distinct from those of traders in the traditional foodstuffs market.

PRICE SETTING

The mechanism by which the women establish the initial price that will set the stage for bargaining is quite a complicated process compared with that employed by local foodstuff traders. This decision-making process highlights the traders' appreciation of the global economic conditions under which they operate. It begins with a careful consideration of the cost of airfare to and from the site of purchase, hotel and food expenses while purchasing items in the foreign land, the cost of the items purchased, and, finally, the import taxes imposed on the goods at Ghanaian ports. Overhead costs such as rents on the shops and warehouses and workers' salaries do not feature directly in the price calculations. Instead, these overhead costs are drawn from the profits of the transnational trader. The total costs incurred in purchasing the global consumer items are generally calculated in three major currencies (the dollar, the pound, and the euro) and then converted to the Ghanaian cedi. Traders who purchase items in countries that do not use those three major currencies first convert the local currency (for example, the Thai baht) into the three major currencies and then convert into Ghanaian cedis to obtain the items' total cost in cedis.

Here, the traders' knowledge of foreign exchange rates comes into play. Traders have access to accurate, daily updates on the currency exchange rates for major international currencies such as the Japanese yen and the European Union euro. A lack of knowledge about such rates could spell financial losses for the traders, so they make an effort to check rates on a daily basis. It is in the dual conversions required by these traders, located at the interface of global and local markets, that the negative impacts of the women's location in a country with a deregulated economy becomes evident. Since the deregulation efforts by the state in the early 1980s, the Ghanaian cedi has not been fixed against any foreign currency. Prices of imported goods are increased in relation to the rates of the cedi's devaluation. In times of relatively stable devaluation rates, this system does not present much of a problem. However, in years of severe devaluations, such as the year 2000,[4] transnational traders face serious hardships.

Given that the women have to be able to return abroad every couple of months to purchase items in hard currency, they have to change the prices of their goods every so often so that consumers will bear the costs associated with the ever-devaluing cedi. Consumers often complain about the insta-bility in prices, which makes them increasingly aware of their decreasing purchasing power. To give consumers some semblance of stability in prices without having to incur the costs associated with devaluation, the traders estimate possible future devaluations of the cedi and include these estima-tions in their calculations of the cost of their items. For example, if the total cost of items is 45 million cedis (US$5,000), then the women should be able to go back in a couple months with $5,000 in hand, at a bare minimum. To ensure this, the women calculate how many cedis they would need in order to buy $5,000 if the going rate for the dollar was increased by approximately 200 cedis. The estimate is based on the rate of recent devaluations. In peri-ods when the Ghanaian currency is devaluing quickly, such as in 2000, the conversions are made at larger intervals of, say, 500 cedis or more. For the example given, a woman would have to ensure that she makes at least 48 million cedis (US$5,333) in order to reclaim the amount she invested in the business. Deviations downward from the estimate of the rate of devaluation simply increase a trader's revenue. Deviations upward from that estimate, however, can severely harm a trader's financial stability.

Likewise, currency devaluations in the countries in which the traders purchase consumer items increase the traders' revenues and profits. The Asian financial crisis of the late 1990s proved especially lucrative in this regard. An interviewee noted how, with the Ghanaian cedi stable against the dollar and the Thai baht devaluing at an alarming rate, she made a huge profit on her trips in 1997. She recounted the fortunes she made that year with a sense of great joy: "I made so much money. I was getting mar-ried in December that year, and I was able to buy all the heavy electrical gadgets and the furniture for our future home with the profits I made from the two trips I took that year. Since then, my profit margin has not been that great, but it is enough to survive on." Such a story is not typical because, more often than not, Ghanaian traders are the ones who have to contend with their national currency plummeting in relation to other cur-rencies. This is especially true for Ghanaian traders who purchase their consumer items in the United States and Europe, where currencies are far more stable than those in the Third World.

Expected profits are included in pricing only after adjustments for devaluation have been made. Usually, a profit margin of between 15 and 20 percent minimum is added. After this, the total cost is divided by the total amount of goods bought to determine the unit price of an item.

At this point, the calculations get even more complicated. The female traders interviewed recounted how prices have to be adjusted at this stage, depending on the kinds of goods they have brought in. Ideally, they know that they should divide the airfare, as well as hotel and food bills, evenly across the number of different items they have bought and then calculate the unit price of each item, based on a portion of the sum of the hotel, food, and transportation bills and the individualized import duty charge and original price of the items. However, to do so would be cumbersome, especially because the women usually bring in at least four or five (and sometimes as many as 20) different types of items. The easiest method is to do an overall calculation but then adjust the prices afterward to reflect the differences in items purchased.

This calculation is not based on the differences in original prices but, instead, on the nature of the goods and the traders' perceptions of Ghanaian consumers' sense of what would be a fair price to pay for an item. In this estimation, a sleeveless dress should cost about 1,000 cedis (US$0.11) less than a similar one with sleeves. Likewise, a three-piece skirt suit should be priced much higher than a two-piece skirt suit. If the base unit price is 70,000 cedis (US$7.77) for a particular kind of skirt, the trader may take 20,000 cedis (US$2.22) off that to price the skirt and add 20,000 to the base unit price to price the skirt suit. The price arrived at by this process establishes the minimum price at which a trader would sell her items, or what traders refer to in the market as the "last price."

The concept of last price is not unique to the global consumer goods market. In the wholesale sections of the traditional foodstuffs market, where price bargaining is more common, traders also have a price below which they are unwilling to sell an item. However, they rarely refer to it as the last price. Instead, they are more likely to say, for instance, "*me de be ma wo* 5,000," which translates loosely as "5,000 cedis [US$0.55] is the price at which I am willing to sell the item." I would argue that the use of the English phrase "last price" to capture the essence of a traditional practice suggests traders' implicit awareness that the goods for which last prices are calculated are distinctly different from locally produced foodstuffs available at the traditional market.

Cognizant of the fact that in the marketing system at work here, prices are not predetermined by the trader, who expects that the Ghanaian consumer will demand price reductions on each item he or she buys, the trader in question then adds another 5,000 to 10,000 cedis (US$0.55 to 1.11) to the "last price" to establish the original price of the item. For example, a lady's blouse bought for a wholesale price equivalent to US$3.50 in Bangkok will retail in Ghana for US$11.50, with the last price pegged at approximately US$11.00.

At this point, one's physical location in Makola Market, which depends on one's awareness of the availability of space and one's ability to pay for the space at the required time, also comes into play in determining the final price of an item. Those transnational traders who are located near the central car park at Makola—the favorite area of the rich and nouveau riche, who would not want to tramp through the chaos, heat, and dirt of the market—increase the final price and therefore move up the last price to increase their margin of profit. When both the "original" price of an item and the last price have been determined, a trader is ready to engage in bargaining with a potential buyer. The nature of bargaining in this market, particularly the language that is used, reflects traders' shrewd awareness of global economic forces.

BARGAINING

Traders in global consumer items, well aware of the integral role that bargaining plays in trading transactions at the market, quote two prices to set the stage for further bargaining when asked about the price of an item. "How much does this item cost?" receives the response, "It is 150,000 cedis [US$16.66]. The last price is 140,000 cedis [US$15.55]." The first price quoted is the bargaining base, and the second price is that at which the trader is willing to relinquish the item (the "real" price). A buyer's request for a further reduction at this point results in the trader's drawing on her awareness of global economic conditions as a bargaining chip to maintain the price, because a reduction is embedded in the last price. The two most frequent arguments provided draw on global currency markets and the original source of the product.

When buyers request price reductions, traders first use the nature of global currency markets as justification for the price at which they are selling an item. A common response is, "That is exactly what the price should be; it is not my fault that the prices are so high. Blame it on the dollar [the constant devaluation of the cedi against convertible currency]." At this point, the potential buyer is left without a retort because the global currency market is not something the trader can manipulate in order to grant the buyer his or her wish. As in the traditional foodstuffs market, buyers who are aware of cheaper prices elsewhere will draw the trader's attention to this fact. It is then that the trader will deploy the second form of argumentation, one that draws on the original source of the product.

The traders of global consumer items at Makola Market exhibit an acute awareness of the existence of what Gereffi (1994) refers to as "triangle manufacturing," although, admittedly, they do not refer to it by that term. Gereffi (1994) argues that the current global production system has a hierarchy of production sites that reflects differences in the quality of items, as well as variations in labor costs and therefore the prices associated with these items. Many large-scale manufacturing companies such as Nike no longer manufacture their items in the United States. The technical aspects of production, such as the development of new designs to suit the tastes of the home market, are left to the American workforce, but the relatively labor-intensive job of production is outsourced to Third World countries such as Mexico and Honduras in Latin America and China and the Philippines in Asia, where production costs are much lower. The third manufacturer in this process is the homeworker in these Third World countries to whom the local manufacturer might outsource part of the production process.

These Third World countries have large pools of labor with a basic level of education as well as good infrastructure, especially with respect to road networks and telecommunications, which enables the parent companies to produce their goods fairly cheaply. Spin-off companies located in the Third World produce cheaper-quality goods in large quantities for the non-US market. These goods, when they find their way onto the Ghanaian market, are relatively cheaper than those purchased directly from Europe or the United States.

The prices of items as set by the transnational traders partly reflect this hierarchy in production. Goods bought directly from the United States and Europe are the most expensive. Next highest in price are goods bought from spin-off companies in the Third World. Third are foreign-made goods purchased from neighboring Togo.[5] These goods, originally from either the West or spin-off companies in Third World countries, are cheaper because the Togolese government allows consumer goods to be brought in without taxation. As long as traders are able to bring these goods into Ghana without paying the taxes imposed by the Ghanaian government, global consumer items purchased in Togo are cheaper. Traders can avoid import taxes by walking across the border with the goods either hidden in bags or, especially in the case of cloth, worn underneath their clothing. Chalfin (2001) notes a similar practice among cloth traders in northeastern Ghana. The traders who engage in such practices are usually small-scale traders who sell their wares on the street corners. Their trading practices are quite distinct from those practiced by the large-scale traders of global consumer items, who own shops and to whom I am referring in this discussion.

The traders of global consumer items use this reality of hierarchical global production as a bargaining chip in haggling with potential customers. Those who buy their products from the United States and Europe, as opposed to Asia, argue that those items should be more costly than ones from Asia. In response to buyers' arguments that their goods are expensive, transnational traders are likely to respond, "This dress is not from Thailand, it is from London; that is why it is more expensive than the others." Likewise, those who purchase their consumer items from Asia argue that their items are not from the neighboring country of Togo, hence the higher prices. In this way, traders produce counter-arguments, depending on their particular location in this hierarchy in terms of the origins of their products.

These two types of arguments clearly distinguish traders who operate at the interface of the global and local markets from those who operate solely within the confines of a local market. Indeed, the unique location of traders of global consumer items has resulted in a unique style of bargaining for consumer goods, which is evident when one compares the nature and outcome of bargaining conversations in traditional foodstuff markets with those of the global consumer goods market.

Uchendu reports a typical price-bargaining session for two red herrings, which the trader quotes as going for 45 centimes. The location is Haiti, and the conversation ensues as follows:

> "Your final price?"
>
> The saleswoman hesitates and then says: "I'll give you them for 40."
>
> "You ask a good deal; do you think people eat up money like that? I'll give you 35."
>
> "You're not serious."
>
> Thereupon the buyer, with an air of indifference, makes as if to take herself off. After a few steps, she turns back and, in a conciliatory tone, says: "Go on, give them me for 35 centimes; if I had 40, I'd give them you."
>
> The seller, simulating a high degree of indignation, explains: "Now, gossip, be off with you."
>
> Disappointed, the buyer moves away, this time for good. She has gone quite some distance, when the saleswoman calls her back and says: "All right, take." [Uchendu 1967:38]

Much closer to home, a typical bargaining session for oil in

Yorubaland, Nigeria, also reported by Uchendu, unfolds in the following manner:

"How much?"

"One shilling and six pence and it is the best you can get."

The buyer leaves the bottle of oil down carelessly. When the trader asks what the matter is, the buyer tells her to try and sell it to someone else for that price. "One shilling and three pence, then," she calls after him as he moves further off.

The buyer still continues his journey.

"One shilling," she cries. [Uchendu 1967:38]

At this point, the buyer becomes interested. He turns back and tells her that he can give her 9 pence and that this is all the money he has. Now, however, it is the trader who holds out. She lets the buyer know that if this is the situation, then the deal is off. The buyer raises the price to 10 pence. Still, the trader will not sell. Nevertheless, she wants to hold the buyer because she knows that he can afford to pay. She then launches into a song of praise for the bottle of real, first-class oil she holds up before the buyer. He finds it difficult to resist her sales skills and finally agrees to pay 11 pence for the bottle of oil.

The implicit assumption in traditional price bargaining, as evident in the two reports above, is that for each commodity there is a price range that is acceptable to both buyers and traders. Bargaining skill determines whether the trader or the buyer walks away from the sale with a deal. In contrast, a typical last-price bargaining session goes like this:

BUYER: "At what price are you selling a yard of this fabric?"

SELLER: "Come in, my dear, it costs 40,000 cedis [US$4.44] a yard. This is what's in fashion now, the multicolored fabric. We're tired of wearing the plain fabrics."

B: "Is it that expensive because it is multicolored and not plain? Prices are lower elsewhere."

S: "My dear, don't compare my fabrics to the old-fashioned kind in other shops. These fabrics are the newest things on the European market, and in modern-day Ghana, as you know, that's what we women also want to wear."

B: "Reduce it for me, okay? I'm buying a lot."

S: "I'll give it to you at 38,000 cedis [US$4.22] a yard."

B: "Oh, can't you give it to me at 35,000 cedis [US$3.88] a yard?"

S: "No, 38,000 cedis a yard is really the best I can do for you. Buy it, my dear, you won't regret doing so. This fabric is good-quality fabric straight from Britain. It isn't like the ones from China [Asia], and so on. This one will not fade. You'll see, you'll be able to wear whatever you make out of this for years to come."

B: "Okay, I'll take it at that price, but it means that I can't buy as many yards as I had initially hoped to buy."

S: "It doesn't matter, it is better to have a few fabrics of good quality that will last you a lifetime than a lot of cheap-quality fabrics which will fade so fast that you will regret having bought them."

The following is another version of a bargaining session, this time for a ladies purse:

BUYER: "I'd like to buy a purse. How much does this one cost?"

SELLER: "200,000 cedis [US$22.22], the last price is 190,000 cedis [US$21.11]."

B: "Wow, that's expensive."

S: "That's the price everywhere, my dear. These are good-quality bags, they come from Italy."

B: "They sure look nice, but I can't afford it. I only have 180,000 cedis [US$20.00]."

S: "That is not enough. If I give it to you at that price, it will be at a loss to me, so try to top it up. Rummage through your bag, you might find some extra money."

B: "I really don't have the extra money, although the bag will go very well with the dress I'm having made for my cousin's wedding."

S: "If you're shopping for a bag for a wedding, this is definitely the one to get. Go and come back when you are paid at the end of the month. I have quite a number in stock."

B: "Okay, I'll do that."

There is far more price flexibility in the traditional form of bargaining than in last price bargaining. In the traditional form of bargaining, a buyer resorts to economic arguments to justify a price reduction, and the seller resorts to economic arguments of a different kind to justify a price hike. Reciprocal price quotations and justifications over a period of time result in a final price that is acceptable to both buyer and trader. On the other hand, in last price bargaining, traders supply justifications for why the price of an item cannot be reduced beyond what has been offered. A buyer's economic argument of inability to pay rarely results in price reductions, because the trader can blame the prices on global forces, over which she has no control. As noted by Potter (1955:108), traders have an undue advantage in this setting because they are selling imported goods whose price and quality are less known to buyers than would be the case with locally produced items. In such a situation of information asymmetry (Akerlof 1970), the traders have an advantage compared to the buyers.

Last price bargaining is very similar to what Firth notes among Malay fishermen. The *mati* price is the bedrock figure below which a Malay fisherman will ideally not sell his products. Firth writes:

> It represents the seller's view of what the price ought really to be, as distinct from his optimistic quotations of what he would like it to be. The serious bargaining normally lies just below this point. The obvious function of the mati price is in giving a focus to the bargaining, in concentrating the differences of view between seller and buyers upon the narrowest range after preliminary variations have been explored. [Firth 1966:195]

Potential buyers who continue to plead for a price reduction after the traders of global consumer items have marshaled the two sets of economic arguments in defense of their prices are most likely to be told indirectly that if they are cash-strapped, then they are better off looking elsewhere for cheaper-quality goods, which they can purchase at a cheaper price.

In situations when a customer genuinely interested in buying an item is short of money and therefore cannot pay the price acceptable to the trader, the trader can also offer her the option of putting the item on layaway. In this case, the buyer pays part of the total cost of the item with the understanding that the remaining amount will be paid at a vaguely specified point in the future, at which point the item will then be transferred to the buyer. A written record is made of the transaction to ensure clarity between the trader and buyer regarding how much is owed on the item.

Though this layaway option is offered to anybody who shows a genuine interest and desire to buy an item at the stipulated price, traders do not consider themselves bound to hold the item until the buyer returns with the rest of the money. The traders do not get information on the buyers so that they can track down the buyers to remind them about the item if they should delay payment.

Just as the transnational traders are unwilling to deposit their foreign exchange in banks only to be told, when they need it, that the banks have insufficient foreign currency available, thus delaying their travel plans, the traders are also unwilling to have their capital locked up in layaways. The practice is to keep the item stored until it is the last one in stock. If at that point the buyer who had put some money down toward it has still not returned and somebody else comes by ready and willing to pay full price, the trader will sell it to the second person and give the original contender a refund when he or she shows up. Any customer who makes a down payment therefore does so knowing that he or she risks losing the item in the end.

One might argue that this "last price" bargaining style is an attempt to maintain cultural practices associated with purchasing, while mimicking the fixed price policies usually associated with shopping in the Western world. Last price bargaining is flexible, though, in that it allows for further reductions in price if the trader so desires. As is often the case with quantity bargaining for local foodstuffs, these price reductions are reserved for those with whom the Ghanaian trader of global consumer items has developed a personalized relationship. Traders develop these personalized relationships with individuals who return to their shops on a consistent basis to purchase items or who introduce friends and acquaintances to the traders. The traders perceive such individuals as loyal customers who need to be maintained, particularly in an environment such as Ghana's, where currency devaluations without a concomitant rise in salaries result in an ever-shrinking population of buyers. Traders attempt to maintain their client base by reserving special offers, such as lower prices, for loyal clients with whom they develop a personalized relationship. In the traders' view, the losses incurred in the short run on an individual to whom they offer their goods without profit are made up for in the long run, either through gaining additional clients or, at worst, selling items at cost so that their capital is not locked up in inventory that is not making any profitable sales.

Anthropologists have documented numerous ethnographic cases of such phenomena. Observed in various parts of the developing world, these relationships are known as *customers* in Jamaica (Katzin 1959), *pratik* in Haiti (Mintz 1961, 1964), *suki* in the Philippines (Davis 1968, 1973;

Szanton 1972), *clientes* in Guatemala (Swetnam 1978), *sedaqa* in Morocco (Geertz 1978, 1979), *onibara* ties among Nigerian traders (Trager 1981), and *casera* in highland Peru (Orlove 1986:93). Such personalized relationships are not confined to the developing world. Though there are no specific words for such relationships in the developed world, they have also been observed between fishermen and buyers in the Maine lobster market (Acheson 1985), in the networks that develop in the securities market (Baker 1984), among Japanese businessmen (Dore 1983), and between art dealers and buyers in the United States (Plattner 1996). These relationships are best defined as

> long lasting dyadic ties formed between individuals operating in the market place. At a minimum, they imply the existence of regular transactions between the individuals. They may also involve extension of credit, concessions in quantity, reduction in price, and multiplex social ties. [Trager 1981:133]

Like their Jamaican counterparts, Ghanaian traders refer to the buyer with whom they have developed such personalized relationships as "my customer." Such customers are given lower prices in a very explicit manner. Traders preface the price of an item with a statement reminding the buyer that she is getting to buy the item at that price because of her relationship with the trader. Occasionally, a trader will grant a personalized relationship status to someone who has not yet acquired that status. Traders will do so if the buyer presents a story that can be justified as unique, such as an out-of-towner who has fallen 5,000 cedis (US$0.55) short of the amount for an item or a resident of the capital city who is 5,000 cedis (US$0.55) short of the amount for an item needed for an impending rite of passage. Otherwise, as mentioned above, the buyer is most likely to be directed elsewhere.

CONCLUSION

When an item is bought outside and sold within the confines of a nation-state, a trader's bargaining chip in the sale of that item is quite different from that used when trading in an item that is bought and sold within the confines of the nation-state. Traders of global consumer items, located as they are at the interface of local and global markets, engage in bargaining with a keen awareness of existing global economic conditions. The language of bargaining in the global consumer goods market reflects the "forces" of globalization. Traders' speeches during bargaining have much more to them than meets the eye. Embedded in these speeches is an awareness of the nature of economic globalization and the limitations it places on the agency of citizens in the developing world. Economic globalization reflected in neoliberal ideology as a development package is Janus-faced. Parts of this ideology, such as the removal of tariff barriers, provide opportunities for trade, but others, such as currency devaluations, sabotage attempts at individual economic success through trade in imported consumer items. These transnational traders' efforts would be further rewarded if they operated in an economy with stable currency.

The end result of this Janus-faced development package is that a new type of price bargaining has emerged, one that allows traders to apply agency in the face of the constraints that the development package imposes on them. This form of bargaining, "last price" bargaining, is restricted, compared with the flexibility in prices that is common with the traditional form of bargaining. Bargaining for global consumer goods has lost its negotiative function. In the sale of global consumer items, bargaining serves only a ritualistic function. Bargaining, in this context, is a ritual that justifies prices that enable traders in global consumer items to make ends meet while they hope, albeit in vain, for a situation in which Ghana's currency will remain fairly stable and even appreciate against international currencies. At ever-increasing prices, in an environment where salaries are rarely adjusted upward to match inflation, turnover is slow and hence profit is low. The women lament this situation as they witness the impact of devaluations in each passing year. As they put it, year in, year out, "these days, people simply do not buy as much as they used to."

About the Author

Akosua K. Darkwah teaches sociology at the University of Ghana, Legon. She holds degrees in sociology from Vassar College and the University of Wisconsin, Madison. Her research interests include gender, globalization, and the changing nature of work, as well as sexuality, in the African context. She helped set up and serves on various committees of the newly established Centre for Gender Studies and Advocacy at the University of Ghana. She is also a board member of the Ark Foundation, a Ghanaian NGO that works with survivors of domestic violence.

Notes

1. At the apex of the pyramid of traders in Ghana's distributive sector are Lebanese, increasingly Asian, and predominantly male traders who may or may not own shops of their own but supply items in bulk to Ghanaian traders who own shops.

These traders are usually second- or third-generation Asians or Levantines born and raised in Ghana by parents who were also traders. For more on this group of traders, see Garlick 1971.

2. In Togo, which borders Ghana to the east, these traders are known as "Mama Benzes," in reference to the Mercedes-Benz vehicles that many of them can afford to drive.

3. Sales and discount offers, a permanent feature of economic life in the West, offer buyers in the Western world the same benefits that bargaining offers consumers in the Third World. The only difference lies in the fact that sales and discount offers force delayed gratification on the citizens of the Western world.

4. That year, the cedi devalued by almost 100 percent over a six-month period.

5. Mention was rarely made of other neighboring countries, such as Nigeria, although some traders purchase items from these countries as well. This has to do with the proximity of Togo, which makes transportation costs associated with this purchasing site much cheaper than for other places.

5

Clothing Difference

Commodities and Consumption in Southeastern Liberia

Mary H. Moran

Then from hut to hut, we spread out your lappas
from the years on the verandas. So the coming
mourners can come and see what a life
you once had.

—*From* For Ma Nmano Jabbeh: A Dirge *by Patricia Jabbeh Wesley*

The Grebo-Liberian poet Patricia Jabbeh Wesley, in a requiem for her
stepmother, uses the image of a "traditional" practice from southeastern
Liberia: that of displaying a woman's accumulated wealth in cloth (*lappas*)
at her wake and funeral to demonstrate "what a life [she] once had" (for
additional contemporary poetry about Liberia, see Wesley 1998, 2003). As
noted by Annette Weiner and Jane Schneider, "throughout history, cloth
has furthered the organization of social and political life. In the form of
clothing and adornment, or rolled or piled high for exchange and heir-
loom conservation, cloth helps social groups to reproduce themselves and
to achieve autonomy or advantage in interactions with others" (Weiner and
Schneider 1989:1).

But cloth has historical importance not only in localized social processes.
In the vast scholarly literature on colonialism, industrialization, and globalization, textiles and apparel also have taken a prominent place in analyses of how imported commodities penetrate and transform local markets.
Jane Collins (2003:27) notes that "for millennia, cloth and clothing have
been trafficked over long distances, linking far-flung regions." For example, Eric Wolf (1982:268–278) has described how early competition among
British, Dutch, and Indian textile producers drove the development of
English industrial technology and of protectionist legislation, leading to

the ultimate demise of Indian handwoven cloth. "Native cloth and clothing thus became invested with meanings forged in the colonial experience" (Collins 2003:28; see also Comaroff 1997). These meanings could vary, from the rejection of local textiles by indigenous elites as a sign of their modernity and sophistication, to an embracing of "native dress" as a symbol of nationalist resistance (Bean 1989).

Manufactured or handwoven, imported or locally produced, cloth and clothing have a long history as communicative devices, as well as a utilitarian value as bodily coverings. Annette Weiner has suggested that the very physical properties of textiles—their ability to combine strength with fragility and possibilities for accumulation with impermanence—allow them to serve as metaphors for expansive social processes including capitalism and political hierarchy (Weiner 1989:34; Weiner and Schneider 1989:6).

Furthermore, it is well known that cloth and clothing operate in highly gendered contexts, in both production and consumption. European women have been recruited for labor in home-based and industrial textile production since the process began. The tradition of the "mill girl" was imported with the new model of factory labor into the New World, where it became central to the emergence of gendered class identities in the United States (for example, Lamphere 1987; Ryan 1981; Schneider 1989; Stone-Ferrier 1989). Apparel has proven itself amenable to the "commodity chain" approach within world systems analysis. As a result, there are numerous "global assembly line" studies of women clothing workers, from the maquiladoras of Mexico to the sweatshops of Asia (for only a few examples, see Dickerson 1995; Gereffi and Korzeniewicz 1994; Gunewardena, chapter 3, this volume; Ward 1993). Yet, Collins (2003) notes the often surprisingly "gender neutral" nature of many workplace ethnographies, and Dunaway (2001) provides a rigorous critique of women's invisibility in the majority of world systems literature (see also Ward 1990, 1993). Many studies of women textile and garment workers focus on the gendered construction of the *women as producers*, not on the *products*, as crucial elements in a particular repertoire of gendered identities. It seems that the current studies of gender as an aspect of textile production and consumption have not exhausted the possibilities of our understanding, even as the body of evidence documenting these processes around the world has grown.

Turning to what has become a separate literature, at the terminal end of the "commodity chain," many studies of consumption similarly lack a clear focus on how products operate to produce and to interact with categories of gender. In a review article, "Consumption and Commodities," Miller (1995) asserts that Marx's work on fetishism, Mauss's theory of the gift, and Appadurai's (1986) work on "the social life of things" have deeply influenced anthropological studies of commodities. Although Miller (1995:156) predicts that, like kinship studies, anthropological analyses of consumption are moving to a view of commodities as "simply a domain through which diverse projects of value are objectified," very little mention is made of these projects' differential impact on women and men.

One exception to this charge is Timothy Burke's (1996) excellent historical study of the marketing of different soap brands to men and women in colonial Zimbabwe, *Lifebuoy Men, Lux Women*. Burke uses a close reading of the colonial and racist discourses constructing the African body as unclean to understand the power of globalized commodities *and* the effects of individual agents making "choices in the marketplace." The global political economy seeks to generate "new needs" for all manner of commodities. Yet, writes Burke,

> the production of these needs was not a consequence of monolithic power acting against powerless subjects, but instead grew out of a massively complex intersection of micropowers and macropowers, local desires and collective interests, imagination and restriction. Moreover, capitalism did not invariably act to flatten out and homogenize African lives for the sake of some global "modernity," but instead actively worked to reproduce and redefine numerous forms of social difference. [Burke 1996:215–216]

Likewise, Jean Comaroff (1997:413) argues that, for the Tswana of South Africa, men and women's clothing styles became fixed as "local" or "folk" during the colonial period, drawing on imported European commodities to "mark the fact that its wearers were being reconfigured as quaint premoderns" within a global British empire. Comaroff (1997:414) demonstrates that foreign commodities, especially those related to the human body, may intrude into local economies that "remain rooted, in important respects, in their own regimes of production and exchange" (for a current example, see Darkwah, chapter 4, this volume). Paradoxically, commodities produced elsewhere can be used to create "indigenous traditions," which are, in turn, employed to "bound local identities" (Comaroff 1997:414).

From 1982 to 1983, I conducted 15 months of ethnographic fieldwork in southeastern Liberia. During that time, I lived with a local family of the Glebo ethnolinguistic group and practiced the standard ethnographic methodology of participant-observation. Trained in the feminist anthropology of the 1970s and 1980s, I was most interested in what has come to be called *intersectionality* in women's lives: the way in which gender inter-sects with other forms of status, prestige, and identity. My work focused on three categories of Glebo women: those who considered themselves "civi-lized" or Westernized; those who considered themselves "native" and were primarily rice farmers; and the "native" market women of the regional cap-ital, who mediated the relationship between producers and consumers of local foodstuffs.

I was also hoping to fill in a significant gap in the ethnographic litera-ture. Although the northwestern peoples of Liberia were well documented and their elaborate secret societies (Poro and Sande) and artistic traditions widely known, very little research had been done on the supposedly "sim-pler" peoples of the southeast. Of those few scholars working in the region, many were historians who were intrigued by the long-standing incorpora-tion of this part of the West African coast into the global economy. As I was to learn, people such as the Glebo had deliberately settled on the coast to gain access to trade with passing European ships. Instead of recent "victims of globalization," these were people who had been actively engaged in large-scale economic transactions for centuries.

After my departure, in late 1983, I had every intention of continuing to work in Liberia, but the civil conflicts of 1989–1997 and 1999–2003 made my return impossible for many years. Luckily, I was able to maintain contact with my foster family during those years and to offer them support during the various periods when they were refugees in the Ivory Coast. I was able to support the educational careers of three of the children through the associate degree level and to pay for, at last count, three weddings and a funeral. During the summer of 2006, I was able to return to Liberia and, briefly, to my field site on the southeast coast, where many people still remembered me and welcomed me back. This analysis, therefore, builds on more than 20 years of engagement with Liberia and Liberians, as well as on my own field data from the 1980s and the historical work of many dedicated scholars.

In what follows, I seek to retain Burke's focus on local agency and dif-ferentiation while documenting the impact of globalizing forces on women's lives in southeastern Liberia, West Africa. Expanding my earlier analysis of prestige hierarchies among Glebo women in the Cape Palmas region (Moran 1990), I focus specifically on cloth and clothing as a "win-dow" through which to view the many and various ways that women become articulated with intruding commodities and political economies. Like Comaroff, I argue that it is impossible to make claims about the impact of globalization on "women" as a generic category, without taking into account the local class-status system, as well as any individual's age and kinship identity. Globalization and the products that circulate in its connections not only create changes in women's lives but also, quite literally, introduce new varieties of womanhood (and manhood) into local contexts.

The origins of local differentiation, in this case, lie in the eighteenth and nineteenth centuries and the incorporation of Glebo men into the West African coastal labor market. The arrival of African American settlers in Liberia in the early nineteenth century, bringing with them their own systems of meaning attached to different kinds of labor and products, created more fine distinctions between men and women of various types. Building on long-standing traditions of expression and communication of relative status through textiles, imported cloth entered local markets and patterns of exchange as both a source of innovation and a reinforcement of existing hierarchies (see also Weiner 1989).

Unlike Latin America, the Caribbean, and Asia, sub-Saharan Africa has generally not been integrated into the global economy as a source of cheap industrial labor for textile and apparel production. Where local textile industries have been set up, these produce largely for the domestic market (see Berger 1992 and Etienne 1980 for examples). Yet machine-made cloth was one of the earliest industrial commodities imported into Africa from Europe and has had the effect of wiping out domestic handweaving industries in numerous locations throughout the continent. In some places, handwoven textiles have survived, moving into the category of luxury and prestige goods, and cheaper, machine-made cloth has become the stuff of everyday wear.

Etienne has carefully documented the incorporation of imported cloth and locally made, industrially produced thread on the Baule people of the Ivory Coast, adjacent to the region of southeastern Liberia where I worked. In precolonial times, Baule women interplanted cotton in their yam fields and spun the fibers into thread, which they gave to their husbands for weaving into cloth. Women, however, "owned" the thread and thus claimed ownership over the final product, which the male weavers turned over to their wives. The women then distributed the cloth to members of their households and made decisions about what portions of it would be saved, given away as gifts, or traded (Etienne 1980:222–224). Always more than simply an item of use value, cloth was "given at funerals, sometimes buried with the deceased, displayed on special occasions and conserved in the sacred treasure that was guarded by each kin-group head" (Etienne 1980:221; see also Darish 1989 and Feeley-Harnick 1989 on the uses of cloth in mortuary practices elsewhere in Africa). Cloth was therefore an element in the ritual and prestige sector of Baule society and was indispensable to long-distance trade with other groups, who brought the Baule such items as cattle, iron, and slaves.

In the 1920s, the French established a textile factory to manufacture thread from locally produced cotton in the Baule homeland; men quickly realized that they could produce woven cloth using purchased, factory-made thread and thus control the final product. Furthermore, the French tried to increase the local supply of cotton by encouraging the Baule to grow it as a cash crop, rather than intercrop it with yams, the subsistence staple. Like other cash crops, cotton soon became a "man's crop" instead of one produced and controlled by women. Factory-produced textiles supplanted the handwoven cloth for everyday wear, and the small stocks of "authentic" cloth became exclusively items of prestige (Etienne 1980:225–229).

Yet, cloth and clothing, whatever the source, remained a store of value and wealth for Baule women. "Whether worn or hoarded, cloth is coveted and continues to represent wealth and status" (Etienne 1980:231). Etienne sees the colonial transformation of cloth from a product of cooperative interdependence between spouses to a new marker of women's dependence on men and a source of distrust and conflict in contemporary Baule marriages. In the classic manipulative magic of commodities, "alienated production means the producer's control of the product is replaced by the product's control of the producer" (Etienne 1980:230). Baule women who now sell their labor as factory workers produce textiles in order to gain cash to buy cloth they cannot rely on men to provide for them. "Thus, multiple processes of alienation converge with the Baule women as their focal point or subject" (Etienne 1980:230).

As the Baule example illustrates, European textiles were introduced into West African systems of prestige and value in which cloth already played a significant role (see, among others, Borgatti 1983; Darish 1989; Feeley-Harnick 1989; Hendrickson 1996; Perani and Wolff 1999; Renne 1995). Unlike the Baule, few indigenous West Africans had the experience of finding a textile factory located in their territory, and groups situated along the coast had a much longer time in which to integrate imported commodities than did the inland-dwelling Baule. The Glebo people of southeastern Liberia, among whom I did fieldwork in the 1980s, have lived along the coast on either side of Cape Palmas since at least the sixteenth century and probably earlier (Davis 1976). Drawn to the seaside from the interior, according to their own accounts, by the lure of trade with passing European ships, the people of the southeast coast were soon importing, using, and deploying a range of foreign commodities including cloth, beads, rum, iron tools, guns, and ammunition. In return, they provided Europeans with the much desired Malaguetta pepper (the "grains" of which gave Liberia its precolonial name, The Grain Coast), ivory, and rice to resupply the ships (Brooks 1972; Davis 1976; Martin 1982).

By the eighteenth century, men from southeastern Liberian communities began working on board merchant and military vessels and traveling "down the coast" to work on contract for two-year periods in onshore enterprises.

> By 1809, according to Thomas Ludlam, former governor of Sierra Leone, they were employed at every factory between Sierra Leone and their Liberian homes and were found on other parts of the coast in groups of 15 to 40. By the 1830's, many were employed on the cocoa plantations of Fernando Po and their shore work during the Niger Expedition of 1833 may have spread their reputation and led to further work. By 1848, they were employed as far south as Calabar. [Martin 1982:2–3]

Known collectively as "Krumen," these male labor migrants became, through their travels and payment for work abroad, the main source of imported goods in their home communities.

An account by Charles Jeannest, a French trader who employed Kruman labor in the Congo in the late 1880s, describes the recruitment process at Cape Palmas at a time when the system of hiring contract labor had been established for several generations:

> It is to Cape Palmas that whites come from all parts of the coast to hire these Negroes, whose reputation for strength and bravery is known everywhere in Africa. As soon as a vessel is sighted a countless number of canoes leave the shore and soon a swarm of blacks invades the deck; each wants to be the first to offer his services. [Jeannest, cited in Brooks 1972:49 n. 159]

Ship captains dealt with established "headmen," who, in turn, recruited a group of young men through kinship and other social linkages. Contracts were for one or two years, during which the laborers received a daily food ration and the assurance of passage home at the end of the term. The migrant worker collected his entire wages at the end of his contract. According to Mary Kingsley, the intrepid British explorer writing in 1897, "he is always paid in goods, in cloth, gin, guns, tobacco, gunpowder, etc." (cited in Brooks 1972:53). Kingsley describes in great detail the care with which these commodities were shipped back to coastal Liberia in pad-locked sea chests, or "Kru boxes." She also speculates on the reports that the materials in those locked boxes were subject to "tax" by the workers' elders back home (Brooks 1972:54–55), a reference to the use of these European products in multiple forms of exchange, prestige competition, and creation of social relations in the coastal Liberian communities.

The context from which these exemplary workers were drawn is the Kruan-speaking region of Liberia, distinct from the better-known Mande-speaking region of the north and west. The languages of the Kruan group are related to the eastern Kwa of the Niger delta and indicate an origin for these people somewhere to the east (Duitsman 1982–1983:28). Among the Kruan languages are Bassa, Kru, Krahn, and Grebo. The coastal Glebo, with whom I worked, occupy a cluster of 13 towns strung out along the shore on either side of Cape Palmas (Europeans extended the linguistic term *Kru* to all the peoples of the southeast). Before the establishment of Liberian gov-ernment control in the early twentieth century, they were organized into loose alliances of autonomous towns, or *dakwe*, with little stratification beyond age and gender and a complex system of local decision making in which even structural subordinates (women and young men) had institu-tionalized means of expression (Moran 1990, 2006). Rain-fed rice was the primary subsistence crop, supplemented by hunting and fishing in the inte-rior forests and along the coast. Glebo towns are still located prominently on the beaches or on narrow spits of land along brackish lagoons—once the favored sites for trading with passing European vessels. Because productive farmland is located farther to the interior, however, many of these towns are literally empty for the greater part of the year, when people relocate as small kin groups to their farm "villages" in the forest.

One puzzling feature of the extensive historical literature on the "Kruman" phenomena concerns both the excellent reputation of the men of this region among Europeans and the very early emergence of the southeast coast as a prime location to hire "free" contract labor. Southeastern Liberia is, demographically, one of the most sparsely popu-lated regions in all of West Africa. Why did men have to be recruited here and transported hundreds of miles to Nigeria, which was then, as now, one of the most densely populated places on the continent? Furthermore, European accounts and, in particular, the guidebooks written for those contemplating entering the West African trade wax almost ecstatic about the trustworthiness, intelligence, and diligence of Kru laborers. A typical comment is this recorded by Laird in his 1837 *Narrative of an Expedition into the Interior of Africa by the River Niger*: "Kru never desert their employers in danger or distress; they are constitutionally brave and are easily kept in order: they are the life and soul of the trade on the coast; without them, the cargoes could not be stowed nor could ships be manned" (cited in Brooks 1972:13). It must be remembered that these glowing reports were written at exactly the same time that discourses of racial inferiority were being developed and refined to justify the slave trade and later European colonial conquest in Africa.

Elsewhere, I have suggested that an explanation for these apparent contradictions lies in the gendered division of agricultural labor in south-eastern Liberian communities (Moran 1986). Simply put, the area of Kru labor recruitment corresponds to the region along the West African coast with the *highest* female labor inputs into agriculture. To the north of the Kruan linguistic area, along coastal Sierra Leone and Liberia,

> rice is planted by broadcasting and hoeing. In parts of the Kruan speaking areas, rice is planted by drilling, with a flat-bladed hoe or stick, a small hole into which rice seeds are dropped....Male labor inputs into rice cultivation tend to be higher in the north-western section of the country....Female labor inputs are higher in the southeastern section where women may do everything except felling the largest trees and the burning. [Carter and Mends-Cole 1982:35–37]

Continuing south past the Kruan speakers to their neighbors in Ivory Coast, the subsistence staple shifts from rice to yams, with an accompanying change in the division of labor. Again, men's work in agricultural production is emphasized. The area of primary male-labor recruitment in the eighteenth and nineteenth centuries, therefore, corresponds to the area where men's contribution to daily subsistence was least important.

Before the demand for migrant labor made this experience literally a rite of passage to adulthood for southeastern men, they were certainly not unoccupied. Men contributed to their communities as warriors, hunters, fishermen, and collectors of forest products. In a system of political offices parallel with those of women, elder men were responsible for the political administration and ritual protection of lineages and towns. Again, it is interesting that the reputation of Kru men as reliable workers was power-ful enough to overcome the contemporary racist stereotype of African men as "lazy" in contrast with their "overburdened" wives. In the 1840s, Dr. Francis Bacon, who lived for several months at Cape Palmas, reported:

> No man who has ever lived among them in their own country could tolerate the statement that a Krooman or Fishman having

acquired money abroad lives in idleness at home supported by
the labour of his wives. They continue, with hardly the exception
of the highest chiefs, a most laborious race....The women are
restricted to particular kinds of labour, household affairs, planting and gathering rice. But the cutting and clearing of the bush,
the building and repairing of houses and canoes, the manufacture of utensils, etc., fishing, and a long list of laborious employ-
ments keep the men as active and industrious as the women.
[cited in Brooks 1972:66]

The extraction of men's labor for periodic employment on European
ships and onshore enterprises, however, did not pose a threat to the basic
day-to-day subsistence system of the southeastern Liberian peoples. As I
have suggested previously, "the fine reputation that Kru workers enjoyed
with Europeans was primarily based on their 'loyalty'; that is, their willingness to work out the duration of their contracts. Might this dedication to
the job not be seen as based on the security of knowing they were not
needed at home rather than on some cultural or psychological peculiarity
of the Kru?" (Moran 1986:122). As elsewhere in Africa, we see the phenomenon of women's subsistence production subsidizing the participation
of men in global labor markets (see Comaroff 1997:414).

Prominent in all the historical accounts of Kru laborers is their insistence on being paid with commodities, not cash, and two of the most important commodities they desired were cloth and European clothing (for
examples, see Brooks 1972:59, 62, 67). As noted above, returning migrants
turned over portions of these goods to patrilineage elders, but cloth, in particular, was featured among the bridewealth gifts exchanged by those same
elders to secure marriages for their junior kinsmen. Cloth was also mentioned as the primary gift of a young man to his mother, sisters, and other
female kin, as well as to sweethearts and potential wives (see the translated text describing Glebo courtship and marriage rituals in Innes 1966).
Throughout a man's life, he would be responsible for periodic gifts of cloth
to his wife, or wives, just as his wife was responsible for feeding him and their
children from her agricultural labors. These gifts came to mark the annual
round of Liberian national holidays and life cycle events such as the birth of
a child. Polygynously married men who wanted to preserve domestic peace
were scrupulous in giving their wives exactly the same amount and quality
of cloth, often even of the same pattern. Co-wives who appeared in public
wearing outfits made from identical cloth were seen as expressing their sat-
isfaction with each other and with the husband's management skills.

Not all the yard goods a woman received were immediately converted into clothing for wear; much was packed away in metal or wooden trunks as a store of value. The cloth women acquired from lovers, husbands, brothers, and sons who participated in the migrant labor trade became their accumulated wealth during their lifetime and a legacy to be passed on to their daughters. A woman's relationship with her male kin and affines (and, under patrilineal logic, both her husband and sons stood in the relation to her of "in-laws") was therefore mediated by gifts of cloth. Just as her agricultural work made possible her husband's "free" participation in the coastal labor market, so too his wages for that labor were converted into consumer goods that she allocated, displayed, and preserved.

From the available sources, it is not clear that there was much of an indigenous weaving tradition in southeastern Liberia, or anything comparable to the complex exchanges between spouses in local cloth production recorded by Etienne for the Baule of Ivory Coast. The African American settlers who founded the colony of Maryland at Cape Palmas in the 1830s seemed most concerned with the state of *undress* they observed among the local Glebo, especially, in the case of women, above the waist (Martin 1968). Although cotton was produced, spun, and woven into cloth in northern Liberia (and there, as with the Baule, men were the weavers), there is little evidence of the southeast as a major site of cloth production. It is likely that the Glebo and other people who later participated in the Kru migrant labor trade were used to trading for most of their textiles and the importation of European machine-made cloth did not eradicate a local industry.

Nevertheless, trade cloth earned by Krumen abroad entered a prestige economy that already allocated value to a range of exotic products. These imported goods had an impact on the "traditional dress" of men and women alike. A long-sleeved white dress shirt, a suit coat, a tie, and a bowler hat supplemented the standard waist cloth for men; in the 1980s, this was considered "traditional" attire for adult males on formal occasions. In addition to the utilitarian or everyday cloths that, in the form of untailored yard goods or lappas, were wrapped around the bodies of both men and women, a variety of luxury textiles, including velvets, brocades, damasks, and lace, and all manner of tailored European clothing entered the coastal communities. Brooks mentions that many nineteenth-century travelers to the region noted the popularity of items of British and American naval officers' uniforms incorporated into warriors' costumes throughout the southeast (Brooks 1972:59, 68; for more on the use of nonindigenous articles in symbolizing the ambiguity of the warrior, see Moran 1997).

The primary context in which I saw these family treasures displayed was on the occasion of women's funerals during my fieldwork in Cape Palmas in 1982–1983. During wake keeping for elderly Glebo women, some of whom had been born to migrant parents "down the coast" in Ghana and Nigeria and some whose husbands had been early-twentieth-century Kru laborers, huge quantities of textiles were used to "dress the room" where the body was laid out. This use of cloth in funeral rites is common throughout Africa. Perani and Wolff (1999:33–39) describe similar displays of cloth to "dress the space" in Kalabari Ijo funerals in Nigeria. Darish notes that, for the Kuba of central Africa, "the display of textiles at funerals powerfully reaffirms the enduring social relationships that encompass the complementary and interdependent efforts of the men and women of the clan section" (Darish 1989:137). Something very similar is accomplished in the display of cloth at a Glebo woman's funeral.

When the death of an elder Glebo man or woman occurs, numerous friends and kinswomen mobilize to make decisions about the use of textiles to mark the event. Close relatives choose the clothing in which the deceased is to be buried. These choices may be contested, and I have observed some corpses go through several changes of apparel before an agreement was reached. White lace curtains must be acquired, if the family does not own enough pairs, to adorn all the windows of the room where the body is laid out for viewing and wake keeping. In the case of a woman, the burial clothes must be in keeping with her fashion sense and interest in fine clothing during life. In one case I observed, there was extended disagreement over which clothes a woman with the reputation of a particularly fine dresser would want to wear for all eternity. "She could *suit*," one informant remarked with emphasis. Obviously, the clothing that accompanies the deceased into the grave is not available for distribution to her survivors, providing some of the context for these arguments. The ability to deploy one's wardrobe with style and taste is highly valued and an integral part of a woman's overall prestige, in life and in death.

Contemporaries of the deceased at the funerals I attended could recount the specific history of particular cloths, identifying the European countries that produced especially fine laces, brocades, or damasks. Walls, ceilings, and furniture were draped with lengths of cloth, some of which appeared to be quite old and suffering the effects of storage in a tropical climate but which still testified to the grandeur of another era. Mourners who come to visit and sit "on the mat" (where female kin fulfill their obligation to cry for the dead) with the women of the family view these cloths as a visible testament to the life of the deceased, discussing and handling the cloth while telling stories about its late owner.

Later, at the "false burial" or "war dance" that is performed for an older man or woman, the cloth is displayed again. Because extended funeral dancing requires advance planning and the collection of numerous resources, it frequently takes place long after the body has been buried. A small, open-sided shelter, or "house," is built to provide a resting place for the spirit of the deceased to observe the dancing when the body is no longer available. In the case of a woman, the *kuu kai* (spirit house) is again draped with cloth, just as the house of the dead woman was decorated during her wake. When I asked about the disposition of the cloth after all the funeral rites had been completed, I was told that it would be divided among the deceased's "family women," including her sisters and daughters.

As Patricia Jabbeh Wesley describes in her poem, this display and distribution of cloth are age-specific duties required of women of adjacent generations, even those living abroad. While living in the United States as a refugee of war, the poet hears of her stepmother's death and comments on the difficulty of meeting her kinship obligations while in "stranger land":

> I spread out lappas for you under the December
> sky while the grass is still wet—lappas upon lappas
> carpet my driveway while dawn comes in with fresh
> dew upon my lawn, and at night, bats cannot hide
> under the eaves of my roof of tarred shingles
> in stranger land. How does a daughter lay out
> The Mat just to wail alone? When our brothers put
> The Mat down, mourners come
> from far away towns, wailing for the Warrior
> Woman's passing. [Wesley in press]

Any given woman's store of imported textiles, therefore, operates in a very specific context as a map of her household's articulation with globalizing forces over the past several centuries. Relative wealth and poverty, success in traveling abroad and returning home with something to show for it, have not been uniformly distributed to all Glebo. In addition to the rich collections of cloth displayed by some kin groups, I observed the hastily contrived funeral of an elderly woman who died impoverished and alone. Distant kin contributed their own cloth to the display in meager amounts simply "for show" and so as not to embarrass the family (see Moran 1990:162–164). Such women either never had the opportunity to accumulate stores of cloth or were forced to sell it as their only source of support in old age.

Even as imported cloth was entering the indigenous system of value, new forms of stratification and prestige were developing because of the coastal trade and the presence of African American settlers and white missionaries in southeastern communities (Martin 1968; Moran 1990). In addition to bringing back European commodities, some migrants returned with facility in new languages, exposure to Christianity, and the rudiments of literacy (Brooks 1972:68). As the Americo-Liberian settlements attempted to establish an administrative hold along the coast, new opportunities emerged for work within the wage sector at home. Coupled with the efforts of white American missionaries to educate and "civilize" the Glebo, a new gendered prestige hierarchy, marked and symbolized by differences in clothing and bodily presentation, was coming into being.

The term *civilized* (*kwi*) has a long history in Liberia and delimits the cultural category of those attached to a "modern" lifestyle of wage work, Western religious and educational institutions, and identification with the nation-state (see Brown 1982; Frankel 1964; Moran 1990; Tonkin 1980, 1981). Although represented as a universal standard that can be achieved through proper educational credentials, training, and outward behavior, civilized status is highly gendered; only women appear to "fall out" of the civilized category and return to "native" status because of economic adversity. A man with a high school education who is unemployed, even impoverished, is still considered civilized, but a woman with a comparable level of education who sells goods in the public market place is most definitely not (see Moran 1990, for a full discussion). The outward manifestation of this status difference is the contrast between the tailored Western woman's dress and the two lengths of cloth, or lappas, worn by "native" women.

Lappas are worn with one length of cloth wrapped around the lower part of the body and tucked in at the waist to form a skirt that falls to about mid-calf or longer. Traditionally, the second lappa was worn higher on the torso, just under the armpits, leaving the shoulders bare, but now it is frequently worn over a tailored blouse or t-shirt. The second lappa, which is associated with marriage, motherhood, and adult status, may be used to cover a baby who is tied onto the back, as a rain cape, as a carrying bag, and for many other purposes. A young girl should properly receive her first full set of two matching lappas from her intended husband as one of the exchanges leading to marriage. Before that time, she wears only the single lappa (as a skirt) with a t-shirt or, in very rural and isolated areas, with no covering above the waist. The cloth for lappas today is commercially produced in neighboring countries such as Ivory Coast or in Asia specifically for the West African market. The colors and patterns are said to be determined by consumer preferences and desire for "African designs." As in the South African case described by Comaroff, the global market has produced a "folk costume" that marks the quintessential "traditional" African native woman, "quaint premoderns on the edge of empire" (Comaroff 1997:413).

The association of dress with status is so strong for the Glebo that *lappa woman* is a synonym for *native woman* and is also used as a designation by the Christian churches in setting tithes for various categories of parishioners. In Cape Palmas in the 1980s, civilized women were assessed an annual donation of three dollars, whereas the lappa woman rate was set at two dollars. Identification with the category of civilized woman and the dress denoting it is quite deeply felt. One friend described her commitment to her children's education by saying that she would "tie lappa and go in the market, never wear dresses again" if this was the only way to keep her children in school (Moran 1990:68–67). The "outside" (secondary) wife of a wealthy, prominent man is called his "lappa wife," in contrast with the officially married "wife of the ring."

Local tailors can fashion Western-style clothing out of the brightly colored, cotton lappa cloth worn by native women, but in the 1980s, most civilized women preferred imported dresses made from solid-color or print polyester for their daily wear. These dresses could be relatively expensive in an isolated region like Cape Palmas, where transportation costs increase the prices of all imported items (see Darkwah, chapter 4, this volume, on the marketing and consumption of imported apparel and fashionable accessories among women in Ghana). Another alternative was the "lappa suit," a tailored garment made from lappa cloth but in which the wraparound waist cloth has been replaced by a fitted skirt with a waistband and zipper and the upper cloth by an elaborate blouse with detailed ruffles, cutwork, and other ornamentation on the sleeves and bodice. Urban professional women favor these suits as an expression of national or authentic "African" identity, yet in Cape Palmas these are seen as modern, sophisticated, and civilized. For formal wear, native but urban-based women, such as market vendors, reach a compromise in combining the elaborate blouse on top with the wraparound length of cloth on the bottom.

Because the distinction between civilized and native status frequently turns on family decisions about which children to send to school or foster out to civilized relatives (and for how long), full siblings often belong to different status categories. All Glebo lineages contain both civilized and native members, who have complex obligations and responsibilities to each other over the course of their lives. Again, these relationships are often most visible at death, when the different forms of expertise and access to resources of civilized and native kin are called upon to complete the full range of Christian, indigenous, and Liberian customary rituals. Civilized male relatives are generally asked to contribute cash, alcoholic drinks, and other purchased commodities to the event; civilized women mobilize to bake biscuits and serve tea at the wake. Civilized women also seem to be frequently called upon to lend the crucial white lace curtains and serve as consultants about the burial clothes, coffin linings, room arrangements, and other important decisions (see Moran 1990). The desire to send a friend or relative into the next world in proper style brings civilized and native Glebo women together in planning and organizing, pooling their knowledge and resources in a common effort despite their differences in status and dress.

A new source of cloth and clothing that has entered the local market in recent decades is the secondhand trade, which brings tons of used clothing into Africa each year (see Hansen 2000). Most men's clothing (civilized and native, because men are not defined by apparel as women are and both civilized and native men wear tailored trousers and shirts) comes from the secondhand trade. Civilized women search for cast-off dresses in the piles of used clothing displayed in markets, and native women mine these markets for blouses and t-shirts to wear with their lappas. Both categories of women search for children's clothing and for items that might be modified into school uniforms.

Civilized and native women alike carry on the tradition of "hoarding" clothing and textiles as a store of wealth. When I was scheduled to return to snowy New England in late December, my civilized Glebo foster mother searched through her trunks and presented me with a beautiful silk coat from China, quilted and embroidered, to keep me warm, she said. I had seen her wearing such a coat at formal events during the "cool" rainy season, when temperatures can fall into the low 70s and Glebo huddle close to their fires and complain about the cold. When I protested that she would have need of her coat and, furthermore, looked so beautiful in it, she opened her trunk and showed me several more just like it, all collected from secondhand markets in Monrovia and stockpiled for such occasions.

Although I never saw the clothing acquisitions of civilized women publicly displayed at their funerals like the untailored lengths of cloth owned by native women, it was clear that textiles still serve as a store of wealth and marker of prestige for women in all status categories. Gifts of clothing between women are also emblematic of kinship and friendship. Just as my foster mother gave me her quilted coat, several friends asked for articles of my clothing when I left Cape Palmas, to remember me by, they said.

The history of specific categories of commodities in particular places clearly illustrates the processes of globalization, dating back to the sixteenth century and with the power to remake local relations of production and exchange. A similar analysis could be applied to the prestige items, including firearms and musical instruments, brought home by migrants for the exclusive use of men, and these processes can be linked to the particular expressions of violence recorded during the Liberian civil wars of 1989–1996 and 1999–2003 (see Moran 1997, 2006). In the case of women's adoption of imported cloth and clothing, there was no local textile industry to displace, and men's absence as labor migrants did not threaten female control over subsistence production. Only by acknowledging women's near monopoly over food production do the growth and development of the Kru labor phenomenon make sense. The contribution of women's labor in subsidizing men's wage work, however, is often missed or ignored by world systems accounts of cores, peripheries, and the commodity chains that hold them together (Dunaway 2001; Ward 1993).

Native Glebo women who began to collect cloth as gifts from wage-working men in the nineteenth and early twentieth centuries were able to accumulate impressive collections, which are still maintained by their daughters and granddaughters. Civilized women, who frequently pay for their status and right to wear Western polyester dresses with economic dependence on husbands and lovers, find themselves in a less favorable position. Barred from the entrepreneurial opportunities of the public market by their desire to wear dresses, these women often resort to covert forms of marketing from a "back door table" or send their children out to hawk baked goods, hard candy, or other small consumer items near schoolyards or crossroads (Moran 1990). Although they may aspire to the independence of having jobs of their own in the wage sector, lack of adequate education, gender discrimination in employment, and limited job opportunities made this impossible for all but a lucky few in the pre–civil war period. Faced with the choice of giving up their dresses for lappas, most civilized Glebo women I knew scraped by as dependent housewives, secondary girlfriends, or family charity cases, perhaps with a small covert business on the side. The women who claimed the right to wear the most highly valued items in the local apparel market were also, ironically, the most vulnerable to the vagaries of globalization.

In tracing the impact of imported commodities in distant places, we must be careful, as Burke (1996:215–216) reminds us, not to reduce these effects to "a consequence of monolithic power acting against powerless subjects" without acknowledging the agency of those who make local meaning out of global products. While I agree with Comaroff that "quaint" native women in colorful lappas are, indeed, a construction of the workings of global capital and colonial empire, it is important not to lose sight of the fact that these women are actively shaping both the reception and valorization of imported commodities. Glebo women of southeastern Liberia *created the market* for certain kinds of cloth in their region, even as their menfolk responded to labor demands originating far beyond their communities. As Darkwah (chapter 4, this volume) reminds us, some women benefit from the changes brought about by globalization, even as others are harmed. In this instance, it is the civilized women who find themselves most dependent on the cash economy and the least advantaged to profit from it. The native women, who use imported commodities to enhance their prestige while maintaining their economic independence, emerge as the best positioned to reap the benefits.

In this account of how cloth and clothing have worked to construct status differences among and between women in the Glebo communities of the southeastern Liberian coast, I have tried to emphasize the agency, creativity, and innovation of several generations of women. As producers, consumers, and interpreters of commodities, the women of coastal West Africa have been deeply implicated in globalization for several centuries. The legacy of that involvement is visible in the multiple status categories a woman must negotiate over the course of her life and in the contents of her "Kru box," ultimately to be seen and appreciated at her funeral.

About the Author

Mary H. Moran is professor of anthropology and Africana and Latin American studies at Colgate University. She has degrees from Mount Holyoke and Brown (1985 Ph.D.). Her first book was *Civilized Women: Gender and Prestige in Southeastern Liberia* (Cornell 1990), and her second was *Liberia: The Violence of Democracy* (University of Pennsylvania 2006). She is currently secretary/treasurer of the Liberian Studies Association. In the past, she served as chair of the Association for Feminist Anthropology, on the American Anthro-pological Association executive board, and as monographs editor for the American Ethnological Society. In 2006, she returned to Liberia for the first time since the war began in 1989; her new research is on men who did not fight in the civil war.

Part II

Racialized Policies, Scarred Bodies
Women Transposing
Neoliberal Violence

6

Progressive Women, Traditional Men

Globalization, Migration, and Equality
in the Northern Periphery
of the European Union

Ulrika Dahl

This chapter is in conversation with and takes issue with some conventional ways of addressing and using the concepts of "gender" and "periphery" within current critical feminist discussions of the very slippery phenomenon of globalization. Critical discussions on the uneven effects of globalization tend to focus on how marginality is experienced in the "global South" and by those originating there, and for very good reason. Western Europe, in contrast, is seen as a strong region, "Europeans" as generally the winners of globalization, and "marginality" as largely experienced by women, migrants, and "racialized others" (compare de los Reyes, Molina, and Mulinari 2003; Lutz 1997). However, as I will argue in this chapter, the sparsely populated, rural northern periphery of Europe shares little (from the perspective of the north) with the *southern* cities, often associated with the positive imaginary of transnational integration and globalization. A marginalized region, the rural north largely remains tied to discourses of underdevelopment and tradition in ways that point to the uneven effects of globalization within Europe. This chapter at once draws attention to a different form of marginality and seeks to complicate the picture of a seemingly homogenous, geopolitical "periphery" in the rural north.

The rural north of Sweden is an area marked by vast distances, sparse population, little economic and population growth, feminized migration, and very little industry. It is a place where globalization is at once an imaginary, a politicoeconomic framework, and an extension of modernization through "development." In the late 1990s, I conducted ethnographic research and collaboration with a wide range of development projects, women's networks, village councils, state agencies, and resource centers based in the county of Jämtland in northern Sweden. My purpose was to explore how men and women understood and experienced regional identity, gender politics, and European integration after Sweden's entry into the European Union (EU).

As a Jämtland-born woman who has pursued educational, career, and life opportunities abroad in international cosmopolitan centers, I myself am an example of the feminization of outward migration that for so long has characterized the region. Through my education at elite institutions in the United States, I was deeply informed by postcolonial critiques of anthropology, and I wanted to return "home" to understand why the vast majority of the northern periphery's inhabitants remain critical of the EU and the European Monetary Union (EMU). I hoped in my dissertation research to bring anthropological tools to bear on a familiar context and to contribute to analyses of European legacies of colonialism and racism. Thus, I found myself particularly attentive to a set of stories about cultural marginality *within* Jämtland that seemed to have elided scrutiny from white feminists.

One might argue that since 1995 Sweden's membership in the EU has provided the main governmental framework through which the complex and contradictory political and economic processes of globalization are mediated. Indeed, to many Jämtlanders I interviewed, the EU largely symbolized increased regulation and bureaucratization. Many argued that on a policy level the EU relies on urban values and encourages increased centralization of decision making. The EU and its emphasis on mobility extend sentiments about the subordination of the rural to the urban, of sparsely populated, "underdeveloped" areas to the crowded cities of the south. However, those pushing for European integration did not take critiques seriously, extending instead long-held negative attitudes of northerners as backward, lazy, and traditional. Others I spoke with argued that Jämtland has benefited from EU membership; the region is now eligible for development funding because of the EU's policies for structural adjustment in the "less advantaged areas." As one government official and EU project evaluator I interviewed put it, "Jämtland gets more than it pays."

Sweden prides itself on having been coined the most gender-equal country in the world by the UN and is often upheld by feminists as a "women-friendly state" (compare Hernes 1987).[1] Swedish policies and strategies for equality implementation not only are well known within Sweden but also have been widely exported and used as models around the world (see Dahl 2005; Kulick 2003; Rabo 1997). In the 1994 EU referendum, women made up a majority of those who voted against EU membership. A common explanation was that women were concerned that European integration might lead to cutbacks in welfare state spending and what that might mean for women. In the rural north, as in most of Sweden, the state has been the main employer of women for several decades, in addition to being a central source of additional temporary, supplementary, and necessary income, through parental leave, unemployment, long-term sick leave, and so on. As some feminist scholars have noted, Swedish women have grown increasingly dependent on the state (rather than on their husbands) in the past several decades.

As several chapters in this volume show, the impact of the growing spread of feminism and equality discourse on the lives of women can be seen as one of the positive effects of global interconnectedness. At the same time, analyses that address only obvious politicoeconomic changes brought about by globalization, it seems to me, ignore the subtle ways in which the neoliberalization of welfare states and the instrumentality of policy are tied to theories of globalization. Less attended to are the very conceptions of gender that gender equality discourse relies on and reproduces. As I argue in this chapter, such understandings of gender tend to reinscribe a developmental model of equality that erases other relations of power while also revealing how the concept of equality itself is relative and produced through comparisons with a less equal "elsewhere."

In this chapter, I draw on ethnographic stories, interviews, informal conversations, and a wide range of public and semipublic documents gathered during 18 months of fieldwork in Jämtland, to challenge what I see as a tendency in analyses of gendered globalization: the assumption that globalization simply impacts men and women differentially. Through cultural analysis of how gender is *talked about* and through a focus on the intersection of neoliberal economic policy and policy on equality between men and women, I hope to show that in the rural northern periphery,[2] experiences with European integration, and therefore with globalization, have had some surprising effects, not only in terms of gendered experiences but also in terms of local understandings of gender and development. In varied discussions about regional development in Jämtland, I argue, women are often described as "progressive" and innovative leaders of development, but men are seen as "traditional" and obstacles to progress. As I will show here, this perspective is linked to views on what counts as effective development and understandings of what equality between men and women means. At the same time, I hope to show that such stories, while focusing on gender, at times run the risk of erasing relations of power *within* Jämtland, including but *not* limited to those based on class and ethnicity and relations between the countryside and the town center. Here I argue that the meaning of gender is an articulation in and an effect of (see Butler 1999) particular discourses of equality, on the one hand, and development and globalization, on the other.

In developing this argument, I draw on work by policy anthropologists Cris Shore and Susan Wright, who have argued that, in late modernity, policy increasingly shapes how people understand themselves as subjects: "By extending hegemony over a population and 'naturalizing' a particular ideology as common sense, policy becomes incontestable, inviolable and beyond political debate" (Shore and Wright 1997:24). They propose that we read policy "not as a discrete local community or bounded geographical area, but as a social and political space articulated through relations of power and systems of governance" (Shore and Wright 1997:14). As policy, as documents of governmentality and as practice, becomes increasingly central to how people understand the relation between gender and power, I argue that this is an area requiring in-depth analysis that does not take gender as an a priori category but as an effect of discursive and material practices. At the same time, as I hope to show, the ways in which differently situated women *utilize* and *draw on* gender and development policies demonstrate agency within marginalization. In the next section, I introduce Jämtland by giving a brief historical background to its situated experiences of marginality and its subsequent resistance to Sweden's EU membership.

LOCATING JÄMTLAND, LOCATING MARGINALITY

Why should a discussion of economic and cultural marginality be concerned with the rural northern periphery? By most accounts, Sweden is a wealthy First World nation with a strong and still relatively well-functioning welfare state and with comparatively little poverty. Even with the past decade's gradual dismantling of the welfare state and rise of "enterprise culture" (see Keat 1991; Strathern 2000) in most western European nation-states, it would be preposterous to speak about economic and cultural marginality in Sweden by some measures. At the same time, the key cultural, technological, and politicoeconomic features often attributed to globalization, such as increased interconnectedness, mobility, and time-space compression, are rarely associated with the vast northern periphery comprising two-thirds of Scandinavia and the north of England, Scotland, and Ireland. The northern periphery continues to be marked by extreme weather, long distances between settlements, little industry, low population density, and high outward migration. Above all, the region and its inhabitants are considered "not quite up to speed" in terms of economic growth and development.

The rural Swedish county of Jämtland, the area at the heart of my research, is approximately the size of Holland but has fewer than 135,000 inhabitants spread over eight municipalities. About 58,000 live in or around the county capital, Östersund. Located in the middle of Sweden, it is part of the two-thirds of the country referred to as *Norrland* (the north). Large parts of Jämtland are also part of Sapmi, the territory inhabited by the indigenous Sami, which stretches across northern Scandinavia and into Russia. The Sami make up roughly 4 percent of the Jämtland population.[3]

Unlike southern Sweden, the north was never populated and ruled by wealthy nobility. Jämtland was the last province to become part of the modern Swedish state, and its modernization began largely with southern Swedish settlers who in the nineteenth century received tax breaks from the Swedish state to settle and farm the rich soil of Jämtland (see Liliequist 1991; Sörlin 1988). The state infrastructure has been primarily concerned with tax collection, military defense, and administration of large natural resources such as timber and hydraulic power. With little significant industry, class differences were, according to my informants, historically reflected in landownership (of woods, in particular). Today class is largely a question of town and country, education, and migration. Aside from leaders of state agencies and professionals such as doctors and lawyers, returned expatriates and successful (tourism) business owners tend to be at the top of the class structure. In past decades, the public sector (municipalities, state agencies, and so on) has become the largest employer in Jämtland, and the county's main revenue comes from tourism, particularly around the mountain region.[4]

The dominant story of Jämtland's marginality, I argue, is highly gendered because it is cast in terms of a problem of growth, both economic growth and, as I will show below, population growth. Women thus hold a peculiar role in Jämtland, where their tendency to migrate out of the province is both a marker of progressiveness and a crisis for the region. Following women's entry into the paid labor market (and the decline of small-scale farming), the public sector has been the main employer of women. Child, medical, and elder care, municipal administrative work, education and custodial work, and often part-time work have dominated women's employment. In recent years, large numbers of women have taken sick leave, in part as a result of physical and emotional burnout from many years of strenuous and underpaid work. Many women I interviewed are engaged in self-development work of various kinds, including alternative medical practices, new age religion, crafts and arts, and service work such as selling beauty products. With property being cheap but taxes high, most people in rural areas subside on far less than urban households. All the persons I interviewed argued that they value the outdoors and the pace of life in rural areas over working too much.

The county's vastness, low population density, and majestic scenery and wilderness make tourism a main source of income, and the regional cultural products require national and European markets. Few other types of businesses have been successful, though in the past decade telecom businesses have been established in several municipalities, employing large numbers of people. In one case, a politician described it as "a positive improvement. Now we see the youngsters wearing suits as they walk around our center." Businesses that establish in the county often receive tax cuts (much like the settlers in the 1800s), but small-scale farmers and local businesses struggle. The county has received development funds from the Swedish state since the 1950s, but the median household income in Jämtland remains below the national average.[5] Experiences with and understandings of globalization in Jämtland must be understood in relation to a longer tradition of "underdevelopment" in relation to the making of modern Sweden and resistance thereto.

In both the 1994 Swedish referendum on EU membership and the 2003 referendum on the EMU, Jämtlanders (along with other northerners) made national headlines by voting strongly against participation. Cast in the national media as evidence of the backward and ignorant ways of northerners, the nearly 80 percent who voted no were ridiculed and scorned. The main explanation for resistance to the EU in 1994 was that Jämtland has a strong regional identity and is unwilling to comply with Swedish national politics. The reason for this, many people would say, is that Jämtland was once, in a mythic "Viking" era, a sovereign "republic" and Jämtlanders are proud and unbendable.[6] People outside Jämtland primarily view this regionalism as a quaint and humorous characteristic of the county. The national media largely interpreted northerners' no vote as reflecting their disinterest in the positive effects of globalization and in keeping with the changing times, rather than as a situated and well-informed critique of a particular political agenda (Dahl 2004). Regionalism and regional identity building might arguably be celebrated and seen as part of globalization, but when regional resistance opposes certain dimensions of economic restructuring and integration, it is ignored.

The Swedish referendum resulted in a 52-to-48 vote in favor of EU membership. Despite many half-joking demands "not that Jämtland leave the EU, but that the EU leave Jämtland" (as the Jämtland Republic's "president"—a well-known musician and actor—once put it), resistance dwindled in the late 1990s. Lena[7] had been active in the "No to the EU" campaign before the 1994 referendum and was working with cooperative development in her village at the time I spoke with her. She explained:

> There is so little resistance to the EU now, it is totally quiet. We voted no, 80 percent of Jämtlanders did. Now almost all of us are sitting here with EU funds and all this paperwork, mad at the bureaucrats. We must do all that they expect us to. Otherwise, we don't get any money. And if Jämtlanders don't get better at fetching the EU money, that is, apply for these funds, then they will be returned. And we get even more reprimanded. "Damned if you do and damned if you don't." That is how it feels.

The northern two-thirds of Sweden are part of the EU's target areas 1 and 2 and are eligible for development funding for "less advantaged areas" marked by what the EU literature describes as "extreme peripherality" (see European Commission 1996). Any group of Jämtlanders, including organizations, resource centers, village councils, and other such actors, was eligible to apply for EU funding for development—that is, if it had access to information about the program and could frame its ideas in the form of a "project" that would meet the funding criteria. A project had to create jobs, increase competence and knowledge among the population, improve the state of *jämställdhet* (equality between men and women), and, ideally, lead to long-term, environmentally sound, sustainable living in the province. In the end, more funding was available than the bureaucrats could spend. One EU official explained that the regional office had to send back money because not enough groups applied for it.

Many Jämtlanders I interviewed shared Lena's frustration. Although EU membership meant new opportunities for development funding, the criteria for content and for carrying out projects were overwhelming. At the same time, Jämtlanders were constantly urged to apply for funding through the complicated and bureaucratic procedures. After funding was secured, the process of running development projects required labor- and time-intensive administration. In most of the projects with which I worked closely, people experienced tremendous frustration with the EU bureaucracy and rarely found that they could achieve what they wanted. Unable to create new jobs, many project workers continued to apply for new funding or went back into unemployment or previous less-desired jobs. Moreover, those who did get funding were, more often than not, already established and powerful groups and actors, including researchers and activists who had transnational connections and the language savvy required to gain funding. These examples, I argue, reveal how policy increasingly shapes people's livelihoods and understandings of themselves.

SEARCH THE OLD, CREATE THE NEW: THE "GENDERED IMPACT" OF GLOBALIZATION

The EU takes equality between women and men very seriously and has earmarked funding for women. Following entry into the EU, great emphasis was placed on encouraging Jämtland women to apply for development funding. A large number of projects, many focusing on promoting equality between men and women and providing particular support for women's entrepreneurship, were created. One example was Search the Old, Create the New, which stated the following in its program proposal:

> We are in a transitional period between two epochs. All experiences, all values we have gathered for a long time have to be merged with new experiences and new knowledge. Out of this melting pot of old and new something good has to be born. Many women feel that they are the losers of today. Continued high unemployment as a result of cutbacks and savings (within the public sector) affect women to a larger degree than men. If we study the world from a global perspective it is still women in almost all cultures who are subordinated [by] traditions and norm systems which devalue them and give them fewer possibilities to affect society as well as their own situation.[8]

With support from the European Union's structural adjustment funds earmarked for equality between men and women (jämställdhet), the project aimed to create livelihoods for long-term unemployed Jämtland women, using a familiar recipe in the 1990s. By utilizing the region's main resources (local history, culture, and crafts) in promoting tourism and small-scale businesses and by developing "networking" and entrepreneurship for women, the goal of this project was to start new (women-run) businesses and a local resource center for women.

The proposal was drafted by a project initiator well versed in the language of development funding applications and reflects how an analysis of "gendered globalizations" is central both to obtaining development funds and to understanding one's gendered place in the world. Here globalization is understood as neoliberal economic change (reflected in cutbacks in the public sector) and late modernity (a period characterized by rapid change away from old traditions) while also reflecting a development narrative of transforming old values into "new knowledge." The analysis presented—that globalization and late capitalist transformations marginalize women and that their subordination is linked to the devaluing of their work—is a familiar one to Marxist feminist anthropologists and other critics of the uneven effects of globalization. In this proposal, the urgency of the situation of Jämtland women was made more powerful precisely by invoking an imagined shared position of women worldwide and a corollary, a sense of universal sisterhood: "women" as a group are the losers in "a transitional period."

This project is one example of how women in Jämtland have responded to and analyzed the impact of that unruly phenomenon called globalization. It also illustrates how globalization and neoliberal strategies for development articulate with "state feminism" as it is expressed through policies of equality between men and women (jämställdhet) in Jämtland. The statement demonstrates agency insofar as it reveals the conscious and strategic invocation of a discourse that carries considerable weight (that of women's position in the world). At the same time, I argue, like much of grand theorizing about gender and globalization, the statement also universalizes and homogenizes women as a group in ways that render inequalities between women, locally and globally, invisible.

To understand such seemingly contradictory moves, we must understand how migration and women's activism are tied in Jämtland and how understandings of gender are tied to economic restructuring. Next, I turn to a discussion of the feminization of migration to and from Jämtland.

"WOMEN ARE FLEEING THE COUNTY!" THE FEMINIZATION OF MIGRATION IN JÄMTLAND

In recent years, feminist scholars have shown that the feminization of migration is a central feature of globalization (see, among others, Brennan 2004; Ehrenreich and Hochschild 2003). Increasingly, women migrate for work, love, and opportunity. Those who leave are often from the global South and often do so in hopes of better lives for their children. In many instances, extended families are supported by the wages earned by these migrant women in wealthy First World nations, wages that are gendered and marginalized. Images of better lives and desirable consumer goods, along with the clearly uneven effects of globalization in "peripheral" places, shape such decisions. Rarely do we hear about migration to and from the rural north, even though it is both a historic and a contemporary effect of global imaginaries and economic restructurings.

In Jämtland, the feminization of migration is nothing new. Like the rural northern periphery of Europe as a whole, Jämtland has been deeply affected by emigration since at least the late 1950s (compare Hansen 1998; Stenvold 2002). Agricultural reform, demand for labor in the industrialized south, and education are among the reasons given for emigration. Swedish ethnologist Kjell Hansen (1998) argues that, paradoxically, migration itself has been seen as the most important indicator of welfare and development in rural inland northern Sweden.

For decades, women have migrated from Jämtland in disproportionate numbers. In the 1970s, as women were entering the labor force en masse in Sweden and tax reforms made it both possible and necessary for married women to work, the explanation given for migration was the lack of jobs for women in Jämtland. Historically, Jämtland's main industries were lumber, a male-dominated sector, and family farming. Since the 1950s and extensive growth of the public sector, the state has provided more than half the jobs in the county. In 1974, the Swedish parliament ruled that regional assistance was needed to create jobs for women (Sundin 1992:106). Since then, the public sector has been the main employer for women in Jämtland, providing largely part-time and, by Swedish standards, underpaid jobs in health care, administration, education, and municipal development. As the effects of the cutbacks in the welfare state began to be felt in rural areas, women were affected greatly. At the same time, many women became long-time unemployed as a result of burnout and physical pain due to heavy repetitive tasks in, among other jobs, caring professions.

As is the case in many parts of the world, gendered yearnings for a cosmopolitan life have also largely shaped young women's desire to move. For women of my generation (born in the 1970s), the main reasons for leaving were the prospects of studies and work abroad. Two very popular routes in the late 1980s and early 1990s were work as nannies and au pairs in European and American cities and work within the service sector in various cosmopolitan centers in the Alps or along the Mediterranean. Others went as far as Tokyo to work as hostesses or, as in my case, to the United States to study. In the late 1990s, as I was interviewing girls and young women in Jämtland, stories of planned emigration persisted, and many interviewees stated that they intended to leave. As one high school girl put it, when asked what she thought she might be doing in ten years: "If I stay here [in the village where she lived], I will either be working as a cashier in the grocery store, or I'll be on sick leave, having ruined my back from working with old people." The public sector and a segregated labor market were still the main reasons for leaving: the girls and women simply did not regard the jobs available as exciting or fulfilling.

Needless to say, migration itself was marked by opportunity, class background, family history, and municipal specificity, but in becoming gendered, it produced a dominant story for the region. By the late 1990s, "the flight of young women" was presented as a serious crisis for the region. As one municipal politician I interviewed noted, "not only do we lose the young women, we lose the next generation as well." Although rarely stated explicitly as such, regional growth was clearly a highly gendered issue: without population growth, there would be no economic growth. Two main strategies were used to try to combat the loss of population: on the one hand, marketing Jämtland as a great place to raise a family (thus attempting to encourage people to move back) and on the other, providing young women with "positive role models" and supporting projects that aimed to offer meeting places for women, where they could discuss and try out ideas for what they wanted to do. Both of these strategies rested on conventional and highly heteronormative (see Rosenberg 2002) assumptions about gender and women's concerns. In both cases, the effect was that the strategies appealed to a very homogeneous group and created a story of who men and women in Jämtland were.

Much emphasis was placed on the great advantages and "good quality of life" in Jämtland for young families. Municipal politicians I talked with explained that their main strategy for combating "the flight of young women" was to provide good schools and day care, great outdoor activities, and safe, friendly, small-scale communities. From a clear understanding that rich natural resources and great outdoors such as those of Jämtland are becoming increasingly scarce in the industrialized world, such arguments, launched in advertising and recruitment campaigns, as well as in local media, often invoked comments on the negative impacts of globalization. For instance, in 2002 a project sponsored by the county council aimed to market Jämtland to an imagined potential group of returned migrants and new settlers. A brochure and website called *Jämtlandsbilden* (The Image of Jämtland) presented life in Jämtland as "a life in luxury," employing a rhetoric that reveals how the very image of what Jämtland has to offer is constructed in dialogue with an imagined urban lifestyle:

> Luxury can be having daycare, people, and experiences with
> nature nearby. Luxury can also be having time for a second cup

of morning coffee because traffic on the way to work does not exist. Luxury to us is not having to have alarms on our houses or gated front doors or not having to deal with the stressful pace of big cities. These are things that we in Jämtland consider self-evident but that are a luxury to big city people.[9]

This approach, I argue, seeks to change the image of Jämtland from one of backwardness and marginality to one of quality of life and "luxury," redefined as closeness to the availability of state services such as day care, nature, and (above all, as emphasized in the brochure) a different relationship to time. The lived experience of life in the rural north is already part of an imaginary in which the urban area is perceived as the norm. The marketing strategy to attract people to Jämtland is to turn the narrative of peripherality around by suggesting that "a life in luxury" is available in the north. Thus, I argue that globalization persists as an imaginary that shapes both dreams of migration and hopes of luring settlers. In such an imaginary, gendered meanings are central. Next, I turn to a discussion of the Women's Resource Center and how EU membership and neoliberalism affected its strategies.

"TO TAKE LIFE AND MATTERS INTO ONE'S OWN HANDS": WOMEN, ACTIVISM, AND POLICY IN JÄMTLAND

Against the backdrop of the gendered history of Jämtland and the feminization of migration, the story of Jämtland's regional women's resource center illustrates how globalization, neoliberal development strategies, and European integration intersect and affect women's activist and development work. By the late 1990s, the Women's Resource Center was the best-known women's organization in the county. The strategy, as summarized by Eva, its main organizer, was simply to listen to what the women themselves wanted and then to offer organizing advice and small stipends to networks of women who wanted to work on issues of local development in their villages and professions. Like the project proposal discussed above, the grassroots organizing often called upon universal models of women's experiences and strategies. The focus was on encouraging women to "take life and matters into their own hands" and to make something of their lives and futures, in Jämtland.

One result was that Jämtland saw the formation of a large number of women's networks with the overall purpose of empowering women to participate in regional politics, development, and employment. The regional women's resource center had support from regional development agencies and the state policy to improve equality between men and women (jäm-ställdhet) and to fight outward migration. The well-documented and nationally known model of organizing used by the resource center was described as a "bottom-up perspective" or as "empowerment." Empower-ment, one woman explained, is "a well-known model that is used by women everywhere, in Africa and India, for example."

The local, national, and international attention given to the work of the Women's Resource Center and what women were doing was, it turned out, not enough. At a time when Jämtland had a woman and self-defined feminist as governor, when increasing amounts of development funding were earmarked for jämställdhet, and when several researchers had begun to suggest that, indeed, what was going on in northern Sweden might be understood as a new women's movement (see Rönnblom 1997:2002), the executive board of the Women's Resource Center decided that the strategy and work of the center's small but energetic staff were "ineffective" and did not generate "growth." Most board members belonged to local business development agencies and funding authorities. They argued that it was hard to see what "concrete effects" the center's efforts would have on regional growth. Emphasis was to be placed on supporting women entre-preneurs, advising women on project ideas, and, above all, administering women's projects.

Mona and Eva, the symbolic leaders of the Jämtland model of mobiliz-ing women, were critical. They felt that it was a top-down approach that would not facilitate grassroots organizing and that it was not in line with the overall goal of their vision for the resource center. Change takes time, they argued, concerned that the new model would leave out too many women. Other women active around the resource center, in particular those who were in favor of supporting women entrepreneurs, insisted that the new model would be more effective in helping women who had ideas and who wanted to develop them. After a heated debate, largely in the media, about the purpose and future of the resource center, Eva and Mona resigned, sad and angry. The story about the unfolding of events surround-ing their resignation framed many discussions not only about women's work but also about the meaning of grassroots in the politics of regional devel-opment in Jämtland. Actors placed themselves within a larger story about regional development through positioning themselves in relation not only to bureaucratic structures but also to either the old or the new resource center.

Aside from revealing different alliances within the women's network movement concerning what women's organizing was supposed to do, the controversy highlighted contestations surrounding the meaning of development and women's role within it. The emphasis on placing matters of development and jämställdhet firmly within a framework that privileges growth illustrates how relations of power were renegotiated following Sweden's entry into the EU. This shift was reflected in the altered metaphors of development in the northern periphery; now empowerment of women as a development strategy was to be enterprised up, literally (see Strathern 2000).

Emphasizing a universal experience of the emancipatory effects of "taking matters into one's own hands," the women's networks embraced neoliberal ideals of individualism and entrepreneurship and became intimately tied to women's progress. In contrast, in a different story of love, work, and migration concerning Thai women who migrate to Jämtland to marry rural Swedish men, progress is understood in very different terms.

PROGRESSIVE WOMEN AND TRADITIONAL MEN

As discussed above, in the late 1990s, as increasingly neoliberal economic politics and cutbacks in the Swedish welfare state began to affect people, development projects became a form of political organizing and a means of livelihood for women. Among other projects, special efforts were made to encourage women, particularly those who were unemployed (often as a result of cutbacks in the public sector), to start their own business. It was an entrepreneurial, neoliberal model that also revealed a broader shift in understandings of work and responsibility: women should now "take life and matters into their own hands."[10] Jämtland women were upheld as innovative and visionary, as leaders of regional development and change, and men were increasingly presented as obstacles to progress. Intimately linked in these stories were gender, development, and regional economic growth.

In the mid-1990s, implementation of Swedish equality policy was moved to county administrations; at the same time, the focus of the policy shifted from women to men (see Dahl 2005). That is, it was assumed that in order to truly change the power relations between men and women, it was necessary to engage and educate men in questions about equality. At that time, a new story about Jämtland began to emerge: it was the traditional men who made women migrate from Jämtland. Gösta was one of the key actors in a county-administered, EU-funded project to engage men in questions of jämställdhet (equality between men and women). He offered a different analysis of the current state of gender relations in Jämtland than that of the project discussed in the introduction of this chapter.

Comfortably seated in his spacious villa with a view of the snow-clad Jämtland mountains, he explained his views on regional development funding and gender equality:

> It is already the case that women stand for much of cultural background and cultural stimulation in rural areas, where many of traditional women's tasks have disappeared. Men tend to be more traditional—he wears his Helly Hansen[11] suit, has his snowmobile, and so on. Many young, especially women, leave rural areas. We felt that if you [only] create opportunities for women to stay here, we run the risk of increasing the gap between men and women, with modern, progressive women and conservative, culturally traditional men in rural areas.

Eva, a night-school teacher involved with the regional women's resource center declared that "Jämtland men simply want to sit on their snowmobiles, wear their Helly Hansen, and they are quite content simply with their fishing poles." Maria, a sociologist who worked as a development project evaluator, explained: "I hear the same thing everywhere I go in rural northern Sweden. The question everyone is asking is, 'What are we to do with these men who do not want to change?'" Lars, another man involved with jämställdhet, insisted that the migration of young women would result in a serious problem of population growth: "There are not going to be any more children in this county because who wants to have a family with a man who is still living in the nineteenth century?"

Gösta's analysis was not unusual. In fact, during that time, people often explained gender relations as central to regional development, and equality was often cast as a narrative of progress. On the one hand, people insisted on describing equality in terms of "how far we've come," both in temporal terms (that is, when compared with "how things used to be") and in spatiocultural terms (for example, "Sweden is the most gender-equal country in the world"). On the other hand, when discussing gender in relation to regional development, people often suggested that, in Jämtland, women were modern and progressive and men were conservative and traditional. For a returned native daughter trained in feminist anthropology and cultural analysis of gender, this local understanding of how gender was linked to regional development, employment opportunities, and sustainability seemed puzzling at first. How was it that men had become the obstacle to progress?

Men and women's ideas about the future of the region tell us much about how gender is understood. One representative of an EU funding agency noted, "Women run the development projects in this county! And for good reasons." He did not know for sure why women were better at development but then thought out loud, mostly to himself, "Perhaps it has to do with their innate ability as mothers to always come up with flexible solutions to problems having to do with feeding their children." Whether one talked to jämställdhet workers, feminists, or representatives for development funding agencies, the idea was that women had "gotten it" but men had not.

Explanations of which properties of female gender made women progressive varied. The EU official insisted that there was something innate in women's biology, some kind of adaptive instinct that had to do with protecting the young. Others invoked the Viking heritage of strong independent women, and a third group argued that women's progressiveness was a result of the heavy emphasis on women's rights through feminism and jämställdhet.

This discussion of the backwardness of northern Swedish men is widespread. For instance, Leontieva and Sarsenov (2003) make similar observations in discussing Russian women who meet Swedish men and are constructed in popular discourse as either "whores" or "mail-order brides." They argue that the media presents men in northern Sweden as "half alcoholic men with saggy clothing, wearing Helly Hansen," in stark contrast to urban men, who are described as civilized and respectful of women (see also Nordin 2005).

The stories of young women "fleeing" the county because of the "traditional" Jämtland men were sometimes juxtaposed with another story of feminized migration: that of Asian women moving to Jämtland. Young, white Jämtland women were seen as being progressive in their move, but Thai women were described in terms of being "imported." Despite being a relatively small number (approximately 200, according to a woman I interviewed), Thai women have a central role in defining the characteristics of progressiveness. Largely migrating as a result of having met Jämtland men, Thai women were described as seeking improvement of their life situation. Yet in doing so they were seen as doing the opposite of what "progressive" Jämtland women were doing by migrating. In marrying the "traditional" Jämtland men, Thai women were assumed to take a traditional subordinate position and to perform household and child care duties that the self-proclaimed progressive Jämtland women were unwilling to do.

For instance, a white Swedish journalist I met at an event that drew a large number of Thai-Jämtland couples, the inauguration of a Thai pavilion in the municipality of Ragunda, said: "What is it with these middle-aged men and their young Thai women? I know what it is. It is because no Jämtland woman in her right mind would put up with these sexist pigs. Of course they have to go elsewhere to find wives; certainly these Asian brides are every man's wet dream!" The journalist's off-the-cuff comment invoked the discourse about backward, traditional men and a racist conception of Asian women. Within an unequal system of power and privilege, Asian women as a group were given certain (gendered) characteristics that placed them below Swedish women. Rarely spoken to or with, but rather about, Asian women were described in racist and stereotypical ways as docile, subservient, sexualized, and oppressed.

The starting assumption for everyday discussions about Thai-Jämtland heterosexual unions was always that Sweden was a better country to live in than Thailand, and especially for women—Sweden being the most equal country in the world (see Kulick 2003). Although Jämtland men were seen as hopelessly backward and traditional, within the global comparative framework of jämställdhet, they were invariably understood to be better than Thai men. In the context of an inherently Swedish vision of jäm-ställdhet as largely concerned with securing equal relations between men and women who live, share children, and work together, the Asian woman as a figure was seen as a threat to equality and to the modernization of Jämtland.

Wanja, a member of the Thai association in Jämtland, reflected on some of these assumptions about Thai women in an interview. Wanja came to Jämtland in the early 1980s after meeting a much older man from Jämtland when he was on vacation in Thailand. The first few years she was miserable, she explained, because she felt very isolated and missed her family. She was also very disturbed by the images of Thai women that she saw in the media, as well as with a discussion of how "immigrants were parasites," as she put it. "I told myself, I'll show them that I'm not like that, I will work hard and show them that I am capable," she explained. Fifteen years later, she was running a successful business with her second Swedish husband. Still, she and her Thai women friends were often frustrated, not only with the racist and sexist attitudes of some Swedish men but also with how women seemed to think that "all Thai women were like that...whores": "When I hear things like that, I think it's terrible. Why do people say things like that when they don't know any Thai women? If they want to know something, they should just ask. But the only question they ask me is, 'What work did you do in Thailand?'"

Wanja's strategy was much like that of the overall approach in Jämtland in the late 1990s (discussed above), namely, to take life and work into her own hands. She had worked hard and made a life for herself. There were many Thai women like her, she said, who ran restaurants, hair salons, and other small businesses. Still, rarely did anyone ask Thai women what they wanted in Jämtland. "Many are isolated. They stay at home with children, or they go to school. We have lots of ideas but nobody asks us."

White "progressive feminist" women's interest in Asian women was limited to talking about them and, at times, to an assumption that they needed to be rescued, both from the traditional men and from their own traditional values. Fueling this view were local media stories about Thai women who were abused by their husbands, who were simply "kept in the house" or "subservient" to Jämtland men.

I would suggest that the construction of women as progressive and men as traditional exemplifies the uneven and contradictory experiences and cultural constructions of globalization in Sweden's rural northern periphery. When long-term residents in the northern periphery often critiqued the relations of power that placed Jämtland at that periphery, they also had an understanding of themselves as more modern and equal than other parts of the world, including neighboring countries that were also becoming part of the EU and the Southeast Asian countries where many dreamed of vacationing. These countries were not seen as "having gotten very far" when it came to jämställdhet, producing a sense that Jämtland, although having a long way to go, was nevertheless distinctly reasonable and modern. Modernity and progressiveness, in other words, are relational categories that gain their meaning as concepts within broader relations of power that are both spatially and temporally mapped.

CONCLUSION

In this chapter, I have sought to offer a glimpse of multiple and rather complicated intersections of "gendered globalizations" in the rural northern periphery of Sweden. Marginality, or "extreme peripherality" as the EU calls it, might, I suggest, be understood both as an effect of geographic location and modernization resulting in a feminized migration and limited opportunity for women and as a powerful discourse about Jämtland that, at times, conceals other relations of power. In Jämtland, globalization has not meant the establishment of large multinational corporations or chains and the exploitation of labor but rather is felt through the presence of EU projects, regulations, and directives and through a shift in how people understand themselves, their position in the world, and their work. As the state's strategy for improving jämställdhet was placed on county administrations, it was also cast in terms of encouraging women to "seize life and work into their own hands" (see Nilsson 1993). What this meant was both an opportunity for women to have agency in determining their own lives and a transformation toward a more neoliberal model of work and personhood that also conceals how larger political and economic processes shape everyday livelihoods. As rural areas began to feel the effects of cutbacks in the public sector, emphasis was instead placed on partnerships between business and local administrations and on entrepreneurship as a way to fight a rather dystopian sentiment about the future of the sparsely populated province.

In this chapter, I have argued that rather than simply a matter of men and women being differently "impacted" by globalization, gender might be understood as an effect of discourses about globalization. For instance, discourses of jämställdhet and development in Jämtland bring an understanding of heteronormative gender relations together with ideas of progress and tradition in a way that serves to naturalize power (see Yanagisako and Delaney 1995). Not only were Jämtland men described as traditional and unwilling to change, but also there was an assumption that they did not want to engage in relationships of equality with women. It was supposedly because of this resistance to change that women had left, so, by extension, these traditional men were at fault for the region's lack of progress. In that sense, the progress of the region not only was understood to be a matter of growth and resources but also was intimately linked to relations between men and women and to reproduction. For the population to grow, then, women had to be encouraged to stay in the county. In the views of jämställdhet workers such as Gösta and other men involved with the men's project, emphasis was placed on changing men.

Such seemingly local understandings of gender were forged in global relations of power. For instance, there was an assumption, particularly among white Swedish women who worked with questions of jämställdhet, that the traditional Jämtland men, rather than strive to be equal with the "progressive" Swedish women, would prefer women who had not been "enlightened" to the qualities of modern Swedish ideas of equality. This discourse was echoed in the national press, where stories about gendered violence were often cast in racialized terms (see, among others, de los Reyes, Molina, and Mulinari 2003). This suggests that globalization produces gendered scripts that require closer analytical scrutiny. Here, a view from the northern periphery might be useful.

Many analyses of globalization, including those that seek to call attention to its negative and uneven effects, tend to assume gender as a stable analytical category, along with other categories of identity. Like other authors of this volume, I wish to bring this stability into question and instead link gender analytically to processes of economic and cultural restructuring associated with globalization. My work shows that the very meaning of womanhood is an effect of an increasingly global discourse of equality, in which feminism itself is a central technology of gender (see de Lauretis 1987) and policy discourse becomes a powerful story that women invoke to position themselves in different ways. Through careful, situated, and in-depth ethnographic analysis, anthropologists can continue to offer nuanced analyses of taken-for-granted categories, processes, and inequalities.

About the Author

Ulrika Dahl holds a Ph.D. in cultural anthropology and women's studies from the University of California, Santa Cruz, and teaches gender studies at Södertörn University College in Stockholm, Sweden. Currently, she has two research projects, one concerning canon formation and intellectual kinship in Nordic gender studies (funded by the Baltic Sea Foundation) and one in which she conducts multisited ethnographic research on queer femininities. An activist teacher and a scholar, she writes regularly for the feminist, queer, and leftist press and is collaborating with photographer Del LaGrace Volcano on a book titled *Femmes of Power: Exploding Queer Femininities*, forthcoming by Serpent's Tail Press.

Acknowledgments

This chapter draws on ethnographic fieldwork conducted from 1998 to 2000, funded by the Wenner-Gren Foundation for Anthropological Research. I thank all the women and men in Jämtland who shared their lives, work, and thoughts with me. I also thank the members of my UC Santa Cruz dissertation committee, Lisa Rofel, Don Brenneis, Donna Haraway, and, in particular, Ann Kingsolver, for all their support. In addition, I thank AnnaCarin Andersson, Kale Fajardo, and Lena Sawyer for ongoing conversation and Kjell Hansen for comments on an earlier draft.

Notes

1. Norwegian feminist scholar Helga Hernes (1987) coined the term *women-friendly* to describe the Scandinavian welfare state model. Feminist political scientists use (and question) this term.

2. The rural north of Sweden comprises, in fact, the northern two-thirds of the nation-state. The *northern periphery*, in this chapter, refers to a region defined as such

by the EU and includes northern Sweden, Norway, Finland, England, Scotland, and Ireland. This "region" shares characteristics such as vast distances between settlements, low population density, extreme climate, and depopulation.

3. This is an estimate. According to the only census ever conducted, in the 1970s there were about 20,000 Sami in Sweden. In Jämtland, there were 12 Sami villages and 99 family businesses managing reindeer. Sapmi website, http://www.samer.se/servlet/GetDoc?meta_id=1145, accessed July 22, 2006.

4. Regionfakta 2007 website, http://www.regionfakta.com/StartsidaLan.aspx?id=2861, accessed March 20, 2007.

5. Statistics Sweden, htp://www.scb.se, accessed March 20, 2007.

6. For an extensive discussion about Jämtland's regional identity, see my doctoral dissertation (Dahl 2004) and Hansen 1998.

7. All names and, in some cases, certain personal details have been changed to protect anonymity.

8. Project description of Search the Old, Create the New, 1998. Unpublished document, courtesy of project leader, on file with the author.

9. Brochure produced by the Jämtland County Administration, on file with the author.

10. As Russell Keat argues in his study of Thatcherite enterprise culture in Britain, the cultural dimension of a shift toward an entrepreneurial model is a shift in understandings of personhood. Enterprising individuals are to be self-reliant and non-dependent. A strong emphasis is on making one's own decisions and, above all, taking responsibility for one's own life (Keat 1991:5).

11. Helly Hansen is a brand of outdoor clothing, generally a bright orange color, popular among hunters and lumbermen in northern Sweden.

7

Neoliberal Policy as Structural Violence

Its Links to Domestic Violence in Black Communities in the United States

William L. Conwill

A few days later he came home late again. Late, loud, and wrong. He accused me of confusing what he had told me about when he would be home. One thing led to another, and in the heat of the exchange he struck me.

I couldn't believe it. At first the blow descended upon me like some scream-ing bat bursting out of lower hell. I must have been in shock. I mean, nobody had ever really attacked me this way. And yet he was doing it again, shoving me into the corner, taking out his Black man frustration on me. Everything inside me began dying.

—Come Out the Wilderness *by Majozo*

In this chapter, I examine the relationship between structural and domestic violence in relation to neoliberal policies in the United States and argue that poverty is a more significant causal factor in domestic violence than racialized identity. First, I want to underscore the neoliberal character of the current structural violence (Harrison 1997a:465) directed against the African American population in the United States, a population that has historically been adversely affected by the nation's economic policies. These policies have long had an impact on families, the same types of impact identified by ethnographers studying the applications and effects of neoliberal policies elsewhere. Underlying my analysis is the relative employability of sex by race (Conwill 1980:89–91); that is, in the United States, African American women are more employable than African American men for the purpose of system maintenance.[1] The jobs for African American women may be more menial and lower paying than those for African American men, but they are also more available. Hence, in the United States, white male dominance is upheld through white female economic dependence, African American male underemployment, and African American female economic sustenance that is independent from African American male economic support. Practices related to this pattern affect both the internal and the external dynamics of the family (Conwill 1980:171–175).

My second objective is to examine the links between structural violence against the African American community and gendered violence in the home. I will use relevant survey literature on domestic violence to do this. Levels of domestic violence in the African American community rise and fall with the intensity of social and economic repression.

Third and finally, I want to represent the links between structural violence against the African American community and domestic violence in the lives of African American women, using qualitative case studies from my community psychology practice. I am, by training, a research clinician. I use theory-based clinical interventions to create or improve evidence-based theory, and vice versa. One of my areas of expertise is black family intervention. For example, I am currently working with the Oregon Social Learning Center (OSLC) to help train staff of the Mental Health Department in Wayne County, Michigan, to serve black families using their Basic Parent Management Training model. My first contact with the OSLC was in 1976, and I have attended numerous multicultural, international training workshops at its headquarters in Eugene, Oregon. The OSLC is renowned for developing a research-based family intervention model over a 30-year period.

STRUCTURAL VIOLENCE, GENDERED ETHNICITY, AND "BLACK MAN FRUSTRATION"

As invariably one of the few black psychologists in cities where I worked, I always situated my private practice where clients from more distressed areas of the African American community could access my services, and I frequently offered reduced-fee sessions. As a result, I built quite unique private-practice bases, including clients who drove in from the suburbs and paid the full fee and others who walked from low-income housing areas and paid a reduced fee. Sometimes I even provided pro bono sessions for those whose need exceeded their ability to pay. The individuals and couples who came to my office felt that I could understand the special circumstances they faced as members of the black community.

The women in these case studies struggle with many of the same issues iterated in the ethnographic literature on women's experiences of global-ization. These concerns include the justification of low wages because of their home responsibilities (Kondo 1995), the exclusion of black men from the workforce, sexual harassment, and the installation of racial hierarchies in the workplace, with black women on the bottom (Yelvington 1995). The women in therapy also decried the lack of affordable child care during work hours and, most sadly, recounted episodes of ongoing sexual abuse of young girls by older (usually teen) male relative babysitters.

In the brief autobiographical account introducing this chapter, Majozo, a literary artist, attributes her experience of domestic violence to her husband's "black man frustration." She describes his aggravating sense of dissatisfaction, his "crisis of masculinity" (Mills 2003:53) as a result of a male's treatment as black. She relates his frustration not to his race or cul-ture, but to his provocation by racist economic policies and black economic distress, which constitute structural violence. Structural violence exists when institutions and policies are designed so that barriers in society result in lack of food, housing, safe and just working conditions, health, educa-tion, economic security, and family relationships. With regard to family relationships, Winter and Leighton (1999) ascribe to structural violence the domestic violence due to dual-income and single parents working to meet the increasing cost of living, latchkey kids, underfunded day care, and escalating violence in the schools.

Structural violence is embedded in our social structures, evincing itself as unequal access to economic resources, as political impotence, as inade-quate education, as inaccessible health care, and as discriminatory treatment under the law (Farmer 2003, 2004; Harrison 1997a:457). In examining the deepening poverty and serious decline in public health conditions related to structural adjustment policies in Jamaica, for instance, Harrison (1997a:452) brings out the inverse relationship between the alarming reduc-tions in government expenditures and the promotion of costly, less acces-sible, privatized health care. Structures of privilege and oppression can become so embedded in our notions of justice and worthiness that they warp our assumptions about who deserves or has a right to societal benefits as fundamental as health care. Farmer (2003:129), noting that managing inequality almost never includes higher standards of care for those whose agency has been constrained, whether by poverty or prison, argues against the sustainability of any policy based on differential valuation of human life.

Because structural inequities are long-standing, they usually seem quite normal, or the way things are and always have been (McGregor n.d.; Winter and Leighton 1999). Victims of structural violence often do not see the systematic ways their lives are orchestrated by the unfair distribution of resources or by human constraints caused by political and economic structures. As a result, victims of structural violence are often blamed, or even blame themselves, for their plight (Winter and Leighton 1999).

According to Winter and Leighton (1999), structural violence frequently leads to direct violence. That is, people who are chronically oppressed often resort to direct violence. Johan Galtung (n.d.), however, presses the point even more strongly: cultural and structural violence *cause* direct violence, using violent actors who revolt against the structures and using the culture to legitimize violence as an instrument, especially against women. This is not to say that variables besides the economic, such as conceptual-integrative complexity (Suedfeld, Tetlock, and Streufert 1992) and social stress (men's "work-hard, play-hard, don't cry" mentality; Lau 2002), do not influence rates of domestic violence. In making the argument that governmental policies are designed to benefit the owners of the means of production at the expense of the family relations of the economically marginalized, particularly black inner-city populations, I will first examine macro-scale demographic indicators and later explore case studies.

PLACING "BLACK MAN FRUSTRATION" IN A GLOBAL CONTEXT

Some of the most promising new approaches to the study of urban economic distress and poverty, especially among African Americans, theorize welfare-state restructuring in connection with larger questions about the restructuring of race, class, and gender relations in the United States and in relation to global shifts in economics and politics (Morgen and Maskovsky 2003). Kingfisher (2002), for example, places the case of poor African American communities in the United States in a global perspective to make the case that the kind of reforms surrounding the US Welfare Reform Act of 1996 constitutes an intrinsic part of the processes of neoliberalism and globalization.

In 1992, Bill Clinton was elected president on the promise to "end welfare as we know it." Working with the Republican Congress that was elected in 1994, Clinton signed the Personal Responsibility and Work Opportunity Act on August 22, 1996, thereby ending the welfare entitlement and replacing it with a new block grant to states to assist the needy. The bill eliminated benefits based on eligibility, as well as the child care guarantee, and set a five-year lifetime limit on assistance. Morgen and Maskovsky (2003) note the parallels between what is happening to African Americans in US inner cities and what is occurring in other places where neoliberal policies include propaganda to reduce expectations that the state will soften the impact of economic policy decisions on those not benefiting from those decisions. Collapsed reliance on male income and the availability of income-production opportunities for females have been associated with increases in domestic violence in a number of international settings where neoliberal policies have also been instituted. In the United States, where gender, race, and class intersections create differences in women's lived experiences, we are not immune from these global processes.

Recent ethnographic research also makes links between historic shifts in the culture and political economy of cities with new modes of survival, resistance, and politicization among the urban poor and integrates Marxist, feminist, poststructuralist, and critical-race approaches to study power relations, governance, and citizenship, as well as difference and inequality (Morgen and Maskovsky 2003). Accordingly, my analysis is in line with more recent ethnographic research that moves beyond the view of the African American urban poor as members of encapsulated worlds, bounded and isolated from history and wider political economic developments (see Goode and Maskovsky 2001; Hyatt 1995).

INNER CITY BLACK COMMUNITIES: "THE SOUTH IN THE NORTH"

In this section, I contrast the global North and South and compare their relationship to that which exists in the United States between the owners of the means of production and the denizens of those areas some call "the South in the North" (Gaventa 1998; Tammilehto 1999), exemplified by US black inner-city communities, Native American reservations, and towns housing maquiladoras along the US-Mexico border.

The contemporary world system is characterized by an asymmetrical relationship between what Robinson (1996) characterizes as a Gramscian hegemonic core in the advantaged countries in the global North and its periphery of cheap and abundant labor in the South. In a global context, *the South* has generally the same meaning as *the Third World, the Third World and the Fourth World,* and *developing countries,* where people are compelled into low-paying wage labor by state-sanctioned forces (Shanahan and Tuma 1994). *Hegemonic* in the usage above and as presented by Wallerstein (1983) denotes wielding power or the preponderance of control in the world economy. The political and social writer Antonio Gramsci posited an implicit complicity between the unquestioned rule makers of society and the unquestioning rule followers, such that the compliance of the latter becomes naturalized.

Within this understanding, then, the North presents itself as having a right to use the South for its own purposes, and the South accepts its treatment as a supplier of the North's needs. The North stands as the core or capitalist class and is seen as controlling the means of and extracting the surplus from production. The South stands as the periphery or the proletarian class having limited control over its labor and receiving minimal compensation for it.

The structural violence in the global South, instituted originally through relations between those whom Fanon (1961) calls the *colonizers* and the *colonized*, can be compared to that established through US internal colonial relations between the owners of the means of production and those traditionally marginalized economically. These internal colonial relations continue to extend deeply into impoverished black urban centers in the United States that house surplus labor pools of the under- and unemployed. Hence, these areas are said to operate as "the South within the North," providing neoliberal capitalists with opportunities for labor exploitation without the costs of providing social benefits, job security, or competitive wages (Bobiwash 2001). In other words, both the global North and South and the global North and "South in the North" exist within an intricate system of complicities and internal power imbalances between blocs within the broader groupings of colonizers and colonized. In reference to black inner-city populations, this relationship has been demonstrated traditionally through the attribution of differential valuations of labor by race and gender (Conwill 1980).

Before describing the historical growth of black inner cities, I first acknowledge the present conceptual and theoretical complexity arising from more recent demographic changes in the black inner city brought on by the new "Great Migration" of blacks from Africa and the Caribbean. Members of these new groups often occupy menial and sometimes professional occupational positions formerly held by African Americans. *Black* does not denote simply the descendents of the Africans formerly enslaved in the United States. The 2000 Census notes that *Black* now means those who report that they are Black, African American, Negro, Afro American, Nigerian, and Haitian. In addition, respondents can now list themselves as black and as members of more than one racial or ethnic category.

Second, besides the national distinctions that are increasingly noted as a feature of black American identity (see Collins 1998b), there are also class differences complicating any simplistic attempts at analysis. For example, many blacks from the Caribbean who live in the United States, that is, more than 70 percent of the Guyanese and 75 percent of the Jamaicans, have postsecondary education and are employed in academia, research, and industry (US Census Bureau 2001). In other words, they are part of what some dub the "brain drain" from the Caribbean. However, even though the "new" blacks can also suffer racialization, I do not focus on them here. Instead, I limit my attention to the descendents of Africans formerly enslaved in the United States.

A Brief History of the Economic Marginalization of the Inner-City Black Community

Before the American Civil War, enslaved and imported Africans in the US South had supplied much of the unpaid labor that produced three-quarters of the world supply of raw cotton. After the Emancipation Proclamation of 1863, black exploitation continued through segregation, poll taxes, literacy tests, grandfather clauses, and other exclusionary practices. The economy of the US South remained heavily agricultural. Most blacks toiled as sharecroppers. They rented land and paid for it by forfeiting most, if not all, of their harvest (US Surgeon General 1999).

With the invasion of the boll weevil in 1892, however, and the subsequent fall of "King Cotton," black agricultural workers were unable to depend on employment in the South's main staple industry. As late as 1910, 89 percent of all blacks still lived in the rural South in legalized subservience and deep poverty. After World War I interrupted the supply of cheap Northern labor provided by European immigrants, and as agriculture became increasingly mechanized, blacks drifted northward to the industrialized cities in the Great Migration in search of jobs (Drake and Cayton 1945). As they moved north and west into cities, many served as a reserve labor force. Following World War II, blacks began to migrate to select urban centers in the West, mostly in California.

The War on Poverty that began in the mid-1960s promised to narrow the economic gap between the privileged and the disadvantaged in America but, in fact, introduced three decades of unraveling and dismantling the safety net for the disproportionately black poor. At the height of the black civil rights uprising, the Moynihan Report (Moynihan 1967), a US Department of Labor document, suggested that the failure of the Negro father to play the role in family life required by American society was at the root of problems in the black family and that nothing could be done to alleviate these problems until American and Negro society changed (Moynihan 1967). The Moynihan Report was long on defining problems and short on proposing solutions. By the late 1960s, cultural and political backlash and policy retrenchment accompanied disavowals of national responsibility for the level of disruption in black families. A generalized persistence of black economic inequality continues today (Conrad et al. 2005).

The Effects of Neoliberal Policy on the Black Community

The 1970s were marked by prolonged declines in wages, increasing poverty, shrinking production of affordable housing, eroding welfare programs, and a rupturing social safety net. With the mechanization of production, the suburbanization of employment, and the closing of central city factories, the inner-city black population became socially isolated (Wilson 1987) and left to fend for itself.

Although these changes affected more whites than blacks, the effect on the black population was more profound. In 1970, for example, black poverty rates in 14 "frostbelt" cities (Indianapolis, Chicago, Milwaukee, Detroit, Philadelphia, Columbus, Baltimore, St. Louis, Boston, Cleveland, Minneapolis, Cincinnati, Buffalo, and Pittsburgh) ranged from 21.4 to 31.9 percent, with a mean of 26.7 percent, and were 2.5 to 3.0 times higher than those for whites. By 1980, black poverty rates had risen to 30.9 percent on average, with some cities, such as Milwaukee, showing a 5:1 ratio of black to white poverty rates (Levine and Callaghan 1998).

The "stagflation"—high unemployment rates coupled with soaring inflation—of the mid- to late 1970s spurred the neoliberal ideology and supply-side economic practices accompanying Reaganomics in the 1980s and the new welfare policies instituted under the Clinton administration in the 1990s, leading to further stress for families at the bottom end of the socioeconomic ladder (see Conwill 2001). The expansion of free trade and the free movement of capital are crucial to supply-side economic theory. Reagan, through his 1981 Program for Economic Recovery, attempted to stimulate supply-side growth by large reductions in tax rates that were intended to encourage investment. Changes in the tax code were some of the most substantial modifications of his administration and totaled $750 billion from 1982 to 1987 (Niskanen and Moore 1996).

Large increases in defense spending, however, and the reluctance of both Congress and the president to make further cuts in domestic discretionary spending and to reform basic entitlement programs hampered Reagan's policy objectives of reducing the growth of government spending, tax rates, government regulation, and inflation. The Pentagon's budget doubled from $158 to $304 billion between 1981 and 1989, and domestic outlays as a share of the gross domestic product fell from 15.3 to 12.9 percent during the same period. The budget for the Department of Housing and Urban Development was slashed from $32.2 billion in 1981 to $7.5 billion in 1988.

Reagan justified his spending cuts in Aid to Families with Dependent Children (AFDC), federal subsidies for child care for low-income families, food stamps, and child nutrition by fictitious tales about obviously black "welfare queens" who did not deserve assistance. Mullings (1997) confronts such hegemonic discourses on welfare reform that racialized and demonized poor women on welfare and condemns the broad-brushed rhetoric reviling welfare dependents as immoral, deviant, and dysfunctional.

In 1992, Clinton promised to "end welfare as we know it." However, the Republican Congress that the American people voted into office in 1994 was also determined to change the existing system. On August 22, 1996, Clinton signed the Personal Responsibility and Work Opportunity Act, which ended the welfare entitlement and replaced it with a new block grant providing $16.5 billion per year to assist the needy. The act also included a five-year lifetime limit on assistance and the establishment of work requirements and led to a dramatic drop in the number of welfare recipients. Government policies that force women into desperate choices while denying responsibility for the results disguise the links between the structural violence of neoliberal policies and the domestic violence we see in the black community, as I will discuss later in my comparison of the experiences of two women under certain neoliberal policies instituted in California and Kentucky. But first, I examine some relationships between economic marginality and domestic violence.

STRUCTURAL VIOLENCE AND DOMESTIC VIOLENCE

Family researchers (Bograd 1999; Jewkes 2002) studying domestic violence have often noted the comparatively higher poverty rates and higher incidences of intimate aggression among blacks. Ethnographers complement their observations with findings from populations in the global South (Armstrong 2004; Grewal and Kaplan 2001:671). The US black population's response to the vicissitudes of neoliberal conditions in "the South in the North" can shed light on the association between neoliberal economic policy and domestic violence elsewhere.

Improving Black Economic Conditions Leads to Decreased Domestic Violence

Blacks' responses under more or less neoliberal economic conditions might help us better understand domestic violence. Rates of domestic violence in the black community under changing economic conditions are of particular interest. According to National Family Violence surveys, rates of severe violence against black women from 1975 to 1985 dropped 43 percent, with no comparable change in spousal violence in white families (Hampton, Gelles, and Harrop 1989). Incidentally, the median income for black families in the 1975 survey was $6,000 less than the overall sample median, and blacks' income in the 1986 survey was comparable to that of the sample median. This suggests that when the median black income was no longer oppressively lower than the sample income, domestic violence among blacks decreased markedly and white rates did not improve. The rates of spousal homicide for all groups peak in the 15- to 24-year-old age category. Rates of domestic violence decline with age among blacks, but not among whites (Burnett and Adler 2006).

The decrease in black family violence has been attributed to a number of factors, including greater age at first marriage, fewer children per family, and higher household income (Hampton, Gelles, and Harrop 1989). Increased educational attainment among black women may also be a factor (Farley 1984). Alternatively, violence in the family is lower when the male is employed for a significant proportion of time, but changes in female employment generally do not have a significant effect on violence, regardless of income level (Kumpfer 1999). Implications for black male employment and gender role issues become clearer in light of the relative employability of sex by race introduced above (Conwill 1980:89–91). In a society in which the breadwinner is a normative role for the male, erosion of employment for black males can have domestic repercussions.

Domestic Violence Is Related to Economic Variables, Not Race

Given how domestic violence measures respond under blacks' varying income conditions, it is fair to ask whether intimate aggression springs from culture or is more related to the structural violence of economic oppression that threatens economic security. A family's descent into poverty brings economic insecurity and threatens the family's very survival. Economic insecurity has been related to domestic violence (Nash 1994). How can we unravel the routine confounding of race and class in the typically lower-class samples of blacks when we try to understand the rates of domestic violence in the black community?

To answer this question, I used a dataset constructed from two waves (1988, 1994) of the National Survey of Families and Households (NSFH) and 1990 US census tract data from a probability sample of more than 9,600 households.[2] I wanted to examine what happens to measures of domestic violence under varying economic conditions. I first needed to standardize a

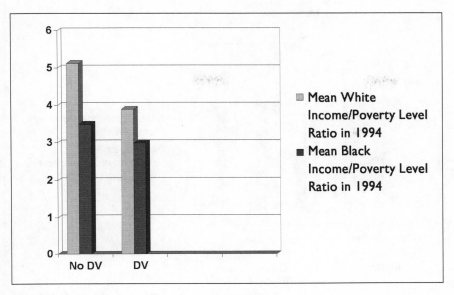

FIGURE 7.1.

Mean black and white income/poverty level ratios and levels of domestic violence (DV) in 1994.

reactive measure of varying household economic conditions hypothesized to covary with measures of domestic violence. I operationalized the notion of economic insecurity (Nash 1994) as the household's approximation to the limit of minimal sustainability. In this statistical analysis, the family's poverty level serves as that boundary, with household income as the numerator in a ratio (income/poverty level) representing the family's level of insecurity. When the ratio is low, economic insecurity is high.

I wondered whether it mattered if a family is black or white when it comes to explaining the differences in levels of domestic violence. To answer this question, I separated blacks from whites in a sample of 5,824 families and examined the difference in ratios between those with and without reports of domestic violence. The estimated means for blacks with and without domestic violence were 3.0 and 3.5, respectively, and the estimated means for whites were around 3.6 and 5.1. Race did not interact with domestic violence at the different income levels.[3] In other words, being black or white had nothing to do with the dissimilarities. Figure 7.1 shows this relationship graphically.

To test the economic insecurity (Nash 1994) hypothesis, I organized the data so that families were grouped together according to the number of times in 1994 they reported domestic violence against the female. In

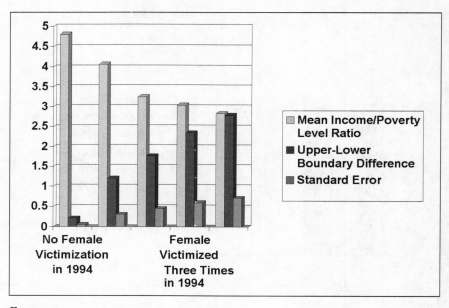

FIGURE 7.2.

Mean black and white income/poverty level ratios at varying levels of female victimization in 1994.

other words, I used the number of times (none, one, two, three, four, or more) black and white households reported incidents of female victimization in 1994 as independent variables. Higher incidences of domestic violence were associated with lower ratios, as shown in figure 7.2. Overall, households reporting no instances had a mean ratio of 4.805. For example, if the household poverty level was $15,000 and a household had an income of $72,075 (that is, $15,000 × 4.805), domestic violence was not found in this sample. Households that reported only one instance of domestic violence had a mean ratio of 4.062. Households reporting two instances had a ratio of 3.249, and those reporting three instances had a ratio of 3.042. Households reporting four or more instances of victimization had a mean ratio of 2.838. These results suggest a clear relationship between economic insecurity and domestic violence.

Couples manage threats to economic security, and the gendered violence that can erupt when coping mechanisms break down, in a number of ways. Some solutions are dysfunctional, and couples may seek help, including therapy. Providing therapy or counseling in these situations is not so much curing as it is assisting in the creation of the circumstances necessary for the couple to engage in the healing process and either to remain united or to separate. The therapist's function, then, is to help induce the set of psychological circumstances for enjoining this process. In many ways, undergoing therapy is a form of self-healing that encompasses recall, abreaction, and the expression and emotional discharge of repressed material by verbalization, especially in the presence of a therapist, as well as problem solving, and decision making.

BLACK WOMEN NAVIGATING STRUCTURAL VIOLENCE AND DOMESTIC VIOLENCE

I have chosen to use two clinical cases involving black women from my practice to show how the structural violence that marginalizes them economically is more responsible for the domestic violence they experience than any essentialized and essentializing notion of violence and race as connected. I do not present a case with a white woman because of the acknowledged tendency of social service agencies to provide more helpful forms of assistance, such as referring white women to actual jobs rather than to workfares, and because of the higher likelihood of white male violence related to white women's seeking and acceptance of work outside the home (McCormack Institute 1997; Riger and Krieglstein 2000). In other words, compared with white men's domestic violence, black men's domestic violence does not appear to be as related to women's attempts to secure employment, indicating a different cultural logic underlying domestic violence in the lower-class white community, such as the assumption that a woman's *need* to work insults the male partner's manhood. In the two case studies below, the women experienced varying degrees of domestic violence related to their economic marginalization, brought on by fiscal decisions that eliminated opportunities for supporting families in their communities.

Case Study 1: Feeling Trapped and Blackmailed

The setting for the first case study is the small San Francisco Bay peninsula community of East Palo Alto, California, which lies "across the freeway" from its affluent neighbor, Palo Alto. For most of its history, East Palo Alto was part of unincorporated San Mateo County. As such, it did not have an official boundary until it incorporated in 1983. However, the area historically regarded as East Palo Alto was much larger than the city's current 2.5 square miles. Large tracts were annexed by Menlo Park and Palo Alto from the late 1940s to the early 1960s.

The original inhabitants were Ohlone (also known as Costanoan) Native Americans. Spanish ranchers later took over, followed by white speculators and settlers. For a time in the mid-nineteenth century, Chinese laborers were prevalent. Asian and Italian flower growers came and went before the flood of middle-class whites attracted to post–World War II housing developments. East Palo Alto later became the largest African American community on the peninsula. Today the city possesses a multiethnic population that includes a large number of Hispanics and Pacific Islanders. People are still drawn to the area for its less expensive housing, proximity to transportation and San Francisco Bay, beautiful rural setting, and desirable weather.

In the 1930s, much of East Palo Alto's business district was made up largely of restaurants, gas stations, and motels catering to travelers, and most businesses clustered along the recently constructed north-south Bayshore Freeway (Highway 101). Bayshore intersects University Avenue, a central thoroughfare linking East Palo Alto to Palo Alto and Stanford University. With the repeal of Prohibition in 1933, a number of liquor stores, bars, and nightclubs sprang up in the area around the Bayshore–University Avenue intersection, attracting people from Palo Alto, which was still "dry," as well as Bayshore travelers. The area drew gamblers and drinkers, earning the name "Whiskey Gulch."

When the University Avenue cloverleaf was built as part of the US 101 freeway project during the 1950s, more than 50 East Palo Alto businesses were forced to relocate. Only five remained, and the business district never fully reestablished. In the following years, abandoned or boarded-up shopping centers became eyesores notorious for loitering and illegal activities. A Safeway grocery store that had operated in Whiskey Gulch since 1959 closed in 1974. The Southern Pacific Railroad closed its East Palo Alto track in 1974. All four of the city's banks left town in the 1980s.

During the 1960s, large numbers of African Americans moved to East Palo Alto as part of "block-busting," aggressive, targeted real-estate tactics that typically began after a black family had moved into a white neighborhood. By the 1970s, East Palo Alto had the largest concentration of African Americans in San Mateo County but lacked opportunities for employment.

Mary and Donald, an African American couple in their mid-20s, moved to affordable housing in East Palo Alto in the late 1970s with their two small children. Donald, a Louisiana native, had never been more than marginally employed since high school and was holding two part-time jobs at the time that I spoke with them. He spent much of his spare time in "Whiskey Gulch" with his male friends. After several years of junior college and part-time work, Mary had recently completed an associate degree and was ready to seek a full-time job on the peninsula. However, this placed Mary in a predicament because she could not afford child care if she went to work. She futilely pressed Donald for more help. He responded with aggression. Mary felt trapped. She felt that she could not afford to stay in her present marriage but that she would lose more if she left.

Donald and Mary were referred to me by a Catholic priest who was counseling them for marital problems. Mary wanted a divorce. Donald interpreted her desire for a divorce as wanting to bring another man into the house with his children. Mary assured Donald that she did not want to leave him to find another man; she just wanted to end their marriage and to move on with her life, come what hardships may. Donald responded that if she divorced him, he would seek child custody and move back to Louisiana. Mary declared that this was tantamount to blackmail. She wanted out of a marriage in which gendered expectations relegated her to both instrumental and affective functions, including daily pressure to be sexual, with little economic assistance from her husband.

Their sex life had deteriorated severely. Donald fluctuated between plaintive pleas for physical affection and vain demands for sex. His male friends taunted him, telling him that he had to "dog" her (treat her badly), to show her who was in charge. He admitted to losing his temper occasionally with his wife and becoming physically aggressive. While listening recently to audiotapes of my sessions with Donald and Mary, I was struck by the nearly overwhelming and abject level of pain expressed in Donald's voice.

Mary confessed to withholding sex, citing fatigue at the end of the day and the need for time to herself. She did not want to have sex unless she desired it, and lately she had not been in the mood. She was dissatisfied with Donald's lack of achievement and stated that she did not want to carry him any longer. She did not want to lose her children either. She reiterated the costs of child care if Donald did not help her by bringing in more money.

As therapy progressed, we talked about ongoing problems in their sexual relationship. She felt that Donald was always putting pressure on her to have sex. She expressed deep shame about her "32-23-32" body. She disclosed that, right after their marriage, she had begun to recoil from Donald's touch.

This led immediately to a second revelation. Right after she had married, she recalled a memory, which she later kept secret from Donald. When she was 6 years old, her 16-year-old male cousin had sexually abused her while babysitting. Her mother came back before her cousin had let her go to bed and asked why she was still up. Her cousin told her mother that Mary had wanted to watch television, but her mother was suspicious. She sent the cousin home and sat Mary down. Her mother asked her repeatedly whether she had been made to do anything. She denied that anything had happened, not wanting to make matters worse. Her mother scrubbed her hands with household bleach. Donald, upon hearing this revelation for the first time, shared his wife's pain.

Mary's mother had been in the same predicament Mary found herself in. Mary's mother futilely wanted more help from Mary's father and was not able to afford child care costs even if she worked outside the home. Her compromise cost her daughter's childhood. Mary felt trapped. She could not afford to stay but felt that she would lose more if she left.

Case Study 2: Once Bitten, Twice Shy

Late 1980s Louisville, Kentucky, is the setting for the second case. Louisville's cultural life revolves around ethnic festivals, sporting events, and the arts. Louisville's black community, like East Palo Alto's, has often sustained structural violence to the benefit of capitalist investors through-out the years. The city's population is one-third African American, and a history of segregated schooling and housing, urban renewal, job discrimi-nation, and poor police–black community relations has long heightened racial issues. Louisville's economic importance declined in the 1960s and 1970s because of "white flight" to the suburbs and the decline of the down-town area, but the city experienced a regrowth in the 1980s. The city's black population has lived mostly in West End low-income housing projects built in the 1950s and 1960s, West End single-family dwellings, and Newburg, an East End section developed primarily to serve African American families of modest to moderate means from the 1950s through the 1970s. Louise was from Newburg.

She was like a number of black women in my private and medical school clinic-based practices in that she became pregnant as a teenager right after high school. Her child's father had no aspirations for continu-ing his education, and her parents did not support the idea of her marry-ing him just because she was pregnant. They put her through college so that she could make a life for herself and her child. She steered clear of both male and female friends. She married a divorced older man when she was in her mid-20s, and he adopted her daughter. The marriage was stormy, ostensibly around parenting issues and finances.

Louise's daughter was a free-spirited, willful young woman who had learned to pit her mother and stepfather against each other to her own advantage. At 17, she was considerably talented, smart, and scheming. She had all the dance, drama, and music lessons her mother had not had and pouted and rebuked her parents whenever they tried to rein her in. When she began sleeping with one of her male classmates, her mother decided that it was time to bring her in for counseling.

Themes in the Cases 1 and 2

Both women described marital relationships with large gulfs between male and female educational level, a commonly cited feature of problematic black relationships. Neurotic consumerism or complaints of lack of funds for household needs sparked the couples' arguments. The women felt that they could not survive economically without their men, but also that they could not advance with them. The men could not compete verbally and intellectually with the women in these arguments and either retreated sullenly or attacked them when no longer able to tolerate defeat.

The women saw themselves as the primary care providers for their children and commandeered the authority to do so. Mary wanted to divorce her husband and keep the children as a single parent. Unfortunately, this configuration is often associated with the entry of women and children into poverty. Donald's counter-threat to sue for custody of the children and move away with them terrified Mary, who did not want to lose her right to protect her children. As for Louise, she formed an alliance with her daughter against her husband. Louise lacked other women friends. She lived vicariously through Carolyn and therefore wanted her to live life large. In both cases, fear for their daughters' plights moved the women to therapy. Both recognized, subconsciously perhaps, that a pattern was about to repeat itself. Inadequate child care is a principal complaint of women living under neoliberal programs. As part of their therapeutic intervention, black women and their partners can benefit from an awareness of the role of neoliberal policies as they manage their family in economically marginalized inner cities.

SUMMARY AND CONCLUSIONS

The bird's-eye view from surveys on domestic violence among US blacks complements findings from local-level ethnographic studies that implicate global processes in domestic violence. Both perspectives coincide with insights garnered from my "frog's-eye" view of case studies of black women in therapy. The case studies flesh out the lived effects of neoliberal restructuring at the intersections of gender, race, and class in the US black community and serve as the basis of recursivity at the ethnographic and survey levels. We have observed, over several decades, the pattern of dislocation of African Americans from the land for survival, coupled with inadequate legal resources, especially for male income production in impoverished black inner-city communities. These conditions elicit predictable responses, such as the fragmentation of household units and the disruption of couple bonds. The experiences of African American women can potentially inform resistance to neoliberal economic exploitation and increased domestic violence in other parts of the world.

The levels of domestic violence we find among African Americans in impoverished inner cities are related to the structural violence waged against poor black communities as discrimination in the workforce, the housing industry, banking, education, and the legal system. That structural violence is dynamically interconnected to globalization (Kingfisher 2002). It is also gendered. For example, the relative employability of men and women by race that we find at the heart of black labor conditions in the United States is related to problems affecting both the internal and the external dynamics of the black family. The erosion of traditional divisions of labor and increased female participation in the workforce at menial wages have affected rates of domestic violence in black inner cities, as well as in the global South. In the two clinical cases presented above, the women experienced domestic violence related to their social and economic marginality. Despite the seeming disparity in their income levels, the issues that drove their actions were the same. In fact, Louise's patterns of anxious consumption uncovered worry about her economic dependency.

Poor child care options appear at the crux of the problem of staying with an abusive spouse. A double bind (damned if you do, damned if you don't) of feeling that they cannot make it without a man and knowing that if they stay, conditions will not improve, paralyzes many women, who choose to stay. Poor child care options are linked to child sexual abuse, which often leads to crippled relationships in adulthood. These relationships that abused women find themselves trapped in are miserable, full of shame, and empty of pleasure.

This multilayered look at domestic violence in the context of neoliberal policy suggests that the intimate experiences of African American women can shed light on the effects of globalization processes on the family and can link African American women, especially those impoverished in the inner city, to women worldwide struggling for human rights for their families and children. It is my hope that these individuals and families see that beyond "black man frustration," they are the target of US domestic neoliberal policy. It is also my hope that, with the help of the realizations explored here, poorly educated, unemployed or under-employed, and otherwise marginalized African American women untrained to view themselves as participants in the struggle for social and economic justice around the globe may organize in solidarity and advocacy in ways heretofore unimagined.

About the Author

William L. Conwill grew up at the edge of a section of Louisville, Kentucky, formerly known as "Little Africa," a haven for antebellum blacks on their way north to freedom. With his training in philosophy (University of San Diego), experimental psychology (California State University, San Jose), and counseling psychology (Stanford University), he has helped develop a number of inpatient and outpatient psychology and behavioral medicine programs (University of Louisville Psychiatry and Behavioral Sciences Department at Hospital Humana-University; Tennessee Department of Health's Lakeshore Mental Health Institute) and has sustained a community-based private consultation and psychological practice for more than 20 years. From 1999 to 2004, he taught mental health counseling at the University of Tennessee. Since 2004, he has been at the University of Florida in the African American Studies Program and Counselor Education Department.

Acknowledgments

I thank Faye V. Harrison, chair of the International Union of Anthropological and Ethnological Sciences' Commission on the Anthropology of Women, for encouraging me to locate my analysis of intersections of gender, race, and class in domestic violence in the black community within a more global context. I am most grateful to Ann Kingsolver for inviting me to join this discussion with ethnologists and ethnographers and for her most helpful directions. I have learned a lot. I am also indebted to the University of Tennessee, Knoxville's Office of Research, Eleanor Read (University of Tennessee database librarian), and Cary Spencer and Mike O'Neil (University of Tennessee statistical consultants). Finally, my thanks go to Marilyn Thomas-Houston, for always pushing me to talk less about statistics and more about people.

Notes

1. See Anthias 1998 for a discussion of racial and ethnicity paradigms and interrelated dimensions of identity formation. See Harrison 1998, 2000 for expansion of the discourse on race and contemporary forms of racism. I use the term *race* to denote racialized ethnicity wherein intergroup antagonisms have escalated to the level of racialized conflicts.

2. The data used in this chapter come from a secondary analysis (Benson and

Fox 2002) of data drawn from waves 1 and 2 of the National Survey of Families and Households (NSFH) and from the 1990 US Census. Information on the history of the survey and the design and content of the questionnaire (Sweet, Bumpass, and Call 1988) can be found online at http://www.ssc.wisc.edu/nsth1.pdf. I focused on the 1994 data, eliminating missing and extremely outlying values. Assumptions such as normality and homogeneity of variance were tested to confirm the robustness of null hypotheses. The Inter-university Consortium for Political and Social Research (ICPSR) at the University of Michigan in Ann Arbor is the distributor of the data used in this chapter, as well as the codebook by Michael L. Benson of the University of Cincinnati and Greer L. Fox of the University of Tennessee.

3. Statistically significant main effects were found for both race $F(1,5824) = 18.226$, $p < .001$ and for the level of domestic violence $F(1,5824) = 8.542$, $p = .003$. No statistically significant interaction between race and level of domestic violence was found $F(1,5824) = 1.509$, $p = .219$.

8

Gendered Bodily Scars of Neoliberal Globalization in Argentina

Barbara Sutton

Much has been written about the globalization of capitalist economies and the neoliberal ideologies that promote this expansion, but few of these analyses look at the bodily dimensions of the economy or address the body in explicit ways (Callard 1998; Harvey 1998). Yet, human bodies fuel economic globalization—literally giving it muscle in factories and other global production sites—and are targets of its consumer products. Whether our bodies are overworked, malnourished, scarred by untreated diseases, altered by cosmetic surgery, or dressed in expensive clothing is often contingent on economic conditions. In a word, structures of inequality, including economic disparities, are embodied. And it is as embodied beings that we transform, resist, and challenge economic forces. This chapter examines women's embodied experiences of neoliberal policies and economic crisis in Argentina, a site that illustrates the bodily implications of globalization.

Globalization processes produce and reinscribe a global hierarchy of bodies, providing adornment, luxury, and costly care for some while drawing on the hard physical labor and depleting the resources of many other bodies. The ways in which different bodies are incorporated in, excluded from, and marked by these processes vary according to social locations based on class, race, gender, age, nationality, and sexual orientation. I explore how socioeconomic developments wrought by neoliberal globalization leave scars on women's bodies and consciousness in Argentina, paying attention to how gender and class locations structure such experiences. These scars not only are imprinted on women's material bodies but are also experienced emotionally. They convey neoliberal globalization's assaults on human dignity as women grapple with declining standards of living, make health and nutrition compromises, deal with the disruption of taken-for-granted body rituals, and cope with the shame and humiliation associated with the rags of poverty.

This chapter draws on and contributes to literature on the body, feminist theory, and globalization. It is based on a 14-month qualitative study in Argentina's capital, Buenos Aires, and its metropolitan area during 2002–2003. I conducted 50 in-depth interviews with women ranging in age from the 20s to the early 60s and from diverse socioeconomic backgrounds.[1] I also interviewed women in four targeted focus groups: lesbians, charity volunteers, domestic workers, and women living in poverty. Additionally, I analyzed print media and conducted ethnographic observations of everyday life and culture, political protest, and women's movement organizing. During interviews, I asked general questions about women's bodily awareness, feelings, and practices, as well as questions regarding the economic crisis, work, sexuality, reproduction, and the meanings of womanhood. Focus groups covered similar themes and showed how gendered discourses are collectively and interactively constructed. For the individual interviews, I developed a technique based on word cards that interviewees could pick and talk about.[2] This method elicited rich narratives about the interconnected nature of multiple bodily experiences, from physical exhaustion and the ignoring of health problems to concerns about beauty and sexual harassment, from embodied experiences of economic marginality to embodied resistance in road blockades and other street protests.

I also joined a vibrant social movement scene that flourished in Argentina as a response to the crisis following the economic collapse of December 2001. I participated in multiple women's movement activities, protests, and networks involving middle-class, working-class, and poor women.[3] I paid particular attention to what women were protesting and how they were doing it. My participation in these events was infused by a deeply felt need to be part of social change, as well as by sociological research interests. My research was not neutral or detached. Not only did I have a political vision of social justice, but also, as a native Argentine (from Buenos Aires) with strong ties to the country, I was personally invested in Argentina's political outcomes. While I took notes, wrote ethnographic reflections, and kept my researcher's radar continuously alert, I also strove to affect the course of events as any other activist would. As a participant in women's movement gatherings and actions, I listened, expressed opinions, shaped discussions, and performed other mundane tasks of activism. I experienced conflict and frustration, as well as the empowering feelings that derive from collective action. The time was ripe both for research and social change.

During the 1990s, Argentina became the star student of the International Monetary Fund (IMF) because the government implemented radical economic restructuring along neoliberal lines. Although the last military dictatorship in Argentina (1976–1983) was a precursor to the application of neoliberal economics—backed by a brutal political regime of torture and "disappearance"—it was during the administrations of elected president Carlos Saúl Menem (1989–1999) and his successor, Fernando de la Rúa (1999–2001), that the model was fully developed. Neoliberal economics during this period of formal democracy exhibited the following general features: the Convertibility Plan, which pegged the Argentine peso to the dollar; the privatization of most state-owned companies; cuts in social expenditures; greater openness of the economy to foreign investment; and the transformation of the labor sector to make business more profitable (Birgin 2000; Dinerstein 2001; Patroni 2002; Wainerman 2003). Despite promises of economic growth and modernization, the economy collapsed, and the country entered a deep social, political, and economic crisis in December 2001 (Cafassi 2002; Galafassi 2003; Pírez 2002; Vezzetti 2002).

Neoliberal programs in Argentina prioritized the profits of big businesses and the payment of an ever-growing debt over expenditures and policies to satisfy the needs of most of the population, including the poor, the working class, and a falling middle class (Argumedo and Quintar 2003; Giarracca and Teubal 2001). These neoliberal measures were supposed to launch Argentina as a successful player in the global capitalist economy, but poverty and inequality grew at home. After the economic meltdown, unemployment rates climbed to 21.5 percent in 2002. Per capita income dropped about 20 percent from 1995 to 2002, and during the same period, the number of people living under the poverty line increased from 29.4 percent to 53.3 percent (De Riz, Acosta, and Clucellas 2002:36). The percentage of people who could not access basic nutrition grew from 7.9 percent in 1995 to 25.2 percent in 2002 (De Riz, Acosta, and Clucellas 2002:49).[4] Currency devaluation, price inflation, declining wages, and the high levels of unemployment during the crisis meant that more and more people had to struggle to make ends meet. Even members of the middle class, who saw their real wages fall and their bank deposits frozen, became impoverished. These numbers only hint at the dire conditions to which most people in Argentina were relegated.

The neoliberal globalization model presents a disembodied approach to the social world, one more concerned about balances, profits, and "rational choices" than about real human beings with bodily needs, desires, and emotions. Globalization is not just about technological development, information flows, and financial exchanges. The globalization of the capitalist economy depends on human bodies (and other-than-human ones) in order to function, because human (embodied) labor and natural resources are extracted for global production and because neoliberal cuts in social expenditures attack bodily integrity to subsidize the "free market." The model does not account for the bodily experiences of the people hit by globalization. The Argentine case shows that neoliberal global restructuring facilitates the exploitation and deterioration of human bodies. Impingement on bodily integrity and human capabilities happens, for example, through worsening work conditions, the decay of health care, and increasing poverty and marginalization. Those coping with or resisting globalization are embodied human beings—not numbers, pie charts, or abstract statistics.

Disembodied economic analyses particularly tend to hide the extent to which neoliberal globalization has drained women's bodily resources. Women and their labor have been traditionally invisible in mainstream economic analyses (Waring 1999), which usually overlook the ways in which neoliberal restructuring transfers the costs of economic crises to women (Benería and Feldman 1992; Elson 1992; Marchand and Sisson Runyan 2000; Moser 1993; Stephen 1997). Yet, the bodies of many women in Argentina have been increasingly exhausted, stressed, and neglected under neoliberalism. Luz, an outspoken activist, observed:

> Now we are the Amazons, you know, the new Amazons of society, but at what cost? We have to work because our husbands are unemployed, go to the *piquete* [roadblock, a form of protest] because we are also unemployed, work in the communal kitchen, take care of the kids. Gee! We have erupted into political life, but at too high a cost. And to some extent, we withstand that and burden our *lomos* [backs], right?... I believe that we demand from our bodies a lot more than men do.

The word *lomo* in this passage evokes an animal's back, perhaps a beast of burden's back, connoting hard labor and underscoring the bodily effects of the economic crisis. Embodying neoliberalism is critical to understanding economic forces as *lived* processes that involve core aspects of individuals' existence. Women's narratives offer a valuable lens through which to learn about embodied "social suffering" (Kleinman, Das, and Lock 1996), resiliency, and resistance in the age of globalization.

THE FLESH OF INEQUALITY

The unprecedented scope of poverty emerging under neoliberalism was something unthinkable in a country that historically prided itself on plentiful natural resources, a large middle class, high levels of education, and relatively high health standards. Despite previous crises, these indicators placed Argentina as one of the most advanced countries in Latin America in terms of human development (De Riz, Acosta, and Clucellas 2002; Uribe and Schwab 2002). Yet, neoliberal economics undermined these trends. Many of the women I met in Argentina knew about the deterioration of social conditions, not just through the media or even through expert reports, but through their personal and embodied encounters with this reality.

The women in this study talked about the economic crisis, poverty, and inequality as they explained their personal lives and bodily experiences or reflected on a social context that affected them in one way or another. Even those who did not experience poverty in their own bodies were at least forced to see it, recognize it, and interpret it. For example, Beatriz, a hairdresser, read the crisis on the bodies of other women in the bus: "Worn out clothing, bad haircuts, discolored hair...shoes that are cheap, broken, torn....This is the crisis." Impoverishment could no longer be ignored. And this "seeing"—seeing with the body and emotions—gave some of the women in the study the impulse to participate in social change.[5]

A Glimpse of the Economic Crisis in Argentina

When the sun starts to go down in the streets of Buenos Aires, large groups of poor men, women, and children begin searching for paper, cardboard, and other recyclable materials, such as copper, bronze, or aluminum. These people, commonly known as *cartoneros/as* (cardboard gatherers), then sell this material to companies (for example, paper manufacturers) that use these supplies. Cartoneros/as sometimes knock on people's doors or simply dig into garbage bags where recyclable products are mixed with food leftovers, diapers, dirt, or other items that more privileged people dispose of. In 2002, an estimated 70,000–100,000 people were scavenging in Buenos Aires and its metropolitan area (De Riz, Acosta, and Clucellas

2002), earning approximately the equivalent of US$50–US$63 per month (Ferreyra 2002).[6]

Fanny, a cartonera who migrated from a rural area to Buenos Aires because of her youngest daughter's health problems, explained why she turned to cardboard gathering: "We are making a living based on this. My husband couldn't find a job, and neither could I. This is feeding us. I have four children." Fanny, along with many others in Argentina, had to resort to alternative means of survival when other avenues were closed under neoliberalism. Fanny described cardboard gathering as physically exhausting, risky, and unpleasant. She pointed out that the bodies of cardboard gatherers, in handling disposed materials, are susceptible to "much infection, many viruses" and other health hazards: "In the last few days, I caught the flu. It rained the whole week, but I still came [to gather materials]. If I don't come, my children do not eat."

A subtler source of risk that cardboard gatherers confront is the social construction of poor people's bodies as suspect. Fanny recalled that a police officer once stopped her under the suspicion that she was involved in a robbery. He left her alone when she showed him the cardboard gatherer ID card that the city government issued for her. As Adair (2002:454) argues, poverty "brands [poor people's bodies] with infamy," making them potentially suspect, sometimes feared, or targets of harassment. Although people with better economic situations may equate the bodies of the poor to those of criminal or dangerous individuals, in fact, the bodies of people like Fanny are inscribed with extreme vulnerability.

Many cardboard gatherers commute from the metropolitan area of Buenos Aires to gather materials. Some of them, like Fanny, have to pay to commute in a special truck. Other cardboard gatherers take the train. Because of the substantial increase of people dedicated to cardboard gathering in the past few years, it has become difficult for them to fit in train cars with their collection carts (De Riz, Acosta, and Clucellas 2002; Reynals 2002). Now cardboard gatherers travel in special trains, which are more rundown, older-looking versions of "regular" passenger trains but still require a fee (although smaller) for transportation. At the train station, "regular" passengers mix with dozens of cardboard gatherers, each group waiting for separate trains. As I watched cardboard gatherers cramming inside their train, I could not help remembering my own privilege. Their train was patrolled by a police officer, had no seats, and, instead of glass, netted wire covered the windows.

A daily ride in the "regular" passenger train, even one of the best ones available in Buenos Aires, also offers a glimpse of the country's dire social situation. Poverty and inequality are visible, unavoidable, and fleshy. In this train, a procession of people struggling to make a living in multiple, sometimes quite original, ways reminds economically advantaged passengers of the collapse of formal employment, rise of impoverishment, high levels of unemployment, and deterioration of social safety nets. Men, women, and children beg for money or offer calendars or religious stamps in exchange for donations. Others sell an array of products ranging from talc that "you can't do without," gadgets small enough "for the lady's purse, and the gentlemen's wallet," city guides, TV remote controls, geography and anatomy pamphlets, candy bars, batteries, pens and pencils, miniature notebooks, and products imported from other countries and sold on the train at bargain prices.

Kids with worn-out clothing offer to sing to better-off passengers or to shake their hands or give them a kiss in exchange for money. A mature man carrying a suitcase cracks jokes reminiscent of Pepe Biondi, a comedian I watched in my childhood. Passengers cannot stop shy smiles escaping from their otherwise serious faces and reward the bogus Biondi with small change. He leaves us with the message that "only love will save the world." A middle-aged woman with disorderly hair, ragged clothes, and seemingly deranged eyes vehemently asks for money for her sick child. She does not elicit sympathetic responses from passengers—most look the other way or concentrate on their newspapers, appearing slightly scared. A man with two legs amputated moves his body on a wood platform with wheels, which he propels with his hands as he requests donations. A blind man asks for help while finding his way in the train corridor with a long stick. A blind woman sings song fragments a cappella, also expecting a few coins. Pop music players and an Andean music group provide some relief to passengers, who welcome the entertainment with handclaps.

The procession of people who completely fell off the edges of the neoliberal economic program coexists with the plainly dressed, working-class passengers (perhaps clinging to increasingly insecure jobs), the young male executive with the elegant suit and dark sunglasses, teenagers in their private school uniforms, the well-groomed woman with fashionable clothing and a stylish hairdo, and foreign tourists in "adventure" outfits looking at a map of the area. The extremely rich usually do not travel in this train. Those who have gained the most from neoliberal globalization often live in gated communities or guarded mansions, own expensive cars, and do not need to take the train. Still, people with relative economic privilege share the train space with those who have to scramble to make a basic living.

Poverty and inequality are right there, on many faces and in the face of others. At the time of my study, many people were either experiencing poverty or were confronted with poverty daily in public spaces such as train stations, street corners, parks, subways, and restaurants far from the poor, heavily populated barrios. Perhaps only the very rich could isolate themselves in their tinted-windowed cars, gated communities, and privatized lives. Yet, the crisis did not leave them completely untouched: rising crime and a wave of kidnappings threatened their valuable property and their bodily security.

For the chronically poor—those whose families had been in this kind of situation for generations—poverty was not new, but it was no less damaging. Although millions of people had been living in shantytowns, in conditions of extreme poverty and violence, long before the 2001 economic collapse, the neoliberal model did little to improve their conditions. When the crisis erupted, these persons had few resources with which to weather it. During the 1990s, isolating the reality of poverty seemed easier as long as the poor remained relatively self-contained in barrios that lacked even minimum services and resources. Some of the women I interviewed lived in this relatively hidden world (hidden, at least, from the better-off), which was nonetheless becoming more familiar to growing numbers of people.

During my fieldwork, I met regularly with women in one of the communal kitchens in a shantytown in metropolitan Buenos Aires. My encounters with these women opened up a world very different from the life of privilege I know. The barrio where the kitchen women live is crowded with basic living structures and houses crammed against one another. From some angles, the barrio looks like an endless labyrinth. Homes stand precariously, made with a mix of whatever materials people could find, including pieces of wood, sheet metal, and bricks. Many houses look half done, in the process of construction. Many do not have doors or windows, but pieces of cloth in their places. To reach the homes of some of the kitchen women, one has to walk along narrow passages in between rows of houses and crisscrossed by a stream of polluted, dark water. With the heat of the summer, the smells of garbage piles and contaminated water become stronger, more penetrating. The houses are generally small, and some of them shelter many people. Neighbors are close and quite exposed to one another. Precarious shelter adds to the list of problems in the shantytown, including drugs, crime, lack of services such as garbage collection, and inadequate access to food and health care.

Many people who live in such shantytowns and other impoverished barrios are unemployed workers who try to improve their conditions and the quality of life in their neighborhoods through collective organizing.

Many became the backbone of the *piquetero/a* movement, which adopted the *piquete* (roadblock) as a protest strategy and engaged in solidarity and productive community projects (Di Marco et al. 2003; Dinerstein 2001, 2003). At the time of my study, piqueteros/as could regularly be seen challenging the centers of power in the heart of Buenos Aires or blocking the bridges linking the city to the surrounding metropolitan area. These men and women were no longer hidden or silent. They became increasingly visible as they put their bodies on the line during marches and at roadblocks. Impoverishment, hunger, and unemployment became more difficult to ignore—obviously present, widespread, and embodied.

In a country that has a history of denying the disappearances, torture, and horror inflicted by the last military dictatorship, the reality of pervasive poverty in the making could, perhaps for a while, still be covered up by politicians and economic elites promoting neoliberalism or overlooked by members of the middle class holding on to the illusions of economic prosperity. However, with the crisis that erupted in the new millennium, this kind of denial was no longer possible. The new disappeared—the "economic disappeared," as they have been called in social movement circles—show their existence with their physical presence when they claim, through individual demands and collective protests, their rights to partake in citizenship and the goods that democracy was supposed to deliver.

EMBODYING GLOBALIZATION: GENDER, CLASS, AND WOMEN'S BODIES

In talking about their lives and bodies, women in this study addressed the direct and indirect effects of neoliberal policies and the economic crisis. Their narratives exposed a matrix of bodily experiences that took specific shapes according to gender expectations and class location. Women with disparate economic conditions had to transform aspects of their lifestyle, with repercussion on their bodies, but poor women had fewer resources in the first place. The bodily grievances that women expressed encompassed not only distress about their reduced access to critical resources to sustain the material body (for example, good-quality food and health care) but also concerns about physical appearance and beauty.

Women's anxieties about their bodily looks, regardless of class, are consistent with social pressures to comply with Western models of beauty, which are magnified in Argentina and especially in Buenos Aires (Sutton 2004). Argentina is an international hub of cosmetic surgery, a place where job ads customarily and explicitly seek job candidates with "good *presencia*" (appearance) and where it is almost a slogan to assert that Argentine women are "the most beautiful in the world" (Hasanbegovic 1998). Furthermore, capitalist globalization is grounded in production geared to promote conspicuous consumption, particularly in relation to physical appearance, which, in turn, plays a prime role in the placement and perception of people in a global social hierarchy. Paradoxically, at the same time that globalization sells products and images of fashion and beauty for the world to consume, it prevents more and more people from meeting such expectations.

Class was a major axis differentiating how economic decline affected women's bodies. For some middle-class women, adjustment entailed switching to less expensive beauty treatments, buying cheaper food, or downgrading their health coverage; for women living in shantytowns, however, adjustment could mean something as basic as the difference between eating and not eating. The narratives of women who grew up in poverty, or whose poverty was deepened with the neoliberal restructuring, prefigured the situation of millions of people, particularly women, as poverty in Argentina became more widespread. Among the bodily problems that poor and working-class women mentioned were difficulty taking care of contraceptive needs, poor diets, inadequate medical attention in public hospitals, physical overwork, little time to rest, and exhaustion from the combination of unpaid work and income-generating activities in a social milieu in which women are still expected to do most of the care and household work.

In the midst of the crisis, newspapers published pieces about the exacerbation of hunger (illustrated by pictures of children with unimaginably thin bodies) and the cuts and changes in people's diets due to worsening economic conditions. By the end of 2002, the prices of nonperishable food products increased about 100 percent, and those of fresh and frozen food products climbed about 70 percent in Buenos Aires and its metropolitan area (Sainz 2002). Many families were consuming less milk and meat (meat being one of Argentina's most popular food sources) and switching to cheaper products (Hicks et al. 2003:15). Because of the gendered division of labor in Argentina, women tend to be especially aware of how adverse economic conditions impinge on their ability to provide a nutritious diet. They are usually in charge of planning, preparing, or directing the preparation of meals. Yet, in a society in which women are generally expected to be self-sacrificing, to not experience appetites, and to bear the brunt of care work, it was not surprising to hear of some economically marginalized women sidelining their own food needs.

Women living in poverty struggled against food insecurity by resorting to multiple strategies, such as looking for leftover foods in garbage bags, begging at supermarkets and private homes, and organizing communal kitchens. The crisis pushed them to the edge, and obtaining minimum amounts of food became ever more difficult. For many mothers, getting enough food for their children was a top priority, with women sometimes silencing their own bodily needs. Alexandra, a young single mother living in a shantytown, showed that lack of food was one dimension of her bodily experiences:

> What happens is that I sometimes have [food], and sometimes I don't. I'm not that worried about it now because my child eats at the *comedor* [communal kitchen]. But in the past, before he went to the comedor, I did get worried...like about him becoming malnourished....That worried me.
>
> *What happens when you don't have food for yourself?*
>
> I drink mate [a caffeinated tea-like beverage].

Because drinking mate was not a long-term solution to hunger or the sense of tiredness she experienced, Alexandra finally decided to overcome her feelings of shame, "lower [her] head," and ask her brother and his wife for help to buy some basic food products. Under the critical economic circumstances in Argentina, Alexandra depended on the goodwill of her relatives (who did not have much money either) and the viability of a nearby communal kitchen to obtain the nutrients that her body and her son's body needed. Alexandra joined the swelling ranks of people who could not find a job to help satisfy basic bodily necessities.

The words of Candela, a 32-year-old unemployed woman living in poverty, also highlight body–economy connections structured by gender and class. Candela was raising her two children and was supported by her husband, who held a low-wage job. She had a hard time finding a job that would allow her to take adequate care of her children. However, she was involved in many kinds of unpaid community activities to improve the quality of life in her neighborhood. She presented a somber picture of how the crisis reached different aspects of her life and body:

> My life was affected because [the prices of] everything increased so much, things increased so much, [that] one income cannot afford what it could afford before. Because my husband continues earning what he earned before, which was barely enough, and now we are lacking [sufficient money]. We don't have enough. And, well, the body is [affected] because, for example,

in the past, when things were cheap, I could think about my teeth, for example, in getting my teeth done. Not now. I don't know, going to the hairdresser [smiling tone]…for example, going to the gym. No, we can't afford those luxuries because money is not enough. It is not enough. With everything that is happening now, it is not enough for anything. I think that if one wants to take a vacation or something in order to relax, to be well, it is not possible. We cannot do it. Well, then regarding food too. In the past, it was possible to eat better, more nutritious [food] for the children, milk every day. Now it is very expensive—[for example] milk and cereals that they love. It is very hard to make the shopping list and have enough money for all those things.

Candela's reflection shows how economic conditions affect a mix of basic bodily needs and the desire for gendered "luxuries." She prioritized some items over others—for example, her children's food needs over her going to the gym, the hairdresser, or the dentist. Yet, in expressing her grievances, Candela referenced social perceptions about the kinds of activities women in Argentina are expected to engage in to look beautiful and feminine. Physical beauty may seem superficial, but many women recognize that they live in a society that judges women by their appearance. The importance of motherhood, another key social expectation of women, also emerges from Candela's narrative. Like other mothers, Candela suggested a sense of connection between her body and her children's bodies. In talking about herself, she slipped to her children's needs and desires (for example, "milk and cereals that they love"), also curtailed under the crisis.

Similarly, the loss of jobs with health benefits, the reduced ability to pay for health services, and the deterioration of the public health system undermined access to health care. Because of economic constraints and consistent with gender norms that expect women to focus their care outwardly, some women neglected signs of illness in their bodies (Di Liscia and Di Liscia 1997; Prece, Di Liscia, and Piñero 1997). Luna and Alondra, both domestic workers, revealed the pressures to ignore their bodies that mothers of limited economic means may experience:

LUNA: Last week I was unwell, but I did not go [to the doctor] because I know I cannot get sick. Because if I get sick, I don't have anyone to look after the girls. Because if I get sick, my girls do not eat. I don't have anyone to take them to school. And if I get sick, I have to get up the next day—no ifs or buts—because I have to get up. So I do not go to the hospital. Even if I'm dying, I will not go, because if I go and they admit me, who is going to take care of my girls?

ALONDRA: And I tell you, I should not get sick, I should not get sick. I have to go to the hospital to do a hormonal analysis, no matter what, and I know that if I go, you see, it takes the whole morning, and I lose those hours of work, and I have to work because that money serves to buy things. So I can't get sick, and I have to do that medical testing, no matter what, rain or shine, every three months. I'm stretching it, stretching it, stretching it…you see, and I don't go.

In addition to household and mothering work, many women had to enter a more precarious formal labor market, do informal work, or devise alternative strategies to replace or supplement the wages of husbands, partners, or family members whose incomes became insufficient or who were unemployed. Under neoliberal globalization, those "lucky" enough to have a job had to cope with greater work insecurity and harsher conditions. Paula, a factory worker, described how the multinational corporation she worked for implemented speed-ups, union busting, and harassment against labor organizers and workers. She spoke of the job-related health conditions that she and fellow female workers developed, including varicose veins, tendonitis, backaches, and problems in the spine and legs:

It was alienating. I would stop to look around and…after an hour, you would look around, and everybody was working like that, and I [thought,] "We are machines." And that's how I started to think, "I am not a machine. The machine is the one in white. I am a person [she laughs]: I am dressed in blue. Identify me." Because we all had blue uniforms and the machines are white…so sometimes, when they wanted to force me to work [I would say], "I am not a machine, I am not a machine" [she laughs]. It horrifies me to reach that point.…I think that I was almost going on that path because I worked too much, but it was also the result of the [economic] need I experienced, to work like that.…But, if you will, I drew a limit and did not continue.

Paula resorted to bodily markers such as workers' clothing as a way to differentiate herself from and reclaim her humanity vis-à-vis lifeless machines. Using her senses, her tiredness, and her embodied consciousness as a compass, Paula rejected the path imposed by neoliberal globalization. She resisted, individually and collectively, working conditions that constructed workers' bodies as disposable. She challenged a gendered division of labor that turned women into "slaves of their workstation" while allowing men relative freedom of movement.

Rising levels of unemployment and underemployment also pushed many people into the streets to try to survive through informal income-generating activities. For example, according to data reported by an association of sex workers, prostitution in the city of Buenos Aires has grown more than 40 percent since the mid-1990s (from an estimated 14,000 in 1995 to 20,000 in 2004), an increase partly blamed on the adverse economic situation (Lladós 2004). As Yamila, who identified as a sex worker, told me: "If there's no work, I will have to continue standing at a street corner. I will have to continue selling my body." Alternative modes of survival such as begging, cardboard gathering, or prostitution, although not illegal, involve considerable stigmatization and bodily risk, including disease, police harassment, and physical violence.

The stories of some of my interviewees reveal the high bodily costs of these informal activities and the ways in which these are gendered. Fanny noted that the hazards of cardboard gathering are not the same for men as for women. The bodies of poor women are coded as targets of harassment in sexualized ways. Fanny talked about some doormen who ask women collectors for sex in exchange for the paper or cardboard they collected within the building. Fanny was emphatic that it is not good for women to be working in the streets at night, but she had few options:

> I can't find work because, really, if I could find it…because this is not…in truth, this is not for women. For men, yes, but not for women. And I think it is not [for women] because the truth is that there are so many things in the streets. Sometimes you can't go out alone. I already told you that the doormen harass you a lot.

Even though being in the streets gathering cardboard is not a sign of Fanny's liberation, but of her lack of other choices, the idea that streets are not for women reverberates with sexist mandates. Her experiences of sexual harassment reinforce cultural norms prescribing that women should stay at home at night and that women in the streets are "asking for it." Fanny used her attachment to a man—by telling doormen that she was with her husband—as a shield against sexual harassment. This is an understandable and effective move, but one that also strengthens sexist prescriptions. In Fanny's case, sexual harassment is a concomitant effect of crisis-induced poverty and of gendered assumptions about her supposedly out-of-place female body.

Fanny's body was also exhausted. Her cardboard-gathering routine would start around 5 p.m. and would not stop until early in the morning of the following day. This work requires not only collecting materials but also sorting them so that they are suitable for sale. Fanny's daily work did not stop there: "I do the household chores, do the laundry, ironing—and my daughter helps me." She excused her husband's avoidance of housework, stating that he was too tired. Fanny had no time to take care of her own body, get medical treatment, or pay attention to her contraceptive necessities. She had an intrauterine device that needed to be removed, but the hassles of a deteriorated public health system and her time constraints made it difficult for her to take care of this. Fanny placed her family's needs before her own. The precarious nature of cardboard gathering intersected with gender norms that construct the female body as a "body for others" (Di Liscia and Di Liscia 1997), jeopardizing Fanny's own bodily integrity.

If women are forced to work harder to offset the impacts of neoliberal economics, if the social support systems that helped to sustain families are under attack, if obtaining adequate health care is increasingly difficult, and if living conditions have generally declined, then we must raise questions about the effects of neoliberalism on women's bodies. The stories of different women in this study reveal intertwined bodily problems, needs, and desires, showing the interaction of material conditions and cultural prescriptions. Some of their bodily troubles were related to bad work conditions or overwork, for example, extreme tiredness or tendonitis due to repetitive motion. In the case of poor women, medical problems tended to worsen because of the inaccessibility of health care and the precariousness of their living situation (for example, a poor woman who was diabetic needed to store her medication in a refrigerator, but because she did not have one, she went without medication). In some cases, bodily problems stemmed from the significant levels of stress women were experiencing. This kind of stress was sometimes an emotional response to a climate of anger, economic insecurity, growing poverty, and uncertainty about the future. These women's suffering, intimately linked to the social context and manifesting concretely in the material body, is the kind of problem that neoliberal gurus will never see as long as they continue to ignore that the policies they make are about embodied human beings.

Embodied Emotions

Unlike the often distant and disembodied appraisals of economic experts, the women in this study talked about the crisis in Argentina in deeply embodied and emotional ways. The crisis was perceived as an all-encompassing, even violent, force affecting body, emotions, relation-ships, and intimate aspects of their lives. Besides enumerating the many ways in which the crisis had diminished their material standard of living, women expressed painful embodied emotions related to their precarious social conditions.

Rosalía, a woman who was running a communal kitchen and other sol-idarity projects, talked about the crisis as something that becomes "part of each of us....It is more than a material economic crisis, since it leads you to depression, tiredness, and not wanting to know about anything else." These emotions were experienced at a bodily level. During a workshop on sexuality I attended at the 2002 National Women's Meeting,[7] some of the participants talked about how the crisis invaded their sexual lives, for exam-ple, how unemployment and economic problems were reflected in a loss of sexual desire. Although feelings such as tiredness, depression, sleepless-ness, and diminished sexual desire may be seen as individual troubles—perhaps more pertinent to the field of mental health—the emotions these women expressed were closely linked to the social crisis, which cannot be solved merely through individualized therapies or efforts.

The material quality of life for Camila, who was part of the impover-ished middle class, also declined with the economic collapse. She linked the crisis to troubling embodied emotions, including lack of energy and negative perceptions of her body: "I'm developing psychosomatic prob-lems because of everything that is happening—the economic crisis. My back hurts a lot. I don't sleep well. I see myself as fat. I can't diet. I don't feel like sacrificing myself with the diet." Resorting to the discourse of psy-choanalysis, which is very influential in Argentina (Plotkin 2001), Camila articulated how the anxiety and discomfort produced by the social crisis resulted in symptoms that connect body and emotions. The crisis affected her body (her back, her sleep) and her perception of her body ("I see myself as fat"). The crisis created a malaise that permeated her whole life. Although Camila's pain was very real, her relative class privilege was evi-dent in that part of her distress was because she "can't diet" and not, for example, because she was unable to get enough food. Camila talked about having to adjust the quality of the food she bought, but she was still able to get the food she needed.

In contrast, Lucía, who lived in a shantytown, faced problems like not having enough food for herself and her five children. Oftentimes she filled her stomach by drinking mate for hours. One of her strategies to obtain food was to dig into garbage cans in search of leftover bread, bones, or lard for stew. She was also a piquetera and a communal kitchen coordinator.

Finding work was a challenge in the midst of a depressed economy and as
the main care provider for her children. In Lucía's case, emotional distress
was related to this kind of scarcity. She used the word *pain* to describe her
feelings about unemployment, poverty, and economic crisis, and she relied
on body language and bodily references to convey her suffering:

> People treat you badly. You go and look for work, and they tell
> you no. And it hurts. Not having a plate of food to give to [your
> children]....I feel bad in that sense. It hurts. It is as if something
> was breaking inside [she touches her chest with her hands]. I say,
> "What have I done to deserve this?" Because it hurts, you know?

Both Camila and Lucía reported embodied pains related to the crisis,
but their different class locations shaped their distress. With the crisis, and
the negative feelings it produced, Camila found it more difficult to sustain
the willpower to maintain the kind of slender feminine body that is at once
a marker of appropriate femininity and a symbol of class distinction. In the
case of Lucía, though she often went without enough food, her body was
not slender. The kind of food she was able to obtain (noodles, bread, lard)
would probably make it difficult to develop that kind of body, even if she
wanted to. Her pain was related to the scarcity of nutritious food and a lack
of access to the means to obtain it, such as regular employment.

Even for those women who were personally affected by the economic
decline but were still able to satisfy basic needs, the climate of social cata-
strophe and the evident suffering of so many people could fuel disturbing
embodied emotions. The reality of poverty demanded the attention of all
members of society, sometimes provoking rejection but in some cases
inspiring a deep embodied understanding. This awareness entails more
than knowing that poverty exists or the poverty percentages and figures.
Jesusa, a middle-class woman, talked about embodied pain:

> To see women scrambling the garbage, with a lot of children, is
> terribly painful, uhhh.
>
> *It's painful at a level of...?*
>
> At a psychic [level], and I think that it is also physical.
>
> *Where do you feel that pain?*
>
> I think that in my stomach, something...visceral! It is terrible,
> terrible, when I drive my car [home] and I see those children at
> 11 p.m., or women with little children, and I say, well, you know,
> in truth, they don't have anything to eat. Nobody likes to do

that!…One thing is to know that poverty exists, and another thing is to see it, to see it and to be in those terribly poor and marginal places and see that those people are really subjected to such violence.

Jesusa's pain was evident in her agitated tone of voice and tearing eyes. She was almost weeping. This passage highlights both the painful reality of poverty and Jesusa's empathy. The fact that her exposure to poverty was through "seeing" and not through her own experience indicates her position of relative class privilege. She went through economic difficulties, but she could still eat daily, receive quality medical attention, access adequate shelter and clothing, and enjoy the benefits of a good education. Yet, her embodied pain ("something…visceral") associated with the suffering of people who are worse off shows that the crisis touched her at a deeper level, beyond concern about her own well-being. In an embodied way, she herself became part of the suffering and shaken "social body." This kind of embodied suffering is different from that of women who have been experiencing poverty in their own flesh. Nevertheless, it points to the fact that the embodied impacts of the economy transcend individuals' particular conditions, blending their lives with other people's and contributing to a collective mood and bodily state of being.

Claudia was a domestic worker who struggled to make ends meet. In Claudia's case, embodied pain was associated both with her own situation—the precarious nature of her life—and beyond. Her feelings extended to the experiences of people she encountered in the streets, saw in overcrowded hospitals, or heard about in the media. During the interview, she also talked about "pain" and related it to the crisis:

> Well, I have many pains, an interior pain for everything that happened to me, you know? You feel that your bones hurt, that your skin hurts, that it is torn apart. Pain when my children are sick.

> *How is that, that your skin hurts or is torn apart?*

> Well, you feel it when…let's suppose that something happens to me, or to my children. You know, when your skin is torn apart, the pain? Like that. When I can't heal my children, I say, "Well, how do I solve this problem?" Do you understand? If your child is hurting because of this or that or if he has to be hospitalized—that kind of pain. Or the pain that I suffer when a kid dies or when I see a barefoot kid begging, a little child, a six-year-old child—that's the pain for me…to see a little child hospitalized,

who is suffering. That's the pain that hurts the most. I suffer a lot
for that. It is an interior pain.

In Claudia's narrative, the embodied pain from her own life was interconnected with the suffering that the sight of poverty in the streets or children
in the hospital provoked in her. The way she talked about poverty shows
that it is not a distant or abstract phenomenon, but something that involves
the body, even if one does not live in extreme poverty oneself.

According to Elina Matoso (2003), with the socioeconomic crisis, the
boundaries between individual bodies and the larger "social body" have
become more fluid, less clearly delimited. As Rosalía pointed out, the crisis is "part of each of us"; it is not something outside that can be held at a
distance. Matoso (2003:24) argues that in the context of the crisis, this
"confusion between the outside and the inside" may provoke a number of
negative bodily feelings, symptoms, and illnesses. Some of the women in
this study expressed a kind of embodied pain that revealed not only their
personal suffering but also a wider "social suffering"—that is, a suffering
intimately related to social problems (Farmer 2003; Kleinman, Das, and
Lock 1996). Their personal difficulties were mirrored by and merged with
those of many other people in Argentina. Yet, while these material, emotional, and bodily problems of women constituted one aspect of the crisis,
the crisis also triggered a renewed impetus for social change in which
women played central roles.

CONCLUDING REMARKS

This chapter examines some of the negative impacts of neoliberal globalization on women's embodied experiences in social conditions of rising
inequality and impoverishment. The economic crisis affected everyone in
Argentina to some extent, but the outcomes of the crisis were clearly not
equally distributed. Gender practices and expectations significantly influ-
enced the ways in which women's embodied experiences were structured.
Among women, class location was also an important factor in how they
weathered the crisis and how their bodily habits and experiences were
transformed. Not surprisingly, women who were already economically marginalized were affected by the collapse of the economy in harsher ways.

The economy is not something "out there," abstract or with little relevance to the body, but a force shaping bodily experiences and consciousness.
The scars of neoliberal globalization on women's bodies were imprinted
through lower quality of work, food, and health care and expressed through
complex embodied emotions. The crisis produced bodies that were more

fatigued, stressed, overworked, and malnourished, as well as sick. In the context of economic insecurity, women's experiences reveal a kind of social suffering that ties body and emotions and connects personal experiences to those of fellow citizens.

My exploration of the embodied dimensions of globalization suggests different levels at which one may "know" impoverishment and which involve the body in distinct ways: (1) to vaguely acknowledge the existence of poverty, something possible only if one is not directly affected; (2) to know the numbers and figures of poverty—a more informed understanding, but the information may seem abstract and disembodied; (3) to see poverty firsthand and perhaps develop a bodily reaction ("visceral," "your bones hurt")—a more embodied recognition of the problem; and (4) to experience poverty in the flesh (living in a shantytown, not being able to satisfy basic needs)—one really knows what poverty is about, so one's understanding is thoroughly embodied. The women I interviewed navigated among these options, but given the context of economic turmoil, the heightened levels of social protest, and the visibility of poverty in the streets, the more removed form of comprehension was becoming less likely or required more active denial efforts.

Despite its negative effects, the crisis also functioned as an opening, an opportunity for many women to reflect on their experiences, to collectively challenge the economic forces that impinged on their lives and bodies, and to confront their social conditions of subordination, including gender inequality. Women were often engines, more or less visible, in many survival struggles, community organizations, and social movement projects. They participated in multiple activities, from communal kitchens to neighborhood assemblies, from popular education and health care projects to collective child care, from subsistence production to bartering clubs, from the recuperation of failed businesses and factories to the transformation of abandoned buildings into cultural and economically productive centers (Chejter 2002; RIGC 2003).

In a time of social breakdown and desperation, women's community and solidarity initiatives took care of many people's problems as individuals. These also contributed to creating and expanding social solidarity ties, promoting social dialogue, and opening paths for a critique of neoliberal globalization and for envisioning alternative ways of living. Argentina has been widely seen as a "social laboratory," with men and women innovating ways of producing goods and services, relating to each other, and organizing politically. Many, like Paula (the factory worker), found opportunities for personal and social change in the midst of the crisis:

The crisis entered everybody's home. In my case, the crisis affected me by leaving me without a job, but it also opened the way for many things for me....The crisis, along with things that you start to observe and do in your life, makes you to try other levels, to want to do other things, to open your mind to see things in a different way....Some people subsist doing many different things, [for example] vegetable gardens. They endure the crisis. I also made handicrafts for a while, but I think that I need to go beyond that if I really want to change things. Because the economic crisis of the country is the political crisis of the country.... Society has to gain consciousness that it is not enough to do things to subsist, you see. One can't leave "subsistence" for the next generations. We need a radical change, I think, so that we don't leave them with debts.

Paula's gain in political consciousness was by no means exceptional. The bleak economic situation catalyzed women's growing participation in social movements and protests. Activist women in Argentina referred to this phenomenon as the "feminization of resistance." For many women, their activism was rooted in embodied economic hardships. In the age of globalization, women's marginalized bodies also became vehicles of courageous resistance.

About the Author

Barbara Sutton is an assistant professor of women's studies at the University at Albany. She holds a Ph.D. in sociology from the University of Oregon (2004) and a law degree from the National University of Buenos Aires (1993), Argentina, where she was born and raised. Professor Sutton's scholarly interests include globalization, body politics, human rights, global justice and women's movements, and intersections of inequalities based on gender, class, race and ethnicity, sexuality, and nation, particularly in Latin American contexts. Her latest research examines racism, citizenship, and democracy in Argentina. She is also co-editing a book with Sandra Morgen and Julie Novkov (Rutgers University Press), which interrogates militarized paradigms of security and explores the linkages among militarization, racism, and gender inequality.

Notes

1. About half of the individual interviewees were activists, including feminists, lesbians, labor activists, piqueteras (road barricade activists), and members of popular assemblies, communal kitchens, leftist political organizations, human rights groups,

and organizations of Afro descendents, Indigenous peoples, migrants, women in prostitution, and people with disabilities.

2. I generated the list of words based on my knowledge of feminist scholarship, body studies, and Argentine culture. Interviewees could add words of their own, although they seldom did. The words are *exercise, pleasure, aging, disability, health, food, sex, art, menstruation, beauty, sports, harassment, childbirth, work, desire, menopause, youth, law, violence, religion, expression, psychoanalysis, movement, skin color, contraception, ethnicity, race, class, reproduction, motherhood, femininity, abortion, economic crisis, politics, appearance, recreation, sexuality, pregnancy, pain, change* (added), and *guilt* (added).

3. For instance, I participated in protests to stop violence against women, to decriminalize abortion, to halt war and state repression, and to demand solutions to hunger, poverty, and unemployment, among others. I took part in the 2002 National Women's Meeting, the Thematic World Social Forum in Argentina, the XXII March of Resistance organized by Mothers of the Plaza de Mayo–Founding Line, the World Social Forum in Porto Alegre, Brazil (to which I traveled, along with a delegation of social movement organizations from Argentina), the International Women's Day march, marches in support of women who "occupied" and recovered a factory abandoned by its owners, marches for peace, and demonstrations in memory of the popular uprising that took place on December 19 and 20, 2001.

4. These figures are even more staggering if one compares similar indicators between the early 1970s and after 2000, when the Argentine economy was visibly crumbling (see Argumedo and Quintar 2003). For example, in 1974 the richest 10 percent had an income 12 times greater than the poorest 10 percent; in 2002 the top 10 percent earned 30 times more than the bottom 10 percent (Argumedo and Quintar 2003:620).

5. See Norgaard 2003 on the connection between embodied emotions and the development of a sociological imagination.

6. Because cardboard gatherers often lack transportation or storage places, they commonly rely on intermediaries, who keep parts of the profits. Some cardboard gatherers organized cooperatives to gain leverage, to improve their conditions, and to avoid abuses from industries or intermediaries (Reynals 2002).

7. The National Women's Meetings are annual events that attract thousands of women from all over the country. The purpose of these meetings is to provide horizontal, autonomous, and democratic structures for women to get to know one another, exchange experiences, debate political views, and generate social change ideas and actions (Alonso and Díaz 2002).

Part III

Servicing Leisure, Serving Class
Women Transgressing
Global Circuits of Care

9

Geographies of Race and Class

The Place and Placelessness of Migrant Filipina Domestic Workers

Rhacel Salazar Parreñas

On any given day, approximately 2,531 workers leave the Philippines to pursue employment opportunities outside the country (Arao 2000).[1] They add to the estimated 7.38 million Filipinos who work and reside in 187 destination countries and territories (Kanlungan Center Foundation 2000).[2] Most are professional women who fill the demand for private domestic work (Parreñas 2001). By domestic workers, I broadly refer to those who provide cleaning and care services in private households. Filipina migrants toil in private households in cities throughout the world, including Hong Kong, Taipei, Tokyo, Los Angeles, New York, Paris, and Rome, to name just a few. In this chapter, I examine the settlement desires of domestic workers in the Filipino diaspora, using interviews I conducted with workers in Rome and Los Angeles as data.[3]

Fitting the classic definition of diaspora as those displaced from a homeland (Cohen 1997), migrant Filipina domestic workers construct the Philippines as "home." Yet they rarely go "home," even though they work hard and spend little abroad in order to accumulate enough savings to return to the Philippines. This ambivalent settlement desire has been observed by Nicole Constable (1999). She noticed that migrant Filipina domestic workers in Hong Kong continuously yearned to return to the Philippines but after they went home, they hastily returned abroad.

Similarly, in Rome and Los Angeles, migrant Filipina domestic workers with legal documents return to the Philippines, on average, only once every four years. When they do, they usually stay no longer than two months. As Constable (1999:203) perceptively notes, migrant Filipina domestic workers perpetually inhabit a state of being "at home but not at home." This is unsurprisingly the case in nations with "illiberal" regimes, such as Singapore, where migrants are restricted to a guest worker status, but this is also the case in nations with liberal regimes, such as Italy and the United States, where migrants are eligible for permanent settlement through labor or marriage (Bakan and Stasiulis 1997; Castles and Miller 2003).[4]

Such ambivalent settlement desires among migrant Filipina domestic workers ill match the common depiction of migrant women in the global North as a group deeply entrenched in the host society. Studies on migrant women in the United States—as well as, but to a lesser extent, Europe—have repeatedly asserted that women prefer permanent over temporary migration (Escrivá 2000; Hondagneu-Sotelo 1994; Pessar 1986; Repak 1995; Singer and Gilbertson 2003); maintain less involvement with hometown association activities than do men and instead engage more frequently with local-oriented organizations (Goldring 2003); and envision their permanent settlement in the host society (Singer and Gilbertson 2003). What explains this gender dichotomy in migrant settlement? According to many (Hondagneu-Sotelo 1994; Pessar 1986; Repak 1995; Singer and Gilbertson 2003), this dichotomy is due to the fact that "women make greater gains in status, autonomy, and resources relative to men" upon migration (Singer and Gilbertson 2003:375). In contrast to women, men may lose status upon migration (Singer and Gilbertson 2003).[5]

There is little exception to the common assertion of this gender binary in migrant settlement.[6] One notable exception is sociologist Cecilia Menjivar's recent study of Central American migrants in San Francisco, in which she questions the assertion that "entry into paid work [is] an unqualified indication of empowerment and improved status within the family for women" (Menjivar 2003:108). Instead, she found the strong possibility of a backlash: when women earn more, men drink more. Similarly, Yen Le Espiritu (2003) observed that women primary earners in the Filipino American migrant community would sacrifice high-paying jobs for lesser earnings in order to retain their husband's status as the primary income earner of their family. Despite these recent contributions, studies on gender and migration continue to insist, for the most part, that men "tend to experience a relatively greater loss of gender and social status" than do women (Goldring 2003). In contrast, women are said to be free of the burdens of this status inconsistency (Goldring 2003). On this basis, studies assert that women, in contrast to men, prefer permanent over return migration.[7]

Studies have slowly begun to acknowledge more nuanced gender processes in migration, illustrating that migration does not involve only a position of gender ascendance for women but instead entails both the reinforcement and transformation of gender (Menjivar 2003) and a simultaneous loss and gain of social status for women (Gold 2003; Kibria 1994). For instance, migration can increase the earning power of women but also weaken the support provided by kin and reduce the social status of the racialized migrant woman vis-à-vis the dominant society (Gold 2003; Kibria 1994). Regardless, studies still conclude, for the most part, that women shun the option of return migration because of the increase in their social status (exceptions to this are Gold 2003; Hirsch 2003; and Menjivar 2003).

Contrary to the findings of most other studies, I have found that migration does not necessarily increase the social status of Filipina domestic workers. In their case, migration usually involves social decline for professionals, racial marginalization, and a new set of gender constraints. In the case of gender, for instance, Filipina migrants may, like other migrant women, successfully escape gender inequalities in their country of origin but face a new set of gender inequalities in their country of destination, one aggravated by race and class and illustrated concretely by their occupational concentration in domestic work (Barber 1997; Glenn 1986; Parreñas 2001). As such, I found that migrant Filipina domestic workers are not as deeply entrenched in the host society as their women counterparts from other countries. This is the case in both Italy and the United States, the two largest destination countries for Filipino migrants in the Western Hemisphere, despite the different contexts of reception in these nations. Although the United States allows permanent residency to labor migrants and Italy grants this right only to "marriage migrants," women hold feelings of curbed membership in both countries. For instance, one domestic worker I met in Los Angeles described the United States as the "United Mistakes of America." In Italy, migrant domestic workers whom I met in the mid-1990s spoke frequently of home as the Philippines.

Unlike their women counterparts from Central America, the Dominican Republic, and Mexico, migrant Filipina domestic workers aspire to return home to the Philippines (Grasmuck and Pessar 1991; Hondagneu-Sotelo 1994; Repak 1995). They imagine, plan, and invest in a future based in the homeland. They are like male migrants in that they maintain concrete ties with sending communities. They remit their foreign earnings regularly;

raise funds for community, education, and church organizations in their hometowns; and finally build homes in their country of origin (Karp 1995; Parreñas 2005). In other words, they remit a significant proportion of their earnings to invest in the reproduction of their families in the Philippines (and not in the host society; Parreñas 2001).[8] Notably, the desire of migrant Filipinas to return home does not necessarily mean that gender inequalities would not welcome them upon their return to the Philippines. For instance, they would still face a sex-segregated labor market and a severe wage gap in the Philippines, which they notably escaped through migration (Parreñas 2005).[9] Not surprisingly, then, they rarely return home, despite vocalizing their desire to do so.

In this chapter, I use the case of migrant Filipina domestic workers to revisit the common assertion in studies of women and migration that gender inequalities in sending countries push migrant women to settle permanently in receiving countries.[10] This problematic assertion assumes that countries of origin provide fewer opportunities for women (Gold 2003; Hirsch 2003) and, in so doing, inadvertently supports the long-dismissed modernization theory of gender that presupposes that disparities in gender relations within the family and society diminish in the movement from tradition to modernity (Kandiyoti 1996).[11] Jennifer Hirsch offers a similar critique:

> Most [studies] found that in fact [migrant] women are more powerful in the United States, primarily because of the social and economic effects of women's participation in wage labor. These studies, however, assumed for the most part that gender in the sending communities was a static set of patriarchal norms, taking these communities to represent the past, the traditional, in contrast to the present or the modern that was found in the United States. [Hirsch 2003:180]

To avoid the inadvertent support of the modernization theory of gender, Hirsh urges migration scholars to view gender as not static in the country of origin. Building from Hirsh's work, I also question the gender binary that dominates our understanding of men and women's migrant settlement. To explain why migrant Filipina domestic workers continue to construct the Philippines as home, I consider how factors besides gender may determine migrant women's settlement. In the case of migrant Filipina domestic workers, I show that race and class inequalities diminish their social status in the host society and consequently propel feelings of sojourn among them.[12]

The ambivalent settlement desires of migrant Filipina domestic workers emerge from their "social location" in the context of the asymmetrical interstices of race, class, and gender (Espiritu 2003; Glenn 1986; Lowe 1996; Menjivar 2003; Trinh 1989; Zavella 1987). Settlement for these women involves their negotiation of status inconsistencies in the multiple and intersecting spheres of race, class, and gender, with the most salient being their loss of social status, from being professionals to becoming domestic workers upon migration. The drastic decline in social status of migrant Filipina domestic workers is illustrated in many forms, including their experience of having domestics in the Philippines and suddenly being one, their low racial status in the host society, and their inability to use their college education.

While acknowledging these various manifestations of social decline, I focus on only one: the spatial manifestation of class and racial inequalities. I do so because the spatial integration of migrants is telling of the extent of their membership (and therefore settlement) in the host society (Soysal 1994; Yeoh and Huang 1998). In this chapter, I illustrate how the peripheral status of migrant Filipina domestic workers constrains their use of space in both the private domain of the employer's household and the public domain of the host society. This spatial displacement is significant because it engenders their sojourner mentality.

This chapter establishes the ambivalent relations to home of migrant Filipina domestic workers. In so doing, it offers a constructive feminist critique of the common reduction of women's migration as emancipation from the imagined gender restrictions of "home" and considers race and class in understanding the settlement patterns of women migrants. I begin with a description of the place of migrant Filipina domestic workers in my research sites of Rome and Los Angeles. Then I address my methodology, after which I proceed to illustrate the spatial displacements of migrant Filipina domestic workers. I conclude by addressing the implications of my observations on the salience of race and class in our understanding of women's settlement patterns in globalization.

ROME AND LOS ANGELES

Filipino migration into Italy officially began in the 1970s, but Filipino migrants did not become a visible presence in Rome until the 1980s. By the late 1990s, Filipinos had become the largest migrant group in the city, representing close to 12 percent of the foreign population in Rome (Collicelli et al. 1997). Local community members estimate the number of Filipinos to be close to 100,000, which is significantly higher than the figure of

24,000 given by the Minister of Interior in 1996 (Collicelli et al. 1997). Since 1998, the annual deployment of overseas contract workers from the Philippines to Italy has reached 20,000 per annum (Philippine Overseas Employment Administration 2005).[13] The destination of half these workers is Rome. Filipinos are residentially dispersed throughout Rome but are most concentrated in the northern periphery, reaching 17.8 percent, and in the areas close to the central train station of Termini, reaching 9 percent in the first district and 11 percent in the second district. The rest of the population is dispersed throughout the 20 districts of the city, reaching no more than 5 percent in each district (Collicelli et al. 1997).

Most Filipinos in Rome are long-term legal residents of Italy. As a receiving state, Italy has granted amnesty to undocumented migrants consistently and generously, for example, in 1987, 1990, and 1995. In Italy, legal migrants hold a *permesso di soggiorno* (permit to stay), which grants them temporary residency. The residence permit can extend to seven years, and for most Filipino migrants, permits are renewable contingent on the sponsorship of an employer, the regular employment of the migrant, and the continual filing of income tax by the employer. Though the residence permit, with very few exceptions, generally restricts the labor market activities of migrants to domestic work, it grants them access to social and health services and rights to family reunification with spouses and children under the age of 18 (Campani 1993). Notably, these rights were bestowed on migrants only upon the implementation of the 1989–1990 Martelli Law (Soysal 1994).

Although most Filipinos in Rome are documented workers, many societal constraints promote feelings of nonmembership among them. One factor is their segregation in domestic service. Another factor is their restricted social integration in Italy, reflected in their avoidance of public spaces of leisure. For example, only 2 of 46 women who participated in my study had ever gone to the movies on their own, that is, without employers or young wards. My own experiences also demonstrate the segregation of Filipinos. To my discomfort, Italians often vocalized their surprise or just stared at me when I entered high-end clothing stores or even neighborhood Italian restaurants. I was not accorded this treatment when accompanied by my white friends (Italians or Americans) because their presence established my identity as a "tourist" whose purchasing power abated my racial othering as a Filipino.

Interviewees explained that they restrict their leisure activities in public social spaces to minimize their expenses (for instance, not eating in Italian restaurants), but without a doubt, their construction as perpetual foreigners in Italy also influences the "self-imposed" restriction of leisure space among Filipinos. It is not surprising that the settlement experiences of migrant Filipinas in Italy feed the intense desire to return to the Philippines.

In the early 1990s, 98.5 percent of Filipinos in Rome performed domestic work (Venturini 1991). In recent years, migrant Filipinos have ventured into other work but, for the most part, remain highly concentrated in low-wage service work, with most of them still in domestic service (Collicelli 1997). In contrast, Filipino migrants in Los Angeles occupy more diverse sectors of the labor market. With roots predominantly tracing back to the post-1965 migration of professionals to the United States, Filipino migrants in Los Angeles have had considerable access to mainstream jobs and are concentrated in wage employment (Portes and Rumbaut 1996). The employment profile of the Filipino population in Los Angeles is quite diverse: 25 percent of Filipinos hold managerial and professional jobs, an equal percentage have low-level professional occupations, and the rest work in lower-end service and manufacturing jobs (Ong and Azores 1994).

Class cleavage has come to define the Filipino migrant community in Los Angeles. The community is distinctly divided between the "haves" and the "have-nots," with migrants obtaining office work (even if low-level) considered the haves and those in low-level service occupations (for instance, hotel and domestic workers) included among the have-nots. From the perspective of domestic workers, the Filipino migrant community is centered on the middle class, which is a group not limited to those in the professional managerial class but includes those employed in low-level professional occupations, such as records processors and office clerks. It is from this perspective that domestics view their "place" in the community.

Filipinos are the second largest Asian immigrant group in Los Angeles. Despite this, they still do not have a visible ethnic enclave economy, meaning "a locational cluster of business firms whose owners and employees are (largely) co-ethnics" (Light et al. 1994:68). Unlike most other Asian immigrant groups in Los Angeles, the Filipino ethnic economy is distributed throughout the city and is not contained within an identifiable enclave. The absence of a Filipino ethnic enclave economy can be attributed largely to their concentration in wage employment.

The geographical constitution of the Filipino community is more discernable by residential patterns. Residential clusters of Filipinos have developed in both the inner city and suburbs. Filipinos are the dominant ethnic group in the suburbs of Carson and West Covina. In the inner city, community insiders identify a few neighborhoods in the vicinity of downtown, for example, certain blocks of Temple Street, as Filipino Town. This neighborhood houses a small number of video rental stores and markets that cater to its predominantly Filipino residents. The other residential clusters of the community include Eagle Rock and Echo Park and extend outside Los Angeles to Cerritos and Long Beach.

Interestingly, the class cleavage in the Filipino community of Los Angeles cannot be easily demarcated according to residential patterns. For most other Asian ethnic groups, inner-city residents are usually more disadvantaged than their counterparts in the suburbs. Yet urban planners have noticed that "inner-city Filipinos are the exception to this pattern" (Ong and Azores 1994:121). Middle-class and working-class Filipinos reside alongside each other in both the inner city and suburbs. Because sharp geographic boundaries do not reflect the class division of the Filipino population, a working-class spatial niche does not cushion the entrance of migrant Filipina domestics into the community. Thus, in spaces of the community, migrant Filipina domestic workers, as members of the have-nots, experience the community from a contentious location, one that always carries a keen awareness of their lesser success than the haves of the community.

Notably, in Los Angeles many of my interviewees were permanent residents of the United States, a status they obtained via marriage or labor certification. Yet they still were ambivalent about their permanent settlement in the United States. The opportunities in the United States—at the very least, the possibility shown by the professional managerial class—gave hope for mobility and instilled desires for permanent settlement. However, the realities of not having similar opportunities as the middle class also enforced sentiments of temporary settlement. Significantly, the realities of domestic work seemed to outweigh the possibilities of class mobility; most of my interviewees claimed to be only temporary migrants in the United States.

METHODOLOGY

This chapter is based primarily on open-ended interviews I conducted with female domestic workers in Rome and Los Angeles: 46 in Rome and 26 in Los Angeles. I based my study on these two cities because they are two main destinations of Filipina migrants among Western countries. To protect the anonymity of informants, I used pseudonyms for all my interviews. I tape-recorded and transcribed fully each of my interviews, which were mostly conducted in Tagalog or Tag-lish (a hybrid of Tagalog and English) and then translated into English. I did not share my interviews with informants, who had knowingly volunteered to participate in my study. Notably, none asked to see the interviews, but many requested and expressed their desire to be video-recorded rather than tape-recorded during our interview. I did not have adequate resources to accommodate this request.

A little less than five months in Rome in 1995 and 1996 gave me ample time to collect 46 in-depth interviews with Filipina domestic workers. The interviews ranged from one-and-a-half to three hours in length. I collected an unsystematic sample of research participants, using chain and snowball referrals. To diversify my sample, I solicited research participants from various sites in the community (churches, parks, plazas). In Los Angeles, I collected a smaller sample of 26 in-depth interviews with Filipina domestic workers. These interviews also ranged from one-and-a-half to three hours in length. I collected these interviews between April and September 1996. My smaller sample is due to the fact that, unlike their counterparts in Rome, Filipina migrants in Los Angeles are not concentrated in the informal service sector. Another factor contributing to the smaller sample in Los Angeles is the relatively small representation of Filipinas among domestic workers. Although present in the ethnic community, Filipinas are but a minority among the larger group of Latina domestics in the area. This is not surprising because Latinos represent the largest racial-ethnic population in Los Angeles.

In the field research site of Los Angeles, tapping into the community began with the network of my mother's acquaintances, friends, and relatives. This network, which is based on a Catholic parish heavily attended by Filipinos, two different hometown associations, the Philippine consulate in Los Angeles, and the ethnic stores frequently visited by my mother, led me to a group of women that represented different regions of the Philippines. To further diversify my sample, I also posted flyers in various ethnic enclave businesses. Two women responded to the flyers. Utilizing networks of domestic workers, the sample of interviewees was collected unsystematically through a snowball method. Participant-observation provided a gateway to the community as I attended meetings of Filipino labor groups, the occasional Filipino town fiestas, and the more frequent Filipino family parties and spent time with domestic workers at their own homes and at their employers'.

Sample Characteristics

While there were distinguishing characteristics between my interviewees in Rome and Los Angeles, they also shared many social characteristics. Differences included region of origin and median age. Interestingly, however, there were more similarities between the two groups. First, most of the interviewees were legal residents of their respective host societies. In Italy, 30 of 46 interviewees had a permesso di soggiorno.[14] Although able to sponsor their children, most of my interviewees had chosen not to. Most maintained transnational families. In Los Angeles, 15 of 26 interviewees had legal documents. Most of the women had acquired permanent legal status via marriage or the sponsorship of a wealthy employer. Yet many had not been able to sponsor the migration of dependents because of the legal bind of having obtained legal status only after their children had reached adult age and were no longer eligible for immediate family reunification.[15]

Another similarity between my interviewees in Rome and Los Angeles was their high level of educational attainment. Most had acquired some years of postsecondary training in the Philippines. In Rome, my interviewees included 23 women with college degrees, 12 with some years of college or postsecondary vocational training, and 7 who completed high school. In Los Angeles, my interviewees included 11 women with college diplomas, 8 with some years of college or postsecondary vocational training, and 5 who completed high school. In both cities, the majority of my interviewees had been professionals or semiprofessionals in the Philippines. Most had been teachers and office workers.

Finally, more than half of my interviewees were married women with children, although, as noted earlier, children were mostly left behind in the Philippines. Only 5 of 26 interviewees in Los Angeles and fewer than half (19) in Rome were never-married, single women. Women with children in the Philippines constituted a greater portion of my sample: 25 of 46 in Rome and 14 of 26 in Los Angeles. The median age of interviewees suggests that the children of the women in Rome were fairly young and in Los Angeles the children were older. The median age of my interviewees in Los Angeles was surprisingly high at 52. The youngest research participant was 33, and the oldest was 68 years old. What explains the extremely high median age of domestic workers in Los Angeles? We can surmise that younger immigrant Filipino women are not attracted to domestic work because of its isolating nature. They can choose to avoid domestic work because, compared with other immigrant groups, knowledge of the English language gives them access to other types of employment. In Rome, the median age of interviewees was 31, significantly lower than my sample in Los Angeles. Only four women fell under the age of 25, and the oldest woman was 66 years old.

RACE, CLASS, AND SPACE: THE PLACE AND PLACELESSNESS OF MIGRANT FILIPINA DOMESTIC WORKERS

To establish the decline of social status for migrant Filipina domestic workers, I now describe their spatial integration in Rome and Los Angeles.

By spatial integration, I speak not so much about their residential patterns of settlement, or in other words, their place in the city. This is because they are dispersed throughout the city of Rome and concentrated as live-in workers in Los Angeles. More precisely, I refer to the limits in the spatial actions in the everyday life of migrant Filipina domestic workers.[16] I speak of the social boundaries that embody their experience of spatiality with the notion that "the partition of space" reflects social inequalities (de Certeau 1984:123; Lefebvre 1977). The everyday practice of migrant life for Filipina domestic workers mirrors their spatial peripheralization by race and class (Yeoh and Huang 1998). We see this not only in their limited spatial movements in the workplace but also in the control of their actions in the public spaces they occupy during their days off. As geographers Brenda Yeoh and Shirlena Huang (1998) have found in Singapore, employers limit the access of domestic workers to public spaces by denying them a day off or by choosing the activities they do during their day off. The spatial peripheralization that confronts Filipina domestic workers in Singapore usually manifests in the extreme form of their segregation in the private sphere. Moreover, among those with the freedom of an actual monthly day off, the experience of spatial peripheralization also emerges in the public sphere in their concentration in "marginal, residual spaces and places associated with outsiders" (Yeoh and Huang 1998:585).

My examination of spatial inequalities in migrant women's lives stems a great deal from the seminal work of sociologist Judith Rollins on the "spatial deference" imposed on domestic workers by their employers, meaning the "unequal rights of the domestic and the employer to the space around the other's body and the controlling of the domestic's use of house space" (Rollins 1985:171; see also Qayum and Ray 2003). In this chapter, I build on the work of Rollins to show how the spatial deference of domestic workers in the workplace extends to the level of society. Albeit coming from the opposite direction, my analysis converges with the call by social geographer Laura Liu (2000:176) to include "immigration into place-based studies of race." Looking at the case of Chinese migration to the United States, Liu makes the important assertion that immigration policies shape the racial dynamics of place. Conversely, the consideration of place could likewise lead us to a better understanding of immigrant processes and the ways that race and class constitute such processes.

As I show, race and class shape the politics of settlement for migrant Filipina domestic workers and determine their spatial incorporation in the communities of Rome and Los Angeles. More precisely, their limited spatial incorporation in both private and public spaces confirms their subordinate status. As briefly addressed earlier, migrant Filipina domestic workers experience the dislocation of nonbelonging upon settlement, meaning that they experience settlement with a sense of constant discomfort (Parreñas 2001). In this chapter, I give greater emphasis to the spatial dynamics of settlement that characterize nonbelonging in the migrant community. In my discussion, I illustrate how the use of space as a framework for analysis magnifies the significance of race and class inequities in the experience of nonbelonging. As I show in this chapter, nonbelonging results from two distinct sources of social exclusion. For women in Los Angeles, it stems from the class stratification in the Filipino migrant community, and for women in Rome, from the racial prejudice permeating dominant Italian society.

I look at space by addressing two questions. First, how does geographical integration influence and shape feelings of incorporation among migrant Filipina domestic workers? Second, how do the politics of space and spatial movements extend our understanding of migrant settlement? It was in addressing these questions that I identified placelessness to define the spatial integration of migrant Filipina domestics in both public and private spheres, or in other words, in their places of leisure (public) and work (private). By placelessness, I do not mean to imply that these women are nomadic. Instead, I refer to the absence of a fixed geographic space that migrant Filipina domestic workers could call their own. A brief example of what I mean by placelessness, for instance, would be the working-class niches they occupy in Los Angeles. I found that these niches are rarely geographically rooted but instead are often only fleeting encounters in public spaces such as buses.

Experiences of placelessness in dominant spaces of society are generally common among migrants. For instance, scholars have repeatedly shown the formation of geographically based ethnic enclaves as a place-based strategy used by migrants to counter their exclusion from dominant spaces in the host society (Light et al. 1994; Zhou 1992). Yet, the shelter of an enclave has not been made available to migrant Filipina domestic workers in either Los Angeles or Rome because many live with their employers or reside with middle-class members of the Filipino migrant community (Ong and Azores 1994). Thus, migrant Filipina domestic workers, as part of the peripheralized workforce, seldom can retreat from their experiences of placelessness. Inside and outside the workplace, placelessness is how migrant Filipina domestic workers experience place. Three key features illustrate what I mean by their placelessness: (1) the limits of their spatial movements in the workplace; (2) their segregation from the dominant public spaces of Rome and the middle-class-centered Filipino migrant community of Los Angeles; and (3) the containment of the places they can truly call their own to fleeting meetings in public spaces such as buses and public parks.

Looking first at the politics of space in the workplace, the constricted spatial movement of domestic workers in their employer's home is telling of what I mean by placelessness. Employers control the spatial movements of domestic workers when they decide on the domestic's integration into or segregation from the family. More often than not, they prefer segregation because they, according to Julia Wrigley (1995), tend to hire those who will demand very few resources in terms of time, money, space, or interaction. Moreover, as noted earlier, they expect spatial deference from domestics (Rollins 1985). The access of domestic workers to household space is usually far more contained than for the rest of the family. In both Los Angeles and Rome, Filipina domestics, including nannies and eldercare providers, had found themselves subject to food rationing, prevented from sitting on the couch, provided with a separate set of utensils, and told when to get food from the refrigerator and when to retreat to their bedrooms.

With spatial deference so established in domestic work, Filipina domestics are often startled when employers fail to enforce segregation. This is reflected in the pride of one woman in Los Angeles, who boasted that her employers did not insist that she use separate utensils in the household: "Here, they are very nice. In other households, the plates of the maids, and the cups and glasses, are different from the employers. Here, it is not. We use the same utensils and plates. They don't care." Her surprise at her employers' lack of concern over crossing the boundaries of spatial deference is telling of its established pattern in the workplace.

The isolation of live-in employment, I should note, also aggravates the spatial segregation of domestic work. In Los Angeles, most migrant Filipina domestics are live-in workers. In contrast, Latina domestic workers, with the exception of eldercare workers (Ibarra 2002), are concentrated in day work (Hondagneu-Sotelo 2001). The difference between Latinas and Filipinos could be attributed not only to the smaller number of Filipino domestic workers, and therefore their less extensive networks and lesser access to different employment opportunities, but also to the concentration of Filipinos in eldercare, which requires 24 hours of on-call labor.

In Los Angeles, we can assume that the recruitment of nurses from the Philippines has led to the creation of the health industry as an ethnic niche for Filipino migrants. This, in turn, has led to the funneling of health care jobs and information to the community. As a result, migrant Filipinos can be found occupying various jobs in different levels of the health industry: medical doctors, physician's assistants, X-ray technicians in hospitals, registered nurses, licensed vocational nurses, nursing aides, and homecare workers for the elderly (Parreñas 2001). Latina domestic workers also do elderly care work, but they are less concentrated in this type of job (Hondagneu-Sotelo 2001).

In Rome, a larger proportion of Filipina domestic workers are day workers, but a sizable number of women are also live-in workers. According to Caritas Roma, 42.1 percent of Filipinos in Rome live in rented apartments, mostly located in the northern periphery of Rome, and 32.9 percent are live-in domestic workers (Collicelli et al. 1997). Often feeling trapped, live-in domestics cannot help but see the enclosed space of the employer's home as a prison. Maria de la Luz Ibarra (2002) has made a similar observation of Latina domestic workers in California. Counting the moments until their days off is usually part of the everyday routine of live-in work. Moreover, live-in domestics often do not have the freedom to leave their employer's home, for instance, to take a lunch break. Instead, they have to ask permission to do so. By being subject to the close scrutiny of employers, domestic workers are without privacy in the private sphere (Rollins 1985; Yeoh and Huang 1998). Privacy is achieved only in the anonymity of public spaces. Yet, surveillance also takes place in the public spaces occupied by migrant Filipina domestic workers.

Generally, the Filipino migrant community does not offer domestic workers an adequate escape from the sense of placelessness they encounter in the workplace, which is defined by spatial deference and segregation. This is the case in both Rome and Los Angeles. In Los Angeles, domestic workers are without a working-class, geographic niche and consequently experience a state of discomfort in the representative spaces of the Filipino community, which they describe as centered on the middle class. I noticed this in the get-togethers I attended frequently with domestic workers. I found that their physical movements were constrained by an invisible class line that separated them from middle-class members of the community. For example, in one get-together I attended with three women, I noticed that they stayed at the far corner of the room and removed from the rest of the crowd during the entire time we were at a party hosted by their hometown association. Migrant Filipina domestics tend to feel discomfort in the middle-class spaces representing the community, despite the fact that their identity as domestic workers is not physically distinguishable. Avoiding the middle class, however, ensures their anonymity, which, in turn, lessens their feelings of discomfort in the community.

Bringing into question romantic notions of the migrant community is the fact that domestics feel that they do not garner support from their middle-class counterparts. As Cherry Jacinto, a domestic worker in Los Angeles, stated:

> There are people here who I knew in the Philippines. I used to feel terrible that they were treating me differently than how they did in the Philippines. They treat you differently just because you are in this situation. They give you attitude. They act like you are below them, telling you that you are a domestic worker. They are not sensitive and don't remember that you were not like this in the Philippines. They don't treat you the same way....It really registers in my mind....What I want is a little bit of respect. There is nothing like that here.

Though some domestic workers described the community as generally supportive, most felt an absence of camaraderie among Filipino migrants. As have-nots in the community, domestic workers are acutely aware of its class divisions. This awareness engenders their cautious behavior in the community and aggravates their sense of placelessness in the United States.

Unlike their counterparts in Los Angeles, migrant Filipina domestic workers in Italy do not have to contend with class-identity conflicts whenever they leave the confines of the workplace. In Italy, migrant Filipinos are restricted, for the most part, to low-wage service work, particularly as domestic workers for individuals and families. Despite the lack of class stratification in the community, Filipino migrant women in Italy also have to contend with a sense of placelessness whenever outside the workplace. Like their counterparts from Los Angeles, they also behave with caution outside the private sphere. In Italy, migrant Filipina domestic workers have to negotiate with a more xenophobic and less welcoming host society than do their counterparts in the United States. Even though Italy historically sent workers to industrial centers of Northern Europe, the recent wave of immigrants has not resulted in compassionate understanding among Italians (Ancona 1991; Veugelers 1994). Instead, it has led to increasing sentiments of nationalism and xenophobia, as shown, for instance, with the victory of the political party Lega, with its anti-immigration platform, in local elections in the north.

We can visualize the placelessness of migrant Filipina domestics outside the workplace in Rome by looking at the geographical constitution of the community. In Rome, the community is geographically situated in what I refer to as *isolated* pockets of gathering, pockets that are located in both public and private spaces. These pockets include, in the private domain, church centers and apartments and, in the public domain, bus stops and train stations. The term *pockets* aptly describes the community's geographic organization by capturing the following central characteristics: (1) the segregation of the social space of migrant Filipina domestic workers from dominant society and (2) the geographic decentralization of Filipinos into multiple sites in the city of Rome.

Even though these pockets can be described as isolated—for example, those in the public domain are usually located in the periphery of the city and have few pedestrian activities—Italians still resent the visibility of Filipinos, as I personally experienced on occasions when Italians yelled at me to get off public phones. One of these unprovoked racial incidents occurred in the central train station and bus stop of Termini in Rome, but another occurred in a neighborhood in the periphery. My experience is not an exception. Many Italians across class backgrounds make known their resentment of Filipinos' use of public spaces to members of the migrant community. It is a frequent and sore topic of conversation. For instance, members of the community were appalled but not surprised when I shared with them the story of how a middle-aged Italian man in a business suit who had been walking in my direction spat on my face after I failed to move aside. As we passed each other, he claimed that his irritation had forced him to do so. This Italian let me clearly know who was to act with spatial deference in the public spaces of Rome. My story provoked mixed reactions. Some members of the community, citing the expression "When in Rome, do as the Romans do," told me that I should have also spat on his face. However, most said that it was better that I did not react at all to the assault and that I kept my dignity by calmly walking away. For many, my experience raised nationalist sentiments, and my "good behavior" signaled the cultural superiority of Filipinos.

With few exceptions, Filipinos tend not to gather in public spaces inhabited or frequented by Italians. Perhaps they do so to avoid confrontations such as the one I had the misfortune of experiencing. Notably, the central train station of Termini is the only site in the city center where Filipinos impose on the public space of Italians. Yet, on any given day off, the bus stops of Termini are never congested with Filipinos in the morning and afternoon; Filipinos seem to congregate there only in the evening. One can imagine that the women crowding Termini at night are just delaying their return to their employer's home, staying a little bit longer, hoping that they might run into a friend they have not seen in weeks. In general, most women do not spend an extended amount of time in gathering pockets in the public domain such as Termini. These areas are often used as fleeting spaces of encounter. For the most part, Filipino migrant domestic workers spend their days off in the private domain, such as apartments and church centers.

In the public domain, the presence of food vendors essentially establishes particular spaces as official pockets of gathering. Ethnic enclave businesses among Filipinos in Italy are restricted to the informal sector. Food vending is a popular informal business. Vendors, who are mostly women, prepack Filipino meals of rice and meat in individual plastic bags to sell to Filipino domestic workers, usually on the afternoons of their days off, Sunday and Thursday. Using paper plates and plastic utensils provided by the vendors, customers eat their meals sitting or standing around the pocket of gathering. Much monitoring of self and others occurs in these public spaces. For example, rarely do migrants litter, and when they do, they usually get reprimanded by those around them. Migrants also keep an eye out for Italian pedestrians and more so Italian authorities. Vendors carry their goods in duffel bags and are ready to run at the first sight of a law enforcement officer, who could fine them for selling food products in violation of health codes.

Vendors also use the trunks of automobiles. In a pocket of gathering, hidden in cars with slightly opened trunks are industrial-size pots containing a selection of dishes to eat for lunch or dinner. Community members know that cars parked with slightly ajar trunks in a pocket of gathering are likely to be stalls of food vendors. During the time of my interviews, I heard of no other ethnic groups selling prepared food informally in the public spaces of Rome. Polish domestic workers congregated in McDonald's and other fast-food establishments, and Peruvians sometimes patronized the businesses of Filipinos. Rarely, however, did Peruvians and Filipinos socialize with each other.

One public pocket of gathering where Filipino vendors used to sell prepacked foods out of large duffel bags was at the Mancini bus stop. They were forced, however, to relocate as a result of constant harassment by the police, who imposed fines and confiscated all their goods. Notably, the police informed the vendors that complaints from Italian pedestrians forced them to penalize the migrant vendors. The actions of the police and the complaints of Italian pedestrians informed migrant Filipinos that they could not impose on the public domain of Italians. They literally had to find a "hidden space" in a public place, meaning a site that had no felt presence in the public social spaces of Italians. Hence, they eventually moved to a new site in the area, one assuredly not at all imposing because it is located underneath an overpass by the Tiber River. This pocket of gathering is not visible from the street level. Quite an unsanitary location, I was told that this area had been abandoned by Albanian refugees and was filled with garbage and tall weeds when the Filipino migrants took over the space.

This "public domain" has since been cleared, though it remains unpaved, and now houses 15 informal business enterprises of eating places, food stores, tailoring shops, and hair salons. These informal businesses are set up in wooden stands along the two structures of the overpass. There is no running water. In the evening, the stoves and portable gas tanks, the sewing machines, and the goods of the food stores are stored in padlocked wooden cabinets built at the premises. Mancini is a one-stop shopping bazaar. Hundreds of Filipinos patronize these businesses every day. This place of gathering under the bridge has given Filipino migrants in Rome a haven from the "public domain" in the public domain. Nonetheless, their very presence under the bridge serves as a reminder that they do not belong in the public social space of Italian society.

Another example of a working-class haven created by migrant Filipina domestic workers is the church center, frequently used as an alternative space to conduct petty retail trade. Filipinos are often uncomfortable in businesses patronized by Italians. To negotiate their placelessness in various public retail venues, they make do with the informal businesses available in various gathering places in the community. Church centers are popular sites for informal, small-scale business activities. This is illustrated by an observation I recorded in my field notes:

> In one church center, I notice that for a span of two hours I had been approached by at least 10 individuals soliciting various commodities. I was given catalogs of Amway and Avon. I was asked to look at a bag of sweaters, which are consigned by a domestic worker for her employer, who owns a boutique. I was approached by a woman about shoes and bags that she sells and orders from a manufacturer in Napoli. A man inquired if I was interested in purchasing bootleg tapes that he had recorded from compact discs....The selection of music ranges from artists such as Air Supply and Whitney Houston to Filipino artists such as April Boys.

Clearly, the church is not just a place of spiritual guidance for migrant Filipina domestic workers. They also use churches to counter their placelessness. However, although a place of gathering, church centers are not truly spaces that migrant Filipina domestic workers can call their own. The use of these places is restricted to limited hours and days. Also, clergy monitor the behavior and attire of domestic workers in these centers. For instance, members of the clergy impose a dress code and literally force out those who they think are dressed inappropriately, such as those wearing miniskirts. "Ill behavior" is also frowned upon. For instance, domestics cannot smoke in these centers. Self-monitoring similar to the kind that takes place in the public domain (for instance, the avoidance of space used by Italians) often occurs at church centers, which domestics tend to leave an hour or two after Sunday morning services.

The geographic formation of the Filipino migrant community into pockets such as the place under the bridge in Mancini shows the segregation of Filipinos from dominant society. On the one hand, these spaces ease the process of settlement, providing migrants with a space of retreat. On the other hand, the formation of these pockets reveals the extension of the spatial deference of migrant Filipina domestics from the private domain of the workplace to the public domain of larger society. The working-class havens of migrant Filipina domestics are hardly ever geographically fixed spaces; they are often passing encounters in buses or on sidewalks. Further, geographically fixed havens such as church centers must be shared and place restrictions on behavior and time of use.

The placelessness of migrant Filipina domestic workers in Rome often translates to their feeling of nonbelonging in Italy. Consequently, many perceive themselves as "guests" in Italy because their citizenship is limited to the status of temporary worker. They view themselves as fortunate guests graciously allowed by the state the privilege of earning the greater income its economy can offer, and they foresee an inevitable termination of their permit to stay—when society no longer needs their labor. They often prepare for the possibility of their mass deportation, a sort of doomsday scenario for temporary workers. The domestic worker Luisa Balila described her readiness for this possibility: "If they send all of us strangers [foreigners] away from Italy, even though my husband and I don't have much money, we have a house [made up of four apartments] that we can go home to....I want to be able to have a consistent income if we decide to go back to the Philippines. We can rent the apartments out."

As illustrated above, the migrant community in Rome centers on the working class—unlike the class-stratified community in Los Angeles. The class-stratified migrant community of Los Angeles does not offer domestic workers a shelter from the private domain of their employer's home, but neither do the working-class niches of Rome. For instance, as illustrated by their eviction from the bus stop to the place under the bridge, the criminalization of their community uproots them, and as illustrated by my experience at public phones, the resentment of Italians establishes the outsider status of Filipinos in Italy.

Interestingly, migrant domestic workers in Los Angeles, like their counterparts in Rome, also form working-class havens. In Los Angeles, I found equivalent pockets of gathering in retirement villages. Usually, domestics met during their employers' nap times. Jovita Gacutan described one such subcommunity of domestics:

> I was able to form a group. We helped each other out....We would always be in my room, which was informally referred to as the Filipino Center in the village. We gave each other moral support. It was because we were all just starting over in this country, and that is why it was in all of us to help each other out.

In other retirement villages, Filipina domestic workers would meet in front of an employer's apartment or house. They had to meet outside because most employers would not tolerate domestics entertaining visitors in their home.

On their days off, Filipina domestics usually leave the subcommunity of domestic workers or the isolation of their employer's home for other subcommunities of Filipinos. The subcommunities they enter as weekend visitors are usually rendered middle-class spaces by the spatial configuration of the community. Occasionally, they are able to form a subcommunity among themselves outside work. An example would be apartments in downtown Los Angeles, where they would congregate on Sundays with domestics whom they had met on a bus or at work. The women with whom I spoke were most comfortable in these place-bound spaces. This was also the case in Rome. However, such private spaces, especially in Los Angeles, were rarely available to them. Family obligations usually took them to the more common, middle-class-centered spaces of the community.

The rarity of meeting other Filipina domestic workers explains why they take advantage of meetings in public spaces. They make public spaces sites for building race and class solidarity. For instance, they use buses as sites for garnering information and resources they need in order to have greater control of their labor. As described by Mila Tizon of Los Angeles:

> Most of the people that I ride the bus with every morning are domestic workers. There are many of us [Filipinos]. There we compare our salaries to know the going rate. We also ask each

other for possible job referrals. We often exchange phone numbers and contact each other.

Public spaces such as parks and buses are where Filipina domestics in Los
Angeles, like Filipina domestics in Rome, forge a consciousness of a collective struggle from their shared experience of marginality in the
employer's home, as well as in the middle-class spaces of the community.
This is where they establish standards of wages and evaluate the fairness of
their working conditions. However, these encounters occur fleetingly and
not in permanent spaces that migrants can call their own.

Notably, these fleeting encounters do not extend to spark interracial
solidarity with others in the margins, for instance, Latinas in Rome and Los
Angeles, with whom they also cross paths on buses and in parks. This tells
us that we cannot assume interracial alliances even among those who share
an economically subordinate status. Language difficulties pose a barrier,
but more significantly, perceived cultural differences discouraged the
Filipino domestic workers I met from reaching out to Latinas they encountered in public spaces. Still, it should be emphasized that migrant Filipina
domestic workers do attempt to counteract and appease their feelings of
nonbelonging with others like them. For instance, as noted earlier, they
create alternative spaces to counter their placelessness in the workplace
and migrant community. However, these spaces do not sufficiently counteract their sense of placelessness in the host society. As noted above, these
places are generally not geographically fixed spaces. Spurred by their
placelessness, migrant Filipina domestic workers resolve the discomfort of
community life by stressing their temporary membership in the host society. I found this to be true even if women qualified for permanent residency in the host society, as was the case with those in Los Angeles.

CONCLUSION

As sojourners, the settlement of migrant Filipina domestics differs
sharply from that of most other immigrant women in the global North.
Spatially displaced by race and class, they are often without a geographically rooted space to call their own. This displacement metaphorically represents their stunted integration into the two host societies I examined. It
also literally tells us that factors besides gender determine migrant
women's settlement. My observations support the call of sociologist Cecilia
Menjivar (2003) not to reduce our understanding of women's settlement
patterns to gender.

Overall, my study suggests that the spatial integration of migrants is an important feature of the context of reception that defines their sense of membership in the immigrant community. This observation has been repeatedly made of male labor migrants but not so much of women.[17] Moreover, it stresses the centrality of race and class in understanding migrant settlement, not just for men but also for women. As I have illustrated, race and class inequities push the desire to maintain ties to the homeland. However, the higher earnings and, accordingly, the gender and economic gains these earnings afford migrant Filipina domestic workers keep them transplanted in the host society.

By underscoring the intersections of race, class, and gender in migrant women's settlement patterns, this study suggests the need to revisit gender analysis of settlement in migration studies and utilize more complex constructions of gender in our study of women's migration. Other gender and migration scholars agree. For instance, Jennifer Hirsch (2003) similarly questions modernization theories of gender and migration by showing in her seminal study of sexuality in a Mexican transnational migrant community that Mexican transnational families experience gender transformations not only after migration but also across generations in Mexico. Evelyn Nakano Glenn (1986), although not looking at settlement patterns per se, describes Japanese women's migration as both gender liberating and debilitating. More recently, anthropologist Patricia Pessar (1999), in an important overview of the state of the literature on gender and migration, warns scholars not to lose sight of the fact that, despite patterns of gender emancipation, patriarchy is not eliminated but instead is somehow retained in the process of migration. I hope that more gender and migration scholars take heed of Pessar's warning and, in so doing, also note feminist historian Joan Scott's (1992) perceptive comment that although gender relations are a reflection of power relations, the dynamics of power are not always literally about gender.

About the Author

Rhacel Salazar Parreñas is professor of Asian American studies and the Graduate Group of Sociology at the University of California, Davis. She is the author of *Servants of Globalization: Women, Migration and Domestic Work* and *Children of Global Migration: Transnational Families and Gendered Woes*. She is currently doing research on migrant Filipina entertainers in Tokyo's nightlife industry.

Notes

1. This figure is based on records of the Philippine Overseas Employment Administration.

2. Destinations of Filipino migrants include territories of various countries, such as the Pacific island territories of the United States, British territories in the Caribbean, and Hong Kong.

3. I would like to acknowledge Nandini Gunewardena and Ann Kingsolver for their editorial comments, as well as Louise Lamphere, Lynn Bolles, Sandy Morgen, Faye Harrison, and Karen Brodkin for the advice I received for improving this chapter. This chapter revisits my previous discussions on the community life of migrant Filipina domestic workers in *Servants of Globalization: Women, Migration and Domestic Work* (Stanford 2005) and in the essay "The Placelessness of Migrant Filipina Domestic Workers," presented at the workshop "Space and Identity: Concepts of Immigration and Integration in Urban Areas" on May 16–17, 2005, at the Woodrow Wilson International Center for Scholars, Washington DC. Support from the Institute for Gender Studies at Ochanomizu University in Tokyo, Japan, allowed me to complete this chapter.

4. See Bakan and Stasiulis 1997 and Castles and Miller 2003 for a discussion of different migratory regimes in globalization.

5. Steven Gold (2003) observes this not to be true for highly skilled male migrants, such as those from Israel, because they achieve greater opportunities for mobility in the US labor market.

6. This is despite the urging of migration scholar Floya Anthias for the need to develop a more complex understanding of the social status of migrant women. As Anthias states, "the multi-faceted and complex nature of women's position does not permit us to see migration in simple terms as either leading always to a loss, or always to a gain, in social status" (Anthias 2000:36). I would also add that women's preference for permanent settlement could also be caused not so much by the reconstitution of gender but instead by the maintenance of "gendered female responsibilities" such as the care of children. Women opt to stay in the host society to secure greater mobility options for their children.

7. In the case of Dominicans, Guarnizo (1997) observed that men send wives back to sending nations to reinstate the "separate spheres" dichotomy in the family. This observation implies the stronghold of patriarchy in some migrant households.

8. For instance, a recent government survey found that between April and September 2002, overseas Filipino workers remitted more than US$1.2 billion dollars to households in the Philippines (Opiniano 2002). Much of this remittance came from the wages of women. Even though the amount of men's remittances outnumbered that of women at a ratio of 2:1, men did not necessarily remit a greater portion of their earnings than did women. Instead, the greater amount of men's remittances was most likely due to their higher average income earnings (Parreñas 2005).

9. For instance, women in the Philippines suffer from a severe wage gap. They earn disproportionately less than men in all sectors of the labor market. A 1995 study reported that for every peso a man made, women earned only 36 centavos in

agriculture, 35 centavos in sales work, 41 centavos in production, and 46 centavos in professional and technical occupations (National Commission for the Role of Filipino Women 1995:172).

10. Following this logic, migration scholars seem to equate women's South to North migration with emancipation on the basis of women's greater access to wage employment in the North (Hondagneu-Sotelo 1994). Although careful to contend that migration emancipates women because of "structural rearrangements" in the household (for example, men and women's equal income contributions) and not feminist ideology per se, scholars—in asserting that gender liberation spurs permanent migration—imply that the gains caused by "structural rearrangements" would somehow disappear upon the return migration of women to the "traditional" sending country.

11. Defining modernization theory, gender scholar of the Middle East Deniz Kandiyoti states: "Modernization theory presupposed a movement from tradition to modernity affecting facets of social life. Disparities in gender relations within the family and society at large could henceforth be explained in terms of relative degrees of modernization" (Kandiyoti 1996:10).

12. Hirsch (2003) insists that class also determines Mexican women's migrant settlement patterns. In her seminal study on the changing contours of sexuality in a Mexican transnational community, Hirsch (2003) points out that class could also deter women's migration. Hirsch observed that not all women wished to leave their rural community in Mexico and join husbands in the North. The material benefits they incur from remittances discourage their migration. This was particularly true for those with a high social status in their hometown, which they were unlikely to wish to trade for the "anonymity and marginality" (Hirsch 2003:182) likely to welcome them in the United States.

13. The number dipped to 12,000 in 2003.

14. The 16 women who reported their status as undocumented were eligible to obtain a permit to stay under the 1995 legislative decree. Because the decree had been in progress during my research, I can safely assume that most of these women are now official guest workers in Italy.

15. See chapter 7 of Parreñas (2005) for a more extensive discussion of loopholes in family reunification policies in the United States.

16. I use de Certeau's (1984:117) notion of space: "Space is a practiced place." Social inequalities manifest in spatial actions.

17. The low status of immigrant men in the labor market is often used to explain their preference for return migration. Singer and Gilbertson (2003), for instance, describe men's low social status as engendering feelings of temporary membership in the host society. As they note, immigrant men's

incorporation in low-status service and factory occupations, restricted spatial movements, and their racialization also shape their experiences. In seeking release from the conditions of their "immigrant" lives in the United States, most men engage in some sort of imagining, planning and investing in a future...in the Dominican Republic through entrepreneurial activities. [Singer and Gilbertson 2003:374]

Notably, this statement also aptly describes the abject experiences of migrant Filipina domestic workers, but, for the most part, the literature has not described the racialization of immigrant women (with the exception of Chang 2000 and Sassen 2003).

10

Sticking to the Union

Anthropologists and "Union Maids" in San Francisco

Sandy Smith-Nonini

> This union maid was wise to the tricks of the company spies.
> She couldn't be fooled by the company's stools.
> She'd always organize...
> We modern union maids are also not afraid
> To walk the line, leave jobs behind,
> We're not just the ladies' aide,
> We'll fight for equal pay, and we will get our way.
> We're workers too, the same as you,
> and we'll fight the union way.
>
> —*from* "Union Maids" *by Woody Guthrie*

Throughout the economic boom of the 1990s, waves of immigrants from Mexico and Central America provided cheap labor for American industries, allowing them to undertake profitable expansions and restructure in the pursuit of maximizing production. Today Spanish-speaking women make up a majority of employees in many workplaces, from chicken-processing and packaging lines to the cleaning staffs of office buildings.

Service sector jobs have been a key growth sector in this postmodern economy, a development driven by several trends, including free trade agreements and altered business practices such as layoffs and outsourcing. Although some well-paid professional jobs are classified as services, most of the growth has been in low-end jobs, disproportionately held by women and minorities. Many are destandardized jobs, notorious for irregular hours, low pay, poor benefits, and abusive conditions. For years, traditional trade unions wrote off service occupations as too difficult to organize because of the fragmented work sites, high worker turnover, and large numbers of immigrants in the workforces. But in the past ten years, several unions, most notably the Service Employees International Union (SEIU) and the Hotel Employees and Restaurant Employees International (HERE), have bucked the odds, developing innovative strategies and diverting enormous resources into organizing workers such as grocery store clerks, janitors, and hotel and restaurant employees.

The convergence of immigration and economic globalization has also been a growth industry for scholars. Anthropologists, like me, who frequently study marginalized populations have often found themselves confronted with the rapid and profound social upheavals resulting from neoliberal policies. Yet writing about injustice is as far as many anthropologists go; seldom do we find ourselves in a position to catalyze social change.

That changed in October 2004, when roughly 6,000 members of the American Anthropological Association (AAA) were finalizing travel plans for attending the AAA annual meeting to be held at the San Francisco Hilton in mid-November. Unbeknownst to most, on September 29 contract renewal negotiations had broken down between a consortium of 14 luxury hotels, known as the San Francisco Multi-Employer Group (MEG), and Local 2 of UNITE-HERE, a giant service workers union formed by the recent merger of HERE with UNITE, a union that had specialized in the garment and textile trades. The deadlock over health care premiums, pensions, wage increases, and contract length led the union to call a two-week strike involving 85 percent of the employees at the major downtown hotels. The strike effectively shut down the city center for tourism and conventions. Within days after the strike began, the hotels in the MEG retaliated; corporate owners locked out more than 4,000 striking workers and began to hire non-union replacements. Angry workers set up picket lines, and the two sides squared off in what promised to be a serious dispute—given that San Francisco has the highest density of unionized hotel workers in the country.

When word got out about the lockout, hundreds of anthropologists refused to cross the picket lines, prompting the AAA board to belatedly change the meeting venue to a non-unionized, Atlanta-based hotel; this hotel, also owned by Hilton, was chosen in a compromise intended to save the AAA from a lawsuit by the hotel chain. Some anthropologists cheered the move because it moved the convention out of San Francisco, but others viewed the trading of an organized hotel for a non-union facility as a sellout. Most of the scholars were inconvenienced, and many lost travel funds. The problems led to a failed annual meeting and an unprecedented debate about the politics of labor within the organization. As 2004 secretary for the Society for the Anthropology of Work, I played a role in advocacy on behalf of labor among AAA members, and I draw on that experience in this chapter, as well as on interviews with hotel workers and union organizers on the picket line in San Francisco and reviews of the literature on service work, gender, and union organizing.

As it happened, the costly and inconvenient last-minute move of the convention initiated a new round of pressure on Hilton negotiators from municipal authorities and helped to end the lockout of workers. The story provides a rare opportunity to examine the impacts of neoliberal restructuring on this predominantly female and foreign-born workforce and to discuss the potential for concrete forms of solidarity between organized academics and a restructured labor movement that is slowly reasserting the primacy of human dignity over profit.

THE TRANSNATIONAL GENDERING OF SERVICE WORK

In the aftermath of the civil rights and feminist movements and after nearly three decades of affirmative action, it is shocking to confront the levels of gender and ethnic segregation that restructured corporate workplaces have produced. The luxury hotel industry is a poster child for the modern patriarchy and apartheid that managers call high productivity. A survey of San Francisco housekeepers in luxury hotels found that 99 percent of room cleaners were women and 96 percent were born outside the United States.

The service economy, which now accounts for a shocking two-thirds of jobs in industrialized countries, in many ways reflects the disparities of wealth in society at large, with high-end and low-end jobs and sharp levels of polarization between those extremes, compared with other job categories (Gray 2004). Changes in women's roles are present at both ends of these extremes. It was a surge of dual-career families, plus hikes in disposable income among upper-income sectors, that helped fuel demand for maids, high-quality ethnic restaurants, and luxury hotel rooms.

At the same time, Mexico's cuts in rural farm subsidies and neoliberal policies such as the North American Free Trade Agreement (NAFTA) have boosted flows of economic migrants from Mexico into the US workforce. The withdrawal of welfare and other social subsidies on the part of the US state have also led to an increase in poor single mothers entering the labor market.[1] Both immigrants and poor women are drawn to low-end service jobs because of their low educational requirements. The hospitality industry has more former welfare participants than any other industry and is one of the largest employers of single mothers (Gray 2004).

Tam (1997) argues that predominantly female jobs pay less because they require lower levels of education and skill, but England, Hermsen, and Cotter (2000) show that cultural devaluation of women's labor also plays a role. They argue that even when jobs are created or restructured outside market forces, managers show a gender bias by tending to assign a low value to types of jobs associated with women, a tendency that reflects the relatively low value assigned to women in the culture. Likewise, Tronto (1989) suggests that Western capitalist society devalues work that involves caring for others (a characteristic of many service occupations) because it is associated with people in a dependent or subordinate position.

Salzinger (2004:1) argues convincingly that global restructuring in the neoliberal model amounts to a "gendered process" because in transnational production "the creation and allocation of labor power is organized around and in terms of tropes of gendered personhood." For example, studies of maquiladoras in the border area show that many employers demonstrate a preference for females, citing their purported higher productivity due to manual dexterity (and some would say more docile reactions to male authority). In contrast, demographic studies show the opposite trend for farmworkers, with growers involved in the H2A "guestworker" program, as well as large non-H2A growers, now mostly hiring newly immigrated males traveling alone, instead of family groups, as in the past, who required more elaborate housing and sought longer-term relationships with growers (Smith-Nonini 2004). Again, it is hard to escape the conclusion that productivity has become the primary criterion shaping job opportunities. Further, given the low wages paid in these settings, such practices lead to fragmented family relationships and a de facto policy of wealth extraction that leaves the costs of social reproduction to impoverished workers in Mexico (Gledhill 1998) and in Spanish-speaking enclaves in the United States—policies that translate into real human suffering and into social costs that are ultimately paid by local communities (Katz 2003).

Huffman (2004) found that gender segregation also functions within a local market. His study of how gender wage inequality varies as a function of a job's ranking in a specific local labor market revealed that female-dominated jobs pay less than comparable male-dominated jobs and that the wage penalty associated with female-dominated jobs is steeper for women than for men in the same jobs.

The above effects on women and minorities are exacerbated by the impacts on the wider working class, which has seen drops in purchasing power of up to 10 percent over the past 30 years, cuts in health coverage, and a widening wealth gap (Ferguson 2005). One study found, for instance, that 62 percent of jobs in the service sector did not even pay workers a living wage (Brocht 2000).

Racial and ethnic differences may actually diminish the visibilities of this increasing poverty from the middle-class perspective. In Karen Sacks' classic study of union organizing at Duke University medical center in the 1970s, she found that poor treatment of workers in low-end jobs was reinforced by Southern paternalism in which "racial differences sharpened, and were often the idiom for expressing class differences" (Sacks 1988:38). More recently, media coverage of Hurricane Katrina showed, to the public at large, the stark racial segregation accompanying poverty in New Orleans and the neglect of this population's needs on the part of authorities.

The growing wealth disparities and newly ascendant forms of ethnic domination (for example, tensions between new immigrants and disenfranchised white workers) have been dubbed "third-worlding" by Kristin Koptiuch to draw attention to the ways in which "exploitative incorporation and hegemonic domination—and its fierce contestation by subjugated peoples—that used to take place at a safe, reassuring distance" (Koptiuch 1997:236) is increasingly a reality here at home. As part of this process, in the competition for "low-end" service jobs, African Americans lose out to more "docile" immigrants, legal immigrants lose out to undocumented ones, men lose out to women, and otherness becomes "reconfigured" through "subtly revised normalizing strategies that mobilize social and cultural difference" (Koptiuch 1997:243), which Koptiuch labels a "neoterritory." This helps explain the labor segregation that Gray (2004) describes in hotels and restaurants, where surveys routinely show a predominance of blacks, Latinos, and women in the undercompensated, high-workload "back of the house" jobs and a predominance of white men (and some white women) in the more sought-after "front" jobs, which involve interaction with customers and result in high tips and more humane working conditions.

MAGICAL REALISM AT THE HILTON: SPA FUSION FANTASIES AND PLANTATION LABOR

Features that distinguish a luxury hotel from a one- or two-star outfit include special amenities such as ballrooms, pools, health clubs, and multiple dining options. For example, the San Francisco Hilton has a health club and something called "Spa Fusion," described on its website as

a 13,000 square foot sanctuary of peace and serenity offering over 47...treatments that blend Eastern healing traditions with

> Western discoveries. Indulge yourself with that special someone
> in the couple's room where side-by-side massages end with a soak
> in a private whirlpool tub for 2. If exercise is your stress reducer
> of choice, check out our health club's full array of equipment
> including cardio-theater aerobic machines and free weights; or
> swim in our heated outdoor pool on the beautiful lanai deck.
> [Hilton Hotels 2005]

It is a fantasy of a simpler life, of voluntary, athletic sweat, of the outdoors—
the things that urban industrialism, including palaces of global tourism
like this one, have helped to make scarce. And beneath that, a personal
fantasy of wealth and specialness that, for many, butts up against American
values of hard work and self-reliance. Writers of ads for luxury goods are
taught to remind clients that they "deserve it," to help overcome our reluctance to indulge.

But around the corner, in the alcove disguised by the potted plant, is
another reality. I imagine that other academics have had the same jarring
experience I had at a recent conference. Attempting a shortcut between
banquet halls, I turned off the richly carpeted promenade, pushed open
the "employees only" doors, and found myself in a suddenly mundane
maze of fluorescent-lit linoleum hallways, lined by cleaning carts and
locker rooms. Only yards away from the gold leaf chandeliers were boisterous kitchens bustling with black and Latino men and women scraping
plates, slicing cheese, and otherwise catering to the guests' needs, imagined and otherwise.

Newspaper reporter Kitty Bean Yancy dipped into this other reality when
she spent a day accompanying a non-unionized housekeeper, Gladis Lee, on
her daily rounds at a 217-room hotel in Annapolis, Maryland. From 8 a.m. to
4 p.m., with a novice worker in tow and Yancy alongside taking notes, the tidy
and efficient Honduran native kept up a nonstop pace squaring off heavy
mattresses and polishing faucets. Yancy wrote:

> A room typically takes half an hour to clean—15 minutes for the
> bedroom, 15 in the bath. It's not as simple as cleaning a house.
> All is prescribed, down to adorning extra rolls of toilet tissue
> with decorative paper bands. A card under the bed boasts: "Yes,
> we've looked under here, too." Grabbing antibacterial cleanser,
> Lee wipes down almost every exposed hard surface—even the
> arms on the desk chair. In the bathroom she scrubs tiles, tub and
> toilet and washes the marble floor on hands and knees....She
> answers questions while in constant motion. [Yancy 2005:1 D]

Lee took only a half hour for lunch and one 15-minute break. At the end of the day she had cleaned all or a portion of 17 hotel rooms. Her pay: $9.75 an hour with no tips. Starting maids earned $7. Divorced, Lee lived with her two school-age daughters and her mother; she spent $500 of her $1,300 monthly salary on rent, an expense that would be far higher near a city like San Francisco. Although the work is exhausting, after 16 years on the job, Lee was happy to have health insurance, sick leave, and vacation time, all benefits that many non-union hotel maids go without. But she acknowledged that the work exhausted her. "I'm tired. Having less rooms to do would be nicer," she told Yancy (2005:1d) at the end of her day.

As Ferguson (2005) notes, unlike manufacturing or telephone call center jobs, most service jobs are resistant to outsourcing. Neither can they be easily replaced by technology—no machine can change a bed or clean a bathtub as well as a human being can. But the working conditions in many corporate service industries are not too far removed from foreign sweatshops or our own half-remembered union-busting past.

Food preparers and servers still make up one-quarter of hotel workers, and housekeepers and cleaners another quarter. The amount of work each worker is asked to do has increased, as has the number of jobs workers are expected to perform. In addition, hours are less certain—workers are now routinely asked to be "on call," which means accepting hours that vary with occupancy rates or event schedules—some weeks with too few hours, others with forced overtime (Ferguson 2005). Likewise, in the past 20 years, establishments have steadily phased out full-time jobs in favor of part-time ones, often with poor or no benefits. The large supply of recent immigrants with low levels of education and few alternative job options in many areas means that employers have few worries about recruitment.

The traditional explanation given by companies for low wages and benefits is competitive pressure, but as Gray (2004) argues, competition does not always explain low wages. Bernhardt (2001) found that hotel workers' wages were stagnant in the 1970s and 1980s, as was productivity, but that when the latter rebounded in the 1990s, wages did not. In 1999 the average wage was only $7.50, yet from 1990 to 1995 productivity grew 12 times faster than wages.

Thus, Gray (2004) argues, it is more accurate to see these jobs as part of a socially structured market. To generate revenue, many hotel firms have opted for consolidation, and others have sold shares and become publicly owned, a change that has led to further emphasis on the bottom line and short-term returns. By the late 1990s, the four largest hotel chains accounted for one-fifth of sales, and the largest 50 accounted for almost half the market, setting them up to dictate industry standards. Surprisingly, large hotel chains, some with profits that exceed 20 percent of revenues, often pay their cleaning and restaurant staffs the least (Ferguson 2005).

Studies have shown that managers play an important role in shaping low-wage service job markets by actively choosing the niche markets in which their company is going to compete and by designing ways to remain "flexible" in response to changes in the market (Ferguson 2005). For major hotel chains like Hilton, management consulting companies are often brought in for advice on this "science" of maximizing productivity. Ads for these services carefully avoid direct reference to sensitive issues such as breaking down room cleaning into minutely timed microtasks that cleaners are expected to master. Euphemisms are preferred. The website for one such firm puts it this way:

> Worldwide hospitality assets represent trillions of dollars in invested capital. This capital frequently fails to deliver financial returns which are commensurate with the operating risks entailed in this hybrid asset type. [We are] engaged at strategic or practical levels to review, suggest, and implement frameworks for value creation or problem correction. It is [our] intent to add value in most instances through direct management of the assignment...co-operating consultants [are] available to [take] charge of tasks...ensuring their timely accomplishment. [Straightline Advisors 2005]

Some large firms now subcontract out aspects of food preparation and laundry. Increasingly, the low wages of subcontractor firms such as Aramark and "temp" agencies cheapen the work of staff employees, constantly lowering the bar for wages and setting higher productivity standards against which full-time staff are expected to compete.

UNIONS AND SERVICE WORKERS

Gray (2004) stresses the importance of drawing on labor history in interpreting the present. Scholars who talk about low-paying jobs as inevitable, or as a natural outcome of the market, ignore the key role that unions played in regulating the market during the post–World War II era, when the union movement helped to turn formerly low-end manufacturing jobs into "good jobs." It was the organized workforce, Gray notes, that required employers to share the profits from increased productivity with workers, an effect that impacted wages even in non-unionized plants as employers tried to make unions less attractive to workers.

By this reckoning, one could say that the low wages characteristic of service jobs in the United States are not a situation inherent to this sector of the economy, but rather a consequence of the low level of institutionalization—referring both to low levels of unionization and to low levels of state oversight or intervention—compared with other labor sectors. Lack of regulation, for example, allows hotels and restaurants to outsource more jobs and to intensify workloads for the work that remains "in house."

Hotel workers do much better when unionized, earning a third more than unorganized workers and achieving better working conditions (for example, lower quotas of rooms to be cleaned in a day; Turner 2001). Hotels in cities with substantial tourism tend to be favorable sites for union organizing. Unlike manufacturing, tourism is a local affair. At least workers know that the hotel is going to stay put and will not relocate to Mexico or China, as do assembly plants (Gray 2004). UNITE-HERE has found that its locals more effectively achieve their goals in labor markets such as San Francisco, New York City, and Las Vegas, which have a high density of unionized low-wage occupations.

Clearly, in advocating on behalf of urban hotel and restaurant workers, UNITE-HERE, which represents 440,000 service workers (including 50,000 hotel workers), has gone to bat for one of the most vulnerable employment sectors in the country. The union's Local 2 in San Francisco represents cooks, room cleaners, bartenders, bellmen, food and beverage servers, housemen, and dishwashers.

In the fall of 2004 as the lockout dragged on, many workers missed rent and mortgage payments and had to take out loans, despite receiving strike pay of $200 a week and $50 in food aid. In comments posted on the union's website (www.unitehere.org/), striking workers often spoke of family concerns. Bertha Lujano, an employee of the Sheraton Grand Hotel in Sacramento, wrote, "I have 2 girls and I'm single mother. I'm Mexican and I am looking for better future for my girls."

Access to health care was in the forefront of strikers' concerns. For Aurolyn Rush, a PBX operator for the Grand Hyatt, San Francisco, a new union agreement meant that a recent personal health crisis did not become a financial crisis: "I was diagnosed with cancer in 1996, six months after I started my job, and I had a reoccurrence last year. If the hotel's current proposal had been in effect, I would not have gotten the care I need. We need a two-year contract so we can engage the employers in a national dialogue to address the issue of rising health care costs." Rush was referring to the local's demand for a two-year contract, from 2004 to 2006, so that contracts for locals in three cities would come up for negotiation at the same time. This would give the union more leverage by allowing it to coordinate work actions for members in all three locations. This demand was a key sticking point in the San Francisco negotiations.

Morena Hernandez, a union member and housekeeper at the Hyatt West Hollywood, spoke of increased work intensity: "I currently clean 16 rooms. Management does not take into consideration the work housekeepers like myself do at the hotel. Many of us often skip our lunch break to finish the work on time."

According to Hartmann, Allen, and Owens (1999), organizing in the service sector tends to benefit women and ethnic minorities disproportionately. Turner (2001) found the union pay advantage to average 38 percent for women, 43 percent for blacks, and 52 percent for Latinos. Thus, a union can play an active role in dismantling the gendered structure of wage labor in services (Gray 2004). Unions can also regulate ethnic segregation. For example, Local 2 is advocating for the legal rights of immigrants and for hiring of more black workers, who today represent only 5 percent of the MEG workforce.

The key to this capacity is UNITE-HERE's success at organizing more than 80 percent of the luxury hotel workforce in Las Vegas, San Francisco, Atlantic City, Chicago, and New York City (Bernhardt, Dresser, and Hatton 2002). This high density of union presence in the market niche "takes wages out of competition" and enhances prospects for union negotiators to influence other aspects of how jobs are structured (Gray 2004). UNITE-HERE has waged these battles using a strategy described by Wial (1993) as "geographic/occupational unionism" (instead of worksite-specific strategies). That is, the union focuses on the types of service work in which workers tend to commit to an occupation in a given geographical area but do not have their job options restricted to a specific workplace.

The strategies applied by UNITE-HERE in San Francisco owe much to the union's Hospitality Industry president John Wilhelm, who led HERE during the 1990s, a period when the union grew by more than 15 percent to more than 275,000 members. Wilhelm speaks of organizing as the union's chief priority and the key to labor's survival in a country where union membership today has sunk to less than 10 percent of private employees. HERE's focus on immigrants represented a new attitude toward immigrants from organized labor, which used to regard illegal immigrants as a threat to American jobs. Today immigrants make up the core of labor's growth segment. Wilhelm's greatest successes in transforming HERE took place in Las Vegas, where the union organized a six-year strike at the Frontier Hotel and Casino and a massive public drive for union recognition before the opening of the MGM Grand, which combined loud demonstrations with aggressive, behind-the-scenes pressure from a well-thought-out corporate campaign (Whitford 2001).

Chandler (2003) studied the experiences of Mexican and Central American women immigrants who found employment in Nevada casinos and became members of HERE. She concluded that the women's experiences advocating for their labor rights through the union had boosted their sense of agency. She documented a transition from their earlier feelings of hopelessness and despair to a sense of personal and collective political power. The union now runs a training academy for hotel and restaurant workers in Las Vegas, which allows it to play a role in controlling quality of work. Through an agreement with local hotels, members who graduate are guaranteed jobs. Unlike some unions, both HERE and UNITE had organized high proportions of women and minority members, reflecting the demographics of the workplaces they represented. The merged union's entire Las Vegas staff now comes out of the rank-and-file membership, according to Neal Kwatra (personal communication, 2004), an organizer in UNITE-HERE's strategic affairs division.

Such a commitment to organizing is not found in most unions, nor even in all locals of the reformed union. In a qualitative survey of 14 regional locals of three unions in northern California, Voss and Sherman (2001) gave high grades to two HERE locals and three SEIU locals for having "revitalized" their locals and placed new resources and priorities on organizing. Interestingly, they found that factors favoring revitalization included a local crisis in leadership, having leaders with previous social movement experience, and support or guidance from the international union. They also found worker-centered approaches, especially educational activities, to be key components of revitalization. Other key factors were strong corporate campaigns, which entail strategies that address the economic ties of employers, and alliances with non-union organizations that provide solidarity and support to union members, not unlike the consumer and church–worker alliances that helped build the United Farm Workers in decades past. Both Wilhelm and UNITE-HERE's president, Bruce Raynor (former president of UNITE), have worked with other movements, and both have long experience with corporate campaigns. The internationals they lead commit a far higher portion of union dues to organizing than do other unions. Organizing now accounts for close to 40 percent of the budgets for service worker unions.

Revitalization is also changing the political landscape of the US labor movement. UNITE had previously stood in solidarity with HERE during the Las Vegas strikes. The merger of the two unions in mid-2004 grew out of their work together the preceding fall on behalf of 4,000 workers who won a strike at Yale University and their collaboration in the Immigrant Workers Freedom Ride to Washington DC. In June 2005, UNITE-HERE joined SEIU, the Teamsters, United Food and Commercial Workers, and the Laborers in a historic split with the AFL-CIO. Leadership of the new "United to Win" coalition formed by the dissident unions criticized the labor federation's leader, John Sweeney, for failing to put enough resources into organizing campaigns. Many hope that these seismic shifts in labor may hold the key to changing US electoral politics. According to Kwatra, "it goes way beyond any individual contract. Growth is what it is about." The outcome of this effort, and its effects on labor's leverage within the Democratic Party, will affect us all.

THE MAIDS AND THE ANTHROPOLOGISTS

I learned of the UNITE-HERE strike on October 16 while attending a small Washington DC conference. In the days that followed, as the Hilton proceeded to lock out the workers, flurries of emails about the strike circulated among anthropologists, especially those individuals and groups working on issues related to labor, immigration, and globalization. Many refused to cross picket lines, spurring the AAA board to consider canceling or moving the meeting.[2] When the Hilton threatened to sue for lost revenues if the AAA moved the convention, the AAA board hastily decided to compromise and to reschedule the meeting for a month later at another Hilton Hotel in Atlanta. The surprise move displeased many pro-labor anthropologists because the new Hilton was also a non-union venue; others were angered by the inconvenience of the new dates and the expense of nonrefundable plane tickets.

Several sections of the AAA, including the Society for the Anthropology of Work, came to San Francisco anyway on the original dates for the convention in mid-November. We held a smaller, "alternative" meeting in a union-friendly hotel. Discussions on academia and labor became central to the new meeting agenda. The move of the convention, which turned out to be the largest meeting cancellation at the San Francisco Hilton during the strike, prompted Mayor Gus Newsom to intervene with Hilton management and to join the picket line himself. The city lost more than $5 million in revenue during the strike as the labor standoff paralyzed San Francisco's tourism. These factors later proved pivotal in helping to end the lockout.

Our planned 11 a.m. solidarity rally on Saturday, November 20, coincided almost exactly with the announcement of the end of the five-week lockout. An irregular procession of professors and graduate students joined the exhausted workers outside the Hilton in a raucous street celebration as they blew whistles, danced, and posed for victory photographs. It was an odd feeling to be in this bustling crowd of multilingual immigrant workers, looking through the plate glass into the cavernous Hilton Hotel lobby absolutely devoid of humans. Had the convention gone ahead as planned, this would have been lunch hour, and scores of our colleagues would be milling about these doors in search of companions, debating restaurant options.

I struck up a conversation with Vilma Campos, a waitress in the Hilton who had been a picket line regular. She said that the main thing that convinced her to go out on strike was the company's announcement that workers would face increases of $119 per month in health care premiums. Previously, the worker portion had been free for individuals or $10 for family coverage. She was delighted to learn that I had worked in El Salvador and told me the story of her flight from the violence caused by civil strife in San Miguel, El Salvador, 21 years ago, accompanied by her aunt, with an 8-month-old baby in her arms and a 5-year-old in tow: "We were very poor. It was a time when bullets were flying, and we thought we could be next."

Campos had gained US citizenship only seven years previously, after waiting many years for approval of her application for political asylum. Thanks to the union, she earned $13 per hour after tips; her husband, a dishwasher, earned $15 per hour—good pay for service work but still a pittance for living in San Francisco. She said that the two of them had managed to send one son to college on those salaries but, after the strike, had to take out a short-term loan to cover their $3,000 monthly mortgage payments. Strike pay from the union just covered the minimal necessities, she said, and after eight weeks on the picket line, Campos was delighted to see the lockout end: "We've been through a lot, out here in the cold, eating bad food, we've had people throw things at us and start pushing matches with us. The corporation is not interested in us. They don't care that we're out here on the street."

Another striker, Anthony Lee, a Chinese American originally from Hong Kong, agreed with Campos that the hike in health insurance premiums was the main grievance for most workers: "They wanted us to pay more, and in our opinion, that is not right. The corporation is making a profit from our business. If health costs go up, that is not our problem, that is a business problem, and it should not be put on the workers." He said that the hike in premiums was especially hard on single mothers with children.

I noticed that nearly all the workers on the picket line were people of color, spanning several ethnicities. I asked Lee how Local 2 managed to avoid schisms with such a diverse membership. He described the local as about a third Asian American, a third Latino, and a third Anglo and said that union meetings routinely involved simultaneous translation and all written materials were printed in three languages.

Our conversation was repeatedly drowned out by a Latino youth who had gotten hold of a megaphone and was leading high-decibel chants: "No more lockout!" and "Who's got the power? We've got the power!" The chants erupted into cheers as groups of fellow strikers got off city buses, holding stacks of yellow flyers announcing the end of the lockout in bold letters—Spanish on one side, English on the other.

During the 60-day cooling-off period that followed, negotiations were to continue while workers returned to work at the 14 hotels involved in the strike. Clearly, the main credit for ending the lockout belonged to the workers, many of whom risked losing their housing and health care to stay on the picket line so long. But "there is no question that the AAA move and decision of other organizations to move were critical to the Hilton administrators' realization that the lockout was not a viable strategy," according to Neal Kwatra of UNITE-HERE, who spoke at an Anthropology and Labor Forum held at the Canterbury the day after the lockout ended. Other key factors, we learned, had been decisions by Kaiser Permanente and other health insurers to extend strikers' health coverage, which also put pressure on the Hilton and other MEG hotels. Likewise, the hotels feared losing revenues during the coming holiday season.

When the rescheduled AAA convention finally took place in mid-December, the vast majority of sessions were cancelled. Only a few hundred of the 5,000 plus members expected showed up. In spring 2005, the renewed labor negotiations continued but bore little fruit. Undeterred by the example of the AAA, the American Philosophical Association's (APA) board also invited controversy within its ranks when its board ignored UNITE-HERE's request to cancel its March 2005 annual meeting in San Francisco. Hundreds of dissident members either boycotted the meeting or shifted their sessions to unionized venues at the last minute (Shrage 2005). The APA's executive director resigned over the controversy, and many members cancelled their membership. When the American Political Science Association later moved its meeting out of San Francisco to accommodate the strike, the organization faced a $450,000 claim from the Hilton Corporation (Brumfiel 2006). The move of the AAA meeting was also costly, although no lawsuit was filed.[3]

One positive outcome of these events was that our internal debate bolstered initiatives already under way to adopt labor-friendly reforms, including the establishment of a Committee on Labor Issues to advise the AAA board on future meeting venues. A vote on the issue in spring 2005 led to a successful resolution that future annual-meeting contracts would be signed with unionized hotels.[4]

PROSPECTS FOR ACADEMIC–UNION SOLIDARITY

UNITE-HERE's success with organizing immigrants and women challenges earlier claims by researchers and labor leaders that these groups are hard to organize. It now appears that such assumptions may also have been "socially constructed" (Crain 1991; Gray 2004). The case for solidarity between social scientists and labor should start with this analysis: who is better positioned than anthropologists to undertake ethnographic investigations that examine stereotypical claims? Further, both sociology and anthropology have models of participatory action research and the developing concept of "public scholarship" to draw on. These strengths should permit us to design projects that deepen our knowledge base about the social life of workplaces and organizing while simultaneously lending solidarity to union struggles (see Durrenberger and Erem 2005; Smith-Nonini 2003).

Academic organizations also have the means to put their members' dues and meeting registration payments to work in ways that benefit workers. The AAA experience with the UNITE-HERE strike illustrates the power that organized academic organizations can wield. According to Kwatra, UNITE-HERE sees potential in outreach to many professional organizations regarding their annual meeting contracts. He estimated that the top-ten academic organizations spend more than $70 million a year on conferences, which translates into one-third of the cash flow for big hotel chains such as the Hilton, Hyatt, and Marriott. In addition to the AAA, the American Sociological Association and the Association of American Geographers have adopted labor-friendly meeting policies.[5]

More union-friendly venues now exist for scheduling academic conferences, thanks in part to UNITE-HERE's strategy of pushing for agreements with developers and municipal authorities at the stage of new hotel development in places such as Las Vegas and Atlantic City, where the gaming industry has led to growth markets. The union has gained more than 20,000 new workers nationwide through such "card-check neutrality agreements," which guarantee a union the right to organize and hold an election that the employer will respect, in return for foregoing the rights to strike or boycott during the organizing effort and limiting the period of contract negotiations. In such a pact, both parties agree to resolve disputes through arbitration, rather than use the National Labor Relations Board, which has often allowed companies to drag out disputes for years, to the detriment of organizing campaigns. The union agrees, in turn, to promote the business. Along these lines, UNITE-HERE is developing a travel and conference-planning division (see www.hotellaboradvisor.info/) to drive business to unionized markets. Kwatra claims that academic organizations will actually save money on hotel facilities by using a union brokerage instead of private meeting planners, which, he noted, receive commissions from hotels and have little incentive to find the most affordable deal for an organization.

The other way academics can work with labor is on their own campuses. We are familiar with student anti-sweatshop campaigns, and some US universities, especially in the northeast, have organized graduate instructors and adjunct faculty. In fact, Wilhelm gained some of his early organizing experience at Yale University's campus in New Haven, where he worked initially as a community activist, then as a union organizer. He was elected as an official of HERE Local 34, Yale's clerical union, and in 1984 he led a precedent-setting 10-week strike that inspired a number of organizing drives on other campuses.

In 2005 a new campaign by SEIU and UNITE-HERE began targeting ARAMARK and other contracting companies that provide food and cleaning services to universities. At Elon University (my former employer) and at Duke University, short campaigns by students, faculty, and the unions in spring 2005 led to pledges of raises for contract workers from both universities. In short, organizing works!

UNRULY SCHOLARS—SOLIDARITY AS PUBLIC SCHOLARSHIP?

Social scientists are also well positioned to challenge the dominant discourses used by companies, including the "corporate" university, to rationalize their practices. As Koptiuch (1997:244) writes, the workplace is "one of the important sites where power relations are being reworked, in a process not unrelated to crisis management on the part of the state." But she adds that work is also one of the "new sites of resistance" to so-called neoliberal realities.

Liberal arts colleges (and some universities) tend to foster a veritable cult of "community" in self-representations of the institution directed at employees, students, and the public, while also laying claim to management practices (for example, contracting) that are depicted as innovative and efficient. Stewart (1987) notes that the postmodern commodity system has a remarkable ability to reinscribe negation as novelty. In her book *Flexible Bodies*, Emily Martin (1994) describes this new virtue as "flexibility." The destabilizing aspects of globalization are recast as mysterious forces that must be harnessed to local benefit by highly trained corporate managers. The marketing of neoliberal practices relies on a universalization of local anxieties about being marginalized, about winners versus losers, about some unnamed aspect of rural life or small towns that is wrong or "backwards" (Castel 1991).

But by definition, real "communities" have many inflexible components. The very notion of community was traditionally based on commitments to place and to people. Communities are places where people raise children and seek to build stable and predictable conditions in which children can flourish. Community is undermined when all the costs of social reproduction are offloaded onto the shoulders of overworked single mothers. Such a situation only postpones and transforms the costs to the wider society as suffering becomes manifest through crime, declining schools, social disorder, and new demands on public programs.

As "knowledge" workers, we academics have our own versions of "contingent" underpaid colleagues, who make up growing portions of many university faculties (for example, nearly one-third of faculty at my former university). Thus, we, too, are caught up in the contradictions of the neoliberal workplace, just as we are part of that wider community that ultimately pays the costs of marginalized labor. For all these reasons, collaborating with labor is in our enlightened self-interest.

But we in the academy also have more power than we realize. UNITE-HERE's struggle offers us a rare opportunity to put our association dues and meeting fees to work on behalf of fair labor, instead of corporate profits. As I remember it, that "employees only" door I pushed open next to the Grand Ballroom swung both ways. It is time we all begin to push it open and see what is going on in the kitchen. In the southeastern United States, where I grew up, "community" (real and imagined) was something that was talked about a great deal—at my grandma's house, when somebody served you a fine dinner, it was just basic good manners to help out with the dishes.

About the Author

Sandy Smith-Nonini is a Wenner Gren Foundation postdoctoral fellow and research assistant professor in the Department of Anthropology, University of North

Carolina (UNC), Chapel Hill, where she is revising a book on the politics of health and violence in El Salvador. She was an assistant professor of anthropology at Elon University from 2000 to 2005 and received the Peter K. New Prize from the Society for Applied Anthropology for previous writings on El Salvador. Since completing her Ph.D. (UNC, Chapel Hill, 1998), she has published articles on social aspects of tuberculosis epidemics in Peru and New York City, on the politics of US farm labor, and on meatpacking in the aftermath of neoliberal restructuring. In 1998, Sandy founded a community group that supports the farmworker movement in North Carolina. Before attending graduate school, she worked as a journalist based in Central America.

Notes

1. This refers to the shrinking of the rolls of Aid to Families with Dependent Children.

2. The leaders of seven of the 44 AAA sections and one committee wrote letters to the AAA board expressing concern and noting that hundreds of their members would refuse to cross the picket line. The AAA board polled meeting registrants on options, and 56 percent of respondents opted either to cancel the meeting or to move it to San Jose, which would have allowed members to use already purchased plane tickets. However, according to board members, this venue posed logistical problems, requiring shuttle buses among several hotels. After deciding to shift the meeting to Atlanta, the board offered to refund registration fees to those who could not attend.

3. Although the AAA was not sued by the Hilton, the organization lost a total of $445,000 from the move of the 2004 meeting. However, more than half of that consisted of registration fees returned to members, not fees paid to the Hilton Corporation (Brumfiel 2006).

4. One caveat of this reform is the lag time for it to take effect. The new policy affects only "new" hotel contracts. The AAA routinely negotiates contracts for annual meetings eight years in advance to lock in favorable room rates. In the next few years, the organization could again find itself caught between its moral commitment to low-wage workers and its contractual obligations (Brumfiel 2006).

5. Other academic organizations that have changed meeting plans or policies since 2004 as a result of the UNITE-HERE hotel strike include the Association for Asian American Studies, the Organization of American Historians, the American Educational Research Association, and the American Political Science Association.

11

"The Caribbean Is on Sale"

Globalization and Women Tourist Workers in Jamaica

A. Lynn Bolles

Tourism is one of the principal agents of globalization. People not only are moving around the world more than ever before, taking advantage of rapid modes of transportation and electronic technology, but also are doing so while on vacation far away from home. By the mid-twentieth century, the Caribbean region had become a prime tourist destination of middle-class visitors looking for affordable adventure. The commonly conjured image of the Caribbean is that of a tropical "island" surrounded by warm aquamarine waters and full of exotic lush flora and other sensual pleasures. Accompanying the scene is the unbridled service of "creature comforts," usually performed by dark-skinned "island" women. In reality, such services can be found in Jamaica, performed primarily by women tourist workers, who have made the country one of the region's tourism leaders. Consequently, tourism, as an emblematic expression of globalization, is played out throughout Jamaica. This chapter examines women tourist workers and their work in the Jamaican village of Negril, focusing particularly on a young woman who manages her family's small establishment on Negril's 7-mile white beach. Her story illustrates how global tourism impacts the lives and livelihoods of women, as well as the larger community of tourist workers.

For my research, I wished to understand how Jamaicans subjectively perceived the nature of their work and workplaces.[1] My interest in tourism emerged from research I conducted in the late 1980s for *In the Shadows of the Sun*, a volume that examines the outcomes of structural adjustment policies (SAPs) on the lives of women and families and the national economies of the Caribbean (Deere et al. 1990). At that time, few academic studies had examined tourism in Jamaica, and most information was generated by the industry itself. Furthermore, the industry and the government were only interested in how to decrease the low-value dimension in tourist revenues. The research on tourism I began resembled studies of factories, but this time on the beach. I was interested in the relationship between women tourist workers and their sites of employment or livelihood and how global economic forces shaped this relationship.

My work took me to multiple sites of tourism in Negril. I observed and conducted interviews with a wide variety of women tourist workers, ranging from small-scale itinerant peddlers to small- and medium-scale tourist hotel owners. My goal was to talk to a wide range of women workers of diverse occupation, age, education, class, and racial and ethnic groups in their work settings, following the ethnographic method. I walked the beach with itinerant trinket vendors, sat with hair braiders as they worked their artistry of beads and braids in kiosks at the edge of other places of commerce, talked business strategies with small hotel owners and managers of all sorts, and observed and participated in tourist weddings held in beachfront or garden gazebos and planned and organized by hotel social-event coordinators. Fieldwork and interviews in Negril occurred over a 3-year period, accounting for the seasonal nature of the business, with tourism high in winter months and low during the summer months; at the end of my research, the industry was reeling from the effects of 9/11. For the most part, my basic research asked what people thought of tourism as a way to make a living.

NEGRIL: SURF AND BUSINESS TURF

Standing in the warm, green Caribbean surf lapping against Negril's 7-mile-long, white sandy beach affords a panoramic view of the beachfront dotted by tourist establishments of various kinds and sizes. Those in the know recognize the small cottages, cabins, and hotels owned by Jamaicans. For the past 30 to 40 years, Jamaicans have made their livelihoods here in these family-owned enterprises. The beach became what it is because of the mid-twentieth-century coconut blight that killed the trees and destroyed the traditional coconut-processing business. Families owned the trees and land and now own those spots on the beach. Besides lodgings, there are cafés, bars, and restaurants of varying sizes that cater to walk-in clientele or visitors who are staying in their lodgings. Women manage many of Negril's locally owned beach establishments. There are water-sport rentals, craft vendors, hair braiders, and masseuses whose stalls, tables, and clotheslines display brightly colored cloth and t-shirts that blow in the breezes. Itinerant vendors, licensed by the Chamber of Commerce, and those without papers, ply their wares of fruit, water coconuts, jewelry, reggae CDs, and "natural" oils up and down the beach. Negril's white sand beach appears to be a lovely place to work. What could be more favorable working conditions than the warm aquamarine sea, a bright blue sky, and the feel of tropical breezes on your skin? That is, of course, until salt stings sunburned skin and the blistering rays of the sun bear down on heads and roast the feet as workers trod the broiling hot sand trying to make a living. Conditions become even more unbearable when the breeze dies down. Working on the beach is not easy.

In the morning, the beach is quiet until 9 a.m., when male water-sports workers and their unemployed male friends begin to gas up Sea-Doos, glass-bottom boats, and paragliders. A male beach attendant rakes the sand in front of establishments so that the area is cleared of debris and seaweed. Early rising guests drink their Blue Mountain coffee in eating places, served quietly by waitstaff of both genders, while other workers restock bars, fold napkins, and prepare for the day. Slowly, women and one or two men craft vendors set up their wares on the beach, unpacking t-shirts, carvings, baskets, and clothing. The clotheslines are soon filled with wraps, shirts with "tropical" prints, and the like. A few cottages and small hotels allow craft vendors to set up shop in tiny spots near their property lines so that they can attract spillover business. Sometimes a hair braider sets up a chair there too. These women workers might be extended kin members of the small cottage owner.

What was just described is the setting of O'Malley's, a group of on-the-beach cottages and cabins and a restaurant. Across the road, Uncle Oscar owns the best "jerk" carryout in Negril. The O'Malleys are a native Negrillian family. The natal home faces the road, and the cottages and cabins were built one by one, starting from the beach and moving back toward the house. Those 14 units were initially tent sites. In the late 1960s and 1970s, hippies camped out in those tents, serviced only by a pit latrine, standpipe-like showers, and no electricity. Now, almost all the cabins have electricity, and all the cottages have their own bathrooms and air conditioning. Over the course of 30 years, the O'Malleys—father and mother—held the business together, building and expanding their enterprise. Failing health finally forced them to relinquish daily operations to their children. However, all their children had left Negril, to live in Kingston or in the United States. Now, the management of O'Malley's is in the hands of Sybil, a granddaughter who grew up in Kingston but spent her holidays in Negril. There on the beach with her grandparents, Sybil learned the business as she was growing up by performing family labor. Sent later by her family to the United States to study business administration, she is educated in all the advanced technological tools of the tourist industry.

Upon her return, Sybil was given the daunting task of "turning the business around." She had to make O'Malley's competitive with other small establishments and, along the way, tackle a long laundry list of steps that required both industry expertise and access to capital. This list included basic upgrades of the property, making sure that basic amenities such as reliable sources of electricity and hot and cold water were available, and joining forces with other small cottage and hotel owners for mutual support and advertising purposes. Sybil's primary mission in turning the business around was to be able to withstand the competition from the new, all-inclusive RIU resort, owned by a Spanish hotel conglomerate that has properties throughout the Caribbean.[2] RIU boasts 400 rooms that skirted the building code by being higher than the blight-ridden "Jamaica Tall" coconut trees. Sybil also had to contend with the fact that RIU's daily all-inclusive rate of US$60 (2001 price) was the same rate charged at O'Malley's and other small hotels. She understood that, given a choice, a first-time international visitor booking a trip to Negril via agents in Europe or the United States would notice the cheap rate for RIU and more than likely choose it over a smaller hotel. How could O'Malley's compete against this global giant? Sybil went about this task in an ingenious manner, drawing not only on her business degree but also on her long years of familiarity with the tourist clientele of Negril and their particular tastes for economical adventure, her long-term networks and relationships cultivated with the Chamber of Commerce, and her thorough knowledge of the Jamaican tourist industry.

Sybil realized that RIU's "pre-fab" rooms (really just a series of concrete boxes affixed to a large structure) had little Caribbean charm, so she targeted certain areas for improving O'Malley's. These included the upgrades she had already identified and developing a joint website along with other small cottage and hotel owners.[3] They decided that the website would feature "real Jamaican-style" not global "glitter" tourism. In addition, Sybil worked with the Chamber of Commerce in a similar venture to gain maximum exposure for O'Malley's. She realized that the focus of the Chamber site on local and small businesses would make a difference. Sybil cultivated her relationship with the director of Negril's Chamber of Commerce, a woman whom Sybil knew as one who "feels" for the small entrepreneur and would extend the support she needed. O'Malley's had relied on a long-established hippie clientele who, now middle-aged, returned with their children and grandchildren for vacations. Yet, their "word of mouth" promotional campaigns could no longer support O'Malley's survival as a domestic, native Negrillian operation, given the incursion of the larger hotel chains. For Sybil, it was a fight to keep Negril from being swallowed up by the all-inclusive resorts owned by Jamaican global giants such as Sandals, Super Clubs, and RIU or by the next foreign investor. Who controls the surf, but more important, the turf of the beach and the community, is part of local engagement with global tourism.

NEGRIL: A PLACE WHERE VACATIONERS DO AS THEY PLEASE

Negril arrived late in the world of tourism, following a slow transformation from a peasant coconut-processing area and fishing village to a place where post-independence middle-class Jamaicans got away from it all and rented cottages and rooms from local people. A few years later, US, Canadian, and European hippies and young professionals on tight budgets came to this relatively secluded, western part of the island. In a semiautobiographical novel, *Banana Shout*, Mark Conklin (2000) recounts how this beautiful isolated village of fisherman and Rastafari slowly encountered the world through an invasion of hippies, draft dodgers, drug smugglers, and other members of the 1970s free love movement. Besides this counterculture group, Negril was now open to all who wanted something different, something very laid-back with a bit of exploration, for their vacation plans. In contrast to the mass-market hotels in the well-established tourist areas of Montego Bay, Negril attracted travelers looking for less luxury, less structure, and more adventure in their stay in Jamaica.

Because of this late entry as a major destination, Negril has a wide range of accommodations—cottages, villas, and hotels of various sizes and themes such as new-age health, sports, and luxury tourism. Negril is one of the original sites of all-inclusive tourism, beginning with the government-built Negril Beach Village, now corporately owned and renamed "Hedonism." Nevertheless, Negril tries to maintain a slow-paced atmosphere indicative of its fishing village roots. Just follow Norman Manley Boulevard, and the four areas of Negril appear. Entering Negril from Montego Bay, one passes the airport and a beachside occupied by five large-size "all-inclusive" resorts. The middle stretch of the road is lined with small- and medium-size, family-owned properties (although a large corporate resort was constructed after the conclusion of this research). These businesses are situated on the beach or have beach access. At Negril Centre, the road turns into a roundabout, with one direction going toward Savanna La Mar and the other leading to the West End Road. On each side of Negril Center are services and offices, including American Express, the Chamber of Commerce, the Jamaican Royal Post Office, banks, restaurants, hotels, and supermarkets. At the West End, cliffs face the sea. Many poor Negrillians live along the West Road, which is also the location of small cottages and secluded small hotels (from inexpensive to luxurious), the famous Rick's Cafe on the Cliffs, and the lighthouse (at the road's end).

There are two extraordinary, celebrated locations in Negril. One is its 7-mile, white sand beach, positioned right in the middle of the area. Geographers list Negril's beach as one of the "world's best," and anyone who has seen it or walked on it knows that the claim of "best" is well deserved. The other celebrated spot is the coral cliff along the West Road. From the cliffs at this most western tip of the island, you can observe the sun setting at sea in all its glory. Negril is a place where vacationers can go as slow as they want or engage in an adventure on land or sea. The village competes with other Caribbean locations for that global tourist trade.

"The Caribbean is on Sale" was a headline for advertisement of a large travel-agent chain promoting the region in the travel section of the *Washington Post*. Like winter coats or bed linen, Negril was "on sale," with implications that this tourist product was reduced in value and with coded implications that the country was for sale too. "The Caribbean is on Sale" signaled a race for the bottom as Jamaica, and Negril in particular, experienced the process of globalization—cheap, open, and competing for global trade. Negril's 7-mile beach affords a view of global capital and local capital at work.

GLOBALIZATION WHILE SMELLING A HIBISCUS IN BLOOM...

The buzzword *globalization* describes the dominating force that has shaped the world since the later part of the twentieth century. According to the United Nations, globalization has fostered interaction and integration among nations, economies, and people (United Nations Development Program 1996–2000). No matter what it is called, globalization is the outcome of the often unconstrained capitalism of the modern period, contributing to social and economic inequality within nations and across the world.

From a gendered perspective, as unequal power relations exist between women and men, it is the former group whose socioeconomic rights are not being advanced by globalization (Steady 2001). Additionally, gender inequality is compounded by other dimensions of difference such as race, class, ethnicity, sexuality, religion, region, and other distinctions that may vary from one culture to the next. For a social analysis of the process and impact of globalization to be meaningful, it must consider the dimensions of the differences just listed. From a nation-state viewpoint, globalization is arguably a mixed blessing that leads to what may be described as a "race to the bottom" for most of the countries of the South (developing countries, or the "Third World"; Steady 2001:3). This race begins when an economy lowers its costs of wages, curtails social welfare spending, and institutes other economic restructuring policies (liberalization, privatization, and deregulation) that open up opportunities for international capital to enter the market freely. Sometimes locally made goods are displaced by imports or are produced solely for a global market. In the short run, the cost of competing in this race is borne by society's most disadvantaged, based on their race, class, gender, ethnicity, age, and the intersection of those factors.

The United Nations Development Program (1989), supported by countless studies, has shown that gender disparities are worsening under globalization. Further examinations also conclude that impoverishment has risen among black women throughout the Africana world in relation to liberalization, privatization, and deregulation policies in the economies of the South. Therefore, to understand how globalization operates on the ground, the relationships among race, gender, and class must be seen as essential organizing principles in theory. For the most part, globalization theories of all stripes have a tendency to ignore discussions of gender. Further, when theory includes the dimensions of gender and class, rarely is race (or ethnicity) factored into the discourse as a category of social life. Only occasionally do studies—across the disciplines—consider all these factors. However, that is the goal of this work on women tourist workers and globalization.

Tourism is a mixed blessing for Caribbean countries, both culturally and economically. Tourism is the world's largest growth industry. The World Tourism Organization predicts that international arrivals will reach the one billion mark by 2010 and estimates recent tourism revenue as approximately $474 billion annually (World Tourism Organization website 2007). In 2003, the Caribbean hosted 16.1 million arrivals, who generated $16.8 billion in revenues. Tourism is considered a service export. In most Caribbean countries, tourism is the main industry, and excluding revenue from remittances from abroad, tourism is the primary earner of foreign exchange.

Even though Jamaica is one of the oldest tourist destinations, called in the parlance of the business "a mature destination," not until the early 1990s did tourism become Jamaica's leading economic sector. Until the latter half of the twentieth century, mining, agriculture, and manufacturing were the top sectors for Jamaica. Through the liberalization, privatization, and deregulation that began in the late 1970s under successive SAPs, tourism ascended to the top. However, turning to this service industry for fiscal sustenance represents a downward spiral in many ways. For example, as early as the 1980s, the Jamaica Tourist Board used promotional slogans such as "Come back to Jamaica, the way it used to be," harkening back to images of the colonial days of solicitous catering and servitude.

Here, I consider three areas. First, how did a service industry replace mining, agriculture, and manufacturing in Jamaica's economy? Second, and central to this chapter, I examine the importance of women workers in the tourist sector. What do women provide that makes them so critical to the success of the Jamaican tourist industry? Finally, I turn to the lived experiences of women tourist workers in Negril who shared their stories with me during my research.

THE PRICE OF SAPS

In 1977, the Michael Manley administration of Jamaica began negotiations with the International Monetary Fund (IMF), a practice that continued over successive governments until the 1990s. The policies instituted at both macroeconomic and sectional levels were designed to correct weakness and deficiencies in the Jamaican economy under the direction of international lending agencies. SAPs implemented over the years, as well as the debt crisis that ensued (through a fiscally debilitating cycle of loans), wreaked havoc on the national economy and the Jamaican people, particularly women (Bolles 1996b; Harrison 1997a). The effectiveness of SAPs is determined by a macroeconomic analytic framework by which economists usually divide goods into two types: tradable and nontradable. As the terms imply, tradable goods have international market potential, and nontradables are produced for domestic consumption. Most SAPs in developing countries focus on raising the prices of tradables and providing incentives for their production instead of nontradables (for example, domestic foodstuffs).

The underlying assumption is that there are no structural barriers to transferring labor from one sort of production to another. However, by this approach, SAPs ignore the sexual division of labor (both at home and on the job) that is the cornerstone of a gendered labor force. For example, during 1993, the beginning of the tourist research in Negril, there was a national increase in female employment (7,400 out of 397,100) in jobs associated with gains in hotel and restaurant services and the apparel sub-sector in export processing zones (EPZs). However, the largest employers were in "elementary occupations" that include street vendors of food and nonfood products and domestic helpers (maids). Female workers in this subset represented 32 percent of all employed women. Clearly, almost a third of female workers were engaged in nontradables, and job creation occurred in sectors prone to variances in tourism and EPZs (Planning Institute of Jamaica 1994). Also of importance, 42 percent of these employed women were heads of households.

SAPs target fiscal expenditures that are deemed too costly when these expenditures interfere with the goal of increasing tradables for the inter-national economic market. Such costly expenditures include food subsidies, health care, domestic food production supports, and education. Jamaica entered its first stand-by agreement with the IMF and World Bank in 1977 to continue its access to credit and trade. Part of the opening up of Jamaica's economy via the prescribed SAPs was to increase the production of tradables. With the election of a conservative government in 1980, Jamaica entered this new economic phase with gusto. The country found itself involved in three new financial and developmental areas: the intro-duction of more SAPs; massive loans from the World Bank, western com-mercial banks, and a variety of international lenders; and US investment in industry, which was facilitated by the provisions of the Caribbean Basin Initiatives I and II trading programs.

The price of gains was high as Jamaicans found themselves subject to violence and hardship due, in part, to the increasing deterioration of social service systems. Even the changing of political leadership, the 1989 re-election of Michael Manley and subsequent re-election of his predeces-sor, Prime Minister P. J. Patterson, has not broken the overseeing of one of the largest privatization drives in the so-called Third World. What privati-zation means, in this case, is increasing foreign ownership of Jamaica's economy. The economy shifted from depending on the revenues of baux-ite mining, agriculture, and manufacturing. Bauxite, a primary mineral resource, follows the wide fluctuations of the international market. So, too, do agricultural products. The seventeenth-century adage "rich like a West Indian" reflected the riches earned by the sugar plantation economy of Jamaica. However, sugar lost currency in the nineteenth century, struggled throughout the twentieth century except in war times, and was buried in the 1980s. Replacing sugar were nontraditional foods such as winter veg-etables and increased coffee production.

Domestic manufacturing competed with imported goods and lost. Instead, EPZs took the primary position in manufacturing, but these have their own Achilles heel for national economies: they decamp as soon as other locations seem more profitable than their current locale. In the mid-1980s, Jamaica's assembly production skyrocketed, fueled by "cheap, unskilled, dead-end labor inputs," also known as female labor, in the EPZs. Trade programs with the United States (807 and 807A) were designed to enhance the international competitiveness of the US clothing industry and not to create a modern manufacturing sector in Jamaica (*Life and Debt* 2001; Watson 1994). Less than a decade later, low-wage Asian labor markets were deemed most profitable, and many EPZs ceased operation and headed to China and other parts of Asia. Of course, other new sectors came on-line, such as the beginnings of an IT industry that received foreign investment, as well as the expansion of food and beverage processing and exports such as Red Stripe Beer, Pick-a Pepper Sauce, and Grace Foods products. However, it was the investment in tourism that provided something old, retooled it, and brought something new to the economy.

GLOBAL TOURISM—SEA, SAND, AND POLITICS

Jamaica's tourist industry began in the late nineteenth century but gained momentum after the Second World War (Taylor 1991). A 1947 Cunard Steamship Line advertisement featured Jamaica as a premier travel destination for the wealthy. Twenty years later, following Jamaica's independence in 1962, tourism had become a way of life for its citizens and a major sector of the economy.

By the 1970s, the affluent, wealthy traveler continued to visit Jamaica, but the majority of guests were middle-class Americans looking for bargains, as well as unaccustomed luxury. Mid-decade, a confluence of events set the course of Jamaican society. First, the price of crude oil increased during the 1974 oil embargo. Revenues from bauxite mining could not keep up with the need for foreign exchange, and the country entered a debt crisis. Second was the destabilization of Prime Minister Michael Manley's 1970s government. His political ideology promoted self-reliance in all aspects of citizenry and questioned the motives of the United States in its economic relations with Jamaica. Manley's leadership in the non-aligned movement and friendship with Cuba raised a "red flag" in the international banking and trade community that eventually led to the first negotiations with the IMF. Third, in the tourist sector, Jamaica pursued at least three marketing strategies. Partly because of the "red scare" and partly because of powerful global market forces, tourist agents and their middle-class, mass-market clients looked elsewhere for their vacation spot. Adding to the problem, many of the international chains left the island.

The first plan to combat the decline of tourism promoted Jamaica as more than a beach; the country as a whole was highlighted, as were alternatives to mass-market tourism, such as more adventure-oriented activities for overseas visitors. The second tourist plan focused on domestic vacationers as the government and its tourist agencies aggressively encouraged middle-class Jamaicans to vacation at home in Jamaica rather than travel to the former colonial mother country, the United Kingdom. Companies were offered tax packages and incentives for their staff to discover their own island, its hotels, beaches, and other accommodations. In addition, Jamaicans living abroad were encouraged to add a hotel vacation segment to their plans when they came home to visit family. The Jamaica Tourist Board had to sell Jamaica to Jamaicans. Jamaicans were also participating more as entrepreneurs. During this moment of self-reliance, the government of Jamaica helped citizens to finance their ownership of hotels. A stipulation was that new owners also had to learn hotel management and develop training sessions for employees. As a result of these initiatives, when the third strategy emerged, hotel owners, managers, and employees were ready. In 1976, the "all-inclusive" resort, Negril Beach Village, owned by Jamaican hotelier John Issa, became the prototype of what was to become one of the most revolutionary products in tourism worldwide (Dunn and Dunn 2002).

In 1980, when a conservative Jamaican government was elected, the Jamaican Tourist Board slogan mentioned earlier, returning to how things "used to be," said it all. The emphasis again rested with the heightened degree of service and seemingly greater degrees of servitude on the part of tourist workers. This campaign intended to lure mass tourism clients back to Jamaica and signaled the beginnings of the transitioning back to mass tourism. Jamaica was "safe" again for middle-class travelers, and the numbers of visitors and the amount of money they spent dramatically increased. But more important, a larger share of the sector comprised a novel type of tourism. Called "all-inclusive," this arrangement was modeled after the profitable French Club Med formula and was already moderately successful in Jamaica. All-inclusive vacationing means that all travel, food, drink, lodging, entertainment, gratuities, and the like are paid in advance to agents located in such places as the United States, United Kingdom, Canada, and Germany; the guest thus does not need to carry money except for souvenirs and personal incidentals. Further, guests do not have to travel outside the resort unless they want to, making the vacation as hassle free as possible. The "all-inclusive" resort is a prime example of global tourism and how it has impacted Jamaica specifically, as well as countries throughout the Caribbean.

When the Peoples National Party regained power in 1989 with a different political philosophy, the tourist sector was flourishing despite infrastructure setbacks caused by Hurricane Gilbert. Working together, government and the private sector poured capital, incentives, and expertise into tourism. Critical to this momentum was investment by Jamaicans. Even pension fund managers invested significant sums in the sector (Dunn and Dunn 2002). By 2002, Jamaicans owned 80 percent of Jamaica's tourist industry. The island's natural beauty, strategic aggressive marketing by the tourist board, and new local captains of industry combined to make Jamaica one of the leaders of global tourism.

Two Jamaicans, John Issa (Super Clubs and Breezes) and Gordon "Butch" Stewart (Sandals and Beaches) broke the American and European lock on all-inclusive holidays. Tourist researchers called this business endeavor "the most important innovation in the Caribbean hotel sector during the last decade" (Curtin and Poon 1988). Both Super Clubs and Sandals are homegrown marketing successes and are copied all over the region. Stewart claimed that their success is based on the value visitors receive for their money: "We have the biggest water sports business and fitness centers, brand-new restaurants, great entertainment. You have quality choices and with all that you end up with value for money you can't get anywhere else in the world" (Pattullo 1996:21).

Originally an owner of a car parts dealership, Butch Stewart started Sandals in 1981 by remodeling an old hotel, turning it into an all-inclusive, "couples-only" resort. Two decades later, the Sandals chain, which also includes properties called "Beaches," owns and operates six hotels in Jamaica, two in St. Lucia, and one each in Antigua, the Bahamas, Barbados, Turks and Caicos, and the Dominican Republic. In 1992, Stewart personally diverted a national foreign-exchange crisis when he deposited US$1 million into Jamaica's commercial banks at US$4 less than the exchange rate. This effort kept the banks and the foreign exchange rate from collapsing. It also encouraged other Jamaicans to put their US dollars into banks, thereby stabilizing the local currency. Another coup for this entrepreneur followed when Butch Stewart relieved the government of its controlling percentage of the national airline, Air Jamaica. Needless to say, Air Jamaica flies to all the countries where a Sandals resort is located, basically making his corporation a totally integrated operation. The Sandals Corporation has won countless awards from the industry.

The Issa family developed one of the first properties for mass tourism

in the 1950s, Tower Island. Now, Issa corporate holdings are found throughout the region under the Super Clubs trademark, and the corporation has
partnered in the rebuilding of tourism in Cuba. However, a key is needed
to truly fathom the complexities of this booming sector. Clearly, Jamaican
tourism is more than resort properties, sunsets, and rum punch cocktails.

THE SPECTRUM OF EDUCATION, COLOR, AND WORK

Tourism as a broadly defined, service-producing sector has for the past
10 years been the largest earner of foreign exchange (US$1.2 billion in
2001) for Jamaica. It employs countless numbers of workers, although the
exact numbers are difficult to tease out of the general employment data
because tourism intersects other sectors, such as transportation, management, and service. For the most part, the majority of workers in Jamaica's
tourist sector are women, employed in a broad spectrum of economic activities, from unskilled domestic workers to highly educated accountants,
bank clerks, and managers with advanced business degrees. The jobs
women acquire often reflect their educational attainment and technical
expertise, which are closely aligned with their class position. Historically,
skin color has been associated with educational attainment and has intersected with social class status. Hence, those with low levels of education still
tend to be of darker skin color than those who have skilled or technical
training. For example, during my study, the women who worked as unli-
censed itinerate vendors were dark skinned and barely literate. Age was
also a factor. One of the most respected market women on the local scene,
who also catered to tourists, was an elderly black woman who had very limited education but was a savvy small businesswoman.

However, with the expansion of education and the emphasis on training and education for the tourist sector, Jamaicans across the color spectrum are now found throughout the various levels of management. At the
time of my research, the manager of a local bank was a highly trained black
woman, as were the night managers at two of the largest resorts in town.
Nonetheless, particularly for women in large corporate-owned establishments, colorism (that is, the practice of favoring lighter skin color) seemed
prevalent both in my observations and in anecdotal evidence. The multilingual women who ran the local tour guide desks in large hotels were
invariably college educated and had traveled to and been educated in the
countries whose languages they spoke—Spanish, Italian, French, and
German. Contention surfaced among educated women who were not university trained but held certificates in hospitality or accounting or had years
of life experience.

Most of the women who talked to me felt that they could not break into the upper echelons of the business because of the color of their skin. They had to rely on luck and "breaks" to be recognized by management above the local level. In tourism, like other sectors of the Jamaican economy, job status oftentimes follows a gradation of color, particularly in sex-segregated occupations such as housekeeper, bar maid, and craft vendor, as well as more nontraditional professions such as hotel manager, dive shop owner, and head chef. All these jobs are also subject to the variances of hurricanes, seasonal business cycles, and overall international economic conditions that allow or discourage individuals from taking a vacation far away from home.

During 2001, the main indicators of the tourism sector were down relative to those of the preceding year because of the economic recession in the United States and other markets and the 9/11 terrorist attacks. To understand the complexities of the tourism industry, we must recognize that tourism is embedded in the structure of the society in which it is located. Jamaican society is highly stratified by race, class, ethnicity, gender, and other marked and unmarked differences. Jamaican culture also reflects the legacy of slavery, as well as a history of indentured relations, colonialism, and neocolonialism. The various social hierarchies and differences of Jamaican society surface in Jamaica's tourism industry, sometimes glossed over for tourist consumption, such as the promotional tag that referenced the way things used to be, harkening back to Jamaica's colonial legacy but romanticizing it for tourist consumption.

As a service sector, tourist work fits neatly into Jamaica's economic hierarchy. In tourism's gender-segmented labor market, women perform the majority of service work. How are these jobs counted? Service work in establishments that pay taxes, such as hotels, banks, and restaurants, is counted and considered a service-producing tradable in the parlance of the gross domestic product. Work categorized in the "elementary occupations" rubric is often not counted but is nevertheless critical to the tourist business; such work includes that of roadside vendors and sex workers. The overall image of women's tourist work is stereotyped as that of chambermaid and sex worker. A study conducted by Dunn and Dunn in 1994 showed that there were actually more men than women working in tourism in Negril. Further, there was a distinctive disparity in income earned by men and women, with males being three times more likely than females to be in the high-income bracket. In their study, Dunn and Dunn (2002: 110–113) show that the employment gender gap has narrowed but women are still earning less than men. Most important, low-skill jobs are the backbone of the business. However, coexisting side by side are avenues for upward occupational and social mobility (Gordon 1989:67–80). Thus, for every dozen or so impoverished women who clandestinely skirt the security guards at any one of Negril's resorts or sell aloe stalks to tourists on the beach, another handful of women own or manage small hotels.

This situation is thus a "mixed blessing" of international trade and investment. Part of Negril's beach became "Margaritaville," a restaurant investment by the US rock-and-roll singer Jimmy Buffet. Margaritas are made with tequila, an agave-based liquor originally from Mexico. With global tourism, the local drink is whatever you make it to be, although rum drinks are also sold at Margaritaville. Although all-inclusive resorts are becoming emblematic of Jamaican tourism, there are still businesses that are family owned and female managed that provide alternative vacation lodging.

CONCLUSION

Globalization has unleashed powerful flows of capital, cultural, and informational systems across our world. In comparison with its predecessors (merchant capitalism, multinational corporations), globalization can be called "turbo capitalism." Entering economies at turbo-charged speeds, globalization seeks out weaknesses and eliminates so-called deficiencies that impede its agenda of privatization, liberalization, and deregulation. Globalization is an integrated phenomenon that brings the entire world into a single, interconnected web (O'Grady 1982:4; Schneider and Susser 2003). Tourism is one of those turbo-charged global industries that feeds off economic weaknesses, often weaknesses resulting from historical legacies of colonialism, greedy regimes, autocratic governments, "special periods" (as in the case of Cuba), or disempowering SAPs (as in the Jamaican situation). Dunn and Dunn (2002:3) suggest that the wider Caribbean region is one of the most tourism-dependent regions of the world, with tourism accounting for one in four jobs and close to a quarter of the gross domestic product (GDP). However, critics (Davidson, Jones, and Schellhorn 2002) point out that tourism is not a magic solution for the nation's ills and in some cases it may even worsen those ills.

Further, tourism, no matter the location, is embedded in the socially constructed setting, where gender, race, sexuality, and power between men and women intersect along class lines. Tourism is a service-based industry that relies on the labor of women in various kinds of economic activities that are usually confined to masculine interpretations of caring, serving, and mothering (Davidson, Jones, and Schellhorn 2002). Promotional images of a Jamaican vacation convey a stereotype of "the brown-skinned/easy and Black/servile, native woman" (Mullings 2002). The image of the sex worker, if not as a personage but as an ideal of the unrestrained seeking of pleasure of all sorts, is clearly coded in the names of resorts such as *Couples* (exclusively for pairs of heterosexual adults) or the even more blatant *Hedonism.*

The situation of tourism in Jamaica, and particularly in Negril, clearly illustrates how this multisector business has almost taken over a country. Here, capital homesteads, looks for sites, establishes its own parameters, and eventually controls the direction of the economy. More women are entering tourist work because the sector is expanding, but where the poor, black, unskilled, and untrained fit into this sector is on the bottom. O'Malley's cottages and cabins are an example of a small local business struggling not to be sucked down to the bottom. Sybil is educated and manages her family enterprise but must also compete with a global conglomerate. For global capitalism, O'Malley's is an ideal weak prey, in a case of not-so-fierce competition. One thing Sybil has that is of incredible value is the family-owned land on Negril's 7-mile, sandy white beach that O'Malley's occupies.

In Jamaica, the situation is complicated in that two of the giants of the industry are homegrown. Butch Stewart and John Issa, with their foreign investors, have made history in the tourist industry. Nonetheless, the corporate headquarters of both Sandals and Super Clubs are not in Jamaica, but in Florida.

Negril represents "the mixed blessings" of globalization. On one hand, certain structures and operations would not be in place if not for trade liberalization, such as access to electronic technology, transportation, construction, and environmentally safe systems of water and waste management to stem the tide of environmental degradation. On the other hand, there is RIU, undermining what makes Negril so special—small cottages, cabins, and restaurants, locally owned by families and managed by their women kin. Sybil O'Malley, one member of an extended family, was given, as she says, the opportunity to "hold on to the land (beach) and the business." Her grandparents sent her to a small college in Connecticut to study business. Back home in Negril, Sybil finds her 14 units pitted against RIU's 400 and must keep pace with new technology in the tourist industry for booking and promotion. She makes sure that her staff has job security, all the while maintaining genuine Jamaican hospitality and forging alliances with other small business owners as they all face the best of the all-inclusive resorts. In her own way, Sybil O'Malley has taken on globalization on her own terms. In this fashion, and in this one aspect of tourism in Negril, a collective of small operators are slowing down the race for the bottom.

About the Author

A. Lynn Bolles is a professor of women's studies and affiliate faculty in anthropology, African American studies, and comparative literature and American studies at the University of Maryland, College Park. She was president of the Caribbean Studies Association and the Association for Feminist Anthropology. Bolles' scholarship focuses on the political economy of women of the African Diaspora.

Acknowledgments

This chapter is a section of a writing project on women tourist workers in Negril. Funding for the fieldwork came from the International Studies, Africa and the Americas Committee, Graduate Research Board, and the College of Arts and Humanities and the College of Behavioral and Social Sciences, University of Maryland, College Park.

Notes

1. Fieldwork and interviews in Negril were conducted over a three-year period (between 1992 and 1994). Follow-up research continued until 2002. I am indebted to all the women who spent time talking to me and sharing their lives and stories. I use pseudonyms here.

2. Ironically, RIU started as a family business in 1953. RIU built a massive hotel at the far end of Negril past the airport, subsequently building a second huge hotel near O'Malley's in 2003.

3. For example, the upgrades included securing the basics, such as reliable electricity and water sources (particularly during drought situations), providing hot water and consistent room amenities, and offering cable television in all rooms.

Part IV

Contesting Marginalities, Imagining Alternatives

Women Transforming Global Coalitions

12

In the Fields of Free Trade

Gender and Plurinational En/Countering of Neoliberal Agricultural Policies

Ann Kingsolver

In the summer of 1993, when the North American Free Trade Agreement (NAFTA) was being negotiated and Mexico's communal *ejido* lands had just been privatized through constitutional changes pushed by the Salinas administration,[1] Diana stood in a row of cucumbers, looking down the hill at the trickle of river the drought had left running through her community in rural Morelos. Her two youngest children were casting a net in the river, trying to catch some fish. Her two eldest children were in Canada doing contract work on a farm where they had gone for several seasons. She and her husband, Leonardo, now held a deed for their ejido plot; the national administration had promoted this aspect of privatization so that land held previously by communities for agricultural use could be sold to corporations (for example, for the construction of factories). Leonardo said that all that had come of this was the ability of the government to tax those holding property deeds for ejido lands, so the household's taxes had increased fiftyfold in the past four years. They, like many other families, had not paid their taxes because they did not have enough money. The loans they and their neighbors had taken out to buy seeds and other agricultural necessities had 20 percent interest rates, compounded monthly. On the day that I talked with them,[2] Diana and Leonardo were trying to decide whether to harvest a crop of cucumbers or leave them in the field.

They had to go a long way to sell the crop, and hiring a truck and workers to help pick the cucumbers would cost more than the cucumbers would bring in the market. Leaving them in the field made sense economically, but like so many other things under a neoliberal policy regime, it did not make sense socially.

That same summer, in eastern Kentucky in the United States, Dot was also balancing the challenges of being a small-scale farmer, a mother, and a partner while making decisions on her tobacco and vegetable farm jointly with her husband, Tommy. Dot was working with a national organization, "Farm Aid" (championed by singer Willie Nelson), and local agricultural organizations to lobby the US government against NAFTA. She said:

> It's a national issue, but it's a local issue that we've taken to heart....Farmers here—I don't want to say that they're not pay-ing attention to what's happening because they are aware of it, but it's that they're so caught up in survival, getting their crop in, getting on to the next step, that they really don't have time to be active....Local involvement was not what it should have been, considering [tobacco] is the primary income in this whole com-munity, but I don't think the total community has a clue what it could do to the economy here....Our organization [Community Farm Alliance] started at the grassroots level....We help each other from county to county. We, as farmers, in our organization basically are against everything that NAFTA stands for at this point.

Dot went on to tell me that she, Tommy, and other farmers were form-ing a collective to work out problems—similar to those experienced by Diana and Leonardo—with marketing vegetables so that they could coor-dinate who would grow cucumbers and who would grow tomatoes and how they would get them to market. She had told someone at the land-grant university to stop doing research for ConAgra and start doing research to help small farmers. In Morelos, Diana and Leonardo had also been work-ing with their community. They had helped build a dam and a bridge to address collectively their problems with access to water. Their local organi-zation was increasingly working together as the state became more a source of tax bills than of farming assistance.

Dot worried about NAFTA because she predicted that competitive tobacco produced in Argentina would enter the North American market through Mexico. Farmers like Diana, protesting at World Trade Organi-zation (WTO) meetings 10 years later in Cancún, Mexico, worried about subsidized farming in the United States taking an unfair share of their agricultural market.

Diana and Dot's analyses of individual and community economic marginalization through agricultural free trade policies resonated with the interpretations of globalization that women and men shared with me in interviews on upcountry tea estates in Sri Lanka in 2004. Saraswati and her mother had lived and worked on a tea estate that had been nationalized and then reprivatized. In this gender-segregated workforce in 2004, women tea workers earned 120 Sri Lankan rupees (approximately US$1.15) per day for plucking tea leaves to be processed and sold in bulk to corporations such as Lipton on the international market. Saraswati, sitting with her infant, friends, and family members in the "lines" (company housing on the estate), told me that I should share her analysis of globalization with those who drank the tea that she and the other workers harvested: "If one person speaks, nobody is concerned about it. If everybody says [something], that is the real satisfaction—the communal voice. It makes a difference. This kind of issue should be taken to the international level, and people at the international level should be told that we are living in such a situation."[3]

In this chapter, I draw on long-term, multisited ethnographic research I have been conducting for 20 years on local interpretations of globalization and plurinational organizing to (a) consider the strategic use of distinctions—for example, North–South, racialization, ethnicity, gender, class, caste, and age—in neoliberal capitalist logic and practice that isolates communities of agricultural workers and promotes their further marginalization from decision making and the economic gains related to "free" market policies; and (b) discuss some analyses and strategies of those working to counter that isolation and strategic alterity.

I am a Euro-American cultural anthropologist from rural Kentucky. The methods I have used in studying interpretations of globalization have included semistructured interviewing and discourse, archival, and spatial analyses. Participatory research has shaped my approach to ethnography. Some of my interviewing on NAFTA, for example, has been done collaboratively with other activist researchers, from Mexico, and all of us—including those interviewed—have used the information from those conversations in our writing.

Because, in this volume, we focus on those most economically marginalized by policies related to all the processes and actions that get glossed as "globalization," we should be mindful of June Nash's (1997b:12) point that ethnographic listening needs to be most attuned to those who have the keenest analytical insights regarding global capitalism: those who have experienced and resisted internal and transnational colonial domination. Diana, and women like Saraswati who live even closer to the economic edge under neoliberal regimes,[4] are frequently the authors of theories and organizational strategies that challenge the way workforces are imagined in debates and documents (like NAFTA) related to neoliberal free trade. Hence, a research question I see as central to the project of this volume was asked in the Second Encounter for Humanity Against Neoliberalism (held in Spain in 1997 as a follow-up to the First Encounter for Humanity Against Neoliberalism, organized by the Zapatistas in Chiapas): "What are the lived experiences of the contemporary neoliberal economic strategies—the faceless rule of markets, wars, cuts in social spending on essential services, pollution and devastation of our natural commons?" (De Angelis 1998:138).

One of our tasks as ethnographers is to document those "lived experiences" of neoliberal restructuring associated with economic "globalization." Another is to challenge the facelessness of those most central to the imposition of those neoliberal capitalist policies. In the United States, Mexico, and Sri Lanka, I interviewed men and women who were members of neoliberal governments and whose occupations situated them in various ways relative to the "free" market, including as authors of free market policies. I also interviewed those most marginalized by neoliberal economic policies. Along the way, I encountered women and men of various class positions organizing against and beyond neoliberal free trade policies. I consider the insights of Patricia Hill Collins (2000) and others vital in recognizing the ways in which class, caste, gender, and racialization, for example, intersect and inform alliances and conflicts of interest within national contexts of the globalized North and South, and not simply between them. In this chapter, I include narratives by those most economically marginalized by capitalist globalization and by those working collaboratively across what might be seen to be different markers of identity or class interests, to design and implement specific alternatives to neoliberal free trade policies. I discuss the organizing strategies articulated by Bertha Luján, a labor lawyer who has participated in transnational collaborative organizing against neoliberal free trade policies through the umbrella organization Red Mexicana de Acción frente al Libre Comercio (RMALC, or Mexican Action Network against Free Trade).

I focus in this chapter on the agricultural sector, which is also a multinational industry. Dot and Tommy were producing burley tobacco, which was sold in a warehouse to a buyer from a transnational tobacco corporation that blends tobacco leaves produced in many nations (including

South Korea, Turkey, Argentina, and the United States) to create a single product, a filtered cigarette, representing the labor of people in multiple countries. Studies of this process can be compared to other analyses of the "global factory." As Diana and Leonardo's children work on a farm in Canada because their family needs to pay the taxes levied through neoliberal policies in Morelos, Mexico,[5] they may be drinking tea produced through the efforts of Saraswati and her coworkers on the tea estate in Sri Lanka. I have written elsewhere (Kingsolver 1991, 2007) about the ways in which ideological constructions of agricultural labor as independent "family farming"—as for Diana and Dot, though not Saraswati—obviate labor organizing among those sharing the lowest-paid and highest-risk work in multinational agricultural industries. It is Saraswati, in the opening example, who calls most directly for global organizing from her perspective as a member of a transgenerational captive labor force. Free trade policies are encountered and countered directly by agricultural workers around the world, then, and their labor is often organized in gendered workforces.

The word *farmer*, itself, may be gendered as male to some readers. As many have written, such gendered notions of agricultural workforces have led to disastrous international economic-development policies based on erroneous assumptions regarding gender-assigned tasks related to planting, harvesting, and marketing. Although I have not separated out gender as a focus separate from its connection to racialization and other strategic justifications for inequitable policies in my research on globalization, gender has sometimes come up specifically in interviews. A retired plantation manager in Sri Lanka, for example, volunteered his view that Sri Lankan men should be ashamed that women do the hard work of bringing international capital to Sri Lanka through their low-wage work in the garment sector, in the transnational domestic labor circuit, and on tea estates (Sri Lanka's three main sources of foreign exchange capital). "It's sad," he told me. "We live on the backs of our women." Women and men's experiences of "free market" capitalism need to be discussed relationally, not in isolation (which is why the concern of this volume is *gendered* globalizations), and analyses of gendered marginalization may, of course, come from men, as in this manager's assessment, as well as from women.

In the rest of this chapter, I address the two purposes of my argument mentioned earlier. First, I examine how the neoliberal capitalist strategy of isolating workforces with at least some shared experiences of economic and cultural marginalization benefits most those central to the implementation of free trade policies. The first section discusses what happened at the WTO meetings in Cancún, Mexico, in relation to the links and wedges between Dot and Diana as farmers in the globalized North and South, respectively. The next section further problematizes the North–South distinction by examining the words of Saraswati and other workers on the tea estates, along with the words of the former president of Sri Lanka Chandrika Kumaratunga, and turns toward strategies of South–South organizing to contest historical North–South relations of infrastructural domination of financial and transport aspects of global production, distribution, and consumption networks. The final section closely examines the strategies of Bertha Luján and others working to craft and implement alternatives to neoliberal free trade policies in Latin America. I argue that lessons learned from gender-focused, transnational organizing efforts about power relations, voice, agency, and the intersections of not only racialized, classed, nation-based, and gendered aspects of identity but also those of shared and distinct concerns have shaped broad-based, transnational "umbrella" organizing strategies to contest neoliberal policies.

This ethnographic project is informed by the analyses of Diana, Saraswati, Dot, and Bertha as much as by those of the other theorists I cite here. Barry Carr (1996:210), in his chapter "Crossing Borders: Labor Internationalism in the Era of NAFTA," comments that although neoliberalism has opened an unprecedented opportunity for grassroots activists to organize across borders and make public statements on transnational policy, the trends in international organizing have been dominated by those in the North "helping" those in the South rather than recognizing expertise in the South. At the 5th International Interdisciplinary Congress of Women in San José, Costa Rica, in 1993, I heard Digna Ribera, speaking as an *indígena* organizer from Costa Rica, say that she was rarely invited to such congresses and that indígena voices should be included more often in international discussions of inequality and the environment (rather than being, as she said, kept in parks) because of the knowledge they bring to what amounts to *everyone's* problems: poverty, inequality, and what's happening to the world's resources. In her words, "We don't have water, we don't have rights to wood, but we have the right to pay *taxes*....We should have more of an administrative role." In 2005, Costa Rican congresswoman Epsy Campbell, the first black woman elected to Costa Rica's legislature, was working from an administrative role in Costa Rica and in alliances across Latin America to see that the voices of Latin Americans of African heritage—who represent the lowest levels of income and political representation (Campbell, personal communication, 2005)—are heard more in national and international contexts (for example, at the current negotiations of the Central American Free Trade Agreement). This chapter, then, is positioned within a much larger project of action and analysis of free trade policies affecting not only those working in the fields but also everyone connected through the neoliberal project.

Barndt (1999) has argued, in a discussion of women and NAFTA, that a focus on the agricultural sector and women's roles as pickers, packagers, and consumers gives us a way to understand viscerally the globalized connections among those of us situated in many different countries and contexts. There can be very different ways of publicizing and addressing those connections, and discussions of globalization (and transnational collaboration and organizing) need to address communications. Of the three women I introduced in the opening part of this chapter, for example, Dot had access to the Internet and eventually began marketing organic tobacco to Europeans via that medium; Diana and Saraswati did not have access to the Internet. However, Diana learned about policy changes and resource availability through her agricultural collective—something Dot was just starting to form. Saraswati said that her union, the Ceylon Workers' Congress (CWC), did not represent her interests because the leadership was upper-caste and shared resources and information within closed family networks. She felt that the working conditions of women on the tea estates were not covered thoroughly or accurately enough in local, national, or international media.

Grassi (1990) has argued the need for South–South participatory and interactive communications networks to challenge Northern domination of global media. Internet sites have helped with transnational communication and activism, including challenges to national governments. (For example, the Ejército Zapatista para Liberación Nacional [EZLN] developed both on-line and armed strategies to challenge the Mexican government on the implementation of NAFTA in 1994.) Organizations like the RMALC have websites that—among other purposes—give other organizations models for writing alternative policy statements when it is time to move beyond critiquing state policy to proposing specific alternatives. It bears noting, however, that accessibility to the Internet continues to vary according to class politics, infrastructural, and organizational considerations. The EZLN, for that reason, used multiple types of media and initiated a public polling process to democratize its shift from a military to a political organization in Mexico (Kingsolver 2001:176–179). Clark and Themudo discuss some of the specific inequities within Internet-based anti-globalization organizing that they have heard voiced:

> Unequal familiarity with new technology and access to resources
> leads to a North–South tension. Many Southern activists see

events such as Seattle and global social movements as very Northern (or US) dominated (O'Brien et al. 2001), focusing primarily on issues of Northern concern (for example, the protection of the US environment, US jobs and US markets; US citizens wanting to have clear consciences about child labour; and reducing pressures for illegal migration). They are angry that issues of concern to the South (such as the way in which agriculture is dealt with in WTO talks) are not addressed. And events that are largely Southern organized (such as the citizens actions at the UN Conference on Trade and Development— UNCTAD—meetings in Thailand in 2000 and the first World Social Forum—WSF) attract very few Northerners. [Clark and Themudo 2003:121–122]

North and South, as rubrics, cannot be too far reified because those governing the nations of the North and South have often been educated together and the movement of people between the physical North and South challenges the notion of distinct publics in many ways. But we can think of nations as distinct policy spheres through which (at least some) people move. Transnational networks, or *meshworks* (Harcourt 2003), are "created out of the interlocking of heterogeneous and diverse elements brought together because of complementarity or common experiences" (2003:78) like the women's movement. One of the challenges of these meshworks is to discern the meaning of policy spheres, how to engage them, and, when necessary, how to change them, especially because the neoliberal shift in many states has represented a shift away from democratic involvement in policy making. The following sections take up the narrative thread of those encountering and countering neoliberal economic policies associated with globalization.

BRINGING THE FOCUS TO THE FIELDS: WHAT HAPPENED AT THE WTO MEETINGS IN CANCÚN?

In analyses of the breakdown of WTO talks in Cancún, Mexico, in September 2003, one current of discourse points to farmers of the North benefiting from state subsidies at the expense of farmers of the South. Such a narrative masks the experiences common to small-scale farmers in the United States and Mexico, like Dot and Diana, despite their obvious differences in median income. That common experience has been one reason for organizing plurinationally against free trade policies in such alliances as the Red Mexicana de Acción frente al Libre Comercio

(RMALC), with which I did ethnographic research in 1995 and which I have followed since.

Ha-Joon Chang (2002) points out that the United States and European nations became developed nations, in part, because of tariffs and protectionism. It is ironic that these nations now lobby hardest for the liberalization of other economies into a global free-trading market. With the implementation of trade liberalization policies, growth in developing countries has declined (Chang 2002). The United States and the European Union (EU) do not form a neat bloc within the WTO's discussions of agriculture, nor do the G-22 nations, which represent collectively "two thirds of the world's farmers and 60% of world agricultural output on five continents" (Johnson et al. 2003:42). Generally, the breakdown of the Cancún talks can be attributed to the unacceptable logic of nations (including the United States) wanting to perpetuate their own protectionist policies and simultaneously pushing for the opening of markets for their agricultural surpluses in G-22 and other nations. South Korean farmer Lee Kyoung-hae committed suicide at the barricades separating the negotiators from the protestors at the WTO meetings in Cancún (Elliott and Denny 2003:21) to demonstrate that removing the WTO from setting agricultural policy within nations was a life-and-death issue. His delegation was joined by thousands of Mexican women and men who were feeling the dire effects of NAFTA and other neoliberal free trade policies in their fields and homes.[6]

What has happened to farmers like Diana and Leonardo in Mexico since the passage of NAFTA? The costs of agricultural production, along with food in the market, have gone up, but the prices received for crops have gone down. For those and other reasons, more than 100,000 farmers in Mexico marched to the Zócalo in Mexico City to protest agricultural policy (Hemispheric Social Alliance 2003:24). NAFTA is not the only transnational neoliberal policy affecting Mexican agriculture; Mexico also has trade agreements with the European Union and with nations in Central America. However, decades of neoliberal policies in Mexico have not countered poverty, as had been promised. Agricultural trade liberalization in Mexico has increased both domestic poverty rates and food prices (Food First 2003a).[7]

The increasing poverty in rural areas of Mexico is mirrored in the United States, which calls into question the pitting of one set of small farmers against another, as in the explanation that subsidies in the United States benefit small farmers like Dot and Tommy but hurt small farmers in Mexico and other countries. US agricultural subsidies impoverish small-scale farmers both in and outside the United States. Most of the agricultural subsidies are going to banks and corporations. The market share of grain has become much more concentrated in just a few corporations. Cargill, ADM, and Zen Noh, for example, export 82 percent of US-produced corn (Memarsadeghi and Patel 2003:3). Meanwhile, economic conditions for most people in the United States have worsened. Since the implementation of NAFTA, approximately 700,000 jobs have been lost in the United States (Food First 2003b), and they have not gone to Mexico, despite Ross Perot's predictions (Perot with Choate 1993). Following trade liberalization in the US agricultural sector, Memarsadeghi and Patel (2003) report that the number of family farmers has decreased, there has been a whitening of the farm population, and malnutrition in the United States has increased. Just as capitalist class interests are allied across national boundaries, so, too, are the class interests of those most marginalized culturally and economically by neoliberal restructuring. It is just that the capitalist class has better control of means of communication (literally owning telephone companies and television stations now, after neoliberal privatization) and is more closely networked (as in the example of neoliberal cabinet members in Mexico and the United States cooperating to promote NAFTA, having studied Milton Friedman's free market policies together in graduate school).

What happened after representatives from Brazil, India, China, and other nations refused to allow the representatives from the United States and the EU to set what the former saw as a trade agenda with disastrous implications for farmers in the global South? Farmers like Diana and Dot, and their coworkers, organized stronger "meshworks" across national contexts to understand the ways in which WTO policies to lower trade barriers have benefited large financial and agroindustrial corporations globally while seeming to pit small farmers against one another in a North–South price war. The lived effects of free trade are by no means even across commodity or geopolitical sectors; individuals have different organizing strategies according to specific sectoral interests. This is taken up in the section on the RMALC and focused organizing efforts countering free trade policies.

SOUTH–SOUTH FREE TRADE: TWO WOMEN'S PERSPECTIVES FROM SRI LANKA

An article in *The Island* (an English-language, daily Sri Lankan newspaper) on October 15, 2003, carried news of then president Chandrika Kumaratunga's speech at the World Economic Forum's East Asia summit in Singapore, after the breakdown of the WTO talks in Cancún, Mexico. She said:

We do not wish to be dictated to. We wish to be active participants in the process of formulating policy. Therefore the World
Trade Organisation and world trade agenda will have to be renegotiated. The principles and underlying positions on trade must
definitely be the same for the developed and developing nations.

We do not comprehend how rich nations demand of us to
abandon to the whims of the global markets vulnerable sectors
of our society…when they practice extensive protectionist policies for these sectors in their countries.

We do not believe in the magic formulae that brandish brilliant
statistics achieved by a privileged few while the majority of our
peoples languish in the ignominy of poverty.

The developed and powerful nations will have to realise there
are millions of humans waiting on the sidelines to share the
fruits of development.

It is time for the rich and developed nations to give their technology, knowledge, and financial assistance not only with the
objective of securing contracts for their nationals, but also to
alleviate poverty.

Her words resonated with those of many other national leaders challenging the WTO, the IMF, the World Bank, and the handful of nations who
maintain elite control of those transnational institutions. In South and
Central America, for example, several newly elected national leaders have
challenged the US-proposed Free Trade Area of the Americas (FTAA).[8]
Because their own nations may be debtor nations these days, national leaders of the global North cannot as easily hold debt over the heads of state in
the global South in their efforts to monopolize the trade agenda and ensure
the inequitable distribution of the profits of "free" trade. Increasingly, even
as one-to-one free trade agreements (for example, a proposed free trade
agreement between Sri Lanka and the United States) are negotiated as
alternatives to the WTO process, there are active South–South trade agreements and trade areas intended to counter neoliberal infrastructural
inequities. Examples include the South Asian Association for Regional
Cooperation (SAARC) formed in 1985 and the Association of Southeast
Asian Nations (ASEAN).

Ananya Mukherjee Reed (1997) points out that regional cooperation
has been challenged by the need to compete as individual nations in the
global market, especially in textile production, but that collaboration has
been increasing. An interesting point of comparison, I think, between the
SAARC nations (India, Bhutan, Sri Lanka, Nepal, Pakistan, Bangladesh,

and the Maldives) and the signatory nations to the North American Free Trade Agreement and the contemplated Free Trade Area of the Americas, is that the SAARC decisions must be unanimous: no matter its size or income, a nation cannot (in SAARC rhetoric, anyway) be bullied out of its sovereignty, its territory, or its economic rights in trade discussions. The South Asia Free Trade Area, or SAFTA (negotiated by SAARC member nations), should be fully implemented by 2010. It will be useful to compare the international dynamics and the well-being of SAARC residents with those within the jurisdiction of NAFTA, which will be fully implemented in 2009.

Both President Kumaratunga and Saraswati have expressed a stated goal to address—immediately and seriously—the poverty experienced by millions of women and men, globally and in Sri Lanka. Saraswati and President Kumaratunga cannot, however, be characterized as having shared interests simply because they both reside in the global South, any more than Diana and US Secretary of State Condoleezza Rice can be said to have shared interests because they both live in the global North. Saraswati, for example, speaks Tamil and practices Hinduism. President Kumaratunga speaks Sinhala and English and practices Buddhism.[9] These distinctions are relevant to the ways in which Saraswati was actively marginalized in the Sri Lankan national context before, during, and since President Kumaratunga's administration (which ended in 2005). Sinhala is the state language and Buddhism is the state religion. Saraswati is first marginalized, then, as a member of a state-marginalized ethnic group. She and other Tamils living on the tea estates are then doubly marginalized by Tamils from the north and east of the island, who do not share their family histories of coming from India to the central hill country of the former British colony of Ceylon as indentured workers.

The Malaiyaha, or upcountry Indian Tamil, population has tended to be concentrated for generations on the estates. In fact, hundreds of thousands of descendants of originally indentured plantation workers from India were left stateless—without national identities or passports—for half a century after Indian and Sri Lankan independence from British colonial rule. President Kumaratunga's government only very recently granted citizenship to the remaining stateless Tamils. Saraswati's family, then, is part of the most marginalized Sri Lankan community (by cultural and national citizenship, ethnicity, caste, language, and income), and President Kumaratunga's position is privileged culturally, as well as politically.[10] These differences mediate powerfully, but do not completely negate, convergence in the two women's strategies to address economic marginality related to globalization.

I am arguing here that even as those participating in capitalist logic practice "strategic alterity," selectively "othering" specific groups at strategic moments by gender, ethnicity, caste, national identity, religion, racialization, age, or other markers of identity in order to justify their low-wage or non-wage position in the labor force,[11] there are at the same time strategic alliances—across these noted differences—to address (sometimes limited) shared concerns. In the case of President Kumaratunga and Saraswati, these are disarticulated. President Kumaratunga called for South–South organization on the state level from a podium, "streaming" immediately into global media, and Saraswati made her call for global organizing in an individual conversation connecting her to the readers of this chapter. They do not strategize together; in fact, Saraswati feels completely marginalized from all political representation in the context of the Sri Lankan state, which she views as oppressive.

There have been many questions in transnational women's organizing about the possibility of, for example, challenging capitalist domination. Some women participate in capitalist strategies even as they challenge them, which might be said of President Kumaratunga's position in guiding economic decision making in the Democratic Socialist Republic of Sri Lanka. Saraswati has little participation, or say, in the marketplace. Yet they both have called, in different venues, for an end to economic disparities, which are so often gendered. As Domitila Barrios de Chungara pointed out to Betty Friedan at the United Nations International Women's Year Tribunal in Mexico City in 1975 (Barrios de Chungara with Viezzer 1978), just because they were both women did not mean that they had a full set of overlapping concerns. Diana and Bertha, in the next section, have many differences—like President Kumaratunga and Saraswati—and some similarities, including being Mexican residents interested in the lived effects of neoliberal policies in agriculture and other sectors of the economy. The RMALC example in the next section demonstrates women's leadership and cross-class, cross-sector organizing for empowerment in the face of free trade policies.

A consideration of the possibilities of such multivocal organizing cannot, of course, ignore the challenges to such collaboration presented by linguistic, class, ethnic, gender, racialized, and other powerful distinctions. Differences within and between North and South women's movements, for example, have been discussed by Hawkesworth (2006:121–145). Alvarez and others (2003) document divisions expressed among Latin American and Caribbean feminist activists, and Macdonald (2003) specifically analyzes exclusionary practices in transnational, anti-NAFTA social movements.

ORGANIZING STRATEGIES OF THE RED MEXICANA DE ACCIÓN FRENTE AL LIBRE COMERCIO (RMALC)

In April 1991, the first Trinational Trade Union meeting took place in Chicago so that labor advocates could compare experiences and plan strategies across North America. Also that month, the RMALC was formed in Mexico. The RMALC is an umbrella organization that collectively facilitates smaller, diverse organizations' crafting of a specific alternative to NAFTA and other free trade policies. Around 100 organizations joined in the RMALC, including labor, environmental, women's, youth, rural, urban, and human rights organizations. Diana's agricultural collective was connected to the RMALC, along with many other rural and urban organizations across Mexico. In turn, representatives of the RMALC met with umbrella organizations from Canada and the United States, including the Action Canada Network, the Québec Coalition on the Trilateral Negotiations, and the Mobilization for Development, Trade, Labor and Environment to organize transnational responses to proposed free trade policies. In October 1991 in Zacatecas, Mexico, representatives of these organizations held, together, the International Forum on Public Opinion and the NAFTA Negotiations: Citizen Alternatives. The RMALC has been involved in organizing a number of conferences bringing various constituencies together—for example, workers for SONY from many different countries or labor union representatives from industries benefiting from and losing out under neoliberal free trade policies.

For Bertha Luján, a labor lawyer and representative of the Frente Auténtico de Trabajadores (FAT), who became a leader in the RMALC (and later the comptroller of Mexico City when Cuauhtémoc Cárdenas became mayor), one of the central roles of a flexible, issue-specific organization like the RMALC was to find legal instruments already signed by the signatory nations negotiating free trade agreements and to try to hold those nations accountable to those existing policies. Examples of such a policy would be the United Nations Universal Declaration on Human Rights and Organization of American States agreements on immigrant workers' human rights. She felt that, case by case, lawyers and judges needed to be made more accountable for their interpretations of changes made in national labor laws accommodating neoliberal models. Bertha Luján argued for a very different kind of plurinational accountability than the control of the IMF, the WTO, and the World Bank. She told me, in an interview in 1995, that the RMALC was monitoring (in collaboration with other umbrella organizations) conditions after NAFTA and was continuing to propose specific alternatives to it, as the RMALC had done when NAFTA was proposed. These alternatives were more akin to the European Union's attention to economic asymmetries among nations involved in transnational trade agreements, to the rights of migrants, and to compensation for those displaced from changing labor markets as a result of neoliberal restructuring.

The RMALC is an example of how national and plurinational cross-class and cross-interest collaborations can be useful. Agrarian, women's, and other worker organizations, for example, had close understandings of how neoliberal policies were affecting the most economically marginalized NAFTA public. Those understandings, coupled with the knowledge of the juridical domain gained by those with more privileged access, like Bertha Luján, resulted in a broad set of analyses formulated into specific policies countering the NAFTA document. Here are some examples.

In 1993, the alternative to NAFTA written by RMALC representatives had, in the labor section, provisions that workers be included in deciding policies that affected them; have rights to organize; have benefits that would be equal for workers in all signatory nations; and work in toxin-free environments. The proposal called for the equal protection of agricultural and manufacturing workers and the observance of protection for migrant workers as already laid out in such agreements as the United Nations Agreement on the Protection of the Rights of Migrant Workers and Their Families, signed in 1990.

The environmental section of the RMALC's proposed alternative to NAFTA called for sustainable development, saying that environmental degradation and economic inequality do not foster sustainability. One of its principles was the "sovereign right of each nation to protect its own resources and the responsibility to avoid doing harm to the environment that affects other nations" (RMALC 1993:7). The proposal called for harmonization without uniformity in the environmental regulations attached to free trade agreements, specifying that one nation not become a toxic-waste dump for other signatory nations (that is, each nation would recycle its own wastes). The specific legal framework, in the environmental section as in the others, was elaborated in this RMALC document, as were specific proposals that groups of NGOs administer oversight of the proposed regulations.

The RMALC proposal on human rights and free trade called for the ratification of the Organization of American States (OAS) and United Nations agreements on human rights and acceptance of the rulings of the Interamerican Human Rights Court, with a commission of NGOs to oversee the human rights of migrant workers.

As noted by Manisha Desai (2002:15), women's transnational solidarity networks have played important roles in working to counter the North to South flow (or return, as we could see it through the lens of dependency theory) of ideas and resources: "At these [transnational organizing] sites, the flow of ideas and activism is no longer unidirectional, from the North to the South, but multidirectional. The ideas and activism are dispersed into varied local sites where they are picked up and refashioned as they resonate in contextualized ways." The RMALC has been accounting for variations in local contexts as its members work toward economic and social harmonization through specific policies. Although the organization began in response to NAFTA proposals, it has continued to respond to free trade policies such as the Central American Free Trade Agreement and Free Trade Area of the Americas. Strategic collaborative concerns have been worked out in person in various conferences and through the RMALC website.

Bertha Luján wrote a chapter called "Citizen Advocacy Networks and the NAFTA" for a book titled *Cross-Border Dialogues* (Brooks and Fox 2002). She notes the positive dynamics associated with globalization, not only the negative ones, including "the growing interrelation between grassroots, citizen, and political organizations" (Luján 2002:212) to "promote citizens' rights over capital" (2002:215). She documents disagreements that arose between labor groups within and between each nation in forging consensus on an alternative to NAFTA and describes the differences in national priorities among transnational NGO solidarity networks (with US groups tending to prioritize environmental concerns, for example, and Mexican groups seeing workers' compensation and the human rights of migrants as top goals). She also notes that Canadian and Mexican NGO alliances critical of neoliberal free trade policies agreed with each other in opposing NAFTA but disagreed over whether alternatives should be proposed. (The Canadian groups did not join the RMALC in going forward with alternative free trade proposals.) In 1996, the Canadian Labour Congress hosted a conference with the trinational alliance organizations, called "Challenging Free Trade in the Americas: Elaborating Common Responses" (Luján 2002:223). As Luján (2002:225) observes, the trinational alliance of hundreds of NGOs has held together beyond its initial purpose of opposing NAFTA to continue with a critique of the proposed FTAA, even as each national alliance focuses its goals in addressing policy at the national level.

The RMALC continues to contest free trade policies, and Foster (2005:215) argues that because of the countering of NAFTA by the RMALC and allied movements, governments negotiating the FTAA have acknowledged officially a role for civil society in the negotiations. The RMALC website includes links to gender-based organizations contesting free trade policies. Those organizations, and their reports, mostly focus on the privatization of water supplies across Latin America, which is a community-based issue of concern to women and men in many contexts.[12] In Bolivia, an organized public stood up to the privatization of the water supply, but the continuing pressure through free trade instruments and organizations is tremendous and the counterpressure must be too.[13] While neoliberal policies are ongoing in their proposals and implementations, the FTAA is another point of convergence for umbrella organizations within which constituencies countering free trade policies have some overlapping goals, including bringing attention to—and addressing—free marketeers' agency in compounding the economic marginalization of those construed as "others" in neoliberal capitalist logic. Daysi Granados, for example, is a Nicaraguan farmer who has stood up with others in her community against the water privatization that corporations are trying to force on Nicaraguans (even though there are national laws against water privatization). She and her colleagues have found support and advice for their efforts via the Internet from activists who successfully countered water privatization attempts in Bolivia (Granados, personal communication, 2005).

CONCLUSION

Women like Diana, Dot, Saraswati, and Bertha have brought expertise learned about the challenges of organizing across many *kinds* of political and identity borders to the current moment of crafting alternatives to neoliberal global capitalist policies (in and beyond the agricultural sector). The RMALC is an example of a solidarity network that brings women's, environmental, human rights, urban, rural, and labor interests to the table with transnational counterparts to negotiate—through very specific policy proposals—a long-term bottom line of social and environmental well-being as an alternative, in global accounting, to neoliberal national administrations' attention to a tenuous, short-term economic bottom line. Those working in agricultural sectors, as in all economic sectors, are affected unevenly by neoliberal restructuring, but the RMALC and other organizations are working to identify those issues and policies that can be supported strategically across interest groups.

Because plurinational alliances of NGOs have become significant venues for not only critique but also action in relation to national and international policies, events, and practices glossed as globalization, I believe that it is important to recognize and document the histories of each of those organizations and to see what lessons they bring to joint organizing efforts. Lessons learned about multivocality and intersectionality through women's transnational organizing now inform those involved in umbrella organizing seeking alternatives to free trade policies that focus on gender-based inequities in relation to other configurations of inequity. The RMALC, for example, is not a women's organization, but women participate in positions of leadership and have crafted policies that resonate with public welfare goals and strategies of the plurinational women's movement. Ximena Bedregal Sáez (1992), in a history of the Mexican women's movement, states that the holding of the International Women's Year Conference (beginning the UN Decade for Women) in Mexico City in 1975 catalyzed widespread organizing efforts among Mexican women during that next decade, with a focus on linking gender and class concerns. I suggest that this history, along with intersections with the labor movement, provided a discourse that has facilitated the very effective work of the RMALC in articulating alternatives to neoliberal trade policies.[14]

Valentine Moghadam (1999) argues that globalization has increased women's participation in the low-wage labor force, as well as the international trade in ideas about feminism and neoliberalism, and that this is an interesting moment for seeing how these factors come together in the union of women's interests across class lines. This was certainly evident in a 1995 gathering of women and men in Mexico City organized through the FAT (Authentic Workers' Front) and the RMALC, in which the conditions for workers (many of them women) around the Pacific Rim were analyzed critically in the context of neoliberal policies. The convergence of plurinational activists in Seattle during the 1999 WTO talks exposed many activists in the United States for the first time to long-term discourses critical of neoliberal policies and established transnational, trans-class, and trans-interest organizing strategies. Staudt, Rai, and Parpart (2001) commented on that moment of convergent interests in "empowerment" and the need for more sustained, cross-context policy efforts, going beyond protests. Activists in the Canadian National Action Committee (NAC) on the Status of Women have made the same observation (Cohen et al. 2002).

Such initiatives *have* been occurring. In August 2001, for example, in Mexico City, 270 representatives of social groups from 39 countries met to form an alliance to counter neoliberal globalization and promote social justice (Global Exchange 2001); a series of forums, often paralleling meetings of national governments and related transnational entities such as the WTO and the International Monetary Fund, was planned at that time. Another initiative was El Foro de los Pueblos (the People's Forum) paralleling the fifth meeting of the WTO in Cancún, Mexico, in September 2003. The Internet site of the RMALC (http://www.rmalc.org.mx) includes a declaration of the Alianza Social Continental (Continental Social Alliance) on the results of the WTO meetings, a description of El Foro de los Pueblos as "an alternative space created by and for Civil Society," and other documents related to ongoing plurinational efforts key to moving beyond simply protesting to evaluating and proposing alternatives to neoliberal state policies.

As Friedman (2003:314) notes, "the transnational women's rights movement substantially changed the framework for understanding global issues." One of those legacies is the increasingly public struggle between a neoliberal, free-market agenda and a social bottom line, as seen in the outcome of the 2004 national elections in India. Documenting the specific contributions of differing organizing histories, including gender-related ones, to plurinational activist alliances is important as these bodies challenge neoliberal states and propose more inclusive alternative policies. The call to organize globally made by Saraswati resonates with the actions of Dot, Diana, Bertha, and many others, through strategic alliances in and beyond the agricultural sector.

In conclusion, I am arguing here that one of the contributions of decades of women's transnational organizing to current, broader-based efforts to analyze and contest the marginalizing effects of free trade policies is the insight that interests need not be completely convergent for strategic alliances to be effective. President Chandrika Kumaratunga, for example, contests marginality within the WTO yet participates in Saraswati's cultural and economic marginalization. This seeming paradox is explained well by Patricia Hill Collins' (2000) concept of the matrix of domination, through which domination, subjugation, and resistance are intertwined, negating, for example, totalizing assumptions of shared interest by gender. I agree with Shirin Rai (2002) that a "politics of engagement" with globalization processes—a transformative politics recognizing the differences between activists—is both possible and necessary. We have learned through discussions of multiply situated viewpoints, as well as the organizing efforts of women like Digna Ribera and Bertha Luján, that strategic actions do not have to involve complete concordance. Just as global capitalist organization and processes can rely on strategic alliances between capitalists who may or may not know one another, strategic contestation of global capitalist practices—and the inequities associated with them—can be enacted by disparately positioned individuals.

About the Author

Ann Kingsolver, associate professor of anthropology at the University of South Carolina, has been interviewing men and women about their views on globalization since 1986 in the United States, Mexico, and, most recently, Sri Lanka. She wrote *NAFTA Stories: Fears and Hopes in Mexico and the United States* (2001) and edited *More Than Class: Studying Power in US Workplaces* (1998). She is general editor of the *Anthropology of Work Review.*

Notes

1. Article 27 of Mexico's constitution was amended to allow for the privatization of ejido lands.

2. The full context of the interviews with Diana and Leonardo (pseudonyms) may be found in Kingsolver 2001:96–99. The names Dot, Tommy, and Saraswati in this chapter are also pseudonyms.

3. B. Sasikumar translated between Saraswati's Tamil and my English in this interview. My fieldwork on globalization in Sri Lanka was supported by a 2004 Fulbright Lecture/Research Award.

4. John Gledhill (1995) observes that the economic problems in the ejido sector in Mexico are not solely due to neoliberal policies, but those policies are the focus of this chapter.

5. See Barrón 1999 for a discussion of Mexican agricultural workers in a Canadian context.

6. See Biswajit Dhar and Sudeshna Dey 2002 for an excellent discussion of the WTO Agreement on Agriculture and the contestation between nations of the global North and South over food security issues.

7. Marc Edelman (2004) discusses famine across Central America as a direct result of trade liberalization in the agricultural sector. In Mexico, Olivia Acuña Rodarte (2003:130) states that since the implementation of free trade policies, approximately 300,000 corn farmers have lost their livelihoods.

8. Itty Abraham's (2005) discussion of increasing counter-hegemonic organizing between Latin American and Asian activists is relevant to this section.

9. See Jayawardena 2002 for a discussion of President Kumaratunga's elite family position, in terms of social and economic capital, in Sri Lanka.

10. For more on the history, working conditions, and citizenship status of estate Tamils in Sri Lanka, see Daniel 1996, Hollup 1994, and Sinnathamby 2004.

11. The fluidity of the category marked as "other" for purposes of inequitable distribution of resources has been well documented by Brodkin (1998:63), Harrison (1995), and Omi and Winant (1994), among others. See Kingsolver 2001, 2007 for further discussion of "strategic alterity."

12. See Ballvé 2005, Olivera with Lewis 2004, and Shiva 2002.

13. Bechtel and a Dutch corporate partner have sued the Bolivian government for $25 million in lost profits after the efforts of many organized women and men in Bolivia were successful in stopping the privatization of public water supplies that was attached to debt renegotiation by the IMF, the World Bank, and the Interamerican Development Bank in 1988 (Women's Committee, Hemispheric Social Alliance 2004:7–8).

14. The collaboration of the RMALC with other umbrella organizations transnationally builds on earlier transnational organizing efforts, begun long before NAFTA negotiations, for example, the transnational monitoring and publicizing of conditions in the maquiladoras, factories in export processing zones in Mexico, documented by the Border Committee of Women Workers (2004).

13

Globalization, *Swadeshi*, and Women's Movements in Orissa, India

Annapurna Pandey

Globalization has produced highly uneven benefits, problems, and responses. Gender, region, ethnicity, and economic conditions have all played a role in the differential impact of the forces of globalization. With case studies from the Indian state of Orissa, particularly of its tribal, or Kond, women, I show how the neoliberal policies associated with the current form of economic globalization (intersecting with earlier policies of "development" and "modernization") have presented both challenges and opportunities for Indian women. Paradoxically, globalization has given the women of Orissa the educational tools and, increasingly, the social and cultural freedom to combat the social problems and dislocations created by economic globalization itself. At the same time, even the gains achieved—as in the case of education—have proved a double-edged sword and, as I will show below in the case of college girls in Kendrapada and Kond women, have come at a heavy price.

In taking advantage of the opportunities afforded by legal equality, enshrined in the Indian constitution and law, and in challenging the inequities of newer economic developments, women activists in Orissa have created a form of feminism that neither rejects tradition outright nor poses women as victims and men as oppressors. Instead, it creates a coalition in which women and men are partners in promoting the interests of the socially disadvantaged. In their organizing, these women have promoted, above all, networking and connectivity. In short, many women in Orissa have a more complex reaction to globalization than being "for" or "against" it. They have sought to take advantage of the benefits of modernity while resisting, and even opposing, its abuses. In the case studies that follow, I hope to show how the culturally distinctive response of Hindu and Kond women in Orissa constitutes a particular form of Indian feminism that emphasizes recognition of cultural identities, that is, a notion of womanhood by which women are defined according to their roles rather than their sex in a common struggle for empowerment and against injustices.

I am a US-based Indian social scientist who is deeply committed to the varied experiences of women in rural, tribal, and urban sectors in India. During my higher education in the post-1975 era (with the declaration of International Women's Decade) in India, I was exposed to the growing interest in the new wave of feminism and its Indian counterpart, Indian feminism, which was growing in popularity. I grew up in the state of Orissa, in an educated, middle-class Brahmin family. As the only daughter with four brothers, I was always aware of both my "privileges" and the conventional constraints of my gender. With parents who supported my education and interest in social issues, I developed early a critical awareness of gender-based expectations in the family and society. I have long been interested in women's experiences in their roles as daughter, wife, and mother and how these roles vary in terms of class, caste, and religion.

For my doctoral dissertation in sociology at Jawaharlal Nehru University in Delhi, I worked on the nature of women's political participation in Orissa. It was disappointing to observe that the grassroots-level women's movement was, at the time, very minimal because of a lack of pre-independence and post-independence gender-based political movements in Orissa, compared with other states in India. Since 1986, I have been working on the nature of women's organization and collective movements in tribal areas, keeping in view the upsurge of industrialization and the development of mining projects in southwestern Orissa. For the past 17 years, I have been teaching about global women's issues of marginality and agency. I have begun new research on the life experiences of Indian diaspora women in California while continuing research in Orissa.

Every year, I go to India for three or more months to work with women in various sectors to see how they are responding to the process of globalization through nongovernmental organization (NGO) networking, grassroots-level knowledge building, or state-promoted development plans and policies. I have been using the participant-observation method throughout my fieldwork in Orissa, and I interview people with a loosely structured, flexible questionnaire that allows me to improvise, depending on the mood of the interviewee and the demand of the circumstances. I do speak the state language, Oriya, and am also very familiar with various regional dialects of Oriya in southern and western Orissa. With a thorough understanding of the available literature on women's issues both in the Western and global South contexts, I use my field experience to challenge some of the available analyses and to develop a specific perspective from the point of view of the specificity of experiences of marginalized women in the context of their location. My research approach for this study has been influenced by, among others, Bauman (1998), Holstein (2005), Kasturi (1995), Mohanty (2003b), Naples and Desai (2002), and Sivaramakrishnan and Agrawal (2003).

ORISSA AND THE KOND WOMEN

Orissa, located in eastern India on the Bay of Bengal, has the dubious distinction of being India's poorest state, an unwanted status previously held by the nearby state of Bihar until 1993–1994. What is striking is that Orissa has tremendous natural resources, including substantial reserves of materials needed to make steel, such as iron ore, coal, dolomite, and limestone. Despite this abundance, previous exploitative efforts to extract these resources have met with opposition from activist environmental groups and tribal development activists. However, the situation may soon change: the current chief minister of Orissa has recently signed several contracts with transnational corporations and organizations to make use of the abundant natural resources and improve the socioeconomic condition of the state.

The situation of women in Orissa also lags far behind that in the rest of India. According to the 2001 census, Orissa has a sex ratio of 972 females per 1,000 males, which exceeds the nationwide average of 933, as well as the sex ratios for many other Indian states. The female life expectancy of 59.71 falls below the national average of 66.91. The infant mortality rate is 92 for females and 98 for males, compared with 67 and 69, respectively, at the national level. Female literacy is 50.97 percent, whereas the male literacy rate is 75.95 percent. The 1991 census found that only 27.28 percent of the total workforce in Orissa comprised women. The unorganized primary sector (for example, agriculture) employed 82.7 percent of the total employed female workers. Of those, around 5.2 percent were engaged in household industries, and other sectors of the economy provided employment to 12.1 percent of female workers. According to the National Family Health Survey, about 48 percent of the female population suffers from nutritional deficiency.

Of the women of Orissa, the most marginalized (along all markers of difference) are the Kond. Tribal members constitute almost one-fourth of the total population of Orissa. Of these, the Kond (including the Kui subgroup) are the most numerous and mainly reside in western Orissa, in the hills and plains of Phulbani, Kalahandi, and Koraput.

To better understand the paradoxes of the impact of globalization on the women of Orissa—whether urban or rural, tribal or Hindu—it is necessary to contextualize the discussion in two ways: first, by understanding the disjunction between formal equality for women and significant deprivation; and second, by underscoring the cultural situation of Indian women, perhaps best exemplified in the concept of *swadeshi* and the ways in which the specifics of cultural reality create, intersect with, and reinforce legal and economic disjunctions.

LEGAL EQUALITY, REAL DEPRIVATION

Women in India enjoy equal constitutional and legal rights because of their significant participation in nation building against the British Raj. But, hand in hand with this "paper" equality, social practices and institutional conventions, as we shall see, effectively deny women the very rights granted. Moreover, the "glorification" of women has similarly been a two-edged sword: since India's independence in 1947, the state has looked upon women as the very emblem of Indian culture and tradition, representing the freedom of the nation, its independence and integrity in a postcolonial setting. Indian state-run television and state-influenced films promote the image of a devoted mother as dependent on her first-born son and of a self-sacrificing wife as the good woman taking care of her children, family, and community and thus upholding Indian values. In response to a question on increasing reports of abuse against women, Lopamudra Mahanty, chief of the Women's Commission in Orissa, has said, "A wife should love her husband, his parents, be a good mother, good woman and most important of all a good house wife" (personal communication, August 28, 1998). In other words, formal legal equality has coexisted with a cultural "typing" of women.

Yet, cultural typing is increasingly in tension with social and economic realities. With industrialization and globalization, the women of India are becoming more and more educated and are joining the professional ranks in significant numbers. The "top ten" students in high schools and colleges across the country are almost always women. Women are represented in political positions at the local, state, and national levels. Thus, in contemporary India, we see two images of women—as the giving mother and achieving worker/active citizen. But, paradoxical and even incongruous as it may seem "under Western eyes" (to use the title of Conrad's novel, also recently used by the Third World feminist writer Chandra Mohanty), the Indian state has endeavored to promote a "happy balance" between the two through popular culture and various development programs. It is widely believed that one can have the cultural cake while eating the economic one too.

Ironically, women's political leadership at the state and national levels mentioned above has not translated into significant progress for women. Hence, we see that, in spite of legal equality for women, real improvement in their daily lives is based on class, caste, region, and family. R. N. Ghosh and K. C. Roy (1997) have argued that legal and constitutional rights in themselves do not necessarily reflect changing social attitudes. It is economic empowerment that ultimately leads to improvement in the status of women. In the Indian context, development and urbanization have led to very uneven results for different categories of women in India. While poor women in rural India have been left behind, middle-class, educated women have been able to improve their economic and social status, thanks to more opportunities for education and employment. Religion has also played a role, with Muslim women held back from opportunities provided to Christian and Hindu women.

In 1971, in response to a request from the United Nations, the government of India appointed a Committee on the Status of Women in India (CSWI) to examine the rights and status of women as guaranteed by the constitution. The committee's comprehensive report (1974) identified a significant gap in women's overall status in relation to education, health, and employment.[1] The Indian government responded in its sixth five-year plan with a developmentalist[2] model aimed at improving the status of women in India, with standards based on those of Western countries. This model assumes that women will take advantage of educational and economic opportunities, the national economy will improve, and overall economic development will be based on large-scale industries and improved production.

Since independence, the government of India has emphasized national economic self-reliance and has realized that women, as half the population, can contribute significantly to this goal. The state of India has proudly described Indian women as "swadeshi," which literally means "of one's own country." As swadeshi, Indian women are the exemplary daughters of the soil who fought side by side with their men to achieve India's independence from British colonial rule and brought in *swaraj* (ruling one's own country).

CHANGING MEANING OF SWADESHI IN CONTEMPORARY INDIA

Ostensibly, swadeshi and globalization are radically opposed. Mohandas Karamchand Gandhi had, starting in 1919, popularized swadeshi as a rallying cry, raising nationalist consciousness against British industry, most notably the mill-woven cloth of Manchester. The swadeshi movement was glossed as *atmashakti* or "self-strengthening" and popularized by Rabindranath Tagore in his nationalistic writings for the Indian public. In this guise, the movement also expressed itself as administrative noncooperation and educational reform (Bose and Jalal 1998). Encapsulated by Gandhi's most potent symbol (which now appears on the Indian flag), the *chakra*, or hand-operated spinning wheel, swadeshi came to denote the desire for self-sufficiency and self-reliance. But it was also from the very beginning connected to Gandhi's adaptation of the concept of swaraj, which drew a philosophical and political analogy between the mastery of individual bodily appetites and desires, on the one hand, and national independence, on the other. Thus, in Gandhi's terms, swadeshi carried a profound significance and does not mean merely the use of what is produced in one's own country. From this perspective, swadeshi is not inexorably opposed to a global perspective: what counts is the *use*, the spirit in which a global perspective is adopted (Mazzarella 2003:5–14).

Significantly, Gandhi himself suggested that the "other" is not per se the enemy. Based on the analogy between the mastery of individual bodily appetites and desires and the mastery of national independence, Gandhi (1997:107) asked, "How can Manchester be blamed? We wore Manchester cloth, and that is why Manchester wove it."

In the name of swadeshi, Gandhi's ideology appealed to the general public in India. Women in large numbers joined the national movement led by Gandhi to fight against British rule in India, and their participation was critical to the success of the struggle for independence. In the process, women's causes, such as education and organizing, and their awareness of swadeshi were incorporated into the nationalist movement. "The increasing political consciousness among women and the integration of their own cause with the Indian national movement helped in further extending the space available to women" (Sethi 1999:341). With India's independence, women gained the right to vote, could participate equally in economic, educational, and political spheres along with men, and achieved legal and constitutional equality.

In sum, in contemporary India, swadeshi has been looked upon as, perhaps paradoxically, a nationalistic welcoming and incorporating of multinational corporations and transnational ideas, thereby exhibiting the depth and power of the nation and the all-embracing nature of the Indian state. I do not mean to suggest, of course, that the "Indian State" is an abstract, faceless, monolithic entity. In fact, a coalition of interest groups is running the state in India. As India has gradually moved from its predominantly agricultural base to an industrialized economy, even agriculture has been heavily mechanized, marginalizing the small farmers dependent on plough agriculture. One hears that rich farmers depend on the exploitation of *dalits* (untouchables), labor unions control various sectors of industries, and in certain regions tribal residents have gained control of the political arena in India.

In any case, swadeshi has taken on the meaning of a resilient tradition that not only can withstand but also absorb neoliberal capitalism, striking what some trumpet as a happy balance between tradition and modernity. As with the multinational corporation, the state also promotes "swadeshi" for women, who are seen as representing India's purity of tradition and at the same time embracing modernity. Unfortunately, the rhetoric of "exemplary daughters of the soil" valorizing the role of Indian women in achieving independence is merely repeating the general pattern that has occurred elsewhere in the nation-building process and in national liberation movements: women become embodied with notions of the "motherland," gaining symbolic value but remaining disempowered by the absence of efforts to address gender disparities, as well as by essentializing conceptualizations and placement of women.

Undoubtedly, globalization has brought new opportunities for many people around the world, and India is no exception. The Indian state has revamped the notion of swadeshi and has accommodated it to openly welcome transnational corporations (Hewlett Packard, Yahoo) and development agencies (the World Bank, the International Monetary Fund [IMF]).

But there are naysayers amidst this public image of the warm embrace of globalization in India (the reader may recall the slogan "India Shining" from the recent election, analyzed so well in the Indian news magazine *Frontline*). According to novelist, architect, and activist Arundhati Roy (2001:26), globalization has also marginalized certain kinds of local knowledge and its producers. For example, there has been a huge rural-to-urban migration in India. From 80 percent at the time of independence, the rural population has dwindled to 65 percent of the country's total. Globalization has created a massive urban proletariat, ever increasing the informal service sector, as discussed further below. The devaluation of local resource and knowledge systems has given rise to new knowledge based on mechanized agriculture and commercialized farming. International loaning agencies are promoting patriarchy, favoring male borrowers over women. According to Roy, there is a lot of money in poverty. She refers to the profit-making scheme of the World Bank and IMF, which give loans to the Third World's poverty-stricken people at high interest rates.

But globalization has had many positive implications as well. Increased access to global media has meant that women in Orissa (my native state and the subject of much of my research), with the help of satellite dishes, are informed daily of rights and opportunities available to women world-wide. Through computers and other media, women in Orissa are network-ing to assert their legal, constitutional, and political rights. So how can we begin to sort out these upsides and downsides to globalization? The ulti-mate balance sheet of globalization is a work for the future, but I offer, in the sections that follow, several ethnographies of women's reactions to globalization that may contribute to an assessment of the gains and losses associated with the impact of global economic developments in a very depressed part of India.

INTRODUCTION TO CASE STUDIES

Since the 1990s, I have been actively involved in several women's orga-nizations: Basundhara, based in Cuttack and Bhubaneswar and devoted to rehabilitation of destitute women and children; Vijaya, focused on women's health and nutrition and collaborating with the Center for Public Health and Environment Education (COPHEE) in rural Orissa; and Ghumusar Mahila Sangathan in Phulbani, aimed at the development of tribal (Kond) women. These organizations focus on social and economic development for women in the villages, tribal regions, and cities of Orissa. In the course of my social science research on women's organizing in different parts of Orissa and in my personal experience as a social activist, I have been struck, time and again, by the differential impact of globalization in the context of Orissa in relation to India, the uneven effects of globalization on women in different regions of Orissa, simultaneous issues of marginalization of women in various sectors, and the multiple levels of contestation voiced by women's organizations at the grassroots level in the state. My ultimate goal has been to begin to understand the complex, and elusive, specific nature of Indian feminism as defined by these women's organizations in relation to the state and the forces of economic globalization.

To return to the question asked by Arundhati Roy—who is benefiting from globalization? I suggest in the following case studies that, at least for the girls in the lower middle class, globalization has not been a boon;

indeed, they are now more marginalized in terms of job opportunities and marriage prospects. For all the vaunted advantages of globalization, and despite legal equality for women and the "affirmative action" focus on disadvantaged groups, women related to political leaders, state bureaucrats, and moneyed groups that support the ruling government party get first priority for whatever jobs are available in the market. Merit is compromised by favoritism. In other words, globalization, rather than level differences, has in many cases intensified class hierarchies among women. T. N. Pandey (2002:6) observes, "Globalization has also polarized and bifurcated our life. It has created a new kind of hierarchy in our society...globalization has promoted and privileged certain people and their products and marginalized others."

The following example supports Pandey's comments and Roy's observation about the way globalization has negatively impacted local cultures. On my visit to India in 2004, I came across a shocking news story that groups of college women were committing suicide in Kendrapara, a suburb of Cuttack in Orissa. Various reporters had investigated this breaking news and discovered that these girls had been secretly used by local political leaders for their sexual gratification, in return for gifts, payment of living expenses, and promises of marriage. These girls, who came from poor families, had lacked the economic means to satisfy desires for such goods as designer jeans, Gucci purses, and Halston perfumes and makeup—desires created by the marketing of products through globalized media. Coming from uneducated or semi-educated families, they were ashamed of their uneducated mothers and barely communicated with them, let alone heeded their advice.

Their college had not helped them and had, in a way, contributed to the tragedy. In the present market economy, many teachers do not teach course material in the classroom, expecting instead that students will come to their homes for expensive tutoring to get their degree. Ironically, college education might be free for girls of marginalized class, caste, and religion, but because of the private tutoring situation, educational success (represented by good grades and passing examinations) remains limited to students from the higher classes. The young women featured in the news story had little chance in the highly competitive job market. Ridiculed for not having jobs after so many years of education, they also had diminished marriage prospects because Indian men perceived their high level of education as threatening. Their desperation for not fitting into either the traditional system or the globalized economy led to their tragic end. They had been truly marginalized by globalization.

In another instance, on a recent trip, my teacher and former colleague Mrs. Manorama Mahapatra shared with me that in the globalized economy, modern consumer goods, such as televisions, refrigerators, gas stoves, and sofa sets, have become the new status symbols in villages. Her niece and her friends are completely absorbed in fashion, competing with peers on looks and ignoring their schooling as a source of useful, marketable knowledge. But neither are they following the local knowledge, as in respecting their elders and doing household chores. The parents are scared of declining marriage prospects for their girls and feel compelled to offer higher dowries to get their daughters married in the same caste, even though the husbands are less educated than their wives.

TRIBAL WOMEN'S EXPERIENCES OF GLOBALIZATION: THE EXAMPLE OF GHUMUSAR MAHILA SANGATHAN (WOMEN JOINING TOGETHER), ORISSA

Traditionally, compared with Hindus, Kond women have enjoyed an equal social status with the men in their society. Kond women can own land and can pass on their lineage to future generations. Women choose their husbands and are not stigmatized if they remarry after the death of their spouse or even divorce their husbands. However, in the course of various development projects, Kond women have come into increasing contact with mainstream Indian society, and many of their beliefs have been threatened by the insurgent Hindu culture. Since the 1990s, the Hindu majority ruling party has emphasized swadeshi to promote Hindu culture and absorb various indigenous cultures into it. There has been a massive Hindu conversion among indigenous groups to make up for the Christian conversion during the British period. Kond women are enticed to follow Hindu customs to become true daughters of mother India. For example, Kond women are under pressure not to remarry and are forced to follow *purdah* (seclusion of women by concealing clothing or physical segregation) to protect themselves from the roving eyes of men.

Sandhyarani Naik, director of Ghumusar Mahila Sangathan (GMS), claimed that, increasingly, Kond women are encouraged to be Hinduized in terms of their dress, use of *sindoor* (vermilion) as a marker of marriage, and dependency on their menfolk for procuring loans from the state. Because Konds are encouraged to attend schools with Hindus, they are constantly teased for their dark skin and distinct demeanor. I learned of several instances of tribal schoolgirls being raped by their nontribal teachers and classmates. As an indication of Hindu–tribal conflict, Kond women were even being used as "bargaining chips" or property to settle scores against the tribals. Mrs. Naik described the current situation: "We had never feared men in our lives. Today we do not own our own lands, our women are constantly harassed by Hindu men in the marketplace and on the street." Kond women have felt threatened by these sinister tendencies, which they traced to plans and policies introduced by the state in the name of "development" and, more recently, to the stress on Hindutva in the process of globalization (for discussion of Hindutva, which promotes Hinduism as a source of personal and national identity, see Savarkar 1969:3–4).

The marginalized status of tribal women in the process of globalization and the "feminist" response are well illustrated in the case of Kond women, who traditionally did not face gender discrimination. They work very hard along with their men for a subsistence living. In comparison with their Hindu neighbors, the favorable sex ratio of women to men in the tribal areas reflects the greater value of women in the tribal society. As a girl, a Kond grows up freely, learning the art of a family trade and all the seasonal planting, weaving, and collecting of forest resources. Unlike the Hindu women of Orissa, a Kond woman—at least until recently, as mentioned above—does not wear vermilion, does not cover her head (reflecting her marital status), and does not wear saris as a marker of her womanhood. Traditionally, a Kond girl wears two pieces of cloth to cover her body according to her cultural customs.

Additionally, the marital customs of Konds and Hindus, particularly in the area of arranged marriages, differ markedly. In the Kond tradition, girls and boys mingle freely in a common community house called the Dhangiri Ghrara. Over time, a Kond girl chooses her partner, based on mutual consent. They go through a simple marriage ceremony and exchange vows in front of the community members. The groom is obliged to pay a bride price to earn the hand of the bride.

One significant example of how globalization has been marginalizing the tribal women is worth mentioning. In the 1960s and early 1970s, the Kondmal area attracted many people from all over India in search of a better life. In the name of progress, massive construction took place in G. Udayagiri (transliterated spelling), the capital city of Phulbani (predominantly a Kond district), which witnessed a huge influx of the mainstream population into tribal areas. Many officials and businessmen were temporarily assigned to work in the forests of Orissa to fulfill government or forestry contracts, build roads, and work in steel mining and other projects.

It became a common practice among these male migrants to marry Kond women with a meager bride price and an exchange of a few gifts.

However, many men were already married, and most had families in their native states. They knew full well that this new marriage was not in compliance with the Hindu Marriage Act (1956), but local custom supporting the independence of Kond women seemed to sanction their living with a Kond woman as their wife. This arrangement must have been extremely beneficial for the man: he got an all-in-one sex provider, caretaker, housekeeper, and cook, all for a meager bride price. In a few years, they would have children. Being the wife of a Hindu, the Kond woman would start wearing vermilion, bangles, and anklets and covering her head as a symbol of marriage. But this fairy-tale marriage would not last long. The men, having a parallel family back home, would eventually come to the end of their business contract or state transfer and would leave the area, promising to return soon to collect their beloved wife and children. Of course, they would never return. This practice created a growing number of dejected wives and children in G. Udayagiri, which became popularly known as Premnagar (Pleasure Town). The town attracted many tourists in search of sexual pleasure for free. The abandoned women were too ashamed to return to their communities.

This major social problem gave rise to an indigenous women's organization known as Ghumusar Mahila Sangathan (GMS) led by a Kond woman, Maka Naik, in 1979. With support of other activist groups and student organizations, GMS attracted much media attention to this issue. GMS challenged the men in court and succeeded in getting traditional marriages recognized as legal. As a result, in 40 cases, women were declared legal wives entitled to financial support (GMS report 1998). The state ultimately acknowledged the helpless situation of these women and provided adequate compensation to them and their children. The men were also charged with human rights violations. Today this practice is uncommon.

More recently, when I last visited in 2004, the community house (Dhangiri Ghara) was almost deserted. When I asked the cause, I was told that rampaging Hindu youth had repeatedly threatened the Konds. Fearing for the safety and security of their women, the Kond community had stopped the practice of young men and women meeting on a casual basis and getting to know each other. Women were wearing vermilion and covering their faces so as not to be teased and mistreated by the mainstream society. Even though there has been a consistent effort to improve the education of boys and girls in the area, the constant threat of rape and abduction of schoolgirls, even by their nontribal teachers, still makes schools unsafe places.

Hence, GMS remains very active in this area in its fight against abuse of women and social injustice inflicted on tribal women. It has been taken over by Maka Naik's daughter-in-law and son, Sandhya Rani Naik and Hemant Naik. Both Mr. and Mrs. Naik are very critical of rising Hindutva and the emphasis on swadeshi to incorporate the tribals into their fold. Taking land, language, and culture as markers of Kond identity, the Naiks are collecting funds from various global organizations to develop a curriculum in traditional Kui language. They attribute the dropout rate of kids in school to the lack of education in their mother tongue and the unfamiliar faces of teachers from the plains who are not very kind to the students. They are very fearful of losing their Kond identity and the independence their women have enjoyed so far.

Mrs. Naik says, "The only way we can preserve our identity is through our language, our hold over our land, and follow our age-old customs." GMS also teaches the indigenous Kui language to emphasize Kond identity and preserve the Kond heritage in the face of tremendous pressure to assimilate to Hindu norms. Another member of GMS observes, "Today with the superimposition of Hindutva, Konds like other tribals are forced to convert themselves to Hinduism, so that they are assured to die as a Hindu, a sure shot to attain salvation." I talked to a few Kond activists in the area. They are bitter about the imposition of cultural values and fear losing their own culture.

Through organizing and networking, the tribal women are able to see the relationship between the multiple levels of oppression they experience as a consequence of their tribal status, gender, and poverty. They see a correlation between rising alcohol consumption by men and their violence toward women, between women's lack of access to the forest resources and their poverty, between gender and sexual exploitation, and between culture loss and identity crisis. GMS today focuses on many aspects of tribal women's problems: poverty, health and nutrition, economy, development, education, biodiversity, training and empowerment, violence against women, media attention, and participation in decision making (Mishra and Ghumusar Mahala Sangathan 2001).

To promote economic, as well as cultural, integration in post-independence India, the state has introduced several development plans to uplift the status of the tribals. Konds are especially recognized as one of the most backward communities in India. The state has been promoting various policies to improve the status of women. However, even though women's well-being has been a primary concern of the state, necessary and beneficial policies are lacking. The state has handed down preplanned policies to the Kond without asking for their input or considering plans arising from the community. I can see, in the development model borrowed from the West, a clear discrepancy between the state's ideology and the existing cultural, social, and economic realities of women in Orissa and elsewhere in India. As Kim Berry (2003:78) observes, "Ideas about women and their needs are created out of and are nested within unequal power relations."

For example, when I visited Kond communities, the women were engaged in collecting kendu leaves, which are used to produce local cigarettes (*bidis*) and various household goods such as brooms, leaf plates, and leaf cups. The government had invested a lot of money to engage Kond women in gainful employment, but what they had produced could not be sold in the open market at the prices the government had set, in competition with the cheaper goods of private suppliers. As a result, these women were not compensated for months for their hard labor. The state had not accounted for the community's needs and desires or women's visions for the use of their labor but had simply assumed that the project was "good" for Kond women and for their community as well.

From this perspective, Kond women have figured as a universal category, lumped together as targets of "poverty and inequality" in the Indian social system. The state, as noted above, follows the development model imposed by the Western world (through strings attached to loans and other conditions) in the name of gender equality. The challenges for a Kond woman, despite her evident poverty and inequality, may not be the same as those a Hindu woman faces, let alone the same in any universal sense. In the words of S. Naik, secretary of GMS, "We want to maintain our identity through our language, culture, customs and tradition. We should be free to practice our own religion. There lies our sense of self."

Upholding the belief that in "caring for mother earth, we care for ourselves," GMS has organized committees to protect the forest. These committees monitor forest use and impose fines on those who illegally engage in logging. The group has also devised projects that include licensing intellectual property rights for knowledge of medicinal plants and setting fair prices for forest products.

With grants totaling $20,250, the GMS has proudly supported the growth of this extensive network of women who are defending and reviving an indigenous, egalitarian culture.

MARGINALIZATION AND WOMEN'S ACTIVISM

Besides the experiences of the tribal (Kond) women detailed above, I have also observed comparable examples of marginalization and resistance among (nontribal) rural and urban women in Orissa. Drawing on my fieldwork, I will cite a few examples of women's organizing and community-building efforts that are designed not only to empower women but also to fight against social problems and injustices women have witnessed and experienced in both the private and public sectors—some as a result of the misguided development efforts mentioned above.

On my last visit to Orissa in 2004, I attended a workshop against alcoholism in Bhubaneswar. In the process of globalization, alcoholism among lower-class and lower-middle-class men who feel cheated and left behind has become a major social problem, not only endangering the lives of chronic drinkers but also ruining their family relationships and their children's futures. Because they cannot afford foreign liquor, they buy locally made "rotgut." During the workshop, various women's organizations shared their experiences combating alcoholism in different parts of the state. A 70-year-old illiterate woman presented a triumphant account of joining with women from her village to smash an illegal "moonshine" tavern serving bootlegged liquor and drag the tavern owner to the local police station. The police had no choice but to arrest the owner. In the woman's own words, "The country liquor factories have ruined our lives. Our husbands, fathers, and brothers have become puppets in the hands of these taverners. They are dead even being alive."

The women attacked the taverns to keep their menfolk away from country liquor and save their family life. Here, women were taking the law into their own hands to promote the well-being of their families. The state, in the guise of excise officers, has been complicit in promoting country liquor. Each one of them gets a fat share of the profit from the illegal enterprises. Women were proving their sense of agency and empowerment as active participants against the system, which had allowed the commercialization of liquor. Women were coming out of the confines of their homes and challenging the social injustice promoted by the state.

In another instance of marginalization in relation to education, an 18-year-old college girl from western Orissa had acid thrown on her face for not marrying a street hooligan. Her face was completely disfigured and required total plastic surgery. Even from the hospital bed, she was determined to fight for justice. I was amazed to see her courage; I heard her telling Saila Behera, the secretary of Basundhara, "Older sister [*apa*], I am not alone in my suffering. I have you and my brothers [referring to the voluntary workers at Basundhara] with me." She got support from various women's groups and other NGOs, which forced the state to take up her case, provide her with the necessary financial assistance, and punish the culprit.

A classic example of globalization spawning at once injustice, marginalization, and women's resistance is provided by the unpleasant ironies of "education," so often taken to be the hallmark of enlightened modernization and development. Schools in Orissa are meant to be a site of women's empowerment. With increasing industrialization and urbanization, tribal girls are attending schools along with Hindu children. The state promotes compulsory high school education for the tribals to bridge the educational gap between various ethnic groups. Girls are offered more and more incentives such as free books, tuition-free education, midday meals, and small scholarships to finish their high school education. Also, the state provides guaranteed positions for women with degrees and diplomas in various public sector jobs. In the process of globalization, educated tribal girls have better opportunities to migrate to urban areas for better jobs. In short, tribal women are beneficiaries of an Indian affirmative action program. It is therefore ironic when schools become the site of exploitation of these disadvantaged people.

On March 11, 1998, a school headmaster, who happened to be a Hindu Brahmin, raped two middle-school girls aged 11 and 12. Sadly, these girls were abused in the process of improving their status. Fortunately, the girls received support from local women's organizations, which, in turn, were able to persuade the state to take up the girls' cases. Despite several threats from the accused and bureaucratic harassment by police and other state government officials, the victims' advocates, the victims, and their families ultimately obtained vindication.

INDIAN WOMEN'S NGO WORK

Yet another sign of hopefulness for the women of Orissa can be seen in an organization called the Center for Public Health and Environment Education (COPHEE). COPHEE was founded as an NGO to fight against various social taboos, stereotypes, injustices, inequalities, and forms of exploitation of the disadvantaged, including women. It was started in rural Jajpur, about 60 km from Cuttack City, by two like-minded social activists and became very active after a powerful cyclone struck the state in October 1999.

COPHEE promotes income-generating activities among women by providing them with savings and credit facilities. The organization has undertaken women's empowerment programs through the formation of women's self-help groups (SHG) in five village *panchayats*[3] covering 45 villages in Jajpur district. Not only do these women's groups work to contribute to family incomes, but also the members, including middle-aged women and teenage girls, focus on family health, education of children, and issues of gender discrimination in public life. The women have successfully waged an anti-tobacco campaign. According to a survey by COPHEE, 47 percent of boys between 12 and 14 years of age use tobacco (or *pan, bidi, gudakhu, gutka,* or *gundi,* locally grown addictives). Shanti from COPHEE shared this story with me: "When a minister from the state had come to inaugurate our school in the village, we demanded from him to stop chewing betel nut to honor our anti-tobacco campaign. The minister was very embarrassed. The best part was it was broadcast all over the state." The members are using street plays, walking in organized marches, and putting up posters to oppose social ills such as tobacco use, dowry, alcohol production and sales, and abuse of women by husbands and in-laws. They are trying to involve entire families in this awareness program.

Members of COPHEE shared many of their dreams and visions with me when I visited them in 2004. At a welcome meeting, several young women and their mothers greeted me at their village school. The welcome song sung by a few teenage girls was very meaningful. Translated, the song went,

> We adorn the whole sky and are like the stars. We can combine the sky, air, earth, water and build a new world order, where there would be no exploitation and no frustration. We are the anchors and hold the oars of our own boat, we can build our own future. We can fill everyone's life around us with the scent of life's flavor.

Urmila, in her 50s, sang a song felicitating Durga, a powerful Hindu goddess. These songs were written by women in the group.

With very few resources, these women are very hopeful, resilient, and actively organizing to improve their situation—not just for themselves but as families incorporating their husbands and emphasizing the education of their children to build a better future. In the process of globalization, they do not want to be left out. Regarding their needs, some high school–educated girls shared, "We would love to have vocational training to get jobs; we would benefit from a computer center. So many of us would be able to connect with the outside world." They dream of having access to computers so that they can learn better skills and have access to various employment opportunities outside their community.

Around lunchtime, I asked, "Would not you like to go home to your menfolks?" They confidently said, "See, our men are here to watch and appreciate our organizing efforts. They encourage us to join the *samitis* [associations] and have learned to adjust their schedules."

To share another instance of women's activism, one recently married COPHEE member was sent back to her parents for not fulfilling dowry demands. The girl and her parents were very worried. They could not afford to go to court or obtain any legal help. COPHEE members came to her rescue. They formed a committee and approached the village heads in the girl's husband's village. A meeting was arranged at which both the parties and COPHEE members were present. After a mutual discussion and intervention from the village panchayat, the husband's family invited the girl back to their home.

As a result of such successful efforts, women feel more confident to take up important issues of human rights and women's rights. While working to resolve many of the problems created by the "development" model, these women are attempting to take advantage of the freedom and opportunities—as they see them—of globalization. Whether their dreams are illusory, only time will tell, but their organizing is very much in the tradition of Indian feminism, which has achieved success by forging partnerships with men, the community, and even the state, which, perhaps dragged kicking and screaming, has been led to uphold its ideology of gender equality.

CONCLUSION

The India of today is a very different country from that of decades past, distinguished by its vibrant economy and fast-rising middle class (larger than the population of the United States) and as a world-class exporter of "knowledge" to the information technology sector (Dash 2005). According to a Goldman Sachs report on India, "India's economy could be larger than all but the US and China in 30 years—that is, India could be the 3rd largest economy in the world before 2035" (quoted in Dash 2005). The overenthusiastic professionals, rising sales of foreign-make cars, as well as new indigenous models introduced by Mahendras and Tatas, and the hustle and bustle in various metropolises make India a principal actor in the globalization play.

Orissa—known as a backward state—also wants to have its share of globalization. In the field of industrial development, the world's largest steel plant, Pohang Steel (POSCO) of Korea, has proposed an $8 billion project in Orissa. Tata Steel is already setting up a new plant in Orissa. Orissa's rich natural resources and outside demands for steel have led approximately seven large steel companies to establish operations in Orissa, as well as almost a hundred small- to medium-scale companies to do the same (with earnings of US$5–US$10 million). Many engineering colleges have also emerged to keep up with the demand for engineering and management degrees. High-tech giants Wipro and Tata Company (TCS) have also decided to open up branches in Bhubaneswar. Girls in middle-class urban families are encouraged to study science, engineering, and computer science to better train themselves in the age of globalization.

Yet, although "women" generically can avail themselves of these rosy opportunities, cultural and social realities often dictate otherwise. For example, just recently a 15-year-old dalit (untouchable) girl, Mamata Nayak, in the village of Narsinghpur, Orissa, became the first girl in her community to graduate from high school. Her plans to become a teacher and educate other dalit girls in her village are threatened because she has to bike through an upper-caste community to go to college. The upper-caste people not only bar her from biking on "their" road but also threaten her family with dire consequences. Her father says, "I do not want to take the risk of waging a battle against the mighty upper caste" (Mishra 2005). Another dalit asks, "Who will come to our rescue? Can the Police and the state protect us and our daughters from the wrath of these people?" (Mishra 2005). This example illustrates the distinctive, culturally rooted forms of marginalization that Oriya women—whether Hindu or Kond (tribal), rural or urban—face and the challenges women's organizations in Orissa and elsewhere in India confront in resisting such abuses and injustices in a globalized world.

The "Janus" head of the Indian state in globalization is especially visible in the cases of education and swadeshi. In the process of globalization, education has played a critical role in rural, urban, and tribal areas. Yet, as I have discussed in this chapter, the process of education and the people in charge of education have marginalized women, especially in the process of modernization, robbing them of their cultural identity, freedom, and sense of self. To explain further, the state has been promoting general higher education with the mushrooming of state-sanctioned private colleges all over the state. However, the state takes no responsibility for providing any meaningful employment for women after their undergraduate or postgraduate degrees. Women who obtain higher education are doubly marginalized because they face higher dowry demands to marry somebody who is equally qualified and feel ostracized for not getting suitable marriage partners.

The state portrays its benevolent image in emphasizing the welfare, growth, and overall development of women. It also uses women as an umbrella category to be defined as "swadeshi," upholders of the nation's values and tradition. But Indian women are not content to succumb to the state's definition of swadeshi: they want the right to modify and refashion it so that they can truly participate in the new opportunities made available to them. Women are redefining their tradition, reinventing their new swadeshi image, not as static or unchanging but rather like a river flowing through many lands, collecting all the treasures, as well as the pollutants. They want to be called swadeshi on their own terms and be free to choose what to accept from it, as well as what to reject as the ills of the past. They do not want to be puppets of the state or globalization. This is the new face of feminism emerging in Orissa in the face of globalization.

About the Author

Annapurna Pandey is a lecturer at the University of California, Santa Cruz. Growing up in India, she followed with interest the work of Prime Minister Indira Gandhi and Nandini Satpathy, who became the first woman chief minister of Orissa in 1972. At Jawaharlal Nehru University in Delhi, she joined others in an intellectual project of critical analysis through sociology and later attended the first women's conference that took place at SNDT University in Mumbai in 1978. For her doctoral dissertation, she explored the nature of women's political participation in Orissa, India. Since 1986, she has been examining women's organization and collective movements in tribal areas, keeping in view the upsurge of industrialization and the development of mining projects in southwestern Orissa. Since 1989, when she moved to the United States, she has continued to return frequently to India and has also been studying the life experiences of women of the Indian diaspora in the Bay area of San Francisco.

Notes

1. Report of the Committee on the Status of Women in India 1974:178–179.

2. I borrow the term *developmentalist model* from Immanuel Wallerstein's keynote lecture "After Developmentalism and Globalization, What?" given at the Development Challenges for the 21st Century conference, Cornell University, October 2004.

3. Panchayats are basic units of administration at the local level, as per the Indian constitution. There are three levels: village, block, and district. The village level is called a panchayat and is run by an elected body of people working for the well-being of the village.

Part V

Concluding Essays

14

Complex Negotiations

Gender, Capitalism, and Relations of Power

Mary Anglin and Louise Lamphere

The essays in this volume demonstrate the importance of feminist ethnographic research in two particularly noteworthy respects. First, the essays illustrate the value of feminist ethnography in documenting the effects of global capitalism at the level of local conditions and women's everyday lives. Moreover, when analyzed through the lenses of gender, race, ethnicity, and class, such ethnographic accounts provide a unique vantage point for understanding the phenomena collectively termed "globalization." Taken as a whole, the essays call for analyses of globalization that are based on nuanced readings of local political economies and the intersecting forces that shape women's experiences in specific settings. Additionally, this kind of ethnographic work necessarily addresses the situated knowledges and specific actions of men and women in local communities. In contrast with the widely held view that transnational processes of economic restructuring and capital accumulation have led—or will soon lead—to economic and cultural homogenization, this volume argues for the recognition of globalization as a highly variable, historically contingent set of processes and for the role of human agency in constructing specific moments, or outcomes, of globalization.

If globalization is not to be construed in deterministic ways, clearly neither can gender relations be viewed as a reflection of static cultural traditions or one-dimensional forms of subordination. Scholars have, instead, examined the variation and subtleties in discourses about women (and men) and documented the deployment of these discourses in settings throughout a number of different countries in the global North and South. As Desai and others demonstrate, women have been powerfully affected by transnational economic policies over the past 40 years (Benería 2003; Bolles 1996a; Desai 2002; Naples and Desai 2002; Sparr 1994). The task undertaken by this volume is to map a range of globalization's gendered consequences by analyzing similarities and differences within women's experiences in particular social and geographic locations. Following the insights of Mohanty (2003b) and other scholars, some of the essays in this volume provide further evidence of points of conflict, as well as mutual interest, between women in the global South and North. Further, these essays suggest the importance of attending to differences among women within the same nation-state (Sharpe and Spivak 2002:610). In many instances, policies of restructuring have benefited some women, especially those with access to economic and social resources, thus sharpening class differences and further exacerbating the vulnerability of other women (and men) within the same country.

It is important to examine gender relations and processes of globalization in the context of capitalist growth in the post–World War II period. Capitalist strategies have built on trends evident in early historical periods, especially when colonialism shaped the relationship between Europe or North America and the rest of the world. The past 30 years, however, have been a period of massive intensification or scaling up of technologies and practices oriented toward capturing natural resources, including indigenous knowledge, and consolidating productive activities for the First World. Transnational corporations and global financial institutions have been the main vehicles for this consolidation. Because of their scale, transnational corporations have been able to reach levels of greater capital accumulation and distribute profits to a range of recipients worldwide. Even so, transnational firms have been only partially successful in securing global domination. They continue to coexist with local economic practices, noncapitalist and capitalist, including economies dominated by state ownership and forms of investment and those controlled by national elites (Benería 1996; Escobar 2001; Gibson-Graham 1996; Gibson-Graham and Ruccio 2001; Roseberry 1997).

Although global capitalism has made national boundaries more porous and encouraged the migration of peoples across the world, this has *not* led to the demise of states or nationalisms. Brodkin suggests, to the contrary, that contemporary forms of capitalism require massive state inter-vention with respect to spheres of production and, increasingly, also of dis-tribution. Constellations of state authority have thus changed, not declined, in response to shifting local and international economic condi-tions and political relations (Brodkin 2000 and Patterson 1999). Accordingly, rather than focus on the entrenched image of the state as a rationalized administrative form, scholars such as Das and Poole (2004:3; see also pp. 9–10, 23) argue that it is more useful to map the power of mod-ern states through the effects of their political, regulatory, and disciplinary practices (Ferguson and Gupta 2002; Roitman 2004). The authors of this volume examine, in detail, two such effects: the consequences of neoliberal approaches to governance and the production of specific forms of ethnic-ity, gender, and nationalism as manifestations of state authority (Williams 1996).

Unquestionably, the nature of globalization has been strongly influ-enced in the past two decades by the neoliberal formulations advanced by the International Monetary Fund (IMF), the World Bank, and the World Trade Organization (WTO). Such formulations are characterized by mar-ket triumphalism and focused on trade liberalization, decreased state expenditures for social programs, the privatization of industry, and the deregulation of labor markets (Kingfisher and Goldsmith 2001). However, neoliberal policies have been implemented inconsistently throughout the global North and South and are the subject of social protest, even in the United States, with its close ties to the World Bank, IMF, and WTO (Cohen et al. 2002; Goode and Maskovsky 2001; Harrison 2004b; Naples and Desai 2002; Nash 2005). In addition, the perspectives and practices of neoliber-alism have been rejected in transnational fora, including "Encounters with Humanity" in Chiapas, Mexico (2001), the UN conferences of the 1990s—including the 1993 World Conference on Human Rights and the Fourth World Conference on Women in Beijing, China (1995)—and the Latin American and Caribbean Feminist Encuentros, which were first convened in 1981 and have continued for the past 30 years. (Alvarez et al. 2003; De Angelis 1998; Friedman 2003; Global Exchange 2001). It is, in other words, vital to speak to both the material effects of neoliberal policies and locally and transnationally orchestrated resistance to their imposition. Kingsolver (chapter 12, this volume) provides a further example of such contestations through the plurinational organizing efforts undertaken by women living and working on the economic edge in Mexico, Sri Lanka, and the United States as the result of neoliberal trade agreements and other free market policies.

As Desai (2002:16–17) observes, notable consequences of neoliberal policies have been the formation of a racialized and gendered global labor force, with the concentration of women's employment in poorly remunerated service sector work; women's increased involvement in the informal sector, for which there is no government oversight; ever greater reliance on women's unpaid labor for services once provided through public programs; and environmental pollution, as well as the depletion of local natural resources on which women and their families rely for subsistence, especially in the global South (see also Bolles 1996; Brodkin 2000; Harrison 2004b; Naples 2002). Discourses of gendered and racial inequality have often colluded with the interests of global and local capitalisms to render certain segments of the population superfluous while disciplining others as members of a poorly remunerated workforce, whose usefulness is measured, in part, by the willingness to undertake waged labor in difficult working conditions (Mills 2003).

Chapters in this volume further document the adverse impact of globalization on women, whether they are women whose countries have suffered from the impact of neoliberal policies or new immigrants who have had difficulty fitting into the economies that beckoned them without treating them as potential citizens with full civil rights. Thus, according to Sutton (chapter 8, this volume), the adoption of neoliberal policies in the 1990s and subsequent collapse of Argentina's economy resulted in high rates of unemployment and the literal embodiment of poverty when women and their families could no longer afford the basics of subsistence. The economy of the Philippines has become ever more dependent on remunerations sent back by Filipinas, who outmigrate in staggering numbers—more than 2,500 women per day—to find global employment. The Filipina domestic workers interviewed by Parreñas (chapter 9, this volume) described their status as that of "placelessness." Racial and class stratification in the host countries of Italy and the United States meant that many Filipinas engaged in socially useful, poorly remunerated domestic labor but were made to feel transient and unwelcome, even when they were eligible for permanent residence. Nonetheless, economic conditions in the Philippines made it impossible for these workers to return "home" except for brief and infrequent visits.

In some instances, it is very difficult for women to develop strategies to resist, or alter, their circumstances. Women often face patriarchal situations at home and in the workplace, or they may be forced into more restrictive roles in exchange for higher status. As an example of the first situation, Gunewardena (chapter 3, this volume) describes young women employed by transnational corporations in Sri Lanka who found themselves in a double bind created by patriarchal relations: they simultaneously had to contend with repressive managerial practices on the factory floor and cultural practices within their families and communities that denied respectability and the potential for marriage to female wage laborers. Moran (chapter 5, this volume) addresses the second situation in her analysis of Liberian women as their situation evolved throughout the nineteenth and early twentieth centuries. To retain the cultural value and dress that distinguish "civilized" from "native" persons, Liberian women were unable to participate in trade at the local markets or publicly engage in other forms of enterprise. Rather, they were forced into the role of housewives dependent on husbands and male kinspeople, for whom there were no comparable restrictions.

Notwithstanding the "appearance of sameness" in gendered hierarchies, considerable variability has been documented in terms of the discursive forms, material practices, and histories informing local regimes of labor in the late twentieth century (Mills 2003:43–44). Thus, in contrast with Moran's account of women accorded cultural value but denied economic opportunities in Liberia, Darkwah (chapter 4, this volume) writes of elite Ghanaian women who drew upon their social standing and access to financial resources in developing new strategies for accumulating wealth *and* status as traders of global consumer goods. As Darkwah's ethnography of Ghana illustrates, middle-class and elite women may experience greater success than their compatriots in putting together viable economic strategies. These strategies may benefit them or push them toward gendered activism, but may also blind them to the situation of women in other class and racial positions.

Moreover, Parreñas (chapter 9, this volume) warns against feminist approaches that imagine a dichotomy between patriarchal cultural traditions in the global South and the emancipatory potential of Northern modernity (Mohanty 2003b; Muratorio 1998). In Parreñas' study, Filipinas experienced more entrenched forms of gendered and racial discrimination in the global North, where they were economic migrants, than in the global South. Conwill (chapter 7, this volume) engages a similar logic when he argues against the popular assumption that working-class African American communities are simply patriarchal and exploitative of women. Conwill attributes the high rates of domestic violence experienced by African American women *not* to racialized traditions of gender inequality, but instead to neoliberal policies that foster conditions of racism, poverty, and psychosocial stress within communities of color in the United States (but see Crenshaw 1991; King 1995; McCall 2005; Mullings 2005; and Mullings and Wali 2001 for alternative readings of these concerns).

On a more hopeful note, several contributions emphasize women's strategies for fighting back or for carving out a niche for themselves that gives them some distance from the transnational corporations that dominate developing economies. Bolles (chapter 11, this volume) argues that the "turbo-charged" industry of Caribbean tourism is fueled by twin histories of colonialism and neoliberalism that result in the exploitation of poor women as unskilled and undereducated laborers. Advertisements for Jamaican tourism, she notes, rely on stereotypic images of "natives" that erase the distinction between sex work and women's labor in the service sector. Smith-Nonini (chapter 10, this volume) likens service sector work in the hotels of North America to plantation labor, framed in this instance by twenty-first-century practices of gendered and racial segregation. Women are active agents in resisting these trends. Bolles finds the "race to the bottom," fostered by neoliberal policies and corporate tourism, to be partially slowed by a small number of Jamaican women operating family enterprises on quite different terms. Likewise, Smith-Nonini juxtaposes the failures of corporate accountability with the 2004–2005 struggle for a new contract in San Francisco by UNITE-HERE (a recent amalgamation of apparel/textile and service unions) and the increased awareness of anthropologists about our unwitting reliance on convention hotels with problematic relations to union labor.

Dahl (chapter 6, this volume) takes up the complex task of analyzing relations of gender, globalization, and modernity through an account of her native Jämtland, a geographic region that remains partially isolated from the rest of Sweden. Dahl found that global discourses of gendered equality and neoliberalism coexisted with masculinist traditions of cultural conservatism in this "northern periphery" of the EU. Yet, the "progressive feminists" studied by Dahl were no less racist or elitist in their interactions with Thai immigrant women than were the "traditional men" of Jämtland. In this respect, Dahl's account resonates with Parreñas' findings on racialized and gendered hierarchies in Italy and the United States.

Like Dahl, Pandey (chapter 13, this volume) returned home in her study of tribal women from Orissa, notable for being the poorest state in India. Yet, whereas Dahl's is a cautionary tale about the technologies of race and gender, as well as the limits of Northern feminism (de Lauretis 1987; Mohanty 2003b), Pandey provides a quite different view of contemporary feminism and gendered alliances in India. Her essay illustrates the ways that Kond women have created an indigenous feminism that is partly based on local cultural tradition and also draws upon the collective efforts of men and women, from multiple generations, against the "benevolent" repressions of the Indian government (see also Channa 2004).

In sum, while demonstrating the value of ethnography for the study of women's lives in the late twentieth and early twenty-first centuries, the essays force us to reconsider local and global capitalism, social inequality, and agency as historically informed, uneven processes. The paradox, as illustrated by these essays, is that the construct of "globalization" becomes more useful through the recognition that it is neither unitary nor deterministic, but a way of calling attention to the particularities of transnational political, economic, and social relations in the twenty-first century. Finally, by refusing to reproduce North–South distinctions discursively in accounting for specific settings and conditions, these analyses of racialized, classed, and gendered differentiation make evident the scholarly and transformative potential of feminist ethnography.

About the Authors

Mary Anglin is an associate professor in the Department of Anthropology and a faculty associate in the Gender and Women's Studies program, in addition to holding joint appointments in the School of Public Health and the College of Medicine, at the University of Kentucky. From 2003 to 2005, she served as president of the Association for Feminist Anthropology and, with Nandini Gunewardena and Ann Kingsolver, co-organized the advanced seminar "Gender and Globalization," which convened in April 2005 at the School for Advanced Research. Her research interests include feminist perspectives on health and social justice, as well as ethnographies of gender, ethnicity, race, and class in Appalachia.

Louise Lamphere is a distinguished professor of anthropology at the University of New Mexico and past president of the American Anthropological Association. During 2001–2002, she was a visiting scholar at the Russell Sage Foundation in New York City. She began her writing in feminist anthropology with the publication in 1974 of *Woman, Culture and Society*, co-edited with Michelle Zimbalist Rosaldo. She has studied issues of women and work for 25 years, beginning with her study of women workers in Rhode Island industry, *From Working Daughters to Working Mothers* (1977). She also coauthored a study of working women in Albuquerque titled *Sunbelt Working Mothers: Reconciling Family and Factory* (1993) with Patricia Zavella, Felipe Gonzales, and Peter Evans and co-edited with Helena Ragone and Patricia Zavella a collection of articles titled *Situated Lives: Gender and Culture in Everyday Life* (1997). Her most recent book is a biography of three Navajo women titled *Weaving Women's Lives: Three Generations in a Navajo Family* (2007).

15

Navigating Paradoxical Globalizations

Ann Kingsolver

Globalization is often spoken of in contradictory terms, or in terms of a paradox. Farhang Rajaee, for example, uses the metaphor of a two-edged sword:

> Globalization operates as a two-edged sword. It emancipates but also represses, and it brings together and unites but also divides and forms new hierarchies....In the areas of culture and politics...the role of globalization is not very clear. At one level, it advocates passive consumption of cultural products and prefers to turn individuals into loyal spectators of the political status quo. At another level, it enables individuals and groups to voice their cultural and political grievances by providing them with more efficient and accessible modes of communication. [Rajaee 2000:96–97]

The authors of the work in this volume recognize and document the ways that structural binaries are powerfully employed in arguments about globalization. Yet those interpretations and experiences of oppression are contextualized within much more multifaceted understandings of power: the matrix of domination (Collins 1991), for example, and Foucaultian (see 1979) concepts of relational and capillary power. This project is situated within a larger intellectual and activist project of understanding the myriad ways that power is asserted and contested in relation to economic, social, and symbolic resources. Claims about the global status (and inevitability) of capitalist projects need to be examined critically (Gibson-Graham 1996; Tsing 2000).

As gender-based discrimination in workplaces informed by "free market" strategies increases, racialized discrimination is also intensifying. This structural violence, as Harrison (2005) argues, is a human rights issue. Globalized rights discourse itself is ironically hegemonic while discussing liberatory projects (Cowan, Dembour, and Wilson 2001:1). Morgen (2005) has suggested that there is a need to focus more specifically on economic rights because maintaining basic subsistence is increasingly challenging for a growing number of people in the world under trade liberalization policies. Gendered effects, and contestations, of global economic changes are refracted through so many circumstances that an ethnographic approach is particularly useful. A historical approach is also vital, as Mary Moran and Lynn Bolles argue; each demonstrates the necessity of looking at historical divisions and cultural constructions of labor in understanding current labor recruitment. As the authors here (and researchers beyond this volume) point out, gendered globalization is not a unified experience of male dominance and female subordination and resistance in capitalist-organized milieux. National leaders implementing neoliberal policies that economically marginalize many in their nations are occasionally women, as we have seen, and some of the sex workers who are beaten or ostracized for providing the very services demanded in the global economy are men and boys. A full consideration of gendered globalizations, then, requires an array of vantage points and collaborations.

In discussing plural globalizations and marginalities, the authors represented in this volume resist the tendency to reduce many (not always coherent) strategies and experiences of economic and power relations to a single expression of "globalization" but recognize the ways that globalization may be employed as a rubric in ethnographic interviews and activist analyses. When heuristically separated (though fused in lived experience), plural globalizations may be thought of in terms of various discourses that rely on assertions of universal legitimacy: for example, structural adjustment discourse imposed upon and within states in the context of transnational trade and debt relations; "globalized" religious or moral discourses; narratives and counter-narratives regarding the history, purpose, and future of capitalist development; and discourses of global resistance, or of alternatives to national and transnational projects of neoliberal economic globalization. In the remainder of this chapter, therefore, I summarize some of the contradictions of globalization noted by the authors in discussions of how individuals such as Dammi in Sri Lanka and Fanny in Argentina have navigated these and other paradoxical discourses of globalization.

Several authors point out contradictions experienced by women in association with the structural adjustment policies that are part of neoliberal economic globalization. Annapurna Pandey points out that hierarchies among women can be intensified within a nation in association with neoliberal economic change, as she has observed in India. Akosua Darkwah describes the way that structural adjustment policies may allow women (especially elites who already have some capital, such as the Ghanaian traders she discusses) to enter the market as transnational traders, even as the currency devaluation associated with those same structural adjustment policies makes their businesses high-risk and unstable. Lynn Bolles describes how some women benefiting from structural adjustment policies end up employing other women in more marginal economic positions, as was the case for women opening tourist facilities in Jamaica, but also how those local managers have difficulty sustaining their businesses (holding on to their property, for example) because of the high taxes imposed under these policies.

Another paradox described by the authors is how women's increased movement and consumption may be facilitated by processes associated with neoliberal economic globalization, yet that mobility and increased consumption may be disempowering. Rhacel Parreñas, for example, shows how Filipina domestic workers' increased earning power and knowledge of transnational spaces are linked to increased marginalization in both their nation of origin and their nation of employment (for example, as their movements are restricted to isolating workplaces). Migration itself, Parreñas argues, is seen as an opportunity for consumption but ends up reinscribing differences and further marginalizing the domestic workers within gendered national and global economic contexts. Barbara Sutton points out another irony of consumption. As women in Argentina consume images of the body dominant in a global capitalist market and desire to embody those images, their diminished health care and wages, and demanding working conditions, distance them simultaneously from the advertised body ideals they are consuming. Nandini Gunewardena discusses the paradoxes of consumption for garment factory workers in Sri Lanka whose attempts to distance themselves from their identities as workers and producers by performing as consumers further necessitate that they earn enough to consume. She raises interesting possibilities for considering the agentive aspects of consumption through her ethnographic analysis of *how* the women make choices in their consumption.

Just as consumption and globalization may not mean the same thing to individuals in different contexts, feminism and womanhood are not understood and employed as concepts in universal ways. Annapurna Pandey refers to a specifically Indian feminism, which she sees as constructed with some different concepts, priorities, and organizing strategies than those used in feminist traditions in the United States and Europe. She found women organizing for social change, including gender-based concerns, in collaboration with men; I have often found similar collaboration in agricultural contexts in which I have interviewed women about their organizing strategies. Ulrika Dahl, writing about gender and development discourse in Sweden, says that a dominant global definition of womanhood and feminist rights discourse is imposed in state contexts, reconstructing gender in local policy discourse. She notes that "gender equality" discourse tends to marginalize discussions of other forms of inequity, such as racialized oppression.

William Conwill discusses the need to consider economic rights and the consequences of ignoring them in neoliberal policy regimes, based on his observation that economic oppression is a stronger factor than racialized oppression in domestic violence, as the structural violence of economic disparities makes its way home. This links to the criminalization of the impoverished that Barbara Sutton observed under neoliberal economic policies in Argentina. Through legal actions, assertions of the state and of marginalization are mobilized (Das and Poole 2004). Religious moral discourse is another venue through which devalorization of the most marginalized workers in a globalized economy is often justified (even as many of those discourses claim empowerment or liberation for the most marginalized). Nandini Gunewardena describes Sinhala Buddhist constructions of women working in the Free Trade Zones as immoral. Similarly, neoconservative Christian moral discourse has been used to justify the marginalization of low-wage workers in US contexts and to assert their responsibility for their own marginality.

Words such as *freedom* and *flexibility* in neoliberal economic discourse may be enticing, but experience contradicts the language. Parreñas points out that the rhetoric of freedom is often an impetus for women who migrate transnationally in search of increased earning power and consumer choice through domestic work. Instead of finding freedom, though, many women find reinscribed and differently inscribed oppression. Sandy Smith-Nonini notes that "flexibility" and "community" are contradictory for low-wage workers. We might argue, then, that the "global community" itself is a contradiction, navigated in very different ways by those most marginalized by neoliberal economic policies than those envisioning that capitalist economic community as policymakers. As Rajaee (2000) notes, global technologies of communication facilitate communication of global strategies; some of those strategies are intended to oppress low-wage labor, and some of them are strategies of resistance, as when social movements mobilize international support. But global communication does not mean, of course, that concepts are being employed or interpreted in the same ways. Annapurna Pandey concludes that women are navigating the contradictions of globalization by using local and national compasses, such as the concept of "swadeshi" in India, rather than through universal understandings of economic organization or marginality.

About the Author

Ann Kingsolver, associate professor of anthropology at the University of South Carolina, has been interviewing men and women about their views on globalization since 1986 in the United States, Mexico, and, most recently, Sri Lanka. She wrote *NAFTA Stories: Fears and Hopes in Mexico and the United States* (2001) and edited *More Than Class: Studying Power in US Workplaces* (1998). She is general editor of the *Anthropology of Work Review.*

16

Reconstituting Marginality

Gendered Repression
and Women's Resistance

Nandini Gunewardena

By taking seriously the ways in which women workers discursively construct their own social locations, practices, and experiences, we can construct a third possibility, one that can inform recent research pointing both to the dangers of romanticizing resistance (Abu-Lughod 1990) and the problems of presenting women as passive victims of structures of oppression (Mohanty 1991).

—*from* Producing Workers *by Leela Fernandes*

Our collective task in this volume is to problematize women's engagement with contemporary processes of globalization as a means to move beyond the naturalization of gender in the operational dynamics of neoliberal capital. As such, central to our analysis is a conceptualization of the gendering of globalization as a purposive strategy, given the tendency of many discussions to gloss over women's particular locations in transnational production. Our point of departure is to examine how and why women configure at the margins of export-oriented industrialization with the emergence of a new industrial division of labor in the 1970s,[1] chartered by transnational firms and spurred by neoliberal economic policies and attendant prescriptions for foreign direct investment. The ethnographic data presented in the chapters permit us to question at least two aspects of the promise of equity alluded to by neoliberal economic theory—the ways in which supposedly impartial market mechanisms are expected to enhance women's roles in the labor market, and the purported possibility for an interdependent, interacting global manufacturing system to bridge the social and income gulf between the global North and South, as well as gender disparities within and between these regions. Yet, as Amin and others (1994) argue, industrial convergence has not resulted in congruence in income levels between the global North and South, contravening the promises and premises of neoliberal economic policies.

As many of the chapters in this volume illustrate, the (re-)construction of marginality in globalization thus appears to occur as the operations of global capital collide with multidimensional axes of exclusion, as ethnicity, race, class, caste, regional affiliation,[2] gender, and citizenship ascriptions,[3] articulate as multiple, overlapping, and seamless oppressions. The ethnographies in this volume, as well as emerging evidence in other sources,[4] illustrate that it is primarily women positioned at the social and economic margins of the global South who suffer most from the dynamics of globalization and that these processes are also implicated in the creation of a racialized, feminized proletariat, as alluded to in many of the chapters. Elucidating these contradictions, for example, are Rhacel Parreñas' exposé of the racialization of Filipina domestic workers, who find themselves placed at the periphery of globalized metropolises such as Los Angeles, Rome, and London; Sandy Smith-Nonini's discussion of the preponderance of women of color in low-wage hospitality industry work; and my (Gunewardena's) documentation of women factory workers from the rural periphery of Sri Lanka incorporated into transnational production at the lowest-paid, unskilled levels. The economic and social divisions ushered in by globalization intersect to reproduce and often exacerbate existing patterns of racial, ethnic, and class subordination along gendered axes, as alluded to in William Conwill's treatise on the disruptions experienced by African American family structures in the United States.

Thus, in the present moment of corporate expansion that constitutes the rubric of globalization, a capitalist hegemony appears to confer deepening economic, social, and political disenfranchisement for low-income women of the global South, as suggested in Ulrika Dahl's analysis contrasting the locations of Swedish women and in-migrating Thai women in Sweden's rural periphery and, to some extent, in Barbara Sutton's discussions of the bodily scars of economic deprivation endured by Argentine women. The racialization of women in the capitalist periphery is embedded in the discourses and practices of the agents of transnational capital and references classic strategies of racial stereotyping that ascribe low capacities to women yet rely ultimately on age-old demarcations of serving and servitude. This is exemplified by Lynn Bolles' insights on how tourism sector workers are characterized in Jamaica and is implicit also in Rhacel Parreñas' juxtapositions of the various streams of migrant women and the complex and constrained interactions with the society at large. Ironically, although women of means have often been able to harness some benefits from new opportunities posed by economic globalization, they, too, have seen a deterioration of their income levels as their clients' purchasing power is diminished, as described in Akosua Darkwah's chapter on middle-income Ghanaian women traders.

DECONSTRUCTING CAPITALIST REGIMES OF POWER: THE DIALECTICS OF REPRESSION, RESISTANCE, AND RECONSTITUTION

We have labored to document the social and economic implications of the transnational production strategy of disproportionately recruiting young women workers, seen as an expendable, low-remunerated, unskilled, devalorized yet highly productive labor force. The diverse ethnographies in this volume vividly capture the power relations and associated material realities in which globalization processes are enmeshed, but the case studies also reveal the dialectical relationships of repression and resistance—borne out not only in women's oppositional practices but also in the contradictory dynamics of accommodation often visible in women's responses to the structures of power they encounter. To this end, the complex and ambivalent subjectivities of women entangled in global production sites and processes imply that the globalization of capital, culture, and consumption belies a crisp dichotomy of consumers versus producers, exemplified, for example, by the way women factory workers in Sri Lanka parody middle-class consumption practices as a form of resistance and the innovative ways in which impoverished Argentine women grapple with the emotional, material, and bodily assaults of neoliberal economic strategies.

Many chapters in this volume add to the growing body of ethnographic data on the numerous ways in which women navigate the repressive effects of the "scattered hegemonies"[5] they encounter in the collusion of global and local capital. Nonetheless, attesting to Leela Fernandes' (1997) cautioning about the production of hegemony as an incomplete and contested process, the case studies reveal how women subordinated by oppressive regimes of capital navigate, negotiate, and often neutralize those structures and processes. In addition to disrupting microregimes of power (for example, in the churches, parks, and public spaces of Rome and Los Angeles, in Accra's Makola markets, on Negril's sandy beaches, in Swedish Jämtland, and in Sri Lanka's garment factories and tea estates), many of the chapters also document how women reconstitute the branded identities, social locations, and power relationships that constrict their lives. Offering insight into the creative ways in which women usurp power and effectively bring about shifts and redemarcations in the contours and reiterations of such power, these narratives enable us to deconstruct the presumed unitary nature of hegemonic oppression.

Expressions of individual and collective resistance form an intrinsic part of, and are vital to, the reconstitution of marginality. However, we are cognizant of Lila Abu-Lughod (1990), Rajeswari Sunder-Rajan (1993), and other transnational feminists' concerns about overinvesting in the expectations of agency, because in some contexts, asserting agency is thwarted by corporeal and symbolic regulation of women's lives that leaves little room for autonomy. Given the daunting implications of this configuration of power, we are increasingly called upon to explore the possibilities of transnational feminist activism as a compelling avenue for countering and confronting the oppressive forces of globalization, as Ann Kingsolver and Annapurna Pandey's chapters document, and, in turn, for the reconstitution of women's marginality in globalization. I turn to this subject in the next section, examining a possible route to overcoming women's subordination in globalization offered by human rights instruments, given the stream of international forums focusing on gender inequities and the transnational feminist movement's reliance on agreements and benchmarks pertaining to women encoded in global human rights conventions.

SUBVERTING HUMAN RIGHTS AND CONSTITUTING ALTERNATIVE VISIONS OF HUMAN RIGHTS

Human rights conventions, pronouncements, and practices have traditionally prevailed largely over the terrain of politics, but not directly over the tyranny of economics. No doubt, transnational feminist praxis is critical for forging a collective transnational platform for reforms that would hasten global gender justice, but the moral weight of human rights instruments is unmatched by the limited accountability of many states entrusted with their enforcement. Tensions inherent in the conflicting authority and mandates of states versus those of border-crossing transnational corporations in a globalized system of production and consumption obscure related issues of governance, transparency, and responsibility in enforcing human rights standards. Although the United Nations conventions pertaining to women (such as the Convention on the Elimination of All Forms of Discrimination Against Women and the Universal Declaration of Human Rights) have been particularly persuasive in assigning legitimacy to the need to safeguard women's human rights, their capacity to serve as a corrective has been limited, outside of a moral consensus. The World Trade Organization (WTO) has served increasingly as the global authority governing matters of transnational production, but gender rights violations have remained outside the dominion of WTO deliberations and, more significantly, beyond its domains of concern.

Thus, in the face of the numerous human rights that globalization subverts, we are left with a vacuum in the accountability needed to translate moral authority into specific corrective strategies. The multiple human rights violations implicated in the current, neoliberal phase of capitalist expansion encompassing the processes of globalization include novel forms of structural domination that have eroded the material, symbolic, and emotional quality of being. The class complicity of *local* capitalists with global capitalism in ways that exacerbate gendered social and economic difference within and across borders is partly responsible for the latter processes. Nancy Naples and Manisha Desai clarify:

> Features of global economic restructuring include a decline in organized labor and formal labor contracts; increasing internationalization of capital; growth in formal and part-time employment; loss of local economic and natural resources; cutbacks in social provisioning associated with the so-called welfare state; restructuring of women's work; and a growing disparity between classes. [Naples and Desai 2002:11]

A gendered labor force that generates capital and enables global capital to thrive and grow exponentially remains unprotected in so many ways, including from risk to life and limb. In contrast, the very powers that reap the benefits of this devalorized labor force have buffered their operations with extensive protective mechanisms that avail unlimited legal and financial protections against every eventuality.[6] As early literature on the industrial division of labor ushered in over the past several decades attests to, despite women's increased economic activity rates, women are still concentrated in low-paid service or agricultural sectors, their work in the unprotected and poorly remunerated informal sector has increased, and their share of unpaid labor in the home has also increased as many states have undertaken cuts in public funding of health, education, and social services, including state-run child care services. In addition, the absence of a living wage and prohibitions on union formation and collective bargaining practices at transnational production sites hint at the violation of fundamental rights inscribed in modern human rights instruments (for example, the International Covenant on Economic, Social and Cultural Rights, in addition to those mentioned above).

Yet, enduring in our task of collective visions of justice, I close with the thought that the increased proliferation of global human rights discourses, the vocal, public dissent over corporate violations, and the arenas and forums for forging transnational corrective strategies (such as the World Social Forum) offer much space for cross-border alliances in the recovery of a globalization of hope.[7]

About the Author

Nandini Gunewardena is a practitioner anthropologist with a Ph.D. from the University of California, Los Angeles. She has more than 14 years of pragmatic experience addressing the concerns of women in several impoverished nations in Asia and more recently the Middle East and North Africa through her work with a number of bi- and multilateral agencies. Her expertise includes community-based research, project implementation, outcome assessments, and policy reform. She returned to academia in 1998, teaching in the departments of anthropology, women's studies, and international development studies at the University of California, Los Angeles. She is currently a faculty member in the human services program at Western Washington University. Her ongoing research focuses on the inequities generated by neoliberal globalization (including the feminization of poverty), women's work in transnational factories, and suicide as a response to economic stressors.

Notes

1. As argued in the landmark volume on globalization by Fröbel, Heinrichs, and Kreye (1980), citing how gender factored into the choices made by transnational firms regarding workers (single, young women) and offshore locations (the global South).

2. Referring to the dominance–subordination relationships that are played out between geopolitical regions located along differential axes of power, such as the global North and South, urban and rural, and elite and indigenous.

3. Meaning the notions of citizenship that are invoked in conferring bona fide belonging and social inclusion in the processes of globalization that form another axis of subordination.

4. As detailed in the introductory chapter of this volume.

5. To borrow Inderpal Grewal and Caren Kaplan's (1994) term.

6. Consider, for example, the NAFTA Chapter 11 clause that allows many rights and protections to transnational corporations in the event they feel that their investors' rights have been violated by a NAFTA country. As clarified by Public Citizen:

The North American Free Trade Agreement (NAFTA) includes an array of new corporate investment rights and protections that are unprecedented in scope and power. NAFTA allows corporations to sue the national government of a NAFTA country in secret arbitration tribunals if they feel that a regulation or government decision affects their investment in conflict with these new NAFTA rights. If a corporation wins, the taxpayers of the "losing" NAFTA nation must foot the bill. This extraordinary attack on governments' ability to regulate in the public interest is a key element of the proposed NAFTA expansion called the Central American Free Trade Agreement (CAFTA). [Online posting available at http://www.citizen.org/trade/nafta/ CH__11/, last accessed February 1, 2007]

7. As suggested by Gustavo Esteva and Madhu Prakash (2004) in their essay on the "international of hope."

References

Abraham, Itty
2005   A Southern Route from West to East. NACLA Report on the Americas 39(2):28–32.

Abu-Lughod, Lila
1990   The Romance of Resistance: Tracing Transformations of Power through Bedouin Women. American Ethnologist 17(1):41–55.

Abu-Lughod, Lila, ed.
1998   Remaking Women: Feminism and Modernity in the Middle East. Princeton, NJ: Princeton University Press.

Acheson, James
1985   Social Organization of the Maine Lobster Market. *In* Markets and Marketing. S. Plattner, ed. Pp. 105–130. Monographs in Economic Anthropology 4. Lanham, MD: University Press of America, Society for Economic Anthropology.

Acuña Rodarte, Olivia
2003   Toward an Equitable, Inclusive, and Sustainable Agriculture: Mexico's Basic Grains Producers Unite. *In* Confronting Globalization: Economic Integration and Popular Resistance in Mexico. Timothy A. Wise, Hilda Salazar, and Laura Carlsen, eds. Pp. 129–148. Bloomfield, CT: Kumarian Press.

Adair, Vivyan C.
2002   Branded with Infamy: Inscriptions of Poverty and Class in the United States. Signs: Journal of Women in Culture and Society 27(2):451–471.

Afshar, Haleh, and Carolynne Dennis, eds.
1992   Women and Adjustment Policies in the Third World. New York: St. Martin's Press.

Aguilar, Delia D.
2004   Introduction. *In* Women and Globalization. Delia D. Aguilar and Anne E. Lacsamana, eds. Pp. 11–24. Amherst, NY: Humanity Books.

Aguilar, Delia D., and Anne E. Lacsamana, eds.
2004   Women and Globalization. Amherst, NY: Humanity Books.

Ahearn, Laura M.
2001   Language and Agency. Annual Review of Anthropology 30:109–137.

Akerlof, George
1970   The Market for "Lemons": Quality, Uncertainty and the Market Mechanism. Quarterly Journal of Economics 84(3):488–500.

Alailima, Pat
2001   Sri Lanka: Growth, Distribution and Redistribution. Colombo: Ministry of Finance.

Alexander, M. Jacqui, and Chandra Talpade Mohanty, eds.
1996   Feminist Genealogies, Colonial Legacies, Democratic Futures (Thinking Gender). New York: Routledge.

Alonso, Graciela, and Raúl Díaz
2002   Encuentros Nacionales de Mujeres: Pedagogías de Viajes y Experiencias. *In* Hacia una Pedagogía de las Experiencias de las Mujeres. Graciela Alonso and Raúl Díaz, eds. Pp. 76–109. Buenos Aires: Miño y Dávila.

Alvarez, Sonia E., Elisabeth Jay Friedman, Ericka Beckman, Maylei Blackwell, Norma Stoltz Chinchilla, Nathalie Lebon, Marysa Navarro, and Marcela Ríos Tobar
2003   Encountering Latin American and Caribbean Feminisms. Signs: Journal of Women in Culture and Society 28(2):537–579.

Amin, Samir, Giovanni Arrighi, Andre Gunder Frank, and Immanuel Wallerstein, eds.
1994   Dynamics of Global Crisis. New York: Monthly Review.

Ancona, Giovanni
1991   Labour Demand and Immigration in Italy. Journal of Regional Policy 11:143–148.

Anthias, Floya
1998   Evaluating Diaspora: Beyond Ethnicity. Sociology 32(3):557–580.
2000   Metaphors of Home: Gendering New Migrations to Southern Europe. *In* Gender and Migration in Southern Europe: Women on the Move. Floya Anthias and Gabriella Lazaridis, eds. Pp. 15–41. Oxford: Berg.

Appadurai, Arjun
1996   Modernity at Large: Cultural Dimensions of Globalization. Minneapolis: University of Minnesota Press.

Appadurai, Arjun, ed.
1986   The Social Life of Things. Cambridge: Cambridge University Press.

Arao, Danilo A.
2000   Deployment of Migrant Workers Increasing. Ibon Facts and Figures 23(8):8.

Argumedo, Alcira, and Aída Quintar
2003   Argentina ante una Encrucijada Histórica. Estudios Sociológicos 21(63):613–642.

Armstrong, E.

2004　Globalization from Below: AIDWA, Foreign Funding, and Gendering Anti-Violence Campaigns. Journal of Developing Societies 20(1–2):39–55.

Aryeetey, Ernest

1994　Private Investment under Uncertainty in Ghana. World Development 22(8):1211–1221.

Babb, Florence

1988　"From the Field to the Cooking Pot": Economic Crisis and the Threat to Marketers in Peru. *In* Traders versus the State: Anthropological Approaches to Unofficial Economies. G. Clark, ed. Pp. 17–40. Boulder, CO: Westview Press.

1996　After the Revolution: Neoliberal Policy and Gender in Nicaragua. Latin American Perspectives 23(1):27–48.

Bakan, Abigail, and Daiva Stasiulis, eds.

1997　Not One of the Family: Foreign Domestic Workers in Canada. Toronto: University of Toronto Press.

Baker, Wayne E.

1984　The Social Structure of a National Securities Market. American Journal of Sociology 89(4):775–811.

Balakrishnan, Radhika, ed.

2002　The Hidden Assembly Line: Gender Dynamics of Subcontracted Work in a Global Economy. Bloomfield, CT: Kumarian Press, Inc.

Ballvé, Teo

2005　¡Bolivia de pie! NACLA Report on the Americas 39(2):40–44.

Barber, Pauline Gardiner

1997　Transnationalism and the Politics of "Home" for Philippine Domestic Workers. Anthropologica XXXIX(1–2):39–52.

Barker, Drucilla K., and Susan F. Feiner

2004　Feminist Perspectives on Families, Work, and Globalization. Ann Arbor: University of Michigan Press.

Barndt, Deborah, ed.

1999　Women Working the NAFTA Food Chain: Women, Food and Globalization. Toronto: Second Story Press.

Barrios de Chungara, Domitila, with Moema Viezzer

1978　Let Me Speak! Testimony of Domitila, a Woman of the Bolivian Mines. Victoria Ortiz, trans. New York: Monthly Review Press.

Barrón, Antonieta

1999　Mexican Women on the Move: Migrant Workers in Mexico and Canada. *In* Women Working the NAFTA Food Chain: Women, Food and Globalization. Deborah Barndt, ed. Pp. 113–126. Toronto: Second Story Press.

Basu, Amrita, Inderpal Grewal, Caren Kaplan, and Liisa Malkki, eds.

2001　Globalization and Gender. Special issue, Signs: Journal of Women in Culture and Society 26(4).

Bauman, Zygmunt

1998   Globalization: The Human Consequences. New York: Columbia University Press.

Bean, Susan S.

1989   Gandhi and Khaki: The Fabric of Indian Independence. *In* Cloth and Human Experience. Annette B. Weiner and Jane Schneider, eds. Pp. 355–376. Washington DC: Smithsonian Institution Press.

Behar, Ruth, and Deborah Gordon, eds.

1995   Women Writing Culture. Berkeley: University of California Press.

Bender, Daniel E.

2004   "Too Much of Distasteful Masculinity": Historicizing Sexual Harassment in the Garment Sweatshop and Factory. Journal of Women's History 15(4):91–116.

Benería, Lourdes

1996   Thou Shalt Not Live by Statistics Alone, but It Might Help. Feminist Economics 2(3):139–142.

2003   Gender, Development, and Globalization: Economics as if All People Mattered. New York: Routledge.

Benería, Lourdes, and Shelley Feldman, eds.

1992   Unequal Burden: Economic Crises, Persistent Poverty and Women's Work. Boulder, CO: Westview Press.

Benson, M. L., and G. L. Fox

2002   Economic Distress, Community Context, and Intimate Violence in the United States, 1988 and 1994. Computer file, ICPSR version. Cincinnati, OH: University of Cincinnati (producer). Ann Arbor, MI: Inter-university Consortium for Political and Social Research (distributor).

Berger, Iris

1992   Threads of Solidarity: Women in South African Industry, 1900–1980. Bloomington: Indiana University Press.

Bergeron, Suzanne

2001   Political Economy Discourses of Globalization and Feminist Politics. Signs: Journal of Women in Culture and Society 26(4):983–1006.

Bernard, H. Russell

2005   Research Methods in Anthropology: Qualitative and Quantitative Approaches. 4th edition. Walnut Creek, CA: AltaMira Press.

Bernhardt, Annette

2001   Hotel Industry Profile. Report prepared for the Russell Sage Foundation Future of Work Case Studies conference, New York, NY, April 21.

Bernhardt, Annette, L. Dresser, and E. Hatton

2002   The Coffee Pot Wars: Unions and Firm Restructuring in the Hotel Industry. Working paper, Russell Sage Foundation, New York.

Berry, Kim

2003   Developing Women: The Traffic in Ideas about Women and Their Needs in Kangra, India. *In* The Cultural Politics of Development in India: Regional Modernities. K. Sivaramakrishnan and Arun Agrawal, eds. Pp. 75–98. Stanford, CA: Stanford University Press.

Birgin, Haydée, ed.

2000   Ley, Mercado y Discriminación: El Género del Trabajo. Buenos Aires: Biblos.

Blim, Michael

2000   Capitalisms in Late Modernity. Annual Review of Anthropology 29:25–38.

Bobiwash, R.

2001   Statement to the World Social Forum from the Forum for Global Exchange and Biocultural Security Directorate, Center for World Indigenous Studies, Port Alegre, Brazil. Electronic document, http://www.cwis.org/fge/swsf.htm, accessed July 30, 2006.

Bograd, M.

1999   Strengthening Domestic Violence Theories: Intersections of Race, Class, Sexual Orientation, and Gender. Journal of Marital and Family Therapy 25:275–289.

Bolles, A. Lynn

1996a   Paying the Piper Twice: Gender and the Process of Globalization. Caribbean Studies 29(1):106–119.

1996b   Sister Jamaica. Lanham, MD: University Books of America.

Border Committee of Women Workers

2004   Six Years of NAFTA: A View from inside the Maquiladoras, with a foreword by Rachael Kamel. *In* Women and Globalization. Delia D. Aguilar and Anne E. Lacsamana, eds. Pp. 90–119. Amherst, NY: Humanity Books.

Borgatti, Jean

1983   Cloth as Metaphor: Nigerian Textiles from the Museum of Cultural History. Los Angeles: UCLA Museum of Cultural History.

Bose, Sugata, and Ayesha Jalal

1998   Modern South Asia. New Delhi: Oxford University Press.

Brah, Avtar

2003   Diaspora, Border and Transnational Identities. *In* Feminist Postcolonial Theory Reader. Reina Lewis and Sara Mills, eds. Pp. 613–634. London: Routledge.

Brennan, Denise

2004   What's Love Got to Do with It? Transnational Desires and Sex Tourism in the Dominican Republic. Durham, NC: Duke University Press.

Brocht, C.

2000   The Forgotten Workplace. Briefing paper, Economic Policy Institute, Washington DC.

Brodkin, Karen
1998   How Jews Became White Folks and What That Says about Race in America. New Brunswick, NJ: Rutgers University Press.
2000   Global Capitalism: What's Race Got to Do with It? American Ethnologist 27(2):237–256.

Brooks, David, and Jonathan Fox, eds.
2002   Cross-Border Dialogues: US–Mexico Social Movement Networking. La Jolla, CA: Center for US–Mexican Studies, University of California, San Diego.

Brooks, George E., Jr.
1972   The Kru Mariner in the Nineteenth Century: An Historical Compendium. Liberian Studies Monograph 1. Newark, DE: Liberian Studies Association in America.

Brown, David
1982   On the Category "Civilised" in Liberia and Elsewhere. Journal of Modern African Studies 20:287–303.

Brown, Stephen Gilbert, and Sidney I. Dobrin, eds.
2004   Ethnography Unbound: From Theory Shock to Critical Praxis. Albany: State University of New York Press.

Brumfiel, Liz
2006   2005 President's Report. Anthropology News 18(3):20.

Buck, Pem Davidson
2002   Worked to the Bone: Race, Class, Power, and Privilege in Kentucky. New York: Monthly Review Press.

Burawoy, Michael
2000a   Introduction. Reaching for the Global. *In* Global Ethnography: Forces, Connections, and Imaginations in a Postmodern World. Michael Burawoy, Joseph A. Blum, Sheba George, Zsuzsa Gille, Teresa Gowan, Lynne Haney, Maren Klawiter, Steve H. Lopez, Seán Ó Riain, and Millie Thayer, eds. Pp. 1–40. Berkeley: University of California Press.
2000b   Grounding Globalization. *In* Global Ethnography: Forces, Connections, and Imaginations in a Postmodern World. Michael Burawoy, Joseph A. Blum, Sheba George, Zsuzsa Gille, Teresa Gowan, Lynne Haney, Maren Klawiter, Steve H. Lopez, Seán Ó Riain, and Millie Thayer, eds. Pp. 337–350. Berkeley: University of California Press.

Burawoy, Michael, Joseph A. Blum, Sheba George, Zsuzsa Gille, Teresa Gowan, Lynne Haney, Maren Klawiter, Steven H. Lopez, Seán Ó Riain, and Millie Thayer, eds.
2000   Global Ethnography: Forces, Connections, and Imaginations in a Postmodern World. Berkeley: University of California Press.

Burke, Timothy
1996   Lifebuoy Men, Lux Women: Commodification, Consumption, and Cleanliness in Modern Zimbabwe. Durham, NC: Duke University Press.

Burnett, L. B., and J. Adler

2006   Domestic Violence. Electronic document, http://www.emedicine.com/emerg/topic153htm, accessed July 30, 2006.

Butler, Judith

1999   Gender Trouble: Feminism and the Subversion of Identity. 2nd edition. New York: Routledge.

Cafassi, Emilio

2002   La Revocación Sonora. Estudios Sociológicos 20(60):677–694.

Callard, Felicity J.

1998   The Body in Theory. Environment and Planning D: Society and Space 16(4):387–400.

Campani, Giovanna

1993   Immigration and Racism in Southern Europe: The Italian Case. Ethnic and Racial Studies 16(3):507–535.

Carr, Barry

1996   Crossing Borders: Labor Internationalism in the Era of NAFTA. *In* Neoliberalism Revisited: Economic Restructuring and Mexico's Political Future. Gerardo Otero, ed. Pp. 209–232. Boulder, CO: Westview Press.

Carter, Jeanette, and Joyce Mends-Cole

1982   Liberian Women: Their Role in Food Production and Their Educational and Legal Status. Monrovia: USAID/University of Liberia, Profile of Liberian Women in Development Project.

Castel, Robert

1991   From Dangerousness to Risk. *In* The Foucault Effect: Studies in Governmentality. Graham Berchell, Colin Gordon, and Peter Miller, eds. Pp. 281–298. Chicago: University of Chicago Press.

Castles, Stephen, and Mark Miller

2003   The Age of Migration, Third Edition: International Population Movements in the Modern World. New York: The Guilford Press.

Chalfin, Brenda

2001   Border Zone Trade and the Economic Boundaries of the State in North East Ghana. Africa 71(2):202–224.

Chandler, Susan

2003   You Have to Do It for the People Coming: Union Organizing and the Transformation of Immigrant Women Workers. Affilia: Journal of Women and Social Work 18(3):254–271.

Chang, Grace

2000   Disposable Domestics. Boston: South End Press.

2004   Globalization in Living Color: Women of Color Living under and over the "New World Order." *In* Women and Globalization. Delia D. Aguilar and Anne E. Lacsamana, eds. Pp. 230–261. Amherst, NY: Humanity Books.

Chang, Ha-Joon

2002 The Real Lesson for Developing Countries from the History of the Developed World: "Freedom to Choose." México, DF: Red Mexicana de Acción frente al Libre Comercio. Electronic document, http://www.historyandpolicy.org/main/policy-paper-09.html, accessed April 6, 2005.

Channa, Subhadra Mitra

2004 Globalization and Modernity in India: A Gendered Critique. Urban Anthropology 33(1):37–71.

Chant, Sylvia, and Nikki Craske

2002 Gender in Latin America. New Brunswick, NJ: Rutgers University Press.

Chant, Sylvia, and Kathy McIlwaine

1995 Gender and Export Manufacturing in the Philippines: Continuity or Change in Female Employment? Gender, Place, and Culture 2(2):147–176.

Chejter, Silvia, ed.

2002 Travesías 11: Globalización y Resistencias. De Viva Voz. Buenos Aires: CECYM.

Clark, Gracia

1994 Onions Are My Husband: Survival and Accumulation by West African Market Women. Chicago: University of Chicago Press.

Clark, John, and Nuno Themudo

2003 The Age of Protest: Internet-Based "Dot Causes" and the "Anti-globalization" Movement. *In* Globalizing Civic Engagement: Civil Society and Transnational Action. John Clark, ed. Pp. 109–126. London: Earthscan Publications, Ltd.

Clifford, James, and George Marcus, eds.

1986 Writing Culture: The Poetics and Politics of Ethnography. Berkeley: University of California Press.

Cohen, Marjorie Griffin, Laurell Ritchie, Michelle Swenarchuk, and Leah Vosko

2002 Globalization: Some Implications and Strategies for Women. Canadian Women Studies/Les Cahiers de La Femme 21/22:6–14.

Cohen, Robin

1997 Global Diasporas: An Introduction. Seattle: University of Washington Press.

Collicelli, Carla, Fabrizio Maria Arosio, Rosario Sapienza, and Fransesco Maietta

1997 City Template Rome: Basic Information on Ethnic Minorities and Their Participation. Rome: Fondazione CENSIS. Electronic document, http://www.unesco.org/most/p97rome.doc, accessed June 28, 2005.

Collier, Jane

1974 Women in Politics. *In* Women, Culture, and Society. Michelle Z. Rosaldo and Louise Lamphere, eds. Pp. 89–96. Stanford, CA: Stanford University Press.

Collins, Jane L.

2003 Threads: Gender, Labor, and Power in the Global Apparel Industry. Chicago: University of Chicago Press.

Collins, Patricia Hill

1998a   Fighting Words: Black Women and the Search for Justice. Minneapolis:
         University of Minnesota Press.

1998b   It's All in the Family: Intersections of Gender, Race and Nation. Hypatia
         13:62–82.

1991   Black Feminist Thought: Knowledge, Consciousness, and the Politics of
         Empowerment. Boston: Routledge, Chapman and Hall, Inc.

2000   Black Feminist Thought: Knowledge, Consciousness, and the Politics of
         Empowerment. 2nd edition. New York: Routledge.

Comaroff, Jean

1997   The Empire's Old Clothes: Fashioning the Colonial Subject. *In* Situated Lives:
         Gender and Culture in Everyday Life. Louise Lamphere, Helena Ragone, and
         Patricia Zavella, eds. Pp. 400–419. New York: Routledge.

Conklin, Mark

2000   Banana Shout. London: Fusion Press.

Conrad, C., J. Stewart, J. Whitehead, and P. Mason, eds.

2005   African Americans in the US Economy. Lanham, MD: Rowman & Littlefield
         Publishers, Inc.

Constable, Nicole

1999   At Home but Not at Home: Filipina Narratives of Ambivalent Returns. Cultural
         Anthropology 14(2):203–229.

Conwill, William L.

1980   A Conceptual Analysis of Black Family Instability. Ph.D. dissertation, Stanford
         University.

2001   Millennial Mandates for Mental Health. *In* Human Services Challenges in the
         21st Century. T. McClam and M. Woodside, eds. Pp. 175–191. Reading, MA:
         Council for Standards in Human Service Education.

Coomaraswamy, Radhika

2000   Unpublished report to the UN Secretary General in preparation for the World
         Conference on Race, Racism, Xenophobia and Related Concerns.

Cowan, Jane K., Marie-Bénédicte Dembour, and Richard A. Wilson

2001   Introduction. *In* Culture and Rights: Anthropological Perspectives. Jane K.
         Cowan, Marie-Bénédicte Dembour, and Richard A. Wilson, eds. Pp. 1–26.
         Cambridge: Cambridge University Press.

Crain, M.

1991   Feminizing Unions: Challenging the Gendered Structure of Wage Labor.
         Michigan Law Review 89:1155–1221.

Crenshaw, Kimberle

1989   Demarginalizing the Intersection of Race and Sex: A Black Feminist Critique of
         Antidiscrimination Doctrine, Feminist Theory and Antiracist Politics. *In* Critical
         Race Feminism: A Reader. Adrienne Wing, ed. Pp. 139–167. New York: New
         York University Press.

1991   Mapping the Margins: Intersectionality, Identity Politics, and Violence against
            Women of Color. Stanford Law Review 43:1241–1279.

Cruickshank, Brodie

1853   Eighteen Years on the Gold Coast of Africa Including an Account of the Native
            Tribes and Their Intercourse with Europeans. London: Hurst and Blacket.

Curtin, Victor, and Auliana Poon

1988   Tourist Accommodation in the Caribbean Bridgetown. Barbados: Caribbean
            Tourism Research and Development Centre.

Dabindu Collective

n.d.   Problems Faced by Women Working in Sri Lanka's Export Processing Zones.
            Electronic document, http://www.amrc.org.hk/Arch/3804.html, accessed
            December, 2006.

n.d.   Report, including personal testimony from Dabindu workers, presented at
            Maquila Solidarity Network conference. Electronic document, http://www.
            maquilasolidarity.org/resources/maquilas/pdf/ ExchangeEng-part6.pdf,
            accessed December, 2006.

Dahl, Ulrika

2004   Progressive Women, Traditional Men: The Politics of "Knowledge" and
            Gendered Stories of "Development" in the Northern Periphery of the EU.
            Ph.D. dissertation, University of California, Santa Cruz.

2005   Scener ur ett äktenskap: Heternormativitet och jämställdhet. *In* QueerSverige.
            Don Kulick, ed. Pp. 48–71. Stockholm: Natur och Kultur.

Daniel, E. Valentine

1996   Charred Lullabies: Chapters in an Anthropography of Violence. Princeton, NJ:
            Princeton University Press.

Daniell, William F.

1856   On the Ethnography of Akkrah and Adampe, Gold Coast, Western Africa.
            Journal of the Ethnological Society 4:1–32.

Darish, Patricia

1989   Dressing for the Next Life: Raffia Textile Production and Use among the Kuba
            of Zaire. *In* Cloth and Human Experience. Annette B. Weiner and Jane
            Schneider, eds. Pp. 117–140. Washington DC: Smithsonian Institution Press.

Darkwah, Akosua K.

2002   Going Global: Ghanaian Female Transnational Traders in an Era of
            Globalization. Ph.D. dissertation, University of Wisconsin.

Das, Veena, and Deborah Poole

2004   The State and Its Margins: Comparative Ethnographies. *In* Anthropology in
            the Margins of the State. Veena Das and Deborah Poole, eds. Pp. 1–33. School
            of American Research. Santa Fe, NM: SAR Press.

Dash, Jnana Ranjan

2005   Orissa 2005. The 36th annual souvenir issue, Journal of Orissa Society of the
            Americas (July):217–220.

Davidson, Penny, Trudy Jones, and Matthias Schellhorn
2002   Women as Producers and Consumers of Island Tourism. *In* Island Tourism and
        Sustainable Development: Caribbean, Pacific and Mediterranean Experiences.
        Y. Apostolopoulos and D. Gayle, eds. Pp. 199–221. Westport, CT: Praeger.

Davis, Ronald W.
1976   Ethnohistorical Studies on the Kru Coast. Liberian Studies Monograph 5.
        Newark, DE: Liberian Studies association in America.

Davis, William G.
1968   Economic Limitations and Social Relationships in a Philippine Marketplace:
        Capital Accumulation in a Peasant Economy. *In* Asian Studies at Hawaii 2. Van
        Niel, ed. Pp. 1–28R. Honolulu: Asian Studies Program, University of Hawaii.
1973   Social Relations in a Philippine Market: Self-Interest and Subjectivity. Berkeley:
        University of California Press.

de Alwis, Malathi
1997   The Production and Embodiment of Respectability: Gendered Demeanours in
        Colonial Ceylon. *In* Sri Lanka: Collective Identities Revisited, vol. I. Michael
        Roberts, ed. Pp. 105–143. Colombo: Marga Institute.

De Angelis, Massimo
1998   Second Encounter for Humanity and against Neoliberalism, Spain 1997, with
        an introduction by Massimo de Angelis. Capital & Class 65:135–157.

De Certeau, Michel
1984   The Practice of Everyday Life. Berkeley: University of California Press.

De Lauretis, Teresa
1987   Technologies of Gender: Essays on Theory, Film and Fiction. Bloomington:
        Indiana University Press.

de los Reyes, Paulina, Irene Molina, and Diana Mulinari, eds.
2003   Maktens (o)lika Förklädnader: Kön, klass och etnicitet i det postkoloniala
        Sverige. Stockholm: Atlas.

De Riz, Liliana, Luis Acosta, and Mariana Clucellas
2002   Aportes para el Desarrollo Humano de la Argentina 2002: Desigualdad y Pobreza.
        Ciudad de Buenos Aires: Programa de las Naciones Unidas Para el Desarrollo.

De Soto, Hernando
1989   The Other Path: The Invisible Revolution in the Third World. New York:
        Harper and Row.

**Deere, Carmen Diana, Peggy Antrobus, Lynn Bolles, Edwin Melendez, Peter Phillips,
Marcia Rivera, and Helen Safa**
1990   In the Shadows of the Sun: Caribbean Development Alternatives and US Policy.
        Boulder, CO: Westview Press.

Derné, Steve
2002   Globalization and the Reconstitution of Local Gender Arrangements. Men and
        Masculinities 5(2):144–164.

Desai, Manisha

2002   Transnational Solidarity: Women's Agency, Structural Adjustment, and
         Globalization. *In* Women's Activism and Globalization: Linking Local Struggles
         and Transnational Politics. Nancy A. Naples and Manisha Desai, eds. Pp.
         15–33. New York: Routledge.

Dhar, Biswajit, and Sudeshna Dey

2002   Global Trade and Agriculture: A Review of the WTO Agreement on
         Agriculture. *In* Development and the Challenge of Globalization. Peter
         Newell, Shirin M. Rai, and Andrew Scott, eds. Pp. 67–87. London: ITDG
         Publishing.

Di Leonardo, Micaela

1991   Introduction. Gender, Culture, and Political Economy: Feminist Anthropology
         in Historical Perspective. *In* Gender at the Crossroads of Knowledge: Feminist
         Anthropology in the Post-Modern Era. Micaela Di Leonardo, ed. Pp. 1–48.
         Berkeley: University of California Press.

Di Liscia, María Herminia, and María Silvia Di Liscia

1997   Mujeres, Estado y Salud: De la Persecución a la Integración. *In* Mujeres y
         Estado en la Argentina: Educación, Salud y Beneficencia. María Herminia Di
         Liscia and José Maristany, eds. Pp. 87–122. Buenos Aires: Biblos.

**Di Marco, Graciela, Héctor Palomino, Susana Méndez, Ramón Altamirano, and
Mirta Libchaber de Palomino**

2003   Movimientos Sociales en la Argentina: Asambleas: La Politización de la
         Sociedad Civil. Buenos Aires: Jorge Baudino Ediciones, Universidad Nacional
         de San Martín.

Dickerson, Kitty

1995   Textiles and Apparel in the Global Economy. Englewood Cliffs, NJ: Merrill.

Dinerstein, Ana

2001   A Silent Revolution: The Unemployed Workers' Movement in Argentina and
         the New Internationalism. Labour, Capital & Society 34(2):166–183.

2003   Power or Counter Power?: The Dilemma of the Piquetero Movement in
         Argentina Post-Crisis. Capital & Class 81:1–8.

Dore, Ronald

1983   Goodwill and the Spirit of Market Capitalism. British Journal of Sociology
         34(4):459–482.

Drake, St. Clair

1987   Black Folk Here and There: An Essay in History and Anthropology, vol. 1. Los
         Angeles: Center for Afro-American Studies, University of California, Los
         Angeles.

1990   Black Folk Here and There: An Essay in History and Anthropology, vol. 2. Los
         Angeles: Center for Afro-American Studies, University of California, Los
         Angeles.

Drake, St. Clair, and Horace R. Cayton
1945   Black Metropolis: A Study of Negro Life in a Northern City. New York:
         Harcourt Brace.

Duitsman, John
1982–1983   Liberian Languages. Liberian Studies Journal 10(1):27–36.

Dunaway, Wilma A.
2001   The Double Register of History: Situating the Forgotten Woman and Her
         Household in Capitalist Commodity Chains. Journal of World-Systems Research
         7:2–29.

Dunn, Hopeton S., and Leith L. Dunn
2002   People and Tourism. Kingston, Jamaica: Arawak Publications.

Durrenberger, Paul, and Suzan Erem
2005   Class Acts: An Anthropology of Service Workers and Their Union. Boulder, CO:
         Paradigm Publishers.

Eames, Elizabeth A.
1988   Why the Women Went to War: Women and Wealth in Ondo Town,
         Southwestern Nigeria. *In* Traders versus the State: Anthropological Approaches
         to Unofficial Economies. G. Clark, ed. Pp. 81–98. Boulder, CO: Westview Press.

Edelman, Marc
2004   The Price of Free Trade: Famine. *In* Anthropologists in the Public Sphere:
         Speaking Out on War, Peace, and American Power. Roberto J. González, ed.
         Pp. 102–104. Austin: University of Texas Press.

Ehrenreich, Barbara, and Arlie Russell Hochschild, eds.
2003   Global Woman: Nannies, Maids, and Sex Workers in the New Economy. New
         York: Owl Books.

Elliott, Larry, and Charlotte Denny
2003   Crisis Talks as Poor Nations Stand Firm. The Guardian, September 13: 21.

Elson, Diane
1991   Male Bias in Macro-Economics: The Case of Structural Adjustment. *In* Male
         Bias in the Development Process. Diane Elson, ed. Pp. 164–190. Manchester:
         Manchester University Press.
1992   From Survival Strategies to Transformation Strategies: Women's Needs and
         Structural Adjustment. *In* Unequal Burden: Economic Crises, Persistent Poverty
         and Women's Work. Lourdes Benería and Shelley Feldman, eds. Pp. 26–48.
         Boulder, CO: Westview Press.

England, Paula, Joan M. Hermsen, and David A. Cotter
2000   The Devaluation of Women's Work: A Comment on Tam. American Journal of
         Sociology 105(6):1741–1760.

Escrivá, Angeles
2000   The Position and Status of Migrant Women in Spain. *In* Gender and Migration
         in Southern Europe: Women on the Move. Floya Anthias and Gabriella
         Lazaridis, eds. Pp. 199–225. Oxford: Berg.

REFERENCES

Escobar, Arturo

1995   Encountering Development: The Making and Unmaking of the Third World. Princeton, NJ: Princeton University Press.

2001   Culture Sits in Places: Reflections on Globalism and Subaltern Strategies of Localization. Political Geography 20(2):139–174.

Espiritu, Yen Le

2003   Home Bound. Berkeley: University of California Press.

Esteva, Gustavo, and Madhu Prakash

2004   From Global to Local: Beyond Neoliberalism to the International of Hope. *In* The Globalization Reader. Frank Lechner and John Boli, eds. Pp. 410–417. Oxford: Blackwell Publishing.

Etienne, Mona

1980   Women and Men, Cloth and Colonization: The Transformation of Production-Distribution Relations among the Baule (Ivory Coast). *In* Women and Colonization: Anthropological Perspectives. Mona Etienne and Eleanor Leacock, eds. Pp. 214–238. South Hadley, MA: Bergin and Garvey.

European Commission

1996   First Cohesion Report. Luxembourg: Office for Official Publications of the European Communities.

Fanon, Frantz

1961   Wretched of the Earth. New York: Grove.

Farley, R.

1984   Blacks and Whites Narrowing the Gap. Cambridge, MA: Harvard University Press.

Farmer, Paul

2003   Pathologies of Power: Health, Human Rights and the New War on the Poor. Berkeley: University of California Press.

2004   An Anthropology of Structural Violence. Current Anthropology 45(3):305–326.

Feeley-Harnick, Gillian

1989   Cloth and the Production of Ancestors in Madagascar. *In* Cloth and Human Experience. Annette B. Weiner and Jane Schneider, eds. Pp. 73–116. Washington DC: Smithsonian Institution Press.

Ferguson, James, and Akhil Gupta

2002   Spatializing States: Toward an Ethnography of Neoliberal Governmentality. American Ethnologist 29(4):981–1002.

Ferguson, Ronald

2005   The Working-Poverty Trap. Public Interest 158 (Winter):71–82.

Fernandes, Leela

1997   Producing Workers: The Politics of Gender, Class, and Culture in the Calcutta Jute Mills. Philadelphia: University of Pennsylvania Press.

Fernandez-Kelly, Maria Patricia

1997 Maquiladoras: The View from the Inside. *In* Gender in Cross-Cultural Perspective. Caroline Brettel and Carolyn F. Sargent, eds. Pp. 525–537. Upper Saddle River, NJ: Prentice-Hall.

Ferreyra, Pilar

2002 Los Cartoneros Porteños Mueven 100 Millones de Pesos Por Mes. Clarín, August 31.

Firth, Raymond

1966 Malay Fishermen: Their Peasant Economy. London: Kegan Paul, Trench, Trubner and Company.

Food First

2003a Food Policy Think Tank Reports Find Trade Agreements Hurt Farmers and Consumers While Benefitting Corporations. Press release. Electronic document, http://www.foodfirst.org/media/printformat.php?id=374, accessed April 6, 2005.

2003b Thousands Mobilize to Derail the Free Trade Area of the Americas. Press release, November 13. Electronic document, http://www.foodfirst.org/media/printformat.php?id=363, accessed April 6, 2005.

Foster, John W.

2005 The Trinational Alliance against NAFTA: Sinews of Solidarity. *In* Coalitions across Borders: Transnational Protest and the Neoliberal Order. Joe Bandy and Jackie Smith, eds. Pp. 209–229. Lanham, MD: Rowman & Littlefield Publishers, Inc.

Foucault, Michel

1979 Discipline and Punish: The Birth of the Prison. Alan Sheridan, trans. New York:
[1975] Vintage Books.

Frankel, Merran

1964 Tribe and Class in Monrovia. London: Oxford University Press.

Freeman, Carla

2000 High Tech and High Heels in the Global Economy: Women, Work, and Pink-Color Identities in the Caribbean. Durham, NC: Duke University Press.

2001 Is Local:Global as Feminine:Masculine? Rethinking the Gender of Globalization. Signs: Journal of Women in Culture and Society 26(4):1007–1037.

Friedman, Elisabeth Jay

2003 Gendering the Agenda: The Impact of the Transnational Women's Rights Movement at the UN Conferences of the 1990s. Women's Studies International Forum 26(4):313–331.

Fröbel, Folkner, Juergen Heinrichs, and Otto Kreye

1980 The New International Division of Labor: Structural Unemployment in Industrialized Countries and Industrialization in Developing Countries. Cambridge: Cambridge University Press.

Frontline

2004   Is India Shining? PBS, February 28–March 12.

Galafassi, Guido

2003   Social Movements, Conflicts and a Perspective of Inclusive Democracy in Argentina. Democracy and Nature: The International Journal of Inclusive Democracy 9(3):393–399.

Galleti, R., K. D. S. Baldwin, and I. O. Dina

1956   Nigerian Cocoa Farmers. London: Oxford University Press.

Galtung, J.

N.d.   After Violence: 3R, Reconstruction, Reconciliation, Resolution. Coping with Visible and Invisible Effects of War and Violence. Electronic document, http://www.transcend.org/TRRECBAS.HTM, accessed July 30, 2006.

Gandhi, Mohandas Karamchand

1997   Hind Swaraj and Other Writings. Anthony Parel, ed. Cambridge: Cambridge University Press.

Garfinkel, Harold

1967   Studies in Ethnomethodology. Upper Saddle River, NJ: Prentice-Hall, Inc.

Garlick, Peter C.

1971   African Traders and Economic Development in Ghana. Oxford: Clarendon Press.

Gaventa, J.

1998   Participation, Poverty and Social Exclusion in North and South. IDS Bulletin 29(1):51–57.

Geertz, Clifford

1978   Bazaar Economy: Information and Search in Peasant Marketing. American Economic Review 68:28–32.

1979   Suq: The Bazaar Economy in Sefrou. *In* Meaning and Order in Moroccan Society. C. Geertz, H. Geertz, and L. Rosen, eds. Pp. 123–224. New York: Cambridge University Press.

Gereffi, Gary

1994   The Organization of Buyer-Driven Global Commodity Chains: How US Retailers Shape Overseas Production Networks. *In* Commodity Chains and Global Capitalism. Gary Gereffi and Miquel Korzeniewicz, eds. Pp. 95–123. London: Praeger.

Gereffi, Gary, and Miquel Korzeniewicz, eds.

1994   Commodity Chains in Global Capitalism. Westport, CT: Praeger Press.

Gero, Joan, and Margaret Conkey, eds.

1991   Engendering Archaeology: Women and Prehistory. Oxford: Blackwell.

Ghosh, R. N., and K. C. Roy

1997   The Changing Status of Women in India: Impact of Urbanization and

Development. International Journal of Social Economics 24(7/8/9):902–917.

Ghumusar Mahila Sangathan
1998   Report. G. Udayagiri, Udayagiri, Kandhamal District, Orissa, India.

Giarracca, Norma, and Miguel Teubal
2001   Crisis and Agrarian Protest in Argentina: The Movimiento Mujeres
            Agropecuarias en Lucha. Latin American Perspectives 28(6):38–53.

Gibson-Graham, J. K.
1996   The End of Capitalism (As We Knew It): A Feminist Critique of Political
            Economy. Oxford: Blackwell.

Gibson-Graham, J. K., and David Ruccio
2001   "After" Development: Re-imagining Economy and Class. *In* Re/Presenting
            Class: Essays in Postmodern Marxism. J. K. Gibson-Graham, Stephen Resnick,
            and Richard Wolff, eds. Pp. 158–181. Durham, NC: Duke University Press.

Gladwin, Christina, ed.
1991   Structural Adjustment and African Women Farmers. Gainesville: University of
            Florida Press.

Gledhill, John
1995   The End of All Illusions? Neoliberalism, Transnational Economic Relations and
            Agrarian Reform in the Ciénega de Chapala, Michoacán. Electronic document,
            http://les.man.ac.uk/sa/jg/jgepubs.htm, accessed April 6, 2005.
1998   The Mexican Contribution to Restructuring US Capitalism. Critique of
            Anthropology 18(3):279–296.

Glenn, Evelyn Nakano
1986   Issei, Nisei, Warbride. Philadelphia: Temple University Press.
2002   Unequal Freedom. Cambridge, MA: Harvard University Press.

Global Exchange
2001   Against Neoliberal Globalization; Toward a World Social Alliance: Call by the
            First International Encuentro of Social Movements. Mexico City, August 14.
            Electronic document, http://www.globalexchange.org/campaigns/alterna-
            tives/alliance081401.html.pf, accessed April 6, 2005.

Gold, Steven
2003   Israeli and Russian Jews: Gendered Perspectives on Settlement and Return
            Migration. *In* Gender and US Immigration: Contemporary Trends. Pierrette
            Hondagneu-Sotelo, ed. Pp. 127–147. Berkeley: University of California Press.

Goldring, Luin
2003   Gender, Status, and the State in Transnational Spaces: The Gendering of
            Political Participation and Mexican Hometown Associations. *In* Gender and US
            Immigration: Contemporary Trends. Pierrette Hondagneu-Sotelo, ed. Pp.
            341–358. Berkeley: University of California Press.

REFERENCES

Goode, Judith, and Jeff Maskovsky, eds.

2001   The New Poverty Studies: The Ethnography of Power, Politics, and Impoverished People in the United States. New York: New York University Press.

Gordon, Derek

1989   Women, Work and Social Mobility in Post-war Jamaica. *In* Women and the Sexual Division of Labor in the Caribbean. Keith Hart, ed. Pp. 67–80. Kingston: The Consortium Graduate School of Social Sciences.

Grasmuck, Sherri, and Patricia Pessar

1991   Between Two Islands: Dominican International Migration. Berkeley: University of California Press.

Grassi, Ricardo

1990   A Network for Culture and Communication. Development, Journal of the Society for International Development 2:105–107.

Gray, Mia

2004   The Social Construction of the Service Sector: Institutional Structures and Labour Marker Outcomes. Geoforum 35:23–34.

Grewal, Inderpal, and Caren Kaplan

2001   Global Identities: Theorizing Transnational Studies of Sexuality. GLQ 7(4):663–679.

Grewal, Inderpal, and Caren Kaplan, eds.

1994   Scattered Hegemonies: Postmodernity and Transnational Feminist Practices. Minneapolis: University of Minnesota Press.

Guarnizo, Luis

1997   The Emergence of a Transnational Social Formation and the Mirage of Return Migration among Dominican Transmigrants. Identities 4(2):281–322.

Gunadasa, Saman

2002   Sri Lankan Government Imposes Longer Hours on Female Workers. Oak Park, MI: International Committee of the Fourth International. Electronic article, September 4, http://www.wsws.org/articles/2002/sep2002/sril-s04.shtml, accessed December 2006.

Gunatilaka, Ramani

1999   Labour Legislation and Female Employment in Sri Lanka's Manufacturing Sector. Colombo, Sri Lanka: Institute of Policy Studies.

Gutmann, Matthew C.

1997   Trafficking in Men: The Anthropology of Masculinity. Annual Review of Anthropology 26:385–409.

Hale, Sondra

1991   Feminist Method, Process, and Self-Criticism. *In* Women's Words: The Feminist Practice of Oral History. Sherna Berger Gluck and Daphne Patai, eds. Pp. 121–136. New York: Routledge.

Hampton, R. L., R. J. Gelles, and J. W. Harrop

1989   Is Violence in Black Families Increasing: A Comparison of 1975 and 1985 National Survey Rates. Journal of Marriage and the Family 51:969–980.

Handler, Richard, and Jocelyn Linnekin

1984   Tradition, Genuine or Spurious. Journal of American Folklore 97(385):273–290.

Hansen, Karen Tranberg

2000   Salaula: The World of Secondhand Clothing and Zambia. Chicago: University of Chicago Press.

Hansen, Kjell

1998   Välfärdens Motsträviga Utkant: Lokal Praktik och Statlig Styrning i Efterkrigstidens Nordsvenska Inland. Lund: Historiska Media.

Haraway, Donna

1988   Situated Knowledges: The Science Question in Feminism and the Privilege of Partial Perspective. Feminist Studies 14:575–599.

Harcourt, Wendy

2003   The Impact of Transnational Discourses on Local Community Organizing. Development, Journal of the Society for International Development 46(1):74–79.

Harding, Sandra

1987   Is There a Feminist Method? *In* Feminism and Methodology. Sandra Harding, ed. Pp. 1–14. Bloomington: Indiana University Press.

Harrison, Faye V.

1995   The Persistent Power of "Race" in the Cultural and Political Economy of Racism. Annual Review of Anthropology 24:47–74.

1997a   The Gendered Politics and Violence of Structural Adjustment: A View from Jamaica. *In* Situated Lives: Gender and Culture in Everyday Life. Louise Lamphere, Helena Ragone, and Patricia Zavella, eds. Pp. 451–468. New York: Routledge.

1997b   Decolonizing Anthropology: Moving Further toward an Anthropology for Liberation. 2nd edition. Arlington, VA: Association of Black Anthropologists and the American Anthropological Association.

1998   Contemporary Issues Forum: Race and Racism. Guest ed. American Anthropologist 100(3):6076–6715.

2000   Facing Racism and the Moral Responsibility of Human Rights Knowledge. Annals of the New York Academy of Science 925:45–69.

2002   Global Apartheid, Foreign Policy, and Human Rights. Souls: A Critical Journal of Black Politics, Culture, and Society 4(3):48–68.

2004a   Everyday Neoliberalism, Diminishing Subsistence Security, and the Criminalisation of Survival: Gendered Urban Poverty in Three African Diaspora Contexts. *In* Mega Urbanization, Multi-ethnic Society, Human Rights and Development. Calcutta: Department of Anthropology, University of Calcutta.

2004b Global Apartheid, Environmental Degradation, and Women's Activism for Sustainable Well-Being: A Conceptual and Theoretical Overview. Urban Anthropology 33(1):1–35.

2005 Introduction. Global Perspectives on Human Rights and Interlocking Inequalities of Race, Gender, and Related Dimensions of Power. *In* Resisting Racism and Xenophobia: Global Perspectives on Race, Gender, and Human Rights. Faye V. Harrison, ed. Pp. 1–34. Lanham, MD: Rowman & Littlefield Publishers, Inc.

Hartmann, H., K. Allen, and C. Owens
1999 Equal Pay for Working Families. Washington DC: Institute for Women's Research Policy.

Harvey, David
1998 The Body as an Accumulation Strategy. Environment and Planning D: Society and Space 16(4):401–421.

Hasanbegovic, Claudia
1998 "Las Mujeres Más Lindas dei Mundo": Un Análisis del Discurso Argentino del Cuerpo Femenino. Paper presented at the 49th European Conference of Latinoamericanists, Halle University, Halle, Germany, September 4–8.

Hawkesworth, Mary E.
2006 Globalization and Feminist Activism. Lanham, MD: Rowman & Littlefield Publishers, Inc.

Hemispheric Social Alliance
2003 Lessons from NAFTA: The High Cost of "Free" Trade. Electronic document, http://www.asc-hsa.org, accessed April 6, 2005.

Hendrickson, Hildi, ed.
1996 Clothing and Difference: Embodied Identities in Colonial and Post Colonial Africa. Durham, NC: Duke University Press.

Hernes, Helga Marie
1987 Welfare State and Political Power: Essays in State Feminism. Oslo: Norwegian University Press.

Hettiarachchy, Tilak, and Stephen L. Schensul
2001 The Risks of Pregnancy and the Consequences among Young Unmarried Women Working in a Free Trade Zone in Sri Lanka. Asia-Pacific Population Journal 16(2):125–140.

Hettige, S. T., ed.
1998 Globalization, Social Change, and Youth. Colombo, Sri Lanka: German Cultural Institute.

Hewamanne, Sandya
2003 Performing Dis-respectability: New Tastes, Cultural Practices, and Identity Performances by Sri Lanka's Free Trade Zone (FTZ) Garment-Factory Workers. Cultural Dynamics 15 (March):71–101.

Hicks, Norman, Sandra Cesilini, Ariel Fiszbein, Vivien Foster, Paula Giovagnoli, Suhas Parandekar, Haeduck Lee, Carolina Mera, Cristóbal Ridau-Cano, María Paula Savanti, Nicole Schwab, Juan Pablo Uribe, and Quentin Wodon
2003   Argentina. Crisis and Poverty 2003: A Poverty Assessment, vol. I: Main Report. World Bank.

Hilton Hotels
2005   Website for Hilton's featured "Spa Fusion" amenities, http://www.spafusion .com/spapackages.html, accessed August 14, 2007.

Hirsch, Jennifer
2003   A Courtship after Marriage: Sexuality and Love in Mexican Transnational Families. Berkeley: University of California Press.

Hollup, Oddvar
1994   Bonded Labour: Caste and Cultural Identity among Tamil Plantation Workers in Sri Lanka. Colombo, Sri Lanka: Charles Subasinghe & Sons.

Holstein, William J.
2005   One Global Game, Two Sets of Rules. New York Times, August 14: 9.

Hondagneu-Sotelo, Pierrette
1994   Gendered Transitions: Mexican Experiences of Migration. Berkeley: University of California Press.

hooks, bell
1984   Feminist Theory from Margin to Center. Boston: South End Press.

Huffman, Matt
2004   Gender Inequality across Local Wage Hierarchies. Work and Occupations 31(3):323.

Hurtado, Aida
1996   The Color of Privilege: Three Blasphemies on Race and Feminism. Ann Arbor: University of Michigan Press.

Hyatt, S. B.
1995   Poverty and Difference: Ethnographic Representations of "Race" and the Crisis of "the Social." *In* Gender and Race through Education and Political Activism: The Legacy of Sylvia Forman. D. Shenk, ed. Pp. 185–206. Arlington, VA: American Anthropological Association.

Ibarra, Maria de la Luz
2002   Emotional Proletarians in a Global Economy: Mexican Immigrant Women and Elder Care Work. Urban Anthropology and Studies of Cultural Systems and World Economic Development 31(3):317–351.

Inda, Jonathan, and Renato Rosaldo, eds.
2002   The Anthropology of Globalization. Oxford: Blackwell Publishers.

Innes, Gordon
1966   An Introduction to Grebo. London: School of Oriental and African Studies.

Jämtland website

2007   http://www.jamtland.se, accessed August 13, 2007.

Jayawardena, Kumari

1986   Feminism and Nationalism in the Third World. London: Zed Books.

2002   Nobodies to Somebodies: The Rise of the Colonial Bourgeoisie in Sri Lanka. Colombo, Sri Lanka: The Social Scientists' Association and Sanjiva Books.

Jayaweera, Swarna

1991   Women, Skill Development and Employment. Women in Development 2, February. Colombo, Sri Lanka: Institute of Policy Studies.

Jewkes, R.

2002   Intimate Partner Violence: Causes and Prevention. Lancet 359:1423–1429.

Johnson, Scott, Jason McLure, George Wehrfritz, and Mac Margolis

2003   The Poor Get Poorer. Newsweek International, September 29: 42.

Kandiyoti, Deniz

1996   Contemporary Feminist Scholarship and Middle East Studies. *In* Gendering the Middle East: Emerging Perspectives. Denize Kandiyoti, ed. Pp. 3–27. Syracuse, NY: Syracuse University Press.

Kanlungan Center Foundation

2000   Fast Facts on Labor Migration. Quezon City: Kanlungan Center Foundation.

Karp, Jonathan

1995   A New Kind of Hero. Far Eastern Economic Review 158:42–45.

Kasturi, Leela

1995   Development, Patriarchy, and Politics: Indian Women in the Political Process 1947–1992. Occasional Paper 25. New Delhi: Center for Women's Development Studies.

Katz, Cindi

2001   On the Grounds of Globalization: A Topography for Feminist Political Engagement. Signs: Journal of Women in Culture and Society 26(4):1213–1234.

2003   Vagabond Capitalism and the Necessity of Social Reproduction. *In* Implicating Empire: Globalization and Resistance in the 21st Century World Order. Stanley Aronowitz and Heather Gwautney, eds. Pp. 255–270. New York: Basic Books.

Katzin, Margaret

1959   Higglers of Jamaica. Ph.D. dissertation, Northwestern University.

Kaufman, Cynthia

2003   Ideas for Action: Relevant Theories for Radical Change. Cambridge, MA: South End Press.

Kearney, Michael

1995   The Local and the Global: The Anthropology of Globalization and Transnationalism. Annual Review of Anthropology 24:547–565.

Keat, Russell
1991   Introduction. Starship Britain or Universal Enterprise? *In* Enterprise Culture. Russell Keat and Nicholas Abercrombie, eds. Pp. 1–20. London: Routledge.

Keating, Christine
2004   Developmental Democracy and Its Inclusions: Globalization and the Transformation of Participation. Signs: Journal of Women in Culture and Society 29(2):417–438.

Kelly, Rita Mae, Jane H. Bayes, Mary Hawkesworth, and Brigitte Young, eds.
2001   Gender, Globalization, and Democratization. New York: Rowman & Littlefield Publishers, Inc.

Kerner, Donna O.
1988   "Hard Work" and Informal Sector Trade in Tanzania. *In* Traders versus the State: Anthropological Approaches to Unofficial Economies. G. Clark, ed. Pp. 41–56. Boulder, CO: Westview Press.

Khuri, Fuad I.
1968   The Etiquette of Bargaining in the Middle East. American Anthropologist 70:697–706.

Kibria, Nazli
1994   Family Tightrope. Princeton, NJ: Princeton University Press.

King, Deborah
1995   Multiple Jeopardy, Multiple Consciousness: The Context of a Black Feminist Ideology. *In* Words of Fire: An Anthology of African-American Feminist Thought. Beverly Guy-Sheftall, ed. Pp. 294–318. New York: The New Press.

Kingfisher, Catherine, ed.
2002   Western Welfare in Decline: Globalization and Women's Poverty. Philadelphia: University of Pennsylvania Press.

Kingfisher, Catherine, and Michael Goldsmith
2001   Reforming Women in the United States and Aotearoa, New Zealand: A Comparative Ethnography of Welfare Reform in Global Context. American Anthropologist 103:716–727.

Kingsolver, Ann E.
1991   Tobacco, Toyota, and Subaltern Development Discourses: Constructing Livelihoods and Community in Rural Kentucky. Ph.D. dissertation, University of Massachusetts, Amherst.

2001   NAFTA Stories: Fears and Hopes in Mexico and the United States. Boulder, CO: Lynne Rienner Publishers.

2007   Farmers and Farmworkers: Two Centuries of Strategic Alterity in Kentucky's Tobacco Fields. Critique of Anthropology 27(1):87–102.

Kirby, Peadar
2006   Vulnerability and Violence: The Impact of Globalisation. London: Pluto Press.

Kleinman, Arthur, Veena Das, and Margaret Lock

1996   Introduction. Daedalus: Journal of the American Academy of Arts and Sciences 125(1):xi–xx.

Kondo, D. K.

1995   Bad Girls: Theatre, Women of Color, and the Politics of Representation. *In* Women Writing Culture. Ruth Behar and Deborah A. Gordon, eds. Pp. 49–64. Berkeley: University of California Press.

Koptiuch, Kristin

1997   Third-Worlding at Home. *In* Culture, Power, Place; Explorations in Critical Anthropology. Akhil Gupta and James Ferguson, eds. Pp. 234–248. Durham, NC: Duke University Press.

Kulick, Don

2003   Sex in the New Europe: The Criminalization of Clients and Swedish Fear of Penetration. Anthropological Theory 3(2):199–121.

Kumpfer, K.

1999   Strengthening America's Families: Exemplary Parenting and Family Strategies for Delinquency Prevention. Washington DC: US Department of Justice.

Lamphere, Louise

1987   From Working Daughters to Working Mothers. Ithaca, NY: Cornell University Press.

Lamphere, Louise, Helena Ragoné, and Patricia Zavella, eds.

1997   Situated Lives: Gender and Culture in Everyday Life. New York: Routledge.

Lancaster, Roger, and Micaela di Leonardo, eds.

1997   The Gender/Sexuality Reader: Culture, History, Political Economy. New York: Routledge.

Lau, B. W. K.

2002   Mental Health in Hong Kong: Desideratum or Mirage. The Hong Kong Practitioner 24:240–247.

LeCompte, Margaret D., and Jean J. Schensul

1999   Designing and Conducting Ethnographic Research. Walnut Creek, CA: AltaMira Press.

Lee, Ching Kwan

1997   Factory Regimes of Chinese Capitalism: Different Cultural Logics in Labor Control. *In* Ungrounded Empires: The Cultural Politics of Modern Chinese Transnationalism. Aihwa Ong and Donald Nonini, eds. Pp. 115–142. New York: Routledge.

Lefebvre, Henri

1977   Reflections on the Politics of Space. *In* Radical Geography. Richard Peet, ed. Pp. 339–352. London: Methuen.

Leontieva, Alexandra, and Karin Sarsenov

2003   Hora eller Brud? Invandrare och Minoriteter 1:14–17.

Lessinger, Johanna
1988   Trader vs. Developer: The Market Relocation Issue in an Indian City. *In* Traders versus the State: Anthropological Approaches to Unofficial Economies. G. Clark, ed. Pp. 139–164. Boulder, CO: Westview Press.

Levine, M. V., and S. J. Callaghan
1998   The Economic State of Milwaukee: The City and the Region. Milwaukee: University of Milwaukee Center for Economic Development.

Lewellen, Ted C.
2002   The Anthropology of Globalization: Cultural Anthropology Enters the 21st Century. Westport, CT: Bergin and Garvey.

Life and Debt
2001   Stephanie Black, dir. Documentary film. New Yorker Films, New York.

Light, Ivan, Georges Sabagh, Mehdi Bozorgmehr, and Claudia Der-Martirosian
1994   Beyond the Ethnic Enclave Economy. Social Problems 41(1):65–79.

Liliequist, Marianne
1991   Nybyggarbarn: Barnuppfostran bland nybyggare i Frostvikens, Vilhelmina och Tärna socknar 1850–1920. Stockholm: Almqvist och Wiksell Intl.

Lim, Linda Y. C.
1983   Capitalism, Imperialism, and Patriarchy: The Dilemma of Third-World Women Workers in Multinational Factories. *In* Women, Men and the International Division of Labor. June Nash and Maria Patricia Fernandez-Kelly, eds. Pp. 216–229. New York: SUNY Press.

Liu, Laura
2000   The Place of Immigration in Studies of Geography and Race. Social and Cultural Geography 1(2):169–182.

Lladós, José Ignacio
2004   La Prostitución Creció Más del 40%. La Nación, May 16.

Lowe, Lisa
1996   Immigrant Acts. Durham, NC: Duke University Press.

Luján U., Bertha Elena
2002   Citizen Advocacy Networks and the NAFTA. *In* Cross-Border Dialogues: US–Mexico Social Movement Networking. David Brooks and Jonathan Fox, eds. Pp. 211–226. La Jolla: Center for US–Mexican Studies, University of California, San Diego.

Lutz, Helma
1997   The Limits of European-ness: Immigrant Women in Fortress Europe. Feminist Review 57 (Autumn):93–111.

Lynch, Caitrin
1999   The Good Girls of Sri Lankan Modernity: Moral Orders of Nationalism and Capitalism. Identities: Global Studies in Culture and Power 6(1):55–89.

Macdonald, Laura

2003   Gendering Transnational Social Movement Analysis: Women's Groups Contest Free Trade in the Americas. *In* Coalitions across Borders: Transnational Protest and the Neoliberal Order. Joe Bandy and Jackie Smith, eds. Pp. 21–41. Lanham, MD: Rowman & Littlefield Publishers, Inc.

Majozo, E. C.

1999   Come Out the Wilderness. New York: Feminist Press.

Marchand, Marianne H., and Anne Sisson Runyan, eds.

2000   Gender and Global Restructuring: Sightings, Sites and Resistances. London: Routledge.

Marques, Margarida, Rui Santos, and Fernanda Araújo

2001   Ariadne's Thread: Cape Verdean Women in Transnational Webs. Global Networks 1(3):283–306.

Martin, Emily

1994   Flexible Bodies: The Role of Immunity in American Culture from the Days of Polio to the Age of AIDS. Boston: Beacon Press.

Martin, Jane

1968   The Dual Legacy: Government Authority and Mission Influence among the Glebo of Eastern Liberia, 1834–1910. Ph.D. dissertation, Boston University.

1982   Krumen "Down the Coast": Liberian Migrants on the West African Coast in the Nineteenth Century. Boston University African Studies Center Working Papers no. 64.

Matoso, Elina

2003   La Piel Herida. Remendada y Suturada. Página 12, February 13.

Mazzarella, William

2003   Shoveling Smoke: Advertising and Globalization in Contemporary India. Durham, NC: Duke University Press.

McCall, Leslie

2005   The Complexity of Intersectionality. Signs: Journal of Women in Culture and Society 30:1771–1800.

McCormack Institute

1997   In Harm's Way? Domestic Violence, AFDC Receipt, and Welfare Reform in Massachusetts. Electronic document, http://www.mccormack.umb.edu/csp/publications/harms%20way.pdf, accessed July 30, 2006.

McGregor, S.

n.d.   Consumerism as a Source of Structural Violence. Electronic document, http://www.kon.org/hswp/archive/consumerism.pdf, accessed July 30, 2006.

Memarsadeghi, Sanaz, and Raj Patel

2003   Agricultural Restructuring and Concentration in the United States: Who Wins, Who Loses? Policy brief no. 6. Food First.

Menjívar, Cecilia
2003   The Intersection of Work and Gender: Central American Immigrant Women and Employment in California. *In* Gender and US Immigration: Contemporary Trends. Pierrette Hondagneu-Sotelo, ed. Pp. 101–126. Berkeley: University of California Press.

Miller, Daniel
1995   Consumption and Commodities. Annual Review of Anthropology 24:141–161.

Mills, Mary Beth
1998   Gendered Encounters with Modernity: Labor Migrants and Marriage Choices in Contemporary Thailand. Identities: Global Studies in Culture and Power 5(3):301–334.

2003   Gender and Inequality in the Global Labor Force. Annual Review of Anthropology 32:41–62.

Mintz, Sidney
1961   Pratik: Haitian Personal Economic Relationships. *In* Proceedings of the 1961 Annual Spring Meeting of the American Ethnological Society. V. E. Garfield, ed. Pp. 54–63. Seattle: American Ethnological Society.

1964   The Employment of Capital by Market Women in Haiti. *In* Capital, Saving and Credit. Ramond Firth and B. Yamey, eds. Pp. 256–286. Chicago: Aldine.

Mishra, Arabinda
2005   Dalit Girl Crosses the Hurdle. The Times of India, August 20. Electronic version, http://timesofindia.indiatimes.com/articleshow/1205566.cms, accessed April 2007.

Mishra, Mamata, and Ghumusar Mahila Sangathan
2001   Tribal Women United against Oppression and for Social Justice. Connect, August 20.

Moghadam, Valentine M.
1999   Gender and Globalization: Female Labor and Women's Mobilization. Journal of World-Systems Research V(2):367–388.

Mohanty, Chandra Talpade
1991   Under Western Eyes: Feminist Scholarship and Colonial Discourses. *In* Third World Women and the Politics of Feminism. Chandra Mohanty, A. Russo, and L. Torres, eds. Pp. 51–80. Bloomington: Indiana University Press.

2003a   Introduction. Decolonization, Anticapitalist Critique, and Feminist Commitments. *In* Feminism without Borders: Decolonizing Theory, Practicing Solidarity. Pp. 1–16. Durham, NC: Duke University Press.

2003b   Feminism without Borders: Decolonizing Theory, Practicing Solidarity. Durham, NC: Duke University Press.

Moraga, Cherríe
2002   Foreword. The War Path of Greater Empowerment. *In* Colonize This! Young Women of Color on Today's Feminism. Daisy Hernández and Bushra Rehman, eds. Pp. xi–xv. Emeryville, CA: Seal Press.

Moran, Mary H.

1986   Taking Up the Slack: Female Farming and the "Kru Problem" in Southeastern Liberia. Liberian Studies Journal 11:117–124.

1990   Civilized Women: Gender and Prestige in Southeastern Liberia. Ithaca, NY: Cornell University Press.

1997   Warriors or Soldiers? Masculinity and Ritual Transvestism in the Liberian Civil War. *In* Situated Lives: Gender and Culture in Everyday Life. Louise Lamphere, Helena Ragone, and Patricia Zavella, eds. Pp. 440–450. New York: Routledge Press.

2006   Liberia: The Violence of Democracy. Philadelphia: University of Pennsylvania Press.

Morgen, Sandi

2005   Comments made in the School for Advanced Research Short Seminar on Women and Globalization. Santa Fe, New Mexico, April 7.

Morgen, Sandi, and Jeff Maskovsky

2003   The Anthropology of Welfare "Reform": New Perspectives on US Urban Poverty in the Post-welfare Era. Annual Review of Anthropology 32:315–338.

Moser, Caroline O.

1993   Adjustment from Below: Low-Income Women, Time and the Triple Role in Guayaquil, Ecuador. *In* Viva: Women and Popular Protest in Latin America. Sara Radcliffe and Sallie Westwood, eds. Pp. 173–196. New York: Routledge.

Moynihan, Daniel P.

1967   The Negro Family: The Case for National Action. *In* The Moynihan Report and the Politics of Controversy. L. Rainwater and W. Yancey, eds. Pp. 41–124. Boston: MIT Press.

Mullings, Beverly

2002   Globalization, Tourism and International Sex Trade. *In* Black Women, Globalization, and Economic Justice. Filomina C. Steady, ed. Pp. 295–329. Rochester, VT: Schenkman Books.

Mullings, Leith

1997   On Our Own Terms: Race, Class and Gender in the Lives of African American Women. New York: Routledge.

2005   Interrogating Racism: Toward an Anti-Racist Anthropology. Annual Review of Anthropology 34:667–693.

Mullings, Leith, and Alaka Wali

2001   Stress and Resilience: The Social Context of Reproduction in Central Harlem. New York: Kluwer.

Muratorio, Blanca

1998   Indigenous Women's Identities and the Politics of Cultural Reproduction in the Ecuadorian Amazon. American Anthropologist 100:409–420.

Naples, Nancy A.

2002   Changing the Terms: Community Activism, Globalization, and the Dilemmas of Transnational Feminist Praxis. *In* Women's Activism and Globalization: Linking Local Struggles and Transnational Politics. Nancy Naples and Manisha Desai, eds. Pp. 3–14. New York: Routledge.

2003   Feminism and Method: Ethnography, Discourse Analysis, and Activist Research. New York: Routledge.

Naples, Nancy A., and Manisha Desai, eds.

2002   Women's Activism and Globalization: Linking Local Struggles and Transnational Politics. New York: Routledge.

Narayan, Kirin

1993   How Native Is a "Native" Anthropologist? American Anthropologist 95(3):671–686.

Nash, June

1979   We Eat the Mines and the Mines Eat Us: Dependency and Exploitation in Bolivian Tin Mines. New York: Columbia University Press.

1994   Global Integration and Subsistence Insecurity. American Anthropologist 96(1):7–30.

1997a   When Isms Become Wasms: Structural Functionalism, Marxism, Feminism and Postmodernism. Critique of Anthropology 17(1):11–32.

1997b   The Fiesta of the Word: The Zapatista Uprising and Radical Democracy in Mexico. American Anthropologist 99(2):261–274.

2001   Mayan Visions: The Quest for Autonomy in an Age of Globalization. New York: Routledge.

Nash, June, ed.

2005   Social Movements: An Anthropological Reader. Malden, MA: Blackwell Publishers.

National Commission for the Role of Filipino Women

1995   Philippine Plan for Gender-Responsive Development, 1995–2025. Manila: Author.

Nielsen, Joyce McCarl, ed.

1990   Feminist Research Methods: Exemplary Readings in the Social Sciences. Boulder, CO: Westview Press.

Nilsson, Agneta

1993   Att ta liv och arbete i Egna Händer: Om projektet Kvinnum i Jämtlands Län. Östersund: Länsstyrelsen.

Niskanen, W., and S. Moore

1996   Supply Tax Cuts and the Truth about the Reagan Economic Record. Electronic document, http://www.cato.org/pubs/pas/pa-261.html, accessed July 30, 2006.

REFERENCES

Nordin, Lissa
2005   När man vill vara sig själv: Om våndan av att vara ensamstående man i nor-
rländsk glesbygd. *In* QueerSverige. Don Kulick, ed. Pp. 24–46. Stockholm:
Natur och Kultur Förlag.

Norgaard, Kari Marie
2003   Community, Place, and Privilege: Double Realities, Denial, and Climate
Change in Norway. Ph.D. dissertation, University of Oregon.

O'Grady, Ron
1982   Tourism in the Third World. Maryknoll, NY: Orbis Books.

Olivera, Oscar, with Tom Lewis
2004   ¡Cochabamba! Water War in Bolivia. Cambridge, MA: South End Press.

Omi, Michael, and Howard Winant
1994   Racial Formation in the United States from the 1960s to the 1990s. 2nd edition. New York: Routledge.

Ong, Aihwa
1987   Spirits of Resistance and Capitalist Discipline: Factory Women in Malaysia.
Albany: SUNY Press.
1997   Spirits of Resistance. *In* Situated Lives: Gender and Culture in Everyday Life.
Louise Lamphere, Helena Ragone, and Patricia Zavella, eds. Pp. 355–370. New
York: Routledge.
2000   The Gender and Labor Politics of Postmodernity. *In* Globalization and the
Challenges of a New Century: A Reader. Patrick O'Meara, Howard D. Mehlinger,
and Matthew Krain, eds. Pp. 253–281. Bloomington: Indiana University Press.

Ong, Paul, and Tania Azores
1994   Asian Immigrants in Los Angeles: Diversity and Divisions. *In* The New Asian
Immigration in Los Angeles and Global Restructuring. Paul Ong, Edna
Bonacich, and Lucie Cheng, eds. Pp. 100–129. Philadelphia: Temple
University Press.

Ontario Human Rights Commission
2001   An Intersectional Approach to Discrimination Addressing Multiple Grounds in
Human Rights Complaints. Discussion document available online at
http://www.ohrc.on.ca/english/consultations/intersectionality-discussion-
paper.shtml or http://www.ohrc.on.ca/english/consultations/intersectionality-
discussion-paper.pdf, accessed December 8, 2006.

Opiniano, Jeremiah
2002   Survey of Overseas Filipinos Shows Increase in OFWs, Remittances. Electronic
document, http://www.cyberdyaryo.com/features/f2003_0512_02.html,
accessed December 19, 2004.

Orlove, Benjamin
1986   Barter and Cash Sale on Lake Titicaca: A Test of Competing Approaches.
Current Anthropology 27(2):85–106.

Ortner, Sherry B., and Harriet Whitehead
1981   Sexual Meanings: The Cultural Construction of Gender and Sexuality.
         Cambridge: Cambridge University Press.

Pandey, Triloki Nath
2002   Some Thoughts on Marginalization and Marginalized Communities. Journal of
         Anthropological Survey of India 51:1–7.

Parreñas, Rhacel Salazar
2001   Servants of Globalization: Women, Migration, and Domestic Work. Stanford,
         CA: Stanford University Press.

2005   Children of Global Migration: Transnational Families and Gendered Woes.
         Stanford, CA: Stanford University Press.

Patroni, Viviana
2002   Structural Reforms and the Labour Movement in Argentina. Labour, Capital &
         Society 35(2):252–280.

Patterson, Thomas C.
1999   Change and Development in the Twentieth Century. Oxford: Berg.

Pattullo, Polly
1996   Last Resorts: The Cost of Tourism in the Caribbean. Kingston: Ian Randle
         Publishers.

Pelto, Pertti J., and Gretel H. Pelto
1970   Anthropological Research: The Structure of Inquiry. Cambridge: Cambridge
         University Press.

Pena, Devon
1997   The Terror of the Machine: Technology, Work, Gender and Ecology on the
         US–Mexico Border. Austin, TX: CMAS Books.

Perani, Judith, and Norma H. Wolff
1999   Cloth, Dress, and Art Patronage in Africa. Oxford: Berg.

Perot, Ross, with Pat Choate
1993   Save Your Job, Save Our Country: Why NAFTA Must Be Stopped—Now! New
         York: Hyperion.

Pessar, Patricia
1986   The Role of Gender in Dominican Settlement in the US. *In* Women and
         Change in Latin America. June Nash and Helen Safa, eds. Pp. 273–294. South
         Hadley, MA: Bergin and Garvey.

1999   Engendering Migration Studies: The Case of New Immigrants in the United
         States. American Behavioral Scientist 42:577–600.

Philippine Overseas Employment Administration
2005   Deployment of Landbased OFWs, by Country: 1998–2003. Electronic docu-
         ment, http://www.poea.gov.ph/html/statistics.html, accessed June 28, 2005.

Pírez, Pedro
2002   ¿Qué Pasó en la Argentina? Algunas Piezas de un Rompecabezas para Intentar
         Entender. Estudios Sociológicos 20(59):455–467.

REFERENCES

Piven, Frances Fox, Joan Acker, Margaret Hallock, and Sandra Morgen, eds.

2002 Work, Welfare and Politics: Confronting Poverty in the Wake of Welfare Reform. Eugene: University of Oregon Press.

Planning Institute of Jamaica

1994 Economic and Social Survey Jamaica 1993. Kingston.

Plattner, Stuart

1996 High Art Down Home: An Economic Ethnography of a Local Art Market. Chicago: University of Chicago Press.

Plotkin, Mariano Ben

2001 Freud in the Pampas: The Emergence and Development of a Psychoanalytic Culture in Argentina. Stanford, CA: Stanford University Press.

Portes, Alejandro, and Ruben Rumbaut

1996 Immigrant America: A Portrait. 2nd edition. Berkeley: University of California Press.

Potter, Dalton

1955 The Bazaar Merchant. In Social Forces in the Middle East. N. S. Fisher, ed. Ithaca, NY: Cornell University Press.

Prece, Graciela, María Herminia Di Liscia, and Laura Piñero

1997 Mujeres Populares: Trabajo, Cuerpo y Salud Familiar. Paper presented at the XX Latin American Studies Association International Congress, Guadalajara, Mexico, April 17–19.

Public Citizen

N.d. NAFTA Chapter 11: Corporate Cases. Electronic document, http://www.citizen.org/trade/nafta/CH__11/, accessed February 1, 2007.

Qayum, Seemin, and Raka Ray

2003 Grappling with Modernity: India's Respectable Classes and the Culture of Domestic Servitude. Ethnography 4(4):520–555.

Rabo, Annika

1997 Free to Make the Right Choice? Gender Equality Policy in Post-Welfare Sweden. In Anthropology of Policy: Critical Perspectives on Governance and Power. Cris Shore and Susan Wright, eds. Pp. 107–135. New York: Routledge.

Rai, Shirin M.

2002 Gender and the Political Economy of Development. Cambridge, UK: Polity Press.

Rajaee, Farhang

2000 Globalization on Trial: The Human Condition and the Information Civilization. Bloomfield, CT: Kumarian Press, Inc.

Rattansi, Ali

2005 The Uses of Racialization: The Time-Spaces and Subject-Objects of the Raced Body. In Racialization: Studies in Theory and Practice. Karim Murji and John Solomos, eds. Pp. 271–302. Oxford: Oxford University Press.

Ray, Raka

2003   On Engendering a Better Life. *In* Feminist Futures: Re-imagining Women, Culture and Development. Kum-kum Bhavnani, John Foran, and Priya Kurian, eds. Pp. 107–111. London: Zed Books.

Reed, Ananya Mukherjee

1997   Regionalism in South Asia: Theory and Praxis. Pacific Affairs 70(2):235–251.

Regionfakta website

2007   http://www.regionfakta.com/StartsidaLan.aspx?id=2861, accessed March 20, 2007.

Reinharz, Shulamit, with the assistance of Lynn Davidman

1992   Feminist Methods in Social Research. New York: Oxford University Press.

Reiter, Rayna R., ed.

1976   Toward an Anthropology of Women. New York: Monthly Review Press.

Renne, Elisha P.

1995   Cloth Does Not Die: The Meaning of Cloth in Bunu Social Life. Seattle: University of Washington Press.

Repak, Terry

1995   Waiting on Washington: Central American Workers in the Nation's Capital. Philadelphia: Temple University Press.

Reynals, Cristina

2002   De Cartoneros a Recuperadores Urbanos. Paper presented at the Seminario Internacional, "Respuestas de la Sociedad Civil a la Emergencia Social: Brasil y Argentina Comparten Experiencias," Facultade de Economia, Administração e Contabilidade, Universidad de São Paulo De Brasil, November 4.

RIGC [Red Internacional de Género y Comercio], ed.

2003   Crisis y Resistencias: Voces de Mujeres. Buenos Aires: RIGC, UNIFEM.

Riger, S., and M. Krieglstein

2000   The Impact of Welfare Reform on Men's Violence against Women. American Journal of Community Psychology 28(5):631–647.

Rimmer, Douglas

1992   Staying Poor: Ghana's Political Economy, 1950–1990. Oxford: Pergamon Press.

RMALC [Red Mexicana de Acción Frente al Libre Comercio]

1993   Agenda Social: Propuestas en Materia Laboral, Medio Ambiente y Derechos Humanos. México, DF: RMALC.

Robbins, Richard H.

2005   Global Problems and the Culture of Capitalism. 3rd edition. Boston: Pearson Education, Inc.

Robertson, Claire

1983   The Death of Makola and Other Tragedies. Canadian Journal of African Studies 17(3):469–495.

1995   Trade, Gender and Poverty in the Nairobi Area: Women's Strategies for
            Survival and Independence in the 1980's. *In* Engendering Wealth and Well-
            Being: Empowerment for Global Change. R. L Blumberg, C. A. Rakowski, I.
            Tinker, and M. Monteon, eds. Pp. 65–87. Boulder, CO: Westview Press.

Robinson, W.
1996   Promoting Polyarchy: Globalisation, US Intervention and Hegemony.
            Cambridge: Cambridge University Press.

Roitman, Janet
2004   Productivity in the Margins: The Reconstitution of State Power in the Chad
            Basin. *In* Anthropology in the Margins of the State. Veena Das and Deborah
            Poole, eds. Pp. 191–225. School of American Research. Santa Fe, NM: SAR
            Press.

Rollins, Judith
1985   Between Women: Domestics and Their Employers. Philadelphia: Temple
            University Press.

Rönnblom, Malin
1997   Local Women's Projects. *In* Towards a New Democratic Order? Women's
            Organizing in the 1990s. Gunnel Gustafsson, Maud Eduards, and Malin
            Rönnblom, eds. Pp. 88–119. Stockholm: Publica.
2002   Ett Eget Rum? Kvinnors organisering möter etablerad politik. Ph.D. disserta-
            tion, Umeå University.

Rosa, Kumudini
1986   Gender and Class Consciousness—Women Workers in Free Trade Zone (Sri
            Lanka). The Hague: Institute of Social Studies.
1989   Women Workers' Strategies of Organizing and Resistance in the Sri Lankan
            Free Trade Zone (FTZ). Institute of Development Studies Discussion Paper
            no. 266. University of Sussex, UK. (Also found in South Asia Bulletin
            10[1]:33–43.)
1995   The Conditions and Organizational Activities of Women in Free Trade Zones:
            Malaysia, Philippines and Sri Lanka, 1970–1990. *In* Dignity and Daily Bread.
            Sheila Rowbotham and Swasti Mitter, eds. Pp. 73–99. London: Routledge.

Rosaldo, Michelle Z., and Louise Lamphere, eds.
1974   Women, Culture, and Society. Stanford, CA: Stanford University Press.

Roseberry, William
1997   Marx and Anthropology. Annual Review of Anthropology 26:25–46.

Rosenberg, Tiina
2002   Queerfeministisk Agenda. Stockholm: Atlas.

Rothstein, Frances Abrahamer, and Michael Blim, eds.
1991   Anthropology and the Global Factory: Studies of the New Industrialization in
            the Late Twentieth Century. New York: Bergin and Garvey.

Rowbotham, Sheila, and Stephanie Linkogle, eds.
2001   Women Resist Globalization: Mobilizing for Livelihood and Rights. New York: Zed Books.

Roy, Arundhati
2001   Power Politics. Cambridge, MA: South End Press.

Ryan, Mary
1981   Cradle of the Middle Class. Cambridge: Cambridge University Press.

Sacks, Karen (Brodkin)
1974   Engels Revisited. In Woman, Culture, and Society. Michelle Rosaldo and Louise Lamphere, eds. Pp. 207–222. Stanford, CA: Stanford University Press.
1979   Sisters and Wives: The Past and Future of Sexual Inequality. Urbana: University of Illinois Press.
1988   Caring by the Hour: Women, Work, and Organizing at Duke Medical Center. Urbana: University of Illinois Press.

Sáez, Ximena Bedregal
1992   Feminist Organizing in Mexico: From Consciousness Raising to Action. In Legal Literacy: A Tool for Women's Empowerment. Margaret Schuler and Sakuntala Kadirgamar-Rajasingham, eds. Pp. 283–297. New York: United Nations Development Fund for Women.

Safa, Helen
1981   Runaway Shops and Female Employment: The Search for Cheap Labor. Signs: Journal of Women in Culture and Society 7:418–433.
1995   Economic Restructuring and Gender Subordination. Latin American Perspectives 22(2):32–50.

Sainz, Alfredo
2002   Desde la Devaluación, Los Productos No Perecederos Subieron un 99,8%. La Nación, November 27.

Salzinger, Leslie
2004   From *Gender* as Object to *Gender* as Verb: Rethinking How Global Restructuring Happens. Critical Sociology 30(1):43, 20.

Sandoval, Chela
2000   Methodology of the Oppressed. Minneapolis: University of Minnesota Press.
2003   US–Third World Feminism: The Theory and Method of Oppositional Consciousness in the Postmodern World. In Feminist Postcolonial Theory Reader. Reina Lewis and Sara Mills, eds. Pp. 75–102. London: Routledge.

Sapmi website
n.d.   http://www.samer.se/servlet/GetDoc?meta_id=1145, accessed August 13, 2007.

Sarker, Sonita, and Esha Niyogi De, eds.
2002   Trans-status Subjects: Gender in the Globalization of South and Southeast Asia. Durham, NC: Duke University Press.

Sassen, Saskia

2000　Cities in a World Economy. 2nd edition. Thousand Oaks, CA: Pine Forge Press.

2003　Strategic Instantiations of Gendering in the Global Economy. *In* Gender and US Immigration: Contemporary Trends. Pierrette Hondagneu-Sotelo, ed. Pp. 43–60. Berkeley: University of California Press.

2006　Cities in a World Economy. Thousand Oaks, CA: Pine Forge Press for SAGE Publications.

Savarkar, V. D.

1969　Hindutva. Bombay: Veer Savarkar Prakashan.

Schneider, Jane

1989　Rumpelstilskin's Bargain: Folklore and the Merchant Capitalist Intensification of Linen Manufacture in Early Modern Europe. *In* Cloth and Human Experience. Annette B. Weiner and Jane Schneider, eds. Pp. 177–214. Washington DC: Smithsonian Institution Press.

Schneider, Jane, and Ida Susser

2003　Wounded Cities: Destruction and Reconstruction in a Globalized World. *In* Wounded Cities: Destruction and Reconstruction in a Globalized World. Jane Schneider and Ida Susser, eds. Pp. 1–23. Oxford: Berg Publishers.

Scott, Joan

1992　Experience. *In* Feminists Theorize the Political. Judith Butler and Joan Scott, eds. Pp. 22–40. New York: Routledge.

Sethi, Raj Mohini, ed.

1999　Globalization, Culture and Women's Development. Jaipur: Rawat Publications.

Shanahan, S. E., and N. B. Tuma

1994　The Sociology of Distribution and Redistribution. *In* The Handbook of Economic Sociology. N. J. Smelser and R. Swedberg, eds. Pp. 733–765. Princeton, NJ: Princeton University Press.

Sharpe, Jenny, and Gayatri Spivak

2002　A Conversation with Gayatri Chakravorty Spivak: Politics and the Imagination. Signs: Journal of Women in Culture and Society 28:609–624.

Shiva, Vandana

2002　Water Wars: Privatization, Pollution, and Profit. Cambridge, MA: South End Press.

Shore, Cris, and Susan Wright, eds.

1997　Anthropology of Policy: Critical Perspectives on Governance and Power. New York: Routledge.

Shrage, Laurie

2005　Which Side Are You On, APA? Hypatia 20(4):234–237.

Silvey, Rachel M.

2000　Stigmatized Spaces: Gender and Mobility under Crisis in South Sulawesi, Indonesia. Gender Place and Culture 7(2):143–161.

Singer, Audrey, and Greta Gilbertson
2003   "The Blue Passport": Gender and the Social Process of Naturalization among Dominican Immigrants in New York City. *In* Gender and US Immigration: Contemporary Trends. Pierrette Hondagneu-Sotelo, ed. Pp. 359–378. Berkeley: University of California Press.

Sinnathamby, M.
2004   Bonded Tea Estate Workers: Still Waiting at the Gates. *In* Sri Lankan Society in an Era of Globalization: Struggling to Create a New Social Order. S. H. Hasbullah and Barrie M. Morrison, eds. Pp. 182–195. Colombo: Vijitha Yapa Publications.

Sivaramakrishnan, K., and Arun Agrawal, eds.
2003   Regional Modernities: The Cultural Politics of Development in India. Stanford, CA: Stanford University Press.

Smart, Alan
1988   Resistance to Relocation by Shopkeepers in Hong Kong Squatter Area. *In* Traders versus the State: Anthropological Approaches to Unofficial Economies. G. Clark, ed. Pp. 119–138. Boulder, CO: Westview Press.

Smart, Josephine
1988   How to Survive in Illegal Street Hawking in Hong Kong. *In* Traders versus the State: Anthropological Approaches to Unofficial Economies. G. Clark, ed. Pp. 99–117. Boulder, CO: Westview Press.

Smith, Linda Tuhiwai
2005   Decolonizing Methodologies: Research and Indigenous People. London: Zed
[1999]   Books, Ltd.

Smith-Nonini, Sandy
2003   Back to "The Jungle": Processing Migrants in North Carolina's Meatpacking Plants. Anthropology of Work Review XXIV(3–4):14–20.
2004   Federally Sponsored Mexican Migrants in the Transnational South. *In* The American South in a Global World. James Peacock, Harry L. Watson, and Carrie R. Matthews, eds. Pp. 59–79. Chapel Hill, NC: University of North Carolina Press.

Sorlin, Sverker
1988   Framtidslandet: Debatten om Norrland och naturresurserna under det industriella genombrottet. Stockholm: Carlssons Förlag.

Soysal, Yasmin
1994   Limits of Citizenship. Chicago: University of Chicago Press.

Spalter-Roth, Roberta M.
1988   The Sexual Political Economy of Street Vending in Washington DC. *In* Traders versus the State: Anthropological Approaches to Unofficial Economies. G. Clark, ed. Pp. 165–188. Boulder, CO: Westview Press.

337

Sparr, Pamela

1994   Feminist Critiques of Structural Adjustment. *In* Mortgaging Women's Lives: Feminist Critiques of Structural Adjustment. Pamela Sparr, ed. Pp. 13–39. London: Zed Books.

Sparr, Pamela, ed.

1994   Mortgaging Women's Lives: Feminist Critiques of Structural Adjustment. London: Zed Books.

Stacey, Judith

1988   Can There Be a Feminist Ethnography? Women's Studies International Forum 11:21–27.

Statistics Sweden website

2006   http://www.scb.se, accessed March 2007.

Staudt, Kathleen, Shirin M. Rai, and Jane L. Parpart

2001   Protesting World Trade Rules: Can We Talk about Empowerment? Signs: Journal of Women in Culture and Society 26(4):1251–1257.

2002   Rethinking Empowerment: Gender and Development in a Global/Local World. London: Routledge.

Steady, Filomina Chioma, ed.

2001   Black Women, Globalization, and Economic Justice: Studies from Africa and the African Diaspora. Rochester, VT: Schenkman Books.

Stenvold, Dag

2002   From Russia with Love? Newspaper Coverage of Cross-Border Prostitution in Northern Norway, 1990–2002. The European Journal of Women's Studies 9(2):143–162.

Stephen, Lynn

1997   Women and Social Movements in Latin America: Power from Below. Austin: University of Texas Press.

Stewart, Susan

1987   Ceci Tuera Cela: Graffiti as Crime and as Art. *In* Life after Postmodernism: Essays on Value and Culture. John Fekete, ed. Pp. 161–180. New York: St. Martins Press.

Stiglitz, Joseph E.

2002   Globalization and Its Discontents. New York: W. W. Norton.

Stone-Ferrier, Linda

1989   Spun Virtue, the Lacework of Folly, and the World Wound Upside-Down: Seventeenth-Century Dutch Depictions of Female Handwork. *In* Cloth and Human Experience. Annette B. Weiner and Jane Schneider, eds. Pp. 215–242. Washington DC: Smithsonian Institution Press.

Straightline Advisors

2005   Website for corporate financial and management consultant agency serving hotels and resorts, http://www.straightline-advisors.com/.

Strathern, Marilyn, ed.
2000   Audit Cultures: Anthropological Studies in Accountability, Ethics and the Academy. London: Routledge.

Suedfeld, P., P. Tetlock, and S. Streufert
1992   Conceptual/Integrative Complexity. *In* Motivation and Personality: Handbook of Thematic Content Analysis. C. P. Smith, ed. Pp. 393–400. Cambridge: Cambridge University Press.

Sunder-Rajan, Rajeswari
1993   Real and Imagined Women: Gender, Culture, and Postcolonialism in India. London: Routledge.

Sundin, Elisabeth
1992   Equality through Regional Policy: Report from a Swedish Project. *In* Rethinking Change: Current Swedish Feminist Research. Maud Eduards, Inga Elgqvist-Salzman, Eva Lundgren, Christina Sjöblad, Elisabeth Sundin, and Ulla Wikander, eds. Pp. 105–130. Stockholm: Humanistisk-Samhällvetenskapliga forskningsrådet.

Sutton, Barbara
2004   Body Politics and Women's Consciousness in Argentina. Ph.D. dissertation, University of Oregon.

Sweet, J. A., L. L. Bumpass, and V. Call
1988   The Design and Content of the National Survey of Families and Households. NSFH Working Paper 1. Madison, WI: Center for Demography and Ecology, University of Wisconsin.

Swetnam, John
1978   Interaction between Urban and Rural Residents in a Guatemalan Marketplace. Urban Anthropology 7:137–153.

Szanton, Maria
1972   A Right to Survive: Subsistence Marketing in a Lowland Philippine Town. University Park: Pennsylvania State University Press.

Tam, Tony
1997   Sex Segregations and Occupational Gender Inequality in the United States. American Journal of Sociology 102:1652–1692.

Tammilehto, O.
1999   Effects of the Production and Consumption Patterns of Industrialized Countries on the Environment in the South. Electronic document, http://www.tammilehto.info/english.htm, accessed July 30, 2006.

Taylor, Frank
1991   The Hell with Paradise: A History of the Jamaica Tourist Industry. Pittsburgh: University of Pittsburgh Press.

Tonkin, Elizabeth
1980   Jealousy Names, Civilised Names: Anthroponomy of the Jlao Kru of Liberia. Man 15:653–664.

1981   Model and Ideology: Dimensions of Being Civilised in Liberia. *In* The Structure of Folk Models. Ladislav Holy and Milan Stuchlik, eds. Pp. 305–330. London: Academic Press.

Torres, Rodolfo D., Louis F. Mirón, and Jonathan Xavier Inda, eds.
1999   Race, Identity, and Citizenship: A Reader. Malden, MA: Blackwell Publishers, Inc.

Trager, Lillian
1981   Customers and Creditors: Variations in Economic Personalism in a Nigerian Marketing System. Ethnology 20:133–146.

Trinh, T. Minh-ha
1989   Woman, Native, Other. Bloomington: Indiana University Press.

Tronto, Joan
1989   Women and Caring: What Can Feminists Learn about Morality from Caring? *In* Gender/Body/Knowledge: Feminist Reconstructions of Being and Knowing. Alison Jaggar and Susan Bordo, eds. Pp. 172–187. New Brunswick, NJ: Rutgers University Press.

Tsing, Anna
2000   The Global Situation. Cultural Anthropology 15(3):327–360.

Turner, B.
2001   Union Innovations: Moving Workers from Poverty into Family-Sustaining Jobs. *In* Low Wage Workers in the New Economy. R. Kazis and M. Miller, eds. Pp. 347–362. Washington DC: Urban Institute Press.

Twine, France Winddance, and Jonathan W. Warren, eds.
2000   Racing Research, Researching Race: Methodological Dilemmas in Critical Race Studies. New York: New York University Press.

Uchendu, Victor C.
1967   Some Principles of Haggling in Peasant Markets. Economic Development and Cultural Change 16(1):37–50.

Ulysse, Gina
1999a   Uptown Ladies and Downtown Women: Female Representations of Class and Color in Jamaica. *In* Representations of Blackness and Performance of Identities. J. M. Rahier, ed. Pp. 147–172. Westport, CT: Greenwood Press.
1999b   Uptown Ladies and Downtown Women: Informal Commercial Importing and the Social/Symbolic Politics of Identities in Jamaica. Ph.D. dissertation, University of Michigan.

United Nations
1995   The World's Women: Trends and Statistics. New York: United Nations.

United Nations Development Program (UNDP)
1996–   Human Development Report. New York: UNDP, University of Michigan.
2000

Uribe, Juan Pablo, and Nicole Schwab
2002   The Argentine Health Sector in the Context of the Crisis. Background Paper
         no. 6. *In* Argentina: Crisis and Poverty 2003, vol. II. World Bank.

US Census Bureau
2001   The Black Population 2000: Census 2000 Brief. Electronic document,
         http://www.census.gov/prod/2001pubs/c2kbr01-5.pdf, accessed July 30, 2006.

US Surgeon General
1999   Mental Health. A Report of the Surgeon General. Washington DC: US
         Department of Health and Human Services, Office of the Surgeon General,
         SAMHSA.

Venturini, Alessandra
1991   Italy in the Context of European Migration. Regional Development Dialogue
         12(3):93–112.

Veugelers, John
1994   Recent Immigration Politics in Italy: A Short Story. *In* The Politics of
         Immigration in Western Europe. Martin Baldwin-Edwards and Martin Schain,
         eds. Pp. 33–49. Portland, OR: Frank Cass.

Vezzetti, Hugo
2002   Scenes from the Crisis. Journal of Latin American Cultural Studies
         11(2):163–171.

Visweswaran, Kamala
1997   Histories of Feminist Ethnography. Annual Review of Anthropology 26:591–621.

Voss, Kim, and Rachel Sherman
2001   Breaking the Iron Law of Oligarchy: Union Revitalization in the American
         Labor Market. American Journal of Sociology 106(2):303–349.

Wainerman, Catalina, ed.
2003   Familia, Trabajo y Género: Un Mundo de Nuevas Relaciones. Buenos Aires:
         Fondo de Cultura Económica.

Wallerstein, Immanuel
1983   The Three Instances of Hegemony in the History of the Capitalist World-
         Economy. International Journal of Comparative Sociology 24:100–108.
2004   After Developmentalism and Globalization, What? Keynote address at the
         Development Challenges for the 21st Century conference, Cornell University,
         Ithaca, NY, October.

Ward, Kathryn B.
1993   Reconceptualizing World System Theory to Include Women. *In* Theory on
         Gender/Feminism on Theory. Paula England, ed. Pp. 43–68. New York: Aldine.

Ward, Kathryn, ed.
1990   Women Workers and Global Restructuring. Ithaca, NY: ILR Press.

REFERENCES

Waring, Marilyn

1999   Counting for Nothing: What Men Value and What Women Are Worth. Toronto: University of Toronto Press.

Watson, Hilbourne A.

1994   Global Restructuring and the Prospects for Caribbean Competitiveness, with a Case Study from Jamaica. *In* The Caribbean in the Global Political Economy. Hilbourne A. Watson, ed. Pp. 67–90. Boulder, CO: Lynne Rienner Publishers.

Weerasuriya, Padmini

2000   The Conditions of the Workers in the Free Trade Zones as a Result of Sri Lanka's Open Economy. Paper presented at the ASEM 2000 People's Forum, "Women's Strategies to Challenge Globalization," Konkuk University, Seoul, Korea, October 17–21. Available online at http://www.tni.org/asem-seoul/008weerasuriya.htm, accessed March 2007.

Weiner, Annette B.

1989   Why Cloth? Wealth, Gender, and Power in Oceania. *In* Cloth and Human Experience. Annette B. Weiner and Jane Schneider, eds. Pp. 33–72. Washington DC: Smithsonian Institution Press.

Weiner, Annette B., and Jane Schneider, eds.

1989   Introduction. *In* Cloth and Human Experience. Annette B. Weiner and Jane Schneider, eds. Pp. 1–32. Washington DC: Smithsonian Institution Press.

Wesley, Patricia Jabbeh

1998   Before the Palm Could Bloom: Poems of Africa. Kalamazoo: New Issues Press, Western Michigan University.

2003   Becoming Ebony. Carbondale: Southern Illinois University Press.

In press   For Ma Nmano Jabbeh: A Dirge. *In* The River Is Rising. Pittsburgh: Autumn House Press. Cited with permission from the author.

Whitford, David

2001   Labor's Best Hope. Fortune 144(8).

Wial, H.

1993   The Emerging Organizational Structure of Unionism in Low-Wage Services. Rutgers Law Review 45:671–738.

Williams, Brackette

1996   The Public I/Eye: Conducting Fieldwork to Do Homework on Homelessness and Begging in Two US Cities. Current Anthropology 36(1):25–51.

Williams, Brackette, ed.

1996   Women out of Place: The Gender of Agency and the Race of Nationality. New York: Routledge.

Wilson, W. J.

1987   The Truly Disadvantaged. Chicago: University of Chicago Press.

Winter, D., and D. Leighton

1999 Introduction. Structural Violence section. Electronic document, http://www.psych.ubc.ca/~dleighton/svintro.html, accessed July 30, 2006.

Wolf, Diane

1992 Factory Daughters: Gender, Household Dynamics, and Rural Industrialization in Java. Berkeley: University of California Press.

Wolf, Eric R.

1982 Europe and the People without History. Berkeley: University of California Press.

Women's Committee/Comité de Mujeres

2004 Women from the Valley of Cochabamba: Water, Privatization and Conflict. Hemispheric Social Alliance Women's Committee Bulletin 1(1):7–8.

Wood, Ellen Meiksins

1997 Back to Marx. Monthly Review 49(2):1–9.

World Bank

2006 Global Economic Prospects: Economic Implications of Remittances and Migration. Washington DC: The World Bank.

World Socialist website

1998 Murderous Conditions in Sri Lankan Free Trade Zones. Oak Park, MI: International Committee of the Fourth International. Electronic document (October 20), http://www.wsws.org/news/1998/oct1998/sl-o20.shtml, accessed December 2006.

World Tourism Organization (WTO) website

2007 http://www.world-tourism.org/facts/menu.html, accessed February 2007.

Wrigley, Julia

1995 Other People's Children: An Intimate Account of the Dilemmas Facing Middle-Class Parents and the Women They Hire to Raise Their Children. New York: Basic Books.

Yanagisako, Sylvia, and Carol Delaney, eds.

1995 Naturalizing Power: Essays in Feminist Cultural Analysis. New York: Routledge.

Yancy, Kitty Bean

2005 Maid for a Day. USA Today, Life, March 25:1d.

Yelin, Louise

2004 Globalizing Subjects. Signs: Journal of Women in Culture and Society 29(2):439–466.

Yelvington, Kevin A.

1995 Producing Power: Ethnicity, Gender and Class in a Caribbean Workplace. Philadelphia: Temple University Press.

Yeoh, Brenda, and Shirlena Huang

1998 Negotiating Public Space: Strategies and Styles of Migrant Female Domestic Workers in Singapore. Urban Studies 35(3):583–602.

REFERENCES

Zavella, Patricia

1987   Women's Work and Chicano Families: Cannery Workers of the Santa Clara Valley. Ithaca, NY: Cornell University Press.

1997   The Tables Are Turned: Immigration, Poverty, and Social Conflict in California Communities. *In* Immigrants Out! The New Nativism and the Anti-Immigrant Impulse in the United States. Juan F. Perea, ed. Pp. 136–161. New York: New York University Press.

Zhou, Min

1992   Chinatown: The Socioeconomic Potential of an Urban Enclave. Philadelphia: Temple University Press.

Index

Pírez, Pedro, 149
place, and spatial integration of migrant Filipina
domestic workers in Italy and US, 180–91
Plattner, Stuart, 81
pockets, and segregation of migrant Filipina
domestic workers in Italy, 185–86, 187–89
Poland, and migrant domestic workers in Italy,
187
politics, and international tourism in Jamaica,
224–27. See also activism
Poole, Deborah, 281, 290
Poon, Auliana, 226
population, loss of in rural northern Sweden, 115
Portes, Alejandro, 177
positionality, as issue in ethnographic research,
29–30
postcolonialism, and patriarchal cultural context
of contemporary Sri Lanka, 47–48, 59n44
postmodernism: and integration of interpretive
and materialist approaches in anthropology,
27; and negation in commodity system, 213;
and service sector jobs in US economy, 197
Potter, Dalton, 79
poverty: and impact of neoliberal policy on black
communities in US, 134–35; and neoliberal
globalization in Argentina, 149, 151–55,
163–64; and wages of women factory workers
in Sri Lanka, 57n27
power: Foucaultian concept of, 5, 41, 57n23,
58n41, 287; gendered repression and capitalist regimes of, 295–96; gender and global
relations of, 123, 279–85; gender as socially
structured relationship of unequal, xiii. See
also empowerment
practice, intellectual and sociopolitical value of
women's stories, 26–27
Prakash, Madhu, 299n7
Prece, Graciela, 158
price, and participation of Ghanaian female
traders in global economy, 71–74, 75, 77–78,
79, 82
privatization: and structural adjustment program
in Jamaica, 223; of water supplies in Latin
American, 251, 255n13
profit margins, of Ghanaian female traders, 72
Program for Economic Recovery (1981), 134
progressiveness, traditionalism and gender relations in rural northern Sweden, 118–22, 123
prostitution, and economic crisis in Argentina,
160
psychoanalysis, and discourse on economic crisis
in Argentina, 162
public sphere, and migrant Filipina domestic
workers in Italy, 185–86, 187–89

Quality of life, and migration in rural northern
Sweden, 115–16
Québec Coalition on the Trilateral Negotiations,
248
Quintar, Aida, 149

Race: and colorism in Jamaica, 227–28; and
impact of economic variables on domestic
violence in US, 136–39; and migrant Filipina
domestic workers, 171–92; structural violence
and gender relations in US, 128–30, 144. See
also ethnicity
racism, and conception of Asian women in rural
northern Sweden, 121
Ragoné, Helena, 14
Rai, Shirin M., 252, 253
Rajaee, Farhang, 287, 291
Rattansi, Ali, 15
Ray, Raka, 15
Raynor, Bruce, 207
Reagan, Ronald, 134, 135
realism, and influence of postmodernism on
anthropological fieldwork, 27
Red Mexicana de Acción frente al Libre
Comercio (RMALC), 238, 241, 242–43,
248–51, 252, 255n14
Reed, Ananya Mukherjee, 245
regionalism, in rural northern Sweden, 110–11
relationships, traditional Ghanaian trade and
personalized, 80–81
religion. See Buddhism; church centers;
Hinduism
Repak, Terry, 172, 173
repression: gendered forms of and women's
resistance in context of globalization, 293–98;
and resistance by women factory workers in
Sri Lanka, 42, 49–52. See also domination;
marginality and marginalization; oppression
residential patterns, of Filipino community in
California, 177–78. See also settlement pat-
terns
resistance: and gendered repression in context
of globalization, 293–98; political conscious-
ness and feminization of in Argentina, 167;
and repression of women factory workers in
Sri Lanka, 42, 49–52; and women's activism in
Orissa, India, 270–72
Reynals, Cristina, 152
Ribera, Digna, 240, 253
Riger, S., 139
Rimmer, Douglas, 66
RIU resorts (Jamaica), 218, 219, 230, 231n2
Robertson, Claire, 66
Robinson, W., 131
Roitman, Janet, 281
Rollins, Judith, 181, 184
Rosa, Kumdini, 38, 40, 52, 55n10, 57n25, 57n32,
58n36
Rosaldo, Renato, 7
Roseberry, William, 280
Roy, Arundhati, 263–64, 264–65

School for Advanced Research Advanced Seminar Series

PUBLISHED BY SAR PRESS

AMERICAN ARRIVALS: ANTHROPOLOGY
ENGAGES THE NEW IMMIGRATION
Nancy Foner, ed.

VIOLENCE
Neil L. Whitehead, ed.

LAW & EMPIRE IN THE PACIFIC:
FIJI AND HAWAI‘I
Sally Engle Merry &
Donald Brenneis, eds.

ANTHROPOLOGY IN THE MARGINS
OF THE STATE
Veena Das & Deborah Poole, eds.

PLURALIZING ETHNOGRAPHY: COMPARISON
AND REPRESENTATION IN MAYA CULTURES,
HISTORIES, AND IDENTITIES
John M. Watanabe &
Edward F. Fischer, eds.

THE ARCHAEOLOGY OF COLONIAL
ENCOUNTERS: COMPARATIVE PERSPECTIVES
Gil J. Stein, ed.

COMMUNITY BUILDING IN THE TWENTY-
FIRST CENTURY
Stanley E. Hyland, ed.

AFRO-ATLANTIC DIALOGUES:
ANTHROPOLOGY IN THE DIASPORA
Kevin A. Yelvington, ed.

COPÁN: THE HISTORY OF AN ANCIENT MAYA
KINGDOM
E. Wyllys Andrews &
William L. Fash, eds.

GLOBALIZATION, WATER, & HEALTH:
RESOURCE MANAGEMENT IN TIMES OF
SCARCITY
Linda Whiteford & Scott Whiteford, eds.

A CATALYST FOR IDEAS: ANTHROPOLOGICAL
ARCHAEOLOGY AND THE LEGACY OF
DOUGLAS W. SCHWARTZ
Vernon L. Scarborough, ed.

THE ARCHAEOLOGY OF CHACO CANYON: AN
ELEVENTH-CENTURY PUEBLO REGIONAL
CENTER
Stephen H. Lekson, ed.

THE SEDUCTIONS OF COMMUNITY:
EMANCIPATIONS, OPPRESSIONS, QUANDARIES
Gerald W. Creed, ed.

THE EVOLUTION OF HUMAN LIFE HISTORY
Kristen Hawkes & Richard R. Paine, eds.

IMPERIAL FORMATIONS
Ann Laura Stoler, Carole McGranahan,
& Peter C. Perdue, eds.

THE ANASAZI IN A CHANGING ENVIRONMENT
George J. Gumerman, ed.

REGIONAL PERSPECTIVES ON THE OLMEC
Robert J. Sharer & David C. Grove, eds.

THE CHEMISTRY OF PREHISTORIC HUMAN
BONE
T. Douglas Price, ed.

THE EMERGENCE OF MODERN HUMANS:
BIOCULTURAL ADAPTATIONS IN THE LATER
PLEISTOCENE
Erik Trinkaus, ed.

THE ANTHROPOLOGY OF WAR
Jonathan Haas, ed.

THE EVOLUTION OF POLITICAL SYSTEMS
Steadman Upham, ed.

CLASSIC MAYA POLITICAL HISTORY:
HIEROGLYPHIC AND ARCHAEOLOGICAL
EVIDENCE
T. Patrick Culbert, ed.

TURKO-PERSIA IN HISTORICAL PERSPECTIVE
Robert L. Canfield, ed.

CHIEFDOMS: POWER, ECONOMY, AND
IDEOLOGY
Timothy Earle, ed.

RECONSTRUCTING PREHISTORIC PUEBLO
SOCIETIES
William A. Longacre, ed.